Sacred Texts of the World

Grant Hardy, Ph.D.

THE
GREAT
COURSES®

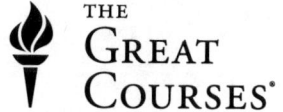

PUBLISHED BY:

THE GREAT COURSES
Corporate Headquarters
4840 Westfields Boulevard, Suite 500
Chantilly, Virginia 20151-2299
Phone: 1-800-832-2412
Fax: 703-378-3819
www.thegreatcourses.com

Copyright © The Teaching Company, 2014

Printed in the United States of America

This book is in copyright. All rights reserved.

Without limiting the rights under copyright reserved above,
no part of this publication may be reproduced, stored in
or introduced into a retrieval system, or transmitted,
in any form, or by any means
(electronic, mechanical, photocopying, recording, or otherwise),
without the prior written permission of
The Teaching Company.

Grant Hardy, Ph.D.
Professor of History and Religious Studies
University of North Carolina at Asheville

Professor Grant Hardy is Professor of History and Religious Studies at the University of North Carolina at Asheville (UNC Asheville). After serving two terms as the chair of the Department of History, he is currently the director of the Humanities Program. He has a B.A. in Ancient Greek from Brigham Young University (BYU) and a Ph.D. in Chinese Language and Literature from Yale University.

Dr. Hardy is the author or editor of six books, including *Worlds of Bronze and Bamboo: Sima Qian's Conquest of History*; *The Establishment of the Han Empire and Imperial China*, coauthored with Anne Kinney of the University of Virginia; and *Understanding the Book of Mormon: A Reader's Guide*. His most recent book is the first volume of the *Oxford History of Historical Writing*, coedited with Andrew Feldherr of Princeton University.

Professor Hardy won UNC Asheville's 2002 Distinguished Teaching Award for Humanities and was named to a Ruth and Leon Feldman Professorship for Outstanding Service for 2009–2010. He has participated in scholarly symposia on Sima Qian and early Chinese historiography at the University of Wisconsin–Madison, Harvard University, and Heidelberg University. He also received a research grant from the National Endowment for the Humanities.

Professor Hardy was raised in northern California and has taught at BYU, BYU–Hawaii, Elmira College, and UNC Asheville. He lived in Taiwan for two years in the 1980s. He and his wife, Heather, have two children. One of his proudest achievements is that he has written or rewritten most of the articles on imperial China for *The World Book Encyclopedia*; thus, his name is in every elementary school library in the country. ∎

Table of Contents

INTRODUCTION

Professor Biography i
Course Scope 1

LECTURE GUIDES

LECTURE 1
Reading Other People's Scriptures 4

LECTURE 2
Hinduism and the Vedas 22

LECTURE 3
What Is Heard—Upanishads 41

LECTURE 4
What Is Remembered—Epics 60

LECTURE 5
Laws of Manu and Bhagavad Gita 79

LECTURE 6
Related Traditions—Sikh Scriptures 97

LECTURE 7
Judaism—People of the Book 115

LECTURE 8
Five Books of Torah 133

LECTURE 9
Prophets and Writings 151

LECTURE 10
Apocrypha and Dead Sea Scrolls 170

Table of Contents

LECTURE 11
Oral Torah—Mishnah and Talmud 189

LECTURE 12
Related Traditions—Zoroastrian Scriptures 208

LECTURE 13
The Three Baskets of Buddhism 227

LECTURE 14
Vinaya and Jataka 246

LECTURE 15
Theravada Sutras 265

LECTURE 16
Mahayana Sutras 284

LECTURE 17
Pure Land Buddhism and Zen 303

LECTURE 18
Tibetan Vajrayana 323

SUPPLEMENTAL MATERIAL

Recommended Texts and Translations 342
Bibliography 346

Sacred Texts of the World

Scope:

Religious texts are, in many cases, the best way to learn about the faith traditions of others. Authoritative and widely available, they offer a window into a new world of ideas and practices. In our rapidly shrinking world, where cultural traditions are converging at an ever-increasing rate, the value of mutual understanding cannot be overstated.

But it would be far too simple to suggest that we can easily discover some universal truth or common ground by a cursory read of another faith's sacred writings. These texts exhibit tremendous variety in content, form, use, and origins. We must approach these texts with an open mind and great care. In so doing, we may find that we learn as much about ourselves and our own beliefs as we do about others'.

The library of world scriptures is huge, and sacred texts can be studied and pondered for a lifetime. Thus, this course will focus on a specific selection of texts. The course provides an overview of the sacred writings of seven major religious traditions, basically in chronological order of the religions' founding, along with descriptions of holy books from another half dozen lesser-known or smaller faiths.

We begin by discussing how to approach reading these texts, then start our journey with the sacred works of the Hindus. Among the many great opportunities here will be a chance to broaden the definition of *text*, for many of these texts defy Western ideas about scripture. We will also look at the related faith of Sikhism, whose relatively recent sacred text occupies a unique role in world religions.

Next, we will study Jewish scripture, including the Tanakh (also called the Hebrew Bible, or the Old Testament by Christians), the Apocrypha, and the Dead Sea Scrolls. We will look at the formerly oral traditions now written down in the Mishnah and Talmud, and we will see why the Jewish relationship to their scripture rightly earns them the title "people of the book." Before moving on, we will also consider the ancient Near Eastern monotheistic religion of Zoroastrianism; its text, the Avesta; and some interesting parallels between this faith and the three great Abrahamic faiths.

The Buddhist canon is the largest in the world, containing about 100,000 pages. We will consider the Tripitaka, or "Three Baskets," of the Buddhist scriptural tradition: the Vinaya (rules for monks and nuns), the Sutras (discourses of the Buddha), and the Abhidharma (works of systematic philosophy) from all of the major Buddhist traditions. After this, we will look at the Jain faith, which arose in a similar time and place as Buddhism. This faith is in the unique position of sharing many of its core principles among its different sects but not sharing its core scriptures.

Confucianism is often thought of as a philosophy rather than a religion, but its texts discuss morality, principles for living in harmony with the universe, rituals for dealing with unseen beings, divination, and temple ceremonies, much like the other scriptures in this course. We will see, however, that although the contents of the Confucian Classics are much like that of other scriptures, their uses are rather different, with a decidedly this-worldly, even political, focus.

Daoism is another great faith of Chinese origin, and its history is entwined with that of Confucianism. Its most famous text, the Daodejing, is fairly well known in the West, but it is only a small section of a much larger canon with a complicated history of development.

We will consider both of these traditions, then turn to Japan for a brief look at two of its native faiths, Shinto and Tenrikyo. One has no official scripture beyond the ancient histories of Japan; the other is a modern faith based in the ideas and the beautiful poetry of its founder.

To most students of this course, Christian scriptures will be among the most familiar, either as part of their faith's own tradition or through the deep influence of these scriptures on Western literature. We will attempt, however, to view these works through fresh eyes as we consider the development and canonization of the Gospels, the letters of Paul and the audience who first read them, and the Apocryphal and Gnostic books that did not make it into the orthodox Christian canon. Then we will look at a late attempt to expand the Christian canon through the addition of the Book of Mormon.

Muslims consider the Qur'an to be the complete and final revelation of God, but it is not the only Muslim text we will consider in this course. In addition to this central and most revered text of Islam, we will look at the legal interpretations of Islamic law passed down through the Hadith, as well as the mystical poetry of Sufism. We will also look at the Baha'i faith, a 19th-century religion that came out of the context of Shia Islam and has its own unique scriptures.

We will end the course with some unusual cases and questions. First, we will ask what happens to a sacred text when the religion it represents is no longer practiced; specifically, we will consider two cases: the Egyptian Book of the Dead and the Mayan Popol Vuh. We will next ask whether explicitly secular writing can take on aspects of the sacred by looking at the place of the U.S. Constitution and the Declaration of Independence in American culture. Finally, we will close with a consideration of how the comparative study of sacred texts might make a difference in our lives as individuals, as members of faith communities, and as citizens of the world. ∎

Reading Other People's Scriptures
Lecture 1

The texts we will discuss in these lectures matter a great deal to a great many people. They have been read and reread, loved and revered for centuries or millennia. People have lived by the books we will discuss and, as we'll see, have sometimes been willing to risk death to preserve them. The library of world scriptures is huge, and in most cases, we come to it as outsiders. But this course provides an overview of the scriptures of seven major religious traditions, as well as holy books of some smaller faiths, in the hope that our study will bring us new insight into global thought, politics, and culture and new wisdom to apply in our own lives.

Preserving Sacred Texts
- Imagine a world in which the printing press had never been invented, where the only books were those that had been painstakingly copied out by hand. How many books would you own, particularly if you had to copy them out yourself? Many people would have only the texts they consider sacred.

- Or from a slightly different perspective, if there were a fire, which books would you try to save? History shows us that this isn't always a hypothetical question.
    o On October 23, 1731, the great classical scholar Richard Bentley was staying at Ashburnham House in London, where the royal library had recently been relocated. About 2:00 am, he awoke to the smell of smoke and jumped out of bed to try to put out a fire that had started near a chimney.

    o As the flames rapidly spread and the paneling caught fire, Bentley ran upstairs and grabbed the Codex Alexandrinus before he escaped the burning building.

    o This book, written in the 5th century, is one of the three earliest and most important manuscripts we have of the complete

Greek Bible (the New Testament plus the Septuagint). The early version of the New Testament that is in the Codex Alexandrinus has been crucial to establishing the most accurate Greek text possible.

- Such tales of sacred texts that have survived through the centuries, sometimes through extraordinary efforts and sacrifices, are not rare. The burning-house scenario is common enough that a section of the Jewish Talmud is devoted to the question of whether it is lawful to rescue sacred writings from a fire on the Sabbath.

- And accidental fires aren't the only concern. From 175 to 183 C.E., teams of carvers in China inscribed the Confucian classics on stone tablets, in part to prevent the repetition of an incident that had taken place 400 years earlier. At that time, the first emperor of China had ordered the destruction of all Confucian writings in private hands and threatened execution for any scholars who persisted in teaching them.

- Most of the Confucian classics survived the first emperor, which is different from the fate of the Zoroastrian sacred texts, most of which were lost in the fires of Persepolis that were set when Alexander the Great invaded Persia in 330 B.C.E. Even today, Zoroastrians lament that they have to make do with fragments of the scriptures that were collected during the Sassanid Empire (c. 3rd century C.E.), which consist of only about one quarter of their original holy writings.

Why Study Scriptures?
- For believers, sacred texts from their own belief systems promise ultimate truth or salvation of some sort. They tell readers how to connect with the divine and offer guidelines for living or even commandments that should not be ignored. But what if you're not a believer in a particular religion? What might be in such texts for you? And why focus on scripture in the first place?
    - There's no question that religion is a significant part of the lives of most people around the world; thus, studying various belief systems offers an important window into understanding global

politics, thought, and culture. In order to understand others, we need some sense of how they see themselves in relation to the cosmos and tradition and other people—and those relationships are often defined by religion.

- Yet religion encompasses much more than just scripture. It includes ritual; ceremonies; such practices as meditation, yoga, or humanitarian service; ecclesiastical organizations; formal theology; sacred spaces and artifacts; ethical codes; a community of fellow believers; and so forth. Why devote a course to scripture?

- We can provide four short answers to this question, the first of which is accessibility. As wonderful as it might be to visit a Zen monastery in Japan, or to observe a pilgrimage in India, or to take part in Holy Week celebrations in Israel, realistically, only a few of us have those opportunities. Sacred texts, by contrast, are readily available in bookstores, libraries, and on the Internet.

- The second reason for studying scriptures is centrality. In most cases, sacred writings communicate core values and beliefs about a religion; sometimes, they are the glue that holds a religion together. For instance, there are several types of modern Judaism, but they all share a reverence for the Torah; Sunni and Shia Muslims all recite the Qur'an; the hundreds of Protestant denominations and subdenominations are united in their reliance on the Bible; and the diverse communities of Hindus look to the Vedas as their most authoritative texts.

- The third reason is comparability. It's true that some religions do not have sacred written texts; instead, they may have oral traditions that are passed down by religious specialists. In fact, most of the scriptures of the larger world religions started as oral traditions that were eventually transcribed into written form. But written texts are, of course, easier to study and compare side by side.
  - For instance, we can investigate the role played by poetry, historical narrative, or law codes in various scriptures. With

printed translations of sacred texts, we can more easily discern the themes, insights, and anxieties that characterize various religious communities.

- o Not all religions use scriptures in the same way, and there is remarkable variety in the types of writings that people hold sacred and the sizes of various canons, but at least written texts give us some common basis for comparison.

- o It is easy to be overwhelmed by the religious diversity of humankind throughout history, but scripture gives us some common ground from which to start a conversation.

- Finally, there is wisdom to be found in sacred texts, even for those who come to a particular scripture as outsiders. These books have survived because people have found them useful, and they frequently offer novel insights or call attention to universal truths.
  - o For instance, reading the Bhagavad Gita and its teachings about acting without attachment to the fruit of actions can make us think more deeply about how much self-interest lies at the heart of what we do. Confucian texts can help us appreciate the degree to which our identities come from our relationships with others.
  - o Note, however, that we can't think of world scriptures as merely books of quotations. Biblical

Ideally, reading other people's scriptures should be more like a window than a mirror; rather than confirming our own assumptions, it should show us ideas we haven't seen before.

7

scholars warn us about the dangers of proof texting—that is, taking a verse out of context to support a point. It's much better to look at scriptural passages in context, to try to understand what the authors had in mind and how believers have interpreted them over the centuries.

Thoreau's Dream

- There has never been a better time for cross-cultural, inter-religious explorations than right now. We can compare our situation to that of an earlier American who was curious about sacred texts from around the world, Henry David Thoreau.
    o From 1845 to 1847, Thoreau lived in a one-room cabin at Walden Pond. He had only few books with him, mostly Greek and Latin classics but also an English translation of the Bhagavad Gita, and he expressed an interest in the Hindu Vedas and the Zoroastrian Avesta, as well.

    o While living at Walden, Thoreau wrote a memoir of a canoe trip he had taken a few years earlier called *A Week on the Concord and Merrimack Rivers*. In this book, he shared a fond dream or ambition: "It would be worthy of the age to print together the collected Scriptures or Sacred Writings of the several nations. ... Such a juxtaposition and comparison might help to liberalize the faith of men."

- Thoreau was a bit too early, but his dream was realized about a half century later when Oxford University published the 50-volume series Sacred Books of the East. It was a groundbreaking scholarly project, with translations of the most significant sacred texts from Hinduism, Buddhism, Confucianism, Daoism, Zoroastrianism, Jainism, and Islam. And all of it is available online today (www.sacred-texts.com).

- Because these are early translations, they're not always as readable or as well organized as we might hope, but the point is that we have at our fingertips everything Thoreau imagined. The trick is knowing where to start, because many of these texts can seem puzzling or strange at first glance. This course is a guide to launch you on a study of these scriptures.

The Benefits of Our Study

- If you approach the study of scripture as a skeptic or an agnostic, you can, like a naturalist, marvel at the variety and creativity of our human species. You may gain an appreciation of what these texts mean to believers and, perhaps, better understand why they have gone to such efforts to preserve, translate, disseminate, and interpret the writings they hold sacred.

- If you are already committed to one of the religious traditions we will survey, you may enjoy learning how people throughout history have made sense of the universe through sacred texts. Through the concerns, critiques, and questions of these historical figures, you may come to see your own tradition with fresh eyes.
  - One of the drawbacks of being religious is that reading your own scriptures is most often a case of rereading. You get comfortable, perhaps even complacent, in hearing the same words again and again. Yet the Jewish philosopher Martin Buber had a point when he observed that people who want to truly open themselves to a sacred text "must take up scripture as if they had never seen it."

  - And that, of course, is exactly what we do when we look at other people's holy books. It's a good reminder of the time when our own scriptural traditions were new to us.

  - Once you've had a chance to stretch your mind a bit, to step outside your own faith community, then you can return to your familiar scriptures with new questions and see things in a new light, from a broader perspective.

Suggested Reading

Feiser and Powers, eds., *Scriptures of the World's Religions*.

Gernet, "Christian and Chinese Visions of the World in the Seventeenth Century" (on Zhang Chao and Christianity).

Levering, ed., *Rethinking Scripture*.

Novak, ed., *The World's Wisdom*.

Smart and Hecht, eds., *Sacred Texts of the World*.

Smith, *What Is Scripture?*

Van Voorst, ed., *Anthology of World Scriptures*.

Questions to Consider

1. Why is studying sacred texts a good introduction to world religions?

2. What would Henry David Thoreau have thought about a course like this one?

Reading Other People's Scriptures
Lecture 1—Transcript

Welcome to a course on *Sacred Texts of the World*. To be honest, I'm a little nervous, because in these lectures I'll be talking about books that matter a great deal to many people. We'll be discussing texts that have been read and reread and have been loved and even revered for centuries, and in some cases for millennia. People have lived by these books, and sometimes have even been willing to risk death in order to preserve them or to stay true to a particular interpretation of them.

As we begin, imagine a world in which the printing press had never been invented; where the only books are those that had been painstakingly and laboriously copied out by hand, page by page. How many books would you own, particularly if you had to copy them yourself? Which books do you love enough to write them out longhand, page after page, letter by letter? Many people would start with texts that they consider sacred. Or from a slightly different perspective—sort of a different question that gets at the same sort of idea—if there were a fire, which books, if any, would you try to save from your house? It's not always a hypothetical question. In the early morning hours of October 23, 1731, the great Classical scholar Richard Bentley was staying at the Ashburnham House in London where the Royal Library had recently been relocated. About 2:00 am, he awoke to the smell of smoke and jumped out of bed to try to put out a fire that had started near a stove chimney. As the flames rapidly spread and the paneling caught fire, he ran upstairs and grabbed the Codex Alexandrinus, which he carried in his arms as he escaped the burning building. (There were some witnesses reported that he had the presence of mind and dignity to put on his great wig before his mad dash to safety with this volume.) Of the 958 volumes in the library, 114 were totally destroyed and another 98 were damaged.

The book that Bentley saved, however, was particularly valuable. The Codex Alexandrinus, written in the 5th century, is one of the three earliest and most important manuscripts of the complete Greek bible (so that's the New Testament plus the Septuagint, which was a Greek translation of the Hebrew Bible; I'll talk more about that in a later lecture). This volume, the Codex Alexandrinus, had been presented to King Charles I in 1627 by Cyril Lucar, the Patriarch of Constantinople. He wanted to thank the English with an extravagant gift for their help in his struggles with the Turkish government. The very early version of the New Testament in the Codex Alexandrinus has been crucial to establishing the most accurate Greek text possible. Today, that book—the very one that was rescued by Richard Bentley almost three centuries ago—can be seen in the British Library; though actually you don't have to go that far anymore: In 2012, the New Testament portion of the Codex Alexandrinus was digitized and put online. With a few clicks on a mouse at your computer, you could be looking at that within minutes.

Such tales of sacred texts that have survived through the centuries, sometimes through extraordinary efforts and sacrifices, aren't rare. The burning house scenario is common enough that there's a section of the Jewish Talmud in the *Tractate Shabbat* devoted to the question of whether it's lawful to rescue sacred writings from a fire on the Sabbath (remember, there were a number of restrictions on all sorts of Sabbath activities, including what you could carry). The rabbis considered whether it makes a difference if the text is a Torah, as opposed to the Writings—and I'll explain those divisions in a future lecture—or if it matters whether the text is written in Hebrew or whether it's a translation into another language; which of those should you rescue, and which would be ok to rescue on the Sabbath or not? But in the end, the consensus is that rescuing scriptures from flames is a good idea, even on the Sabbath. By coincidence, October 21, 1731, the very day that Richard Bentley sprinted through the smoke to grab the Codex Alexandrinus, was a Sunday. I know that Sunday is the Christian Sabbath rather than the Jewish Saturday, but it does appear that Bentley did the right thing, at least according to two religions traditions.

These are just accidental fires. In the late 2nd century C.E.—C.E. and A.D. are going to be pretty much the same, except C.E. doesn't make everything revolve around Jesus, so there's C.E. that equals A.D. and B.C.E., "Before the Common Era," is going to be B.C., "Before Christ"; so in this course, I'll use B.C.E. and C.E.—when the rabbis were putting together the earliest portion of the Talmud (that's going to be the Mishnah), craftsmen in China were carving the Confucian classics on stone tablets. For eight years, from 175–183 C.E., teams of carvers inscribed about 200,000 characters on 46 stelae that are seven feet tall and maybe three feet wide, in part to prevent any repetition of the famous burning of the books that happened 400 years earlier when the First Emperor of China (he's also known as Qin Shi Huangdi) ordered the destruction of all Confucian writings in private hands and he threatened execution for any scholars who persisted in teaching them. Most of the Confucian classics survived the First Emperor, which is different from the fate of the Zoroastrian sacred texts, most of which were lost in the fires of Persepolis that were set when Alexander the Great invaded Persia in 330 B.C.E. Even today, Zoroastrians lament that they've had to make do with fragments of the scriptures that were collected during the Sassanid Empire, and that's about in the 3rd century C.E. We'll see in a later lecture, there's a huge timespan between the composition of the Zoroastrian scriptures and when they were first written down. Today, the scriptures that we have from that tradition consist of only about a quarter of the original holy writings.

Aren't you a bit curious about what's in these books that mean so much to people? Sacred texts aren't just significant writings in a culture, they're often considered the most important books—the kind that people were willing to copy by hand or to rescue from destruction—and they're frequently the first texts to be translated into foreign languages. I want to get things right in this course, but because sacred texts can often be studied and pondered for an entire lifetime, I'm well aware that some of my listeners may know more about a particular book or a scriptural tradition than I'll ever know. I only have one lifetime to work with here, and lots of traditions. The library of world scriptures is huge, and in most cases I, like you, am an outsider. I'll provide an overview of the sacred writings of seven major religious traditions, basically in the chronological order based on when their writings were first composed; and then in between, I'll give you descriptions of holy books from another half dozen lesser-known or smaller faiths. But at the outset, it's worth considering why it might be useful to read other people's scriptures.

It's easy enough to understand why someone might want to spend time with their own sacred texts. For believers, these are books that promise ultimate truth or salvation of some sort. They can tell you how to connect with the divine and offer guidelines for living and even commandments that can only be ignored at one's spiritual peril. But what if you're not a believer in that particular religion? What if you're not really moved or motivated by their claims to transcendent truth or doctrinal authority? What might be in those texts for you, and why focus on scripture in the first place?

There's no question that religion is a significant part of the lives of most people around the world, so studying various belief systems offers an important window into understanding global politics, thought, and culture. In order to get along with others, to know them for who they truly are, you need some sense of how they see themselves in relation to the cosmos and to their own native traditions, or ethnic traditions, or religious traditions, and the way they relate to other people; and those relationships are often defined by religion. Yet religion encompasses much more than just scripture: There's also ritual and ceremonies; practices such as meditation, yoga, or humanitarian service; there are ecclesiastical organizations; there's formal theology; there are sacred spaces and pilgrimages to go visit those places; there are sacred artifacts, and ethical codes; there's a community of fellow believers; the list goes on and on.

Why have a whole course devoted to scripture? I can give you four quick reasons now, and then I'll save another for the end of the lecture (build up some suspense here). The first advantage of focusing of scripture is accessibility. As wonderful as it might be to visit a Zen monastery in Japan, or to observe a pilgrimage in India, or take part in Holy Week celebrations in Israel, realistically only a few of us will have those opportunities; and even if we have a few of those chances to see those things in person, you won't get to see those kinds of ceremonies or opportunities for lots of religious traditions. Our time, our travel is limited. But sacred texts are readily available in bookstores; they're in the libraries, they're on the Internet. If you're curious about Buddhism, Islam, Daoism, or Sikhism, take a look at the writings that they hold, and that would be an easy, safe way to go. You can read as much as you like or as little, and on your own time schedule with no pressure, no embarrassment. If someday you want to follow up with a visit to a worship service or with conversations with actual believers, you'll have a basic understanding of the tradition and something to talk about. It's always good to say, "I've read a little bit from the Bhagavad Gita" or "I've read a little bit from the Qur'an and tell me about this" or "this is what I thought about it."

The second reason—the first is accessibility—is centrality. Sacred writings are generally not peripheral to religious traditions; in most cases they communicate core values and beliefs, and sometimes they're the glue that holds a religion together. For instance, there are several different types of modern Judaism, but they all share a reverence for the Torah; Sunni and Shia Muslims all recite the Qur'an; the hundreds of Protestant denominations and sub-denominations are united in their reliance upon the Bible; and the even more diverse communities of Hindus look to the Vedas as their most authoritative texts.

Reason number three is comparability. It's true that some religions don't have sacred written texts; instead they may have oral traditions that are passed down by religious specialists, and this is often the case for indigenous religions of Africa, the Americas, or the South Pacific. That's not necessarily a bad thing; and, in fact, many, even most, of the scriptures of the larger world religions started out as oral traditions that were eventually transcribed into written form. But written texts are surely easier to study side-by-side in comparative ways. For example, we can investigate the role played by poetry, by historical narratives, or by law codes in various scriptures. With printed translations of sacred texts, we can more easily discern the themes, the insights, and the anxieties that characterize various religious communities. Not all religions use scriptures in the same way—for instance, in a later lecture we'll see that Shinto, the traditional religion of Japan, is a notable outlier in this respect—and there's remarkable variety in the types of writings that people hold sacred and how large their canons are, but at least we're sort of comparing apples to apples here. It's easy to be overwhelmed by the religious diversity of humankind throughout history, and scripture gives us something of a common ground from which to start a conversation.

Fourth reason: I think that there's wisdom to be found in sacred texts, even for those who come to a particular scripture as outsiders. These are books that have survived because a lot of people have found them useful or inspiring, and they frequently offer novel insights and fresh perspectives, or even just call attention to truths that seem to be universal. For instance, reading the Bhagavad Gita and its teachings about acting without being attached to the fruit of actions has made me think more deeply about how much self-interest there is at the heart of most of what I do. Confucian texts have helped me appreciate how much of my identity comes from my relationships with others. When I first heard the Buddhist doctrine of the five aggregates—and we'll hear about that later; about how there's no such thing as a permanent, eternal self but we're made up of kind of a temporary combination of five strands of things: your body, sensations, perceptions, psychic dispositions, and consciousness—when I first heard about that doctrine, I realized that my own ideas about the soul and the body were too simplistic, and I became more aware of impermanence. After reading Daoist scriptures, I think differently about death and how my body will eventually be recycled by nature; and perhaps that's not such a bad thing, or such a scary thing. My point is that I'm not Buddhist, or Daoist, or Hindu, but I nevertheless find meaning and am enriched by those traditions for my own ideas about how the world works and my relationship to the cosmos. I love Confucius's injunction that the only time your parents should worry about you is when you're sick; and the observation from the Buddhist Dhammapada that all we are is the result of what we've thought; and the assurance from the Qur'an that God is nearer to us than our jugular vein or that there's no compulsion in religion; and on and on.

But I don't want you to think of world scripture as quote books that you can pick and choose from at your leisure. Biblical scholars constantly warn us about the dangers of "prooftexting"; that is, taking a verse out of context to support whatever point you're trying to make. Perhaps you've seen those religious discussions in which two people throw down Bible quote after quote, sort of like cards in a poker game; and no one wins and only hard feelings result. It's much better to look at scriptural passages in context; to try to understand what the authors had in mind, how they fit into the larger scheme of things, and how believers have interpreted them over the centuries. That's the sort of overview that this course is going to provide.

Ideally, reading other people's scriptures will be more like a window than a mirror. Rather than just looking for confirmation of our own assumptions—where you say, "Look, that guy must be inspired because he agrees with me"; rather than that—reading sacred texts can show us things that we haven't seen before. I don't think that deep down all religions are pretty much the same; in fact, quite the opposite: There are fundamental differences in the ways that people of various faiths understand the basic problems of life, as well as the solutions they put forward. I don't think it's the case that all religions are equally true; I guess that's an opinion you can make on your own. Even if they aren't all true, they can all be legitimate; and what I mean by that is we can say, "I see your point, and I can see that you have good reasons for believing that way, even if in the end I'm going to disagree."

If done right, reading the sacred texts of other religious traditions can offer a door to understanding, a bridge to harmony, and mutual respect that acknowledges profound differences as well as similarities. But how do we do this? The good news is that there's never been a better time for cross-cultural, interreligious explorations than right now. We can compare our situation to that of an earlier American who was very curious about sacred texts from all around the world, and his name was Henry David Thoreau.

You may recall that for two years, from 1845–1847, Thoreau lived in a tiny one-room cabin he'd built for himself at Walden Pond. He had only few books with him—they were mostly Greek and Latin classics—but he also had an English translation of the Bhagavad Gita, the central text in Hinduism, and he expressed considerable interest in the Hindu Vedas and the Zoroastrian Avesta as well (we'll have lectures about all of those). In the chapter about "Reading" from his book *Walden*, he complains that the best books aren't read even by good readers. He refers to Western classics, talks a little about how they're more neglected than he'd want them to be, and then he continues by saying, "As for the sacred Scriptures, or Bibles of mankind, who in this town can tell me even their titles? Most men do not know that any nation but the Hebrews have had a scripture. A man, any man, will go considerably out of his way to pick up a silver dollar; but here are golden words, which the wisest men of antiquity have uttered."

While living at Walden, Thoreau wrote a memoir of a canoe trip that he'd taken a few years earlier with his younger brother. This memoir was called *A Week on the Concord and Merrimack Rivers*. In this book, he shared a fond dream or an ambition. He said:

> It would be worthy of the age to print together the collected Scriptures or Sacred Writings of the several nations, the Chinese, the Hindoos, the Persians, the Hebrews, and others, as the Scripture

> of mankind. ... Such a juxtaposition and comparison might help to liberalize the faith of men. This is a work which Time will surely edit, reserved to crown the labors of the printing-press.

It's kind of lofty, eloquent language; you can probably tell when I'm speaking and when I'm quoting Thoreau.

Thoreau was a bit too early, but his dream was realized about half a century later—this dream of a compilation of all the scriptures and sacred texts of the world—when Oxford University published the series Sacred Books of the East in 50 volumes under the direction of Max Muller; so it was published from 1879–1910. It was a groundbreaking scholarly project with translations of the most significant sacred texts from Hinduism, Buddhism, Confucianism, Daoism, Zoroastrianism, Jainism, and Islam, and it's all online today at www.sacred-texts.com, you can look at it there. These are early translations, so they're not always as readable or as well organized as those you might find in, say, the Penguin Classics series; but the point is, you've got all of that at your fingertips, everything that Thoreau imagined. We'll be coming again and again back to Max Muller and his Sacred Books of the East, partly because it was such a groundbreaking series. This was the first time that many of these texts had ever been translated into English, published, and made available, accessible, to outsiders.

When you're faced with such a plethora of texts to choose from, the trick is knowing where to start, because many of these texts can seem puzzling or even strange at first glance. It's like you're strolling along a beach. There are shells all about; some are obviously lovely, others may be broken or half-buried in the sand and it takes a little more effort to appreciate them or imagine the living beings that they once shaped and sustained. In this course on *Sacred Texts of the World*, I can give you a quick tour of the shore. I can let you know which shells are most common, why they look the way they do, how they're related to other shells, and where they come from. Here, finally, is the fifth reason to read other people's scriptures: If you're skeptical or agnostic about religion, you can, like a naturalist on the beach, marvel at the variety and creativity of, in this case, our human species. You may gain an appreciation of what these texts mean to believers, and perhaps a better understanding of why they've gone to such efforts to preserve, translate, interpret, and disseminate the writings that they hold sacred. If you're already committed to one of the religious traditions I'll be talking about, you, too, may enjoy learning about how people throughout history have made sense of the universe through sacred texts. But there's an added benefit for you: By recognizing and articulating near similarities or even radical differences, we can better perceive the doctrines, the sensibilities, and the features of our own scriptures; and we might find that some of our common assumptions are inadequate. It's good to be challenged in our beliefs and perhaps in our unbelief's as well.

In this course, I'm going to introduce you to some intelligent, moral, spiritually-attuned women and men who see the world quite differently from how you're used to looking at it, whoever you are. They're going to have concerns, critiques, and questions that perhaps haven't really occurred to you before. Sometimes this may lead to a sort of crisis of faith, but it might also allow you to look more deeply into your own tradition with fresh eyes; and that's often a good thing. For example, Thomas Merton, generally considered one of the most influential Catholic authors of the 20th century, was a monk who lived a life of prayer, contemplation, and silence since he lived in a Trappist monastery (it's part of the Trappist tradition to not say very much) in Kentucky for 27 years, so he could hardly be accused of having a wishy-washy attitude toward his own faith. Nevertheless, Thomas Merton was deeply interested in other religions. He wrote several books about them, and shortly before his death he gave lecture in which he said, "I believe that by openness to Buddhism, to Hinduism, and to these great Asian traditions, we stand a wonderful chance of learning more about the potentiality of our own traditions"; and I think by "the potentiality of our own traditions" he meant "our own Christian traditions"

One of the drawbacks of being religious is that reading your own scriptures is most often a case of rereading. These are often texts that you've not only read before, but perhaps have grown up with. You've heard them in church, or in synagogue, or in a mosque, or elsewhere; you've seen them illustrated; they're very comfortable, very familiar. Perhaps it's a little too comfortable; you may even be complacent in hearing the same words and the same stories again and again. You know what they mean and how they apply to you. Yet the Jewish philosopher Martin Buber had a point when he observed that people who want to truly open themselves to a sacred text "must take up scripture as if they had never seen it." That, of course, is exactly what we do when we look at other people's holy books. It's a good reminder of the time when our own scriptural traditions were new to us. It's sort of like when my cello teacher—and I took cello lessons as an adult, so this wasn't as a child—sometimes she used to bow with her left hand and press the strings on the fingerboard with her right, which is the opposite of the way you'd do it, and she'd do this just to try to remember how it feels when it's all completely new to you.

In this way, as we talk about scriptures of other religious traditions that perhaps you're not familiar or maybe you've never even heard of before, it gives you a chance to think about how it would be to come to your own tradition afresh. Hopefully after you've run through this course—and then I hope that you'll eventually read some of these texts—that it'll be a little bit like rereading; it won't be completely new to you, you'll have some idea of what's going on. Then once you've had a chance to stretch your mind a bit, to step outside your own faith community, you can then return to your own familiar scriptures with new questions and see things in a new light or from a broader perspective.

I'm quite fond of Zhang Chao's description of lifelong learning. Zhang was a 17th-century Chinese scholar—he was a writer as well—who'd studied Confucianism, Daoism, and Buddhism, and he'd even talked to Jesuit missionaries, which was kind of a new thing in China at the time. This quote is about reading in general, but I think that his insights apply to rereading sacred texts. Zhang Chao said:

> Reading books in one's youth is like looking at the moon through a crevice; reading books in middle age is like looking at the moon in one's courtyard; and reading books in old age is like looking at the moon on an open terrace. This is because the depth of benefits of reading varies in proportion to the depth of one's own experience.

What we bring to texts often shapes what we get out of them, so even a single, much-read scripture can mean different things to a person at different stages of life. It's the added experience that leads to deeper, richer meanings.

Let's gain some knowledge and experience with sacred texts of the world, beginning in our next lecture with scriptures that belong to what's probably the oldest continuously-practiced religious tradition on the planet: Hinduism. I'll see you then.

Hinduism and the Vedas
Lecture 2

If you come to the study of sacred texts from a Judeo-Christian background, you probably have a certain concept of "scripture": Such texts are written books that claim some sort of divine origin; they tell us about the life or ideas of the founder of the religion; they are considered especially sacred and authoritative by believers; and so on. But one of the interesting things about studying world religions is that it gives us an opportunity to rethink our assumptions, and most of what we think about scriptures doesn't apply to the sacred texts of Hinduism. In fact, as we'll see, the Vedas—the holiest and most powerful scriptures in the Hindu tradition—seem to break all these rules.

Ideas about Scripture
- In a Judeo-Christian conception, "scripture" has certain attributes: First, it refers to a written book that claims some sort of divine origin. Such texts tell us something about the life or ideas of the founder of the religion and are considered especially sacred and authoritative by believers, who study and consult them regularly for guidance and wisdom. Finally, scriptures serve as a source of doctrine for the religion, defining beliefs and revealing truths about the universe.

- Interestingly, most of these assumptions about scripture don't apply to the sacred texts of Hinduism.
    - Rather than a single book of scripture, Hindus have hundreds of sacred texts, and they have traditionally valued oral rather than literary transmission. Their holiest compositions, the Vedas, were thought to be too sacred to put into written form; instead, they were memorized by ritual specialists, the Brahman priests.

    - There is no founder of Hinduism. In fact, the term "Hindu" itself was created by Westerners in the 18th century to refer to the many religious beliefs and practices of people living in the

Indian subcontinent. What we term "Hinduism" encompasses a tremendous variety of beliefs, rituals, and deities, but there is no single person who started it all.

- Some parts of the Hindu canon are considered more sacred than others; oddly enough, the Bhagavad Gita, probably the most beloved and widely read Hindu scripture, is not in the most sacred category of Hindu texts. In addition, there isn't a strict boundary between scripture and commentary.

- Sacred texts are important in Hinduism, but they are not central to the religion in the way that the Bible is in Judaism or Christianity; in fact, ordinary Hindus are familiar with but don't generally read the scriptures. Many believers consider taking part in festivals, pilgrimages, the worship of icons or images, devotional offerings, and hospitality or the performance of one's duty to family and community as more important to religious life than scriptures.

- Perhaps the strangest thing about Hindu scripture from a Western perspective is that the Vedas—the holiest and most powerful scriptures in the tradition—don't convey much cognitive information. The content matters less than their ritual function. They are chanted in an ancient language that even the priests who are performing the ceremony may not understand. They don't tell about the gods so much as directly connect believers with divinity or with the harmonious order of the universe.

Basic Framework of Hindu Sacred Texts
- The key distinction in Hindu sacred texts is between Shruti ("What Is Heard") and Smriti ("What Is Remembered"). Shruti—basically, the Vedas—is considered to have been revealed. (The Vedas consist of four collections of hymns known as the Samhitas, along with their oldest commentaries, the Brahmanas, Aranyakas, and Upanishads.) Ancient sages called *rishis* ("seers") perceived these mantras ("sacred syllables") resonating through the cosmos and passed them on to their disciples orally. According to some Hindus,

the Vedas were written by God; others hold that they are eternal and uncreated.

- o The oldest of the four Samhitas, the Rig Veda ("Knowledge of the Verses"), dates to perhaps 1500 B.C.E. and consists of 1,028 hymns, divided into 10 books. The poems are addressed to various gods and were meant to be chanted as an accompaniment to rituals or fire sacrifices.

- o The Sama Veda ("Knowledge of the Chants") includes songs and melodies used in sacrifices, with words mostly taken from the Rig Veda and instructions on their recitation.

- o The Yajur Veda ("Knowledge of the Ritual Directions") has prose formulas and prayers chanted by priests in rituals.

- o The Atharva Veda ("Knowledge of the Atharvans [Priests]") consists of incantations and magical spells to ward off evil spirits and illnesses, to gain a husband or a wife, or to prevent miscarriages and charms to speak when one is building a house, going into battle, worried about crops or family arguments, or even gambling. This last Veda is the latest—dating to perhaps 800 B.C.E.—and is not considered quite as authoritative as the other three.

- Each of the four Samhitas is associated with texts called Brahmanas (ritual handbooks); Aranyakas, or "Wilderness Books", which are explanations of symbolism and the inner meaning of ritual; and Upanishads (meaning "sitting near" [the teacher]), which are philosophical expositions of such concepts as *atman* (the soul) and *brahman* (ultimate reality). The Upanishads form the basis of Hindu philosophy, and with them, we finally get an emphasis on ideas and knowledge rather than ritual.

- Altogether, the four Vedas (Samhitas plus their three collections of associated texts) make up the Shruti.

- The second major category is Smriti, "What Is Remembered." These texts were produced after the Vedas and are thought to have been written by humans, but they are nevertheless inspired.
  - Although they are not as holy or as authoritative as the Vedas, these texts have probably played a more important role in the everyday lives of Hindus for the last 2,500 years.
  - The Smriti include the two epics, the *Ramayana* and the *Mahabharata* (200 B.C.E.–400 C.E.); the Dharma-shastras (200–300 C.E.), regulations for everyday living; and the Puranas (400–1000 C.E.), myths and legends about the gods.

Gayatri Mantra and the Vedas
- Every morning at dawn and every evening at twilight, millions of Hindus recite the Gayatri mantra, an invocation to the three realms of earth, atmosphere, and sky.
  - The meaning of the mantra is something like: "We meditate on the adorable glory of the radiant sun; may he inspire our intelligence," with an implication that sun equals light, which equals knowledge, which equals consciousness.
  - But the mantra is always recited in Sanskrit, a language not spoken in India today. As Professor of Religion Robert Lester explains, giving voice to the ancient syllables, "harmonizes the body, mind, and spirit with the physical worlds and the primal, universal forces."
  - The Gayatri mantra has been known as the "mother of Veda," and it was taught to young upper-caste males as part of the ceremony that began their study of the Vedas.
- In traditional India, there were four major castes: Brahmans, priests/teachers; Kshatriyas, warriors/rulers; Vaishyas, farmers/merchants; and Shudras, laborers/servants. (The so-called untouchables, now referred to as Dalits, were without caste.) Only the three highest castes were allowed to participate in Vedic religion because they claimed descent from the Indo-Aryan migrants that came to India

around 1500 B.C.E.—the originators of the Vedas—and only they could study the Vedas (though Brahmans were the specialists).

- The Vedas were in existence for more than 1,000 years before they were written down, and for the next two millennia they were still mainly transmitted orally from teacher to student, because transcribing the sacred words was thought to diminish their power or even to be sacrilegious.

- The Brahmans took their duties seriously and jealously guarded the sacred words that had been entrusted to them. There were, however, Hindu reform movements in the 19th century that encouraged all Hindus to recite the Gayatri mantra, regardless of caste or gender, and that practice has continued to the present.

- Even now, although most Hindus would describe the Vedas as their most sacred scriptures, they probably don't know much about their contents, because the Vedas are hardly ever encountered apart from ritual functions, in which they are always chanted in Sanskrit.

Contents of the Rig Veda
- Scholars of religion sometimes talk about the "Protestant bias," that is, looking at other faiths through the lens of the Christian Reformation: assuming that scriptures are at the heart of a religion, that the oldest texts represent its purest form, and that those documents can best be understood through textual criticism, historical analysis, and translation. This approach may give us a somewhat skewed view of Hinduism.
    o Still, the pioneering Protestant scholars of the 19th century, particularly Max Müller (1823–1900), did amazing work in building bridges and promoting inter-religious understanding.

    o Müller, a German religious scholar, worked for 24 years to produce the first scholarly edition of the Sanskrit Rig Veda, using only handwritten manuscripts. Such devotion to other people's sacred texts is admirable, even if the European approach was foreign to Hinduism.

Selections from the Rig Veda

Hymn to Agni:

I extol Agni, the household priest, the divine minister of the sacrifice, the chief priest, the bestower of blessings.

May that Agni, who is to be extolled by ancient and modern seers, conduct the gods here.

Through Agni may one gain day by day wealth and welfare which is glorious and replete with heroic sons.

(1.1; Embree, 9)

Hymn to Soma:

I have tasted the sweet drink of life, knowing that it inspires good thoughts and joyous expansiveness to the extreme, that all the gods and mortals seek it together, calling it honey. ...

We have drunk the Soma; we have become immortal; we have gone to the light; we have found the gods. What can hatred and the malice of a mortal do to us now, O immortal one?

(8.48; Doniger, 134)

- Burial Hymn:
- Go away, death, by another path that is your own, different from the road of the gods. I say to you who have eyes, who have ears: do not injure our children or our men. ...
- Open up, Earth [for ashes]; do not crush him ... wrap him up as a mother wraps a son in the edge of her skirt.
- (10:18; Doniger, 52–53)

- The Rig Veda consists of 1,028 hymns, divided into 10 books. Most of these are praises and petitions to the gods; references to myths; and hymns addressed to the sky and earth, storm gods, solar gods, and the components of sacrifices. There are also injunctions to moral behavior and touching burial hymns. The hymns in the 10th book tend to address more universal or philosophical themes.
  - Some of the hymns from this book concern creation, but these seem to be contradictory. Sometimes, the universe comes from sacred speech, nonexistence, a mother goddess, or a primordial giant who was sacrificed; there is a hymn that suggests that even the creator himself may not know exactly how it happened.
  - The fact that most English anthologies include some of these hymns about the origins of the cosmos is another example of Protestant bias. We care about creation stories because the Bible starts with a dramatic example, and we're curious about other people's beliefs on this issue.

- It's important to keep in mind that when we read translations of sacred texts, looking for bits of wisdom or beauty or poignancy, we are doing something that is rather foreign to the texts themselves. Analyzing and discussing the meaning of specific passages might seem natural in an academic lecture series, yet for Hindus, the Vedas are not supposed to be understood cognitively so much as experienced in a traditional setting of sound, color, fragrance, movement, and devotion.

Suggested Reading

Denny and Taylor, eds., *The Holy Book in Comparative Perspective.*

Doniger, trans., *The Rig Veda.*

Edgerton, trans., *The Beginnings of Indian Philosophy.*

Flood, *An Introduction to Hinduism.*

Griffith, trans., *The Hymns of the Rig Veda.*

Holm, ed., *Sacred Writings*.

Mittal and Thursby, eds., *The Hindu World*.

Questions to Consider

1. What are the two major categories of Hindu sacred texts?

2. Why did the Hindus value oral over written scriptures?

3. How are the Vedas different from scriptures in the Judeo-Christian tradition?

Hinduism and the Vedas
Lecture 2—Transcript

Hi, welcome back. I imagine that most of those listening to this lecture are coming to the study of sacred texts from a Judeo-Christian background, or at least have a familiarity with that tradition. When we think of scripture from that perspective, we might have in mind something like the following: Scripture is a written book that claims some sort of divine origin that tells us something about the life or ideas of the founder of the religion, and that is considered especially sacred and authoritative by believers, which they study regularly and look to for guidance and wisdom, and that defines their beliefs and reveals truths about the universe.

One of the great things about studying world religions is that it gives us a chance to rethink our assumptions, and most of these statements don't really apply to the sacred texts of Hinduism. I'll go back through the list, and then we'll see how it looks from the Hindu perspective: First, a scripture is a written book. Actually, rather than a single book of scripture, Hindus have hundreds of sacred texts, and they've traditionally valued oral rather than literary transmissions. So their holiest compositions, the Vedas, were thought too sacred to put into written form; instead, they were memorized, generation after generation, by ritual specialists, who were the Brahman priests. Second, the descriptions tell us something about a founder; but there's no founder in Hinduism. In fact, the term itself, *Hinduism*, is a word created by Westerners in the 18th century to refer to the many religious beliefs and practices of people living in the Indian subcontinent; the word *Hindu* is an Old Persian word for people living beyond the Indus River. What we term *Hinduism* encompasses a tremendous variety of beliefs, rituals, and deities, though they generally share a reverence for the Vedas, and that's going to be the subject of this lecture. Together, they constitute the world's oldest living religious tradition. But there's not one person who started it all; and, in fact, there's not even one religion, it's more like a family of related religions.

Second is that scriptures are especially sacred. Some parts of the Hindu canon are indeed considered more sacred than others; and oddly enough, the Bhagavad Gita, probably the most beloved and widely-read of the Hindu scriptures, isn't in the most sacred category of Hindu texts. In addition, there isn't a strict boundary between scripture and commentary in the sense that "this is scripture and everything that comes after is commentary"; so some explanatory works eventually made it into the canon and continued to be written into the 17th and 18th centuries. There's no Hindu Pope or All-Church Committee to decide what is or isn't scripture; it's more a matter of tradition or denominational lineages, and it's much more flexible than in Judaism or Christianity.

Remember we said that scripture is studied by believers. Ordinary Hindus may try to live their lives in accordance with principles from the Dharmashastras (we'll hear more about those in a later lecture); they may have learned important life lessons from listening to Hindu epics like the *Ramayana* and the *Mahabharata*; and they've heard the Vedas chanted at festivals and life cycle rituals like weddings; but they generally don't read or study the scriptures. That's mostly left to the Brahmans, the uppermost of the caste system. Other members of the three upper castes—and those are defined as people who have been "twice-born" through initiation—have access to sacred texts, but it's part of caste duty only for Brahmans to read and to study them. One exception may be the Bhagavad Gita, which is kind of read and studied by lots of Hindus, regardless of their caste. Sacred texts are important in Hinduism, but they're not central to the religion in the way that the Bible is in Judaism or Christianity, or perhaps the Qur'an is in Islam. Many believers would consider taking part in festivals, pilgrimages, the worship of icons or images, making devotional offerings, showing hospitality, or doing one's duty to family or community, all those things may be more important to their religious life than scriptures; and, as I said, the Vedas in particular are a concern of the religious elites rather than of the masses.

We said before that scriptures are oftentimes a source of doctrine; and perhaps the strangest thing about Hindu scripture, at least from a Western perspective, is that the Vedas—the holiest, most powerful, awe-inspiring scriptures in the tradition—don't convey much cognitive information; their content matters less than their ritual function. They're chanted in an ancient language (in early Sanskrit), and even the priests doing the ceremony may not understand exactly what things mean; the priests are mostly concerned with the exact pronunciations of the sacred words. The Vedas are directed towards practical ritual processes; and rather than telling worshippers something about the gods, they actually connect them with divinity, or with the harmonious order of the universe. Perhaps it's good that we're starting our survey of the sacred texts of the world with some scriptures that seem to break all the rules.

Here's the basic framework of Hindu sacred texts. The key distinction is between Shruti (that's what's heard) and Smriti (what's remembered). Shruti—and that's basically the Vedas—is considered to have been revealed; so the Vedas consist of four collections of hymns known as the Samhitas, along with their oldest commentaries, the Brahmanas, the Aranyakas, and the Upanishads. Ancient sages called *rishis* (and that means "seers") perceived these mantras (those are "sacred syllables") resonating through the cosmos and passed them on to their disciples orally through direct, sort of face-to-face communication. According to some Hindus, the Vedas were written by God; others hold that they were eternal or uncreated. The word *Veda* means "knowledge."

The oldest of the four Samhitas, the Rig Veda (which means "knowledge of the verses"), dates to perhaps 1500 B.C.E. and consists of 1,028 hymns divided into 10 books. The poems are addressed to various gods such as Indra, who's the thunderbolt-wielding warrior god; Agni, the god of fire; and Soma, who's a personification of a mysterious hallucinogenic substance. These were meant to be chanted (all these hymns) as an accompaniment to rituals or fire sacrifices. The Sama Veda—which means "knowledge of the chants," and this is the second of the Samhitas—includes songs and melodies used in sacrifices, with the words mostly taken from the Rig Veda and then instructions on their recitation. The third of the Samhitas is the Yajur Veda—"knowledge of ritual instructions," it means—and that has prose formulas and prayers that are chanted by priests in rituals. Finally is the Atharva Veda—and that means "the knowledge of the atharvans," it's another word for "priests"—and that consists of incantations and magical spells to ward off evil spirits or illnesses: to gain a husband or a wife, or to prevent miscarriages; and there are charms to say when one's going to build a house or going into battle, when a person is worried about crops or family arguments, or even to bring luck to gamblers; it's a very practical sort of scripture. This last Veda, the Atharva Veda, is the youngest of the four

Samhitas. It perhaps dates back to 800 B.C.E., and it's not considered quite as authoritative or as prestigious as the other three.

Each of the four Samhitas is associated with texts called Brahmanas, and those are ritual handbooks with very detailed instructions about how these rituals and chants are to be performed and enunciated. There are also Aranyakas, and those are "Wilderness Books" that are explanations of symbolism and the inner meaning of ritual. The idea there is that the information they contain is so holy that it can't really be taken into cities; it needs to stay out in the countryside. The fourth part of the Vedas are the Upanishads, and that means "city near"; the idea is students would sit near a teacher and hear these explanations. The Upanishads are philosophical expositions of concepts within the Vedas such as *atman* (which is the soul) and *brahman* (ultimate reality). The Upanishads, the latest of these Vedic texts, form the basis of Hindu philosophy, and with them we finally get an emphasis on ideas and knowledge rather than ritual and ritual instructions. There are 108 classic Upanishads, of which about 13 are considered the most important. They were written from 700–200 B.C.E., and I'll talk more about that in the next lecture.

All together, the four Vedas—so it's the Samhitas plus their three collections of associated texts; so each of the Samhitas has Aranyakas, Upanishads, and Brahmanas—all those together make up Shruti. It's a lot of literature to memorize, and different Brahmanic families specialized in different texts.

The second major category of Hindu scripture is Smriti, "what is remembered." These texts were produced after the Vedas and are thought to have been written by humans; so they're not eternal, or they're not written by the gods, but they're nevertheless inspired. While they're not as holy or as authoritative as the Vedas, they've probably played a more important role in the everyday lives of Hindus for the last 2,500 years. The Smriti include the two epics, the *Ramayana* and the *Mahabharata*, and those were written from maybe 200 B.C.E.–400 C.E. (we'll talk more about those in Lecture 4); the Dharma-shastras, from 200–300 C.E., are regulations for everyday living, like the Laws of Manu (we'll hear more about that in a future lecture); and the Puranas of 400–1000 C.E. are myths and legends about the gods. Altogether, those make up Smriti, "what's remembered."

I realize that this is a lot get your head around, and we'll spend the next few lectures talking about several of the most important texts in these broad categories, but the Vedas are a special case. For other Hindu scriptures, the meaning of the words matter—there are stories, doctrines, and rules that can be analyzed and understood—but the Vedas are revered for their sound rather than the meaning. How exactly might this work for ordinary Hindus?

Every morning at dawn and every evening at twilight, millions of Hindus recite the Gayatri Mantra. It begins with the line *"Om bhur bhuvah svah."* The first syllable, the famous mantra "Om," doesn't mean anything, but it channels the cosmic, mystical vibration of ultimate reality. One of the Upanishads says:

> The word which all the Vedas repeat, and what they say is (equivalent to) all austerities, seeking which men led the religious life, that word I declare to you summarily. It is Om. For this syllable alone is Brahman; for this syllable alone is the supreme; for knowing this syllable alone, whatever anyone wishes, that is his.

The next three words are invocations of the three realms: the Earth, the Atmosphere, and the Sky. Then follows three lines of the mantra proper, taken from a hymn to the Sun in the Rig Veda. I don't know Sanskrit, I'm not Hindu, so I won't attempt to pronounce these sacred words; but you should go to YouTube, where you can hear chanted versions or versions set to music, often repeated 108 times (that's a sacred number). These videos routinely get millions and millions of hits. The Gayatri Mantra may be off your radar, but it obviously means a great deal to many, many people. The meaning of the mantra is something like "We meditate on the radiant glory of the sun; may he inspire our intelligence," with the idea that the sun is connected with light, which is connected with knowledge and consciousness. But the Mantra is always recited in Sanskrit, even though no one in India today speaks Sanskrit as their first language; in fact, it's a dead language, older than Greek or Latin. Yet giving voice to those ancient syllables again and again, as Robert Lester explains. He says: It "dispels the darkness, destroys the effects of bad deeds and harmonizes the body, mind, and spirit with the physical worlds and the primal, universal forces" What a lovely way to start and to end one's day. The Gayatri Mantra has been known as the "mother of

Veda," and it was taught to young upper-caste males as part of the ceremony that began their study of the Vedas.

In traditional India, there are four major castes: There are the Brahmans, who are the priests or teachers; the Kshatriyas, the warriors or rulers; the Vaishyas, who are farmers and merchants; and finally the Shudras, who are laborers or servants. The so-called untouchables, now referred to in India as Dalits, were out of the system; they were without caste or outcastes. Only the three highest castes were allowed to participate in Vedic religion, since they claimed descent from the Indo-Aryan migrations that came into India around 1500 B.C.E. Those were the people that originated the Vedas, and only they could study them later; though the Brahmans—remember that's the uppermost of the castes—were really specialists who memorized the Vedas and kept the traditions and rituals going.

You can imagine the effort and care that it took to memorize long, complex scriptures in an ancient language and then pass them on exactly over the course of many centuries. The Vedas were in existence for over a thousand years before they were ever written down, and for the next two millennia they were still mainly transmitted orally from teacher to student since transcribing the sacred words was thought to diminish their power or it might even be sacrilegious. One of the Aranyakas states that a student "should not recite the Veda after he has eaten meat, seen blood or a dead body, had intercourse or engaged in writing." One of those may seem a little bit strange to you; I can imagine the taboos against sexual activity, or eating meat, or seeing dead bodies, but writing's put in that same category? There's something wrong about written scripture from the Vedic perspective.

The Brahmans took their duties seriously, and they jealously guarded the sacred words that had been entrusted to them. The 19th-century scholar Max Müller, who edited the 50-volume Sacred Books of the East, reported hearing of "an [English] gentleman who had a very sacred hymn of the Veda, the Gayatri, printed at Calcutta." Müller continues: "The Brahmans were furious at this profanation, and when the gentleman died soon after, they looked upon his premature death as the vengeance of the offended gods."

There were, however, Hindu reform movements in the 19th century that encouraged all Hindus to recite the Gayatri Mantra, regardless of caste or gender, and that practice has continued to the present. Even now, however, although most Hindus would describe the Vedas as their most sacred scriptures, they probably don't know much about their contents because the Vedas are hardly ever encountered apart from ritual functions, where they're always chanted in Sanskrit by Brahmans taking care to reproduce exactly the correct pronunciation, and the exact pitch and rhythm. (By the way, Brahman experts in the Vedas were called "Pandits," which is where we get our English word *pundit*.)

So far, we've encountered some important ideas that will reappear later in the course in other religious traditions. For example, Zoroastrianism and Sikhism have sacred poetry as more important than prose. Another similarity that we'll see is that Buddhists also began with scriptures that were transmitted orally, and they were keenly aware that once things are written down, you lose that direct connection between teacher and student; of always encountering sacred texts in the presence of someone who's already mastered them. We'll again see the importance of recitation in original languages in both Judaism and Islam, and Muslims themselves have a long tradition of memorizing their scripture; actually memorizing the whole Qur'an. Mantras are used extensively by Tibetan Buddhists, who like Daoists and Mormons are wary of sacred words being taken out of their original ritual contexts. Speaking of being taken out of context, the Gayatri Mantra was used in the theme song for the 2004 TV series *Battlestar Galactica*. I know that Hindu reformers wanted it more widely used and spread, but I'm not sure what they would've thought about that. The significance of miraculous syllables left its traces in Christianity. You may know that the New Testament was written in Ancient Greek, even though Jesus and his disciples spoke Aramaic. The gospel of Mark, telling the story of Jesus raising a young girl from the dead, says: "He took her by the hand and said to her, 'Talitha cum,' which means, 'Little girl, get up!'" Do you see what's happening there? Mark wants you to hear those exact Aramaic words that Jesus spoke, even if you don't understand Aramaic. In fact, he does this three more times in his gospel, where he gives you an Aramaic phrase that was said by Jesus. I'm not saying that Christianity got this from Hinduism—in fact, that's not the case—but you see a similar sense that the exact words matter sometimes, even if you don't understand the content.

At this point in our lecture, however, you may be a bit frustrated. "Yes," you say, "I understand that the Vedas are valued more for their ritual function than for their content; that people hearing the sounds of ancient Sanskrit at festivals, weddings, and funerals know that those words have been carefully and lovingly preserved through the centuries, even if very few at the ceremony, including the priests, really know what they mean. But still, I want to know, what's in the Vedas? What are they saying?" It's a natural question, particularly for people coming from a Judeo-Christian background. Religious Studies scholars sometimes talk about the "Protestant Bias"; that is, looking at other faiths through the lens of the Christian Reformation: Assuming that scriptures are at the heart of a religion; that the oldest texts represent the purest form of that faith; and that those documents can best be understood through the scholarly endeavors of textual criticism, historical analysis, and translation. This approach may give us a somewhat skewed view of Hinduism, but there's no question that the pioneering Protestant scholars of the 19th century did amazing work in building bridges and promoting interreligious understanding.

I keep coming back to the example of Max Müller. He lived from 1823–1900. He was a German Lutheran who lived most of his life in England as a professor at Oxford. At a time when no one in the West really knew what was in the Vedas and when there were only handwritten manuscripts because the text had never been published before, not even in India, Müller worked for 24 years with manuscript collections in Paris and London to produce the first scholarly edition of the Sanskrit Rig Veda in six volumes. (Somewhat ironically, Müller himself never visited India throughout his life.) Müller thought of the Rig Veda as the oldest book in the world, and one that would provide a key to the earliest, most primitive forms of language, thought, religion, and society. He translated many of the hymns into English as part of his Sacred Books of the East series, and then Ralph Griffith translated the whole thing in 1896 based on Müller's Sanskrit text. Even Brahmans in India came to appreciate Müller's labors as they began to investigate their own traditions with the tools of modern scholarship.

Such devotion to other people's sacred texts is admirable, even if the European approach was foreign to Hinduism. As the Harvard scholar Wilfred Cantwell Smith observed, "Turning the Hindu *Veda* into a written book is an entrancing instance of 19th-century Western cultural imperialism, here quietly imposing the Western sense of 'scripture.'" But the results are fascinating. Let's look at some of the examples from the Rig Veda, the oldest and most prestigious of the four Vedas. The book begins with a hymn to Agni, the god of fire, which sometimes speaks of him as a god of the priests, as a priest of the gods, and as the sacrificial fire itself:

> I extol Agni, the household priest, the divine minister of the sacrifice, the chief priest, the bestower of blessings. May that Agni, who is to be extolled by ancient and modern seers, conduct the gods here. Through Agni may one gain day by day wealth and welfare which is glorious and replete with heroic sons.

As I mentioned earlier, the Rig Veda consists of 1,028 hymns, divided into 10 books. Most of these are praises and petitions to the gods, like the one you just heard; petitions to Agni, Indra, and Soma being the most popular. There are references to myths, such as how the sky-warrior Indra defeated a dragon-like creature and thus released the life-giving, monsoon-bringing waters; and the entire ninth book of the Rig Veda is devoted to hymns to Soma, a mysterious, intoxicating substance that was crucial to the sacrificial rites. It says there:

> I have tasted the sweet drink of life, knowing that it inspires good thoughts and joyous expansiveness to the extreme, that all the gods and mortals seek it together, calling it honey. … We have drunk the Soma; we have become immortal; we have gone to the light; we have found the gods. What can hatred and the malice of a mortal do to us now, O immortal one?

Other hymns are addressed to Sky and Earth, to storm gods, to solar gods and other deities, and to the components of sacrifices; so there are hymns to the priests, the clarified butter, and speech. In a hymn to Varuna, the guardian of the cosmic order who sees everything and punishes transgressors, we hear a plea for forgiveness: "Was the offense so great, Varuna, that you want to crush your friend and praiser? O you who are impossible to deceive, wholly self-sustaining, you will explain this to me. I would swiftly humble myself before you with reverence to be free of guilt."

There are also injunctions to moral behavior. One of the hymns says: "Whoever has food and acts ungenerously toward someone desiring food, his heart hardens and then later his unsympathetic friend also gives no food"; so the idea is if you have food and you don't give it to someone else, in another day you're going to be hungry and someone is going to withhold from you. Then there's a touching hymn in which the mourners plead with Death not to take anyone else: "Go away, death, by another path that is your own, different from the road of the gods. I say to you who have eyes, who have ears: do not injure our children or our men." That's followed by a tender request to the grave that says: "Open up, earth [the idea is that they're going to bury ashes here]; do not crush him … wrap him [up' as a mother wraps a son in the edge of her skirt."

The last two hymns come from the tenth book of the Rig Veda, which is thought to be one of the later parts of that Samhita. The hymns in that section tend to address more universal or philosophical themes, and so they're commonly included in anthologies of world scripture. In fact, it's rare to see any English selections that don't include one or more hymns from Book 10 about creation. These seem to be contradictory. Sometimes the universe comes from sacred speech or from nonexistence, or from a mother-goddess. There's a story about a primordial giant who was sacrificed by the gods and then his various body parts became the earth and the sky, the sun and the moon, animals, and the four human castes with the Brahmans coming from his head, the warriors coming from his arms, the farmers coming from his thighs, and then the Shudras, the servants, coming from his feet at the bottom; so a sense of the social order comes from this guide. There's also a hymn from this 10th book about creation or about other things like creation that suggests that even the Creator himself might not know exactly how this all came into being.

Yet the very fact that the English anthologies always include something about the origins of the cosmos is itself another example of Protestant Bias. We care about creation stories because the Bible starts with a dramatic example in Genesis, and we're curious about other people's beliefs on the matter. It came as a shock to Western scholars to discover that the Chinese don't really have any ancient creation myths. Where the world came from wasn't a burning question for them, they were much more interested in the origins of human culture; things like agriculture, marriage, and writing that were thought to have been produced by ancient sages.

There are all sorts of interesting things in the Vedas; but it's important to keep in mind that when we read translations looking for bits of wisdom, beauty, or poignancy, we're doing something with these sacred texts that's rather foreign, at least foreign from a Hindu perspective. Analyzing and discussing the meaning of specific passages might seem natural in a college class or an academic lecture series like this one, yet for Hindus the Vedas aren't really supposed to be understood cognitively so much as experienced in a traditional setting of sound, color, fragrance, movement, and devotion.

In the next lecture, we'll take up the latest layer of the Shruti—remember, that's the part of the Hindu scriptures that's "what is heard," the most sacred part—and we'll be looking particularly at the Upanishads, which are philosophical texts whose ideas have been vigorously analyzed and debated throughout Indian history. We'll be on more familiar territory here; but even so, as we bring this lecture on the Vedas to an end, it's good to be reminded of the immense variety of world scriptures and the different ways that people have used and been inspired by them. Today, Max Müller is remembered as a founder of the field of religious studies, but his ideas on the origins and historical development of religions have mostly been superseded. Nevertheless, you'll still often hear his famous quote about how religion can only be understood through comparison. Max Müller said: "He who knows one, knows none."

What Is Heard—Upanishads
Lecture 3

In the last lecture, we talked about the broad category of Hindu sacred texts known as Shruti—"What Is Heard." These revered texts were known as the four Vedas; each begins a Samhita, used primarily in rituals and sacrifices. Eventually, the sacred sounds of the archaic Sanskrit hymns became more important than the meaning, and exact instructions for performing the rituals, called Brahmanas, along with some speculations about their religious significance, the Aranyakas, were attached to the Samhitas and became components of the Vedas and, thus, Shruti. The latest stage in the development of Shruti came with texts known as the Upanishads. These compositions, also memorized and transmitted orally for many centuries, consist of explorations and elaborations of key themes in the Vedas.

European Interest in Indian Culture
- The beginnings of European scholarship on Indian culture came in the 18th century, when the British East India Company took over large portions of the Asian subcontinent, starting with Bengal in the northeast.
    o Sir William Jones was a British civil servant in Bengal with an astonishing facility in languages. In 1786, Jones gave a lecture noting distinctive similarities among Greek, Latin, and Sanskrit, and he suggested that they were related as descendants of an earlier language that later scholars would call Indo-European. It was a startling hypothesis that turned out to be correct.

    o Most European languages, along with Persian, Sanskrit, Bengali, and Hindi, belong to the Indo-European language family, which means that English is more closely related to Sanskrit than, say, Japanese is to Chinese. In Jones's time, it also meant that studying the ancient texts of India might yield clues to the origins of European culture.

- In 1818, the German philosopher Arthur Schopenhauer wrote, "I anticipate that the influence of Sanskrit literature will not be less profound than the revival of Greek in the fourteenth century," and he asserted that the best way to understand his own philosophy was to start with the Upanishads. But not many Europeans had read them in 1818, much less the older Samhitas, which hadn't yet been translated.
    o The archaic language of the Samhitas was difficult, and most of the few manuscripts that were available were in poor condition.

    o In addition, Henry Thomas Colebrooke, another British civil servant in Bengal and one of the few Europeans with enough Sanskrit to have dipped into the Samhitas, warned his colleagues that what they contained was not rewarding.

    o A few excerpts of the Samhitas were published in the 1830s, but full translations would have to await the efforts of Müller and others in the late 19th century.

- By contrast, the Upanishads had long been important in Indian philosophy, and Europeans had a shortcut to them. In 1657, a Muslim Mughal prince in India named Dara Shikoh had produced a Persian translation of 50 Upanishads. A century later, in 1755, the French adventurer and scholar Abraham Anquetil Duperron came across two copies of the Persian version, which he translated into Latin and published in 1801.

- There was a German translation from Sanskrit in 1832, followed by an English rendition in 1853. Müller himself published a careful translation of 12 Upanishads as two volumes of his *Sacred Books of the East* series in 1879 and 1884. In his introduction, Müller defended the value of Asian scriptures while trying to temper the unreasonable enthusiasm of those who assumed they were full of ancient wisdom and eternal truths.

Overview of the Upanishads
- The first Upanishads date from about 700 B.C.E. There are generally thought to be 108 classic Upanishads, all composed within a 1,000-year period, but there are now more than 200 texts that are considered by at least some Hindus to be Upanishads. In this collection, 12 or 13 Upanishads are regarded as the most important and authoritative.

- The Upanishads feature some sort of instruction, often a dialogue between a teacher and student or a debate or lecture; these pedagogical interactions sometimes include gods and women. The word "Upanishad" literally means "sitting by the side of"; thus, this is the sort of transmission of wisdom that eager students would have wanted to overhear.

- The earliest of the Upanishads are prose collections of miscellaneous materials, while the later principal Upanishads are verse compositions with a devotional focus. They are all suggestive and exploratory rather than definitive about their ideas.

- Two Upanishads are considered to be the earliest—the Brihadaranyaka and Chandogya; they are the longest, as well.

The Brihadaranyaka Upanishad
- Book I of the Brihadaranyaka begins with a cosmic reinterpretation of the horse sacrifice, one of the most elaborate and prestigious rituals in ancient India, which could be undertaken only by a king.
    - It is doubtful that this ritual was performed very often, but the Brihadaranyaka invites listeners to view it in metaphorical terms, as something to be meditated on rather than physically enacted. It begins with a chapter imagining the world as a sacrificial horse, in which dawn is the horse's head; the sun, its eye; the wind, its breath; and so on.

    - This sort of microcosmic/macrocosmic thinking is common in the Upanishads, where connections are drawn between something close at hand and the larger universe, though the microcosm is more often the worshipper's own body.

- o Some scholars have suggested that the main issue seems to be control; by learning to control one's mind through meditation or one's breathing and bodily positions (as in Yoga), humans can put themselves in harmony with the cosmos and gain power over things that otherwise would be beyond us, such as a good harvest, the gods, or life and death.

- After the passage reinterpreting the horse sacrifice, the Brihadaranyaka moves to various stories of creation and discussions of how humans are connected to the gods and the natural world. Two key terms here are *brahman* (ultimate reality) and *atman* (the self or soul). The great mystery to be realized is that *atman* is *brahman*. Our individuality is an illusion; at a deeper level, we are one with the universe.

- Book II follows with a dialogue in which a king teaches a Brahman priest about *brahman*.
  - o The king uses a concept that will reappear several times in the Upanishads, that there are four modes of consciousness: wakefulness (ordinary life), dreaming (which seems real but is an illusion), dreamless sleep (loss of one's sense of self), and pure consciousness (beyond the other three, in which one merges with *brahman*).

  - o A later Upanishad analyzes the sacred syllable *Om* as comprised of three sounds—*a*, *u*, *m*—each of which represents one of the first three modes of consciousness, and the silence that follows as a manifestation of *brahman*, the oneness of the universe.

- We next hear the story of the sage Yajnavalkya, who is asked by one of his wives to teach her the knowledge that leads to immorality. He explains that *atman* and *brahman* are identical; there is ultimately no difference between self and other.

- In Book III, Yajnavalkya debates eight teachers about the meaning of ritual, the number of gods, life and death, and *brahman* and *atman*. In Book IV, he discusses with a king several mistaken ideas about *brahman*, as well as what happens at the moment of death and reincarnation.
  - The idea of reincarnation, or samsara, is a key concept in the Upanishads. People are reborn into better or worse human situations or even as animals, but not randomly. Our next lives are determined by our actions (karma), as judged against our duty or moral responsibilities (dharma).

  - Those who can free themselves from desires—who understand that they are, in actuality, *brahman*—can escape rebirth and gain immortality by merging with the infinite.

- In Book V, Prajapati, the creator god, teaches his children—gods, humans, and demons—about *brahman*, speech, fire, and breath. Perhaps most memorably, he teaches them "the divine voice that the thunder repeats": DA DA DA, which is short for *damyata, datta, dayadhvam*, "Be self-controlled, give [to others], be compassionate."

- Book VI includes an argument among the bodily functions about which is superior (breath wins), and another teacher/student dialogue, this time about different types of fire and reincarnation. The Brihadaranyaka concludes with several rituals and spells for love, fertility, childbirth, and so on.

Other Upanishads and Their Influence
- The second early, lengthy Upanishad, the Chandogya, is famous for its recounting of a dialogue between a father and his son, in which the father teaches the absolute oneness of *atman* and *brahman* through a series of metaphors—how nectar from many flowers comes together in honey, water in many rivers comes together in the ocean, and so on. After each example, he concludes with the observation, "You are That."

- The Brihadaranyaka and Chandogya Upanishads are key texts in Vedanta philosophy. "Vedanta" means "the end of the Vedas" and is a term used to describe the Upanishads as a whole, but it later became the name of the preeminent school of Indian philosophy that emphasized the underlying unity of the universe.

- The 8th-century philosopher Shankara argued that *brahman* is the only thing in existence, eternally and without attributes; everything else is an illusion. But later Upanishads were more devotional and seemed to discuss *brahman* in more personal terms, as if it could be identified with a god.

- Other Indian philosophers found support in the Upanishads for dualism (the idea that individual selves are dependent on *brahman* but not identical to it) and theism, in which liberation from reincarnation comes not from knowledge of ultimate reality but from devotion to a god or goddess who, in return, would save his or her followers.

• One of the most famous of the later Upanishads is the Katha, which tells the story of Nachiketa, a young boy who is granted three wishes by Yama, the god of death. Yama teaches the boy about reincarnation, *atman* and *brahman*, and the importance of meditation, self-discipline, and Yoga.

• In the 19th century, German Idealists, English Romantics, and American Transcendentalists all found the Upanishads electrifying. Later, the great 20th-century poet T.

Ralph Waldo Emerson retold the story of Nachiketa and Yama in his essay "Immortality."

S. Eliot titled one section of his poem *The Waste Land* "What the Thunder Said" and included the Sanskrit terms corresponding to DA DA DA from the Brihadaranyaka Upanishad.

- In 19th-century India, at a time when many were feeling the humiliation of British colonialism and imperialism, religious leaders looked to the Upanishads for inspiration as they developed what has been called Neo-Vedanta: the re-creation of Hinduism as a modern, unified, tolerant religion based on the ideals of non-dualism, meditation, and Yoga.

- The Upanishads may or may not speak to your own religious sensibilities, but it's hard not to empathize with the basic impulse behind them. In the Brihadaranyaka, we hear the plea: "Lead me from the unreal to the real! Lead me from darkness to light! Lead me from death to immortality!"

Suggested Reading

Goodall, trans., *Hindu Scriptures*.

Olivelle, trans., *Upanisads*.

Radhakrishnan, trans., *The Principal Upanishads*.

Roebuck, trans., *The Upanishads*.

Questions to Consider

1. Why were Europeans initially more interested in the Upanishads than in the Vedas?

2. What are the major concepts developed in the Upanishads?

What Is Heard—Upanishads
Lecture 3—Transcript

Hello again. We've been talking about the broad category of Hindu sacred texts known as Shruti, "what is heard." These are the most sacred Hindu scriptures. In fact, they were long considered too sacred to put into writing, so instead they were memorized, recited orally, and passed down by word of mouth from generation to generation by religious specialists, the Brahman priests. These revered texts are known as the four Vedas: the Rig-Veda, Sama-Veda, Yajur-Veda, and the Atharva-Veda. Each begins a Samhita, usually used primarily in rituals and sacrifices; those are the hymns. Eventually, the sacred sounds of the archaic Sanskrit poems became more important than the meaning, and exact instructions for performing the rituals, called Brahmanas, along with some speculations about their religious significance, called the Aranyakas, were attached to the Samhitas and those became themselves components of the four Vedas, and thus it's all Shruti.

The latest stage in the development of Shruti came with texts known as the Upanishads. These compositions, also memorized and transmitted orally for many centuries, are more philosophical and consist of explorations and elaborations of key themes in the Vedas. With the Upanishads, we've moved from ritual texts to wisdom texts; and this might help explain one of the mysteries of Western scholarship on the history of India: Even though it was well-known that the Vedas were the most sacred texts of Hinduism, the Upanishads were translated first into European languages.

In the lecture, we'll be looking at several of the most important Upanishads; but we'll also take notice when outsiders start to get excited about Indian sacred texts, and when Hindus themselves want to reconnect with their scriptures in new ways. As I'll keep repeating throughout this course, sacred texts matter a great deal to a lot of people, many of whom structure their entire lives according to scriptural precepts; and we'll see how many individuals, both believers and outsiders, devote years or even decades to editing, translating, and commenting on these texts. Indeed, one of the characteristics of sacred texts is that they tend to attract a lot of interpretations and commentaries. There's a tremendous drive to try to understand such works in coherent, systematic ways.

The beginnings of European scholarship on Indian culture came in the 18th century when the British East India Company took over large portions of the Asian subcontinent, beginning with Bengal in the northeast. Sir William Jones was a British civil servant in Bengal with an astonishing facility in languages. He'd learned Greek, Latin, Hebrew, French, Italian, German, Spanish, Persian, and Arabic as a young man (that's a lot of languages to try to get under your belt); and by the end of his life—he only lived until he was 47—he'd mastered 13 languages and was reasonably fluent in another 28. Naturally, when he arrived in India, he was curious about the ancient Classical language of Sanskrit, which like Greek and Latin was no longer spoken by the masses.

In 1786, Jones gave a lecture noticing distinctive similarities between Greek, Latin, and Sanskrit and he suggested that those languages were related as descendants of an earlier language that later scholars would call Indo-European; so it's a similar situation to how Italian, French, Spanish, and Portuguese are all offshoots of Latin, the so-called Romance languages or Roman languages. It was a startling hypothesis—that Greek, Latin, and Sanskrit were all sister languages—but it turned out to be correct. Most European languages, along with Persian, Bengali, Hindi, and Sanskrit belong to the Indo-European language family, which means that English is more closely related to Sanskrit than, say, Japanese is to Chinese; those come from entirely different language families even though they use the same Chinese characters, or kanji as the Japanese call them. This language family connection also meant that studying the ancient texts of India might yield clues as to the origins of European culture; and many people wondered at the time: Couldn't there be treasures of wisdom hidden in those archaic Sanskrit texts that are equal to our own Classical heritage of Greek and Latin?

The 19th-century German philosopher Arthur Schopenhauer, who is famous for his melancholy reflections on suffering and on the fundamental irrationality of the universe, wrote in 1818: "I anticipate that the influence of Sanskrit literature will not be less profound than the revival of Greek in the 14th century" (he was talking about the Renaissance, right?). Schopenhauer went on to assert that the best way to understand his own philosophy was to start with the Upanishads. In 1918, not many Europeans had read the Upanishads, much less the older Samhitas, which hadn't even been translated yet.

The Samhitas were tough going. The archaic language was very difficult and there weren't many manuscripts, most of which were in rather poor condition with copying errors, omissions, and physical deterioration. You have to remember that these manuscripts were written on dried palm leaves and then they were kept in a humid climate where they were eaten by insects and stuff, and there was sort of an aversion from the very beginning to writing this stuff down. Remember, the Vedas were still mostly the concern of priests, and they valued the oral tradition above all. In addition, Henry Thomas Colebrooke, another British civil servant in Bengal and one of the few Europeans with enough Sanskrit to have dipped into the Samhitas, warned off his colleagues with an essay in 1805 that concluded by noting that they "are too voluminous for a translation of the whole; and what they contain would hardly reward the labor of the reader, much less that of the translator." This became something of a self-fulfilling prophecy. There were a few excerpts of the Samhitas published in the 1830s, mostly from the Rig Veda, but full translations would have to await the efforts of Max Müller and others in the late 19th century.

By contrast, the Upanishads had long been important in Indian philosophy, and Europeans had a shortcut: In 1657, a Muslim Mughal prince in India named Dara Shikoh had produced a Persian translation of 50 Upanishads. A century later, in 1755, the French adventurer and scholar Abraham Anquetil-Duperron—we'll see him again in the lecture on Zoroastrian scriptures—came across two copies of the Persian version, which he translated into Latin and published in 1801. This was the translation that Schopenhauer swooned over, proclaiming that "In the whole world there is no study ... so beneficial and so elevating as that of the Upanishads. It has been the solace of my life; it will be the solace of my death!" (That's from a Latin translation that he was reading.) There was a German translation from Sanskrit in 1832, followed by an English rendition in 1853; and then none other than Max Müller himself published a careful translation of 12 Upanishads as two volumes of his Sacred Books of the East series, one volume in 1879 and another in 1884. Indeed, Müller's translation of the Upanishads was the first volume in the series; he wanted to start it with a bang with something he really believed in. In his introduction, Müller both defended the value of Asian scriptures to those who believed that they were nothing more than superstition and ignorance, while at the same time trying to temper the unreasonable enthusiasm of those who assumed that these obscure, unknown books were full of ancient wisdom and eternal truths. He basically said, "I'm giving you complete translations rather than highlights, and then you can see for yourself that there are wonderful insights alongside passages that may seem strange, confusing, or even a little bit dull." Müller was anxious to give people a full view of the text rather than just a few selections to either prove they were worthless or prove they were wonderful; he's a very responsible scholar.

We'll keep that caution in mind that there are wonderful things and then also some strange things as I provide a rather thorough description of one of the oldest of the Upanishads, followed by some themes and highlights from later examples. Of course, the first question is: How many are there? The first Upanishads date from about 700 B.C.E., and there are generally thought to be 108 Classic Upanishads, all composed within a thousand year period. But there are now over 200 texts that are considered by at least some Hindus as Upanishads, and they continued to be composed into the modern era, including a 17th-century Upanishad dedicated to Allah, which was evidently written to impress India's Muslim overlords. Such are the wonders of an open canon; the lists of sacred texts just get longer and longer as the needs arise for new revelations or scriptures. In this rather large collection of 108 or maybe even 200 Upanishads, there are 12 or 13 that are regarded as the most important and authoritative, especially since the great 8th-century philosopher Shankara wrote commentaries on 11 of those.

The Upanishads feature some sort of instruction—often a dialogue between a teacher and student, or they might have a debate or a lecture—and these pedagogical interactions sometimes include gods and women as well. The word *Upanishad* literally means "sitting by the side of," so this is the sort of transmission of wisdom or understanding that eager students would've wanted to have overheard. The earliest of the Upanishads are prose collections of miscellaneous materials with a number of contradictions and repetitions, while the later principal Upanishads are verse compositions with a devotional focus. But they're all suggestive and exploratory rather than definitive about their ideas. They don't offer systematic philosophical analyses; it's not the sort of thing that we'll see in Greek philosophy with Aristotle. We'll see that in Indian history as well, but it'll come later in the sutras and the commentaries of the six schools of Classical Indian philosophy. Two Upanishads are considered to be the earliest—the Brihadaranyaka and Chandogya—and they are the longest as well, since together they constitute about two-thirds of the length of the major Upanishads.

Are you ready for a quick tour of the six books of the Brihadaranyaka Upanishad? Even its name shows that it was an early outgrowth of Aranyaka texts—those are wilderness books; remember, the teachings that were too sacred to be discussed within city limits—and those texts offered reflections on the deeper meanings of the Vedic rituals. Book One of the Brihadaranyaka begins with a cosmic reinterpretation of the horse sacrifice. This was one of the most elaborate and prestigious rituals in ancient India, which could be undertaken only by a king. A fine, fast horse was allowed to roam wherever it wanted for a year, an entire year, and it was guarded by the king's troops who sort of followed it around; and any place that this horse travelled was proclaimed part of the kingdom and then was conquered (I guess there were armies coming behind this horse). Every day, back at the palace, special sacrifices were offered, and the priests recited legends and stories in 10-day cycles. Finally, the horse was brought back to court where it was bathed and slaughtered, and then its various parts were cooked and offered in sacrifice.

It's doubtful whether this particular ritual was performed very often, but the Brihadaranyaka invites listeners to view it in metaphorical terms: as something to be meditated upon rather than physically enacted. It begins with a chapter imagining the world as a sacrificial horse, where dawn is the horse's head, the sun is its eye, the wind its breath, the sacrificial fire is its open mouth, the sky is its back, the atmosphere its belly, the earth is its hoof, and so on, with various body parts corresponding to the stars, the seasons, the rivers and mountains, and plants and trees. You sort of have to imagine that you're living within this sacrificial horse. It says that when the horse shakes, that's what causes thunders; when it urinates, that's the rain. This sort of microcosmic/macrocosmic thinking is common in the Upanishads, where connections are drawn between something close at hand and then the larger universe, though the microcosm is more often the worshipper's own body; so you imagine parts of your body correspond with parts of the cosmos. Some scholars have suggested that the main issue here seems to be control: By learning to control one's mind through meditation, or one's breathing and bodily positions as in Yoga, humans can put themselves in harmony with the cosmos and gain power over things that otherwise would be beyond us; things that people worry about like a good harvest, weather, or the gods, even life and death.

After the passage reinterpreting the horse sacrifice, the Brihadaranyaka quickly moves to various stories of creation and to discussions of how humans are connected to the gods and to the natural world. Two key terms are *brahman* (that means ultimate reality) and *atman* (the self or soul), and the great mystery to be realized is that *atman* equals *brahman*; they're in some ways the same. Our individuality, our sense of self, our soul is an illusion, and at a deeper level we're one with the universe. It says: "If a man knows 'I am brahman' in this way, he becomes this world."

Book Two then follows with a dialogue in which a king teaches a Brahman priest about *brahman*. Those words are sometimes spelled the same way; sometimes the Brahman, the priest, is spelled with an "-in" at the end, oftentimes it's with an "-an" and that makes it look the same as *brahman*. The words are related; I'm going to distinguish them by saying "Brahmin" and "Brachman," and I'll do a little more with the "h" articulation there so that you can tell the difference between Brahman the priest and *brahman* the ultimate reality. We have an interesting situation: We have a king who belongs to the Kshatriya class—these are the rulers and the warriors—who's spiritually more advanced than a priest; he's teaching the priest about the nature of reality. The early Upanishads were composed at about the time that Buddhism and Jainism began to have an identity distinct from Hinduism, and it's significant that both Mahavira, the founder of Jainism (sort of the founder of Jainism; we'll talk about that in another lecture) and the Buddha were Kshatriyas rather than Brahmans.

There must've been many such discussions as new tensions arose in the old social order. The king—remember, we're talking about this passage from the Brihadaranyaka—uses a concept that will reappear several times in the Upanishads, that there are four modes of consciousness: wakefulness, which is ordinary life; dreaming, which seems so real but actually is an illusion; dreamless sleep, where you lose your sense of self; and then pure consciousness, which is beyond those other three modes of being, and that's where one merges with *brahman*. A later Upanishad analyzes the sacred syllable *Om* as comprised of three sounds—"a," "u," "m"—each of which represents one of the first three modes of consciousness; and then the silence that follows that syllable is a manifestation of *brahman*, the oneness of the universe.

Next, we hear the story of the sage Yajnavalkya, who was coming to the fourth stage of his life—so there are four stages in life: a student, a householder, a forest dweller, and a wandering ascetic—and as he was reaching that last stage of wandering ascetic, he was making arrangements for his two wives to be taken care of after he left so he could devote himself exclusively to spiritual matters. One of his wives, Maitreyi, asked him, "Even if I were given all the riches in the world, would that bring immortality?" "No," he answered. She said, "Then teach me the knowledge that leads to immortality." Yajnavalkya explained how *atman* and *brahman* are identical and that there's ultimately no difference between self and other.

In Book Three, Yajnavalkya debates eight teachers, one after another—including a female teacher—about the meaning of ritual, the number of gods, life and death, and *brahman* and *atman*. Then in Book Four, he discusses with a king several mistaken ideas about *brahman*, as well as what happens at the moment of death and reincarnation. The idea of reincarnation, or samsara, is a key concept in the Upanishads. People are reborn into better or worse human situations, or even as animals, but not randomly. When you die, you're going to come back to this earth in another body of some form, as a human or even as an animal, but it's not, as I said, random. Our next life is determined by our actions, which are called karma, and those actions are judged against our duty or our moral responsibilities, and this is often called dharma. Yajnavalkya explains that by doing good things we become good, and by doing evil deeds we become evil; and then this: "He, with his action, is attached to that same mark to which his mind is bound. When he reaches the end of the action he did here [the end of the karma], he comes back from that world to this one, to act again." But those who can free themselves from desires, who understand that they are, in actuality Brahman, can escape rebirth and gain immortality by merging with the Infinite. In our society, sometimes we think about reincarnation as being a wonderful thing; you can remember back when you were usually royalty or some famous person. But in Hinduism, it's not a great thing; this world is full of sorrow and misery, and the ultimate goal is to try to escape this cycle of birth and death and rebirth and re-death that goes on and on.

In this idea of reincarnation, dharma (of duty), and karma (of this sort of cosmic justice), there are similarities to Buddhism here—we'll see this in a later lecture—but there are also some crucial differences. Buddhists don't believe that there's a permanent soul or an *atman* at all, and they reject the authority of the Brahman priests, the Vedas, and the Upanishads. We'll see more of this later.

Back to the Brihadaranyaka Upanishad: Next, we get the story of Yajnavalkya teaching his wife Maitreyi all over again; you get the same story with just some minor variations—there are some repetitions here—that make it seem like this was originally an oral composition (it was an oral composition) that was put together over time. In Book Five, Prajapati, the creator god, teaches his children—and his children include gods, humans, and demons—about *brahman*, speech, fire, and breath. Perhaps most memorably, he teaches them "the divine voice that the thunder repeats," "DA DA DA," which turns out to be short for "damyata, datta, dayadhvam," which means to "Be self-controlled, [to] give [to others], [and to] be compassionate." Imagine in a rainstorm that nature itself is calling us to moral action. You hear that thunder and think "DA DA DA"; be compassionate and such.

Book Six includes an argument among bodily functions—so different parts of the body are arguing—as to which is superior (breath is the one that wins that argument); and there's another teacher/student dialogue, this time about different types of fire and reincarnation. The Brihadaranyaka concludes with several rituals and spells: spells for love, for getting pregnant, for not getting pregnant, for safe childbirth, for getting different types of children; so much for being free from desires. But one of the great things about Hinduism is its inclusiveness; there are different stages of life, and what's appropriate for householders might not be as beneficial for wandering ascetics. I suppose that everything's encompassed within *brahman*; and, as you can see, a lot of things are enclosed within this one Upanishad. It's quite eclectic in its content.

There are other principal Upanishads that are worth mentioning, if only briefly. The second early, lengthy Upanishad, the Chandogya, is famous for its recounting of a dialogue between a father and his son, where the father teaches the absolute oneness of *atman* and *brahman* through a series of metaphors: how nectar from many flowers comes together into honey; or how water from many rivers comes together into the ocean; or how the life-force is distributed throughout a tree and all of its constituent parts; and how a pinch of salt is distributed throughout a cup of water. What it's basically saying is these many things seem distinct, but they're actually all the same. After each example, the father concludes with the observation "You are That." When we're talking about water coming from all the streams into the ocean, that's what you are; and eventually, the idea is, when you can escape from reincarnation you yourself will be like a drop of water being reabsorbed into the great ocean of being.

The Brihadaranyaka and the Chandogya Upanishads are key texts in Vedanta philosophy. *Vedanta* means "the end of the Vedas," and it's a term that's used to describe the Upanishads as a whole, but later it became the name of the preeminent school of Indian philosophy that emphasized the underlying oneness or unity of the universe (I guess the word *universe* has the word *unity* sort of written into it). The 8th-century philosopher that I mentioned earlier, Shankara, who wrote important commentaries on the principal Upanishads, argued that *brahman* was the only thing in existence, eternally and without attributes; everything else is an illusion, a temporary illusion. But remember, the Upanishads were not works of systematic philosophy, and later Upanishads, written in verse rather than in prose, were more devotional and seemed to talk about *brahman* in more personal terms, as if it could be identified with a god such as Shiva, Vishnu, or Ishvara. Other Indian philosophers found support in the Upanishads for dualism—that individual selves are dependent on *brahman* but they're not identical to it; so it's a different take on the nature of reality—and there were still other Indian philosophers who promoted a form of theism, in which liberation from reincarnation comes not from a knowledge of ultimate reality, not from understanding the oneness of *brahman* and *atman*, but rather from devotion to a god or a goddess who in return would save his or her followers.

These devotional practices are part of the origins of what we today call Hinduism. Scholars often refer to the early Vedic rituals as Brahmanism—the religion of the Brahman priests—though some of the later Upanishads even disparage the ancient sacrifices, the ones that would've been done to the accompaniment of Vedic recitations, as "unsteady boats," as a lower form of worship that appealed to the ignorant. You can see there's a tremendous variety in the Hinduism.

One of the most famous of the later Upanishads is the Katha Upanishad, which tells the story of Nachiketa, a young boy whose father gave away everything as an act of religious devotion. When Nachiketa (the son) pointed out that his father hadn't given away himself, hadn't given away his son, the father in anger gave him to Yama, the God of Death. Yama happened to be out at the time, so Nachiketa waited for three days in the underworld. Yama was a bit surprised when he got back home, and apologizing for being inhospitable he agreed to grant Nachiketa three wishes. His first wish was to be able to return home and be welcomed back by his father; his second wish was an explanation of the fire sacrifice; and then his third wish was to know what happens after death. Yama hesitated, offering him wealth, or pleasure, or a long life instead; but Nachiketa persisted—he wanted to know what happened after death—and at last Yama taught him about reincarnation, about *atman* and *brahman*, and the importance of meditation, self-discipline, and Yoga.

I'm particularly fond of the Isha Upanishad, which offers a number of paradoxes reminiscent of the Daoist Daodejing, as we'll discover in a later lecture. Others have also found this brief, two-page composition especially insightful; it's usually put first in Indian collections of the Upanishads. Speaking of *brahman*, ultimate reality, the Isha Upanishad says:

> It moves—yet is does not move
> It's far away—yet it is near at hand!
> It is within this whole world—yet
> it's also outside this whole world.

> When a man sees all beings
> within his very self,
> and his self within all beings,
> It will not seek to hide from him.

In the 19th century, German Idealists, English Romantics, and American Transcendentalists all found the Upanishads electrifying. For instance, Ralph Waldo Emerson retold the story of Nachiketa and Yama in his essay "Immortality," and in "The Over-Soul" he wrote: "We live in succession, in division, in parts, in particles. Meantime within man is the soul of the whole; the wise silence; the universal beauty, to which every part and particle is equally related, the eternal ONE." You can hear the influence of the Hindu Shruti quite clearly in those words of Emerson's. The great 20th-century Modernist poet T. S. Eliot titled one section of his poem *The Waste Land*, "What the Thunder Said," and he includes in that section the Sanskrit terms corresponding to "DA DA DA" from the Brihadaranyaka Upanishad (remember the thunder saying "Be self-controlled, give, be compassionate").

In 19th-century India, at a time when many were feeling the humiliation of British colonialism and imperialism, religious leaders such as Vivekananda were looking to the Upanishads for inspiration as they developed what's been called by some scholars "Neo-Vedanta"; it's basically the recreation of Hinduism as a modern, unified, tolerant religion based on the ideals of non-dualism, meditation, and Yoga. Vivekananda also spread such ideas in the West through his writings and lecture tours in Europe and America, beginning with his groundbreaking speech at the 1893 Parliament of World's Religions in Chicago. He was the first Hindu that many Americans had ever seen.

The Upanishads may or may not speak to your own religious sensibilities—this idea of oneness with the whole, or that the cosmos is within us and we're within it—but it's hard not to empathize with the basic impulse behind them. In the Brihadaranyaka, we hear the plea: "Lead me from the unreal to the real! Lead me from darkness to light! Lead me from death to immortality!" I'll conclude with one last quotation: the first verse of the Isha Upanishad. Mahatma Gandhi, writing in 1937, said "If all the Upanishads and all the other scriptures happened all of a sudden to be reduced to ashes, and if only the first verse in the Isha Upanishad were left intact in the memory of Hindus, Hinduism would live forever." Are you ready for that one verse? It's this: "Know that all this, whatever moves in this moving world, is enveloped by God. Therefore find your enjoyment in renunciation; do not covet what belongs to others." I like that: "find your enjoyment in renunciation; do not covet what belongs to others." Indeed, those are words to live by.

What Is Remembered—Epics
Lecture 4

We've had two lectures on the Hindu sacred texts categorized as Shruti ("What Is Heard"), consisting primarily of the Vedas, including both the Samhitas and Upanishads. These scriptures were the particular concern of the Brahman priests and represented an elite form of the religion, focused on ancient ritual and meditative philosophy. However, ordinary Hindus were more likely to look to Smriti ("What Is Remembered") for guidance in their daily lives. Smriti encompasses a vast body of literature and several key genres: epics, Puranas, and Dharmashastras. In this lecture, we'll talk about two Hindu epics: the *Ramayana* and *Mahabharata*.

Defining "Dharma"

- The *Ramayana* and *Mahabharata* are mythic narratives of gods and kings. One thread that runs through both is the idea of dharma. This term can be translated as "sacred duty" or "morally upright behavior," but it's more than that.

- *Dharma* is probably the closest term in traditional India to what we in the West might call "religion," yet it's not just a set of beliefs and practices. Rather, it's a conglomeration of principles that gives meaning and shape to all of life and, indeed, provides order throughout the cosmos.

- The word *dharma* comes from a Sanskrit word meaning "to support or uphold"; eventually, it came to be used to refer to the eternal laws that maintain the world. It is a manifestation of order, harmony, and truth. Although there are universal aspects to dharma, it is not the same for everyone. Your dharma depends, to some degree, on your gender, caste, family situation, and stage in life.

The *Ramayana*

- The *Ramayana*, traditionally ascribed to a poet named Valmiki, appears to have been composed between 200 B.C.E. and 200 C.E., probably by multiple individuals. It's a lengthy epic of about 25,000 verses, divided into seven books.

- The *Ramayana* begins with a framing story, in which the poet Valmiki is commissioned by the creator god Brahma to tell the story of Rama, the king of Kosala.
    - Valmiki does so and then teaches his epic poem to his disciples, especially the twins Lava and Kusha, who spread it far and wide.
    - Eventually, King Rama himself learns of the epic and invites the twins to his court so that he may hear it. Thus, the story is about Rama, and he's also the audience for it.

- What follows is the epic itself. The former king of Kosala appealed to the gods for a son. At the same time, various deities complained to Lord Brahma about a demon or ogre named Ravana, who was oppressing the world. The god Vishnu agreed to take on human form to defeat Ravana and, thus, was born as Rama. In other words, Rama is an avatar of Vishnu.

- As a young man, Rama and his brother Lakshmana take a journey to save a sage from demons. While away from court, they hear of a marriage contest for a woman named Sita who had been found as a baby in a furrow of a plowed field and had been adopted by a king. Rama wins the contest and returns to the capital, Ayodhya, with Sita as his wife.

- Years later, the old king wished to make Rama his successor, but one of his wives intervened, claiming two wishes that she had been promised earlier: to make her own son the heir apparent and to have Rama exiled into the wilderness for 14 years.

- - The king is brokenhearted but cannot go back on his word. And Rama is happy to accept exile rather than see his father proven untruthful. Sita and Lakshmana, unable to bear life without Rama, accompany him into the wilderness.

  - Here, we see examples of dharma in action—Rama is the perfect son, who sets aside his own feelings and ambitions to obey his father, and Sita shows herself to be the perfect Hindu wife, completely devoted to her husband.

- But there is trouble ahead for this ideal couple. An ogress tries to seduce Rama and Lakshmana, and when she is rebuffed, she complains to her brother Ravana, the 10-headed demon-king of the island kingdom of Lanka. He kidnaps Sita, but Rama learns the identity of her captor. He soon teams up with Hanuman, the monkey-hero to find her.

- Hanuman takes a great leap over the ocean to the island of Lanka, where he finds Sita and offers to carry her back, but she refuses, saying that her husband must rescue her. Then follows a long account of the war between Rama and Ravana, before Ravana is finally defeated and killed.

- Afterward, Rama accuses Sita of having been unfaithful to him with Ravana. She protests that she is innocent and offers to undergo public ordeal by fire to prove it. When she is vindicated, Rama welcomes her as his wife, explaining that he had never doubted her virtue but had to put her to the test to prove her innocence to others. The couple returns in triumph to Ayodhya, and Rama takes the throne. Some versions of the epic end here, but Valmiki's Sanskrit version has one more chapter.

- A few years later, Rama hears that some of his people still doubt Sita's fidelity. Uncomfortable with the uncertainty, Sita decides to leave, even though she is pregnant. She takes refuge with the poet Valmiki and gives birth to twins who grow up to become disciples of the poet: Lava and Kusha.

The most popular Hindu holiday, Diwali, in part commemorates the lighting of the palace lamps when Rama and Sita returned from exile.

- o In other words, Rama's own lost sons are now reciting to him the story of his own life. Rama is joyfully reunited with them and invites Sita to return to the palace.

- o Sita, however, calls upon her mother, the goddess Earth, to witness her longstanding devotion and purity; she then descends into the earth as it opens to receive her. Rama is heartbroken until the god Brahma reminds him that he is an incarnation of Vishnu, and he will once again be with his beloved wife in heaven.

- The *Ramayana* has much to say about dharma with regard to gender roles, kingship, family relationships, honor, interactions with the gods, and the place of sacrifice, violence, and even poetry within a well-ordered, harmonious life. The story is also integral to Indian culture.

- Not many Hindus have read the Vedas, but hundreds of millions have read the *Ramayana* in vernacular languages or have seen versions on television or in reenactments. Indeed, Rama is widely worshipped in India (as an avatar of Vishnu).

- Further, Rama's influence is not confined to India. His story has been transformed into beloved national epics in Indonesia, Malaysia, the Philippines, Thailand, Burma, and Cambodia. There are Buddhist, Jain, and even Muslim versions of the tale, which can be found throughout South and Southeast Asia in temple architecture, dance, and drama.

The *Mahabharata*

- The *Mahabharata* ("Great Epic of the Bharata War") is much longer, more complicated, and more morally ambiguous than the *Ramayana*. The *Mahabharata* comprises 75,000 to 100,000 verses in 18 books. It is ascribed to the poet Vyasa, who like Valmiki, is both the author of the epic and a character in it.

- This epic has a similar setting to the *Ramayana* and was composed at about the same time (300 B.C.E.–300 C.E.), but it is much darker in tone. It is the story of a family that tears itself apart and, in the process, brings ruins to the whole country.

- The story begins with a king who had two sons. The oldest son, Dhritarashtra, should have been the next ruler, but because he was born blind, the kingdom was given to the younger son, Pandu.
    - Pandu had five sons—or so it seemed, but their actual fathers were gods: Yudhisthira, the son of Dharma personified; Bhima, the strong one; Arjuna, the great archer; and the twins Nakula and Sahadeva. These five Pandava brothers are all married to the same woman, Draupadi.
    - When Pandu died, the blind Dhritarashtra became regent, and naturally, his eldest son, Duryodhana, expected to inherit the kingdom, though Yudhisthira, the son of Pandu and the oldest of all the cousins, had a stronger claim.

- The blind king divides the realm in two, but this does not satisfy Duryodhana, who tries to kill the Pandavas and eventually challenges Yudhisthira to a game of dice. Yudhisthira, whose dharma does not allow him to back down from a challenge, loses everything, including his brothers and their wife Draupadi. Ultimately, the losers promise to go into exile for 12 years and remain in disguise for another year, after which time, the winners will hand over the kingdom.

- After the Pandavas fulfill the terms of their agreement, the cousins refuse to give up their kingdom. There seems to be no alternative but war. On the eve of the battle, Arjuna does not want to fight, because he knows that he will be killing relatives, teachers, and friends the next day, but the god Krishna, who is acting as his chariot driver, explains that doing one's duty is required by dharma. (This famous episode is later known as the Bhagavad Gita.) In the 18-day war that follows, nearly everyone on both sides dies.

- The Pandavas are victorious, but peace is still elusive. Several years later, most of their chief allies are slaughtered in a drunken brawl, and Krishna himself is accidentally killed by a hunter. Yudhisthira abdicates the throne, leaving the kingdom to a younger kinsman while he, his four brothers, and Draupadi try to reach Indra's heaven in the Himalayas.

- Along the way, everyone dies except for Yudhisthira and his devoted dog, who turns out to be the god Dharma; they both are taken into Indra's heaven. However, Yudhisthira is shocked to discover his archenemy Duryodhana in heaven, while his four brothers and Draupadi are in hell. He chooses to go to hell to be with his family; the vision then dissolves, and he is told that he has passed the final test. All are reunited in heaven.

- This summary doesn't even begin to touch on the poignancy and richness of this narrative, which includes framing stories, hundreds of subplots and digressions, sacred vows, terrifying curses, and more. The ideal of dharma is constantly sought for and questioned, as even the heroes make terrible mistakes and the gods themselves encourage humans to act in ways that seem ethically troubling. But the *Mahabharata* offers plenty of material for thinking about the deepest questions of life. One of its constant refrains is: Dharma is subtle.

- If the *Ramayana* is the more beloved of the two epics, the *Mahabharata* is similarly well-known and pervasive throughout India; indeed, Bharat is what Indians call their own county. The *Mahabharata* is a national epic and a work of profound religious devotion and insight. It is not surprising that it is often referred to as the Fifth Veda.

Suggested Reading

Brockington and Brockington, trans., *Rama the Steadfast*.

Dass, Gucharan, *The Difficulty of Being Good*.

Doniger, *The Hindus*.

Goldman et al., trans., *The Ramayana of Valmiki*.

Mittal and Thursby, eds., *The Hindu World*.

Narasimhan, trans., *The Mahabharata*.

Smith, trans., *The Mahabharata*.

Venkatesananda, *The Concise Ramayana of Valmiki*.

Questions to Consider

1. What are the basic stories of the *Ramayana* and the *Mahabharata*?

2. Why have these epics become so popular and influential?

What Is Remembered—Epics
Lecture 4—Transcript

Hello again; thanks for joining me. We've had two lectures on the Hindu sacred texts categorized as Shruti, "what's heard," and those consist of the Vedas, and including both the Samhitas and the Upanishads. These scriptures were the particular concern of Brahman priests and they represented an elite form of the religion, focused on ancient ritual and meditative philosophy. Ordinary Hindus were more likely to look to Smriti, "what's remembered," for guidance in their ordinary lives. Smriti encompasses a vast body of literature, but in the next two lectures I'll introduce some of the key genres: epics, Puranas, and Dharma-shastras.

But first, a caution: Hinduism is a religious tradition characterized by astonishing diversity; there are actually only a few statements that we could make about it that would be universally accepted. For instance, we might say that Smriti generally comes after Shruti; that they are thought to have human authors rather than divine origins; and that they're secondary in importance in Hinduism. But at the same time, we've seen how some Upanishads continued to be written into the early modern era, long after the composition of the *Ramayana*, the *Mahabharata*, and the Laws of Manu, to name the three most significant Smriti. Some consider Vyasa, the legendary author of the *Mahabharata*, to be an incarnation of the god Vishnu; and the most popular, beloved text in Hinduism, the Bhagavad Gita, though it's an excerpt from the *Mahabharata* and is clearly within the Smriti category, is treated like an Upanishad and it's often considered as if it were Shruti. Those boundaries often aren't as clear cut as we might expect. Remember, Hindu sacred texts, like Hinduism itself, are often very flexible and fluid; they resist strict classifications.

In this lecture, we'll talk about the two Hindu epics, the *Ramayana* and *Mahabharata*. These are mythic narratives of gods and kings from long ago, and Indians refer to them as *itihasa*, which means "that's how it was"; they're history-like texts, except they include a lot of interactions with the gods, they're mythical as well. Like the Shruti, these tales were originally oral compositions, but unlike the Vedic hymns, they were adapted, expanded, and translated into vernacular languages over generations. Whereas correctly pronouncing the sounds of the ancient Sanskrit syllables of the Vedic hymns was considered more important than knowing what they meant, for the epics, it's the stories that matter; people know exactly what's happening when they hear these and hear them recounted.

As we review some of the main characters and plotlines, I want you to keep in mind two things: First, even though some of the details may seem strange or even a bit bizarre, I want you to imagine what it would be like if you'd grown up with these tales. What if they were as familiar to you as, say, the stories of Adam and Eve, Noah's Ark, David and Goliath, or Jonah and the Whale? You might imagine how Indians might react to stories of fire coming from heaven, of talking donkeys, walking on water, and other things from the Western Bible. The second thing is I want you to listen for a thread that runs through all of these narratives. Okay, here comes one of those generalizations about Hinduism that I warned you about; but I'm pretty confident about this one. As the scholar Wendy Doniger says, "The Hindus regard the Epics both as great poems and as great textbooks; we may think that they are about the war of the Bharatas and the battle between Rama and Ravana, but the Hindus think that they are about dharma." It's actually all about dharma; that's the thread that ties them together. But what exactly is dharma?

Dharma can be translated as "sacred duty" or "morally upright behavior," but it's more than that. It's probably the closest term in traditional India to what we in the West might call "religion"; yet it's not just a set of beliefs and practices. Rather, it's a conglomeration of principles that gives meaning and shape to all of life and, indeed, dharma provides order throughout the cosmos. Dharma comes from a Sanskrit word that means "to support" or "uphold." Eventually it was used to refer to the eternal laws that maintain the world; they uphold or support the world as we know it. Dharma is a manifestation of order, harmony, and truth; and although there are universal aspects to it, it's not the same for everyone. Your dharma depends to some degree on your gender, your caste, your family situation, and your stage in life. Dharma is more straightforward in the shorter of the two epics, the *Ramayana*, where Rama is thought of as the ideal man and Sita the ideal woman. We'll start there; and, by the way, *Ramayana* means "The Way of Rama."

The *Ramayana*, traditionally ascribed to a poet named Valmiki, appears to have been composed between 200 B.C.E. and 200 C.E.—so 400 years there that it was added to or put together—probably composed by multiple individuals. It's a lengthy epic poem of about 25,000 verses (so those are couplets, 50,000 lines or so), and it's divided into seven books, which makes it almost twice as long as the *Iliad* and the *Odyssey* put together.

The *Ramayana* begins with a framing story. The poet Valmiki is conversing with a divine seer named Narada. Valmiki asks if there are any truly superior men in the current age, and Narada tells him the story of Rama, the king of Kosala. Not long thereafter, Valmiki curses a cruel hunter and in so doing he invents a new form of Sanskrit verse—it must've been a particularly potent kind of curse that he gave—and then he's visited by the creator God Brahma who commissions Valmiki to use this poetic form to tell the story of Rama; that's the story that he's just heard. Valmiki does this, and then he teaches his epic poem to his disciples, especially the twins Lava and Kusha, who spread it far and wide (remember those two figures, Lava and Kusha). Eventually, King Rama himself hears of this epic, this story, and invites the twins to his court, where he hears a performance. The story is about Rama, but Rama's also the audience for it; he's listening to a story about himself. It takes place—this performance takes place—as part of one of those legendary horse sacrifices that goes on and on for a year.

Then after that—this is still the introductory material in the *Ramayana*—follows the epic itself. The former king of Kosala, wishing to have a son, appealed to the gods with prayer and sacrifices. At the same time, various deities complained to Lord Brahma about a demon or an ogre named Ravana who'd been given the gift of being invulnerable to all attacks by the gods and was oppressing the world. The gods couldn't really do anything about that because of that gift that he had, but they realized that this gift didn't make Ravana impervious to humans; so the great god Vishnu agreed to take on human form—he comes down, he's born to this earth, he takes on human form—in order to defeat Ravana, and so he was born as Rama. In other words, Rama is an avatar of Vishnu.

As a young man, Rama and his brother Lakshmana take a journey to save a sage from demons; and while they're away from court, they hear of a marriage contest for a woman named Sita (the name means "furrow." She'd been given that name because she'd been found as a baby in the furrow of a plowed field and had been adopted by the king. The contest that would result in her marriage was to lift and to string a massive bow that had been given to the king by the god Shiva. Rama was the only contestant able to do this, and so he returned to the capital Ayodhya with Sita as his wife; she was the prize that was given for winning this particular contest. Years later, the old king wished to make Rama his successor, but one of his wives, who'd long ago been promised two wishes, claimed one of those wishes at that very moment, and the wish she wanted was to make her own son the heir apparent rather than Rama. The second gift that she asked for was she asked the king to exile Rama into the wilderness for 14 years. The king was brokenhearted, but he couldn't go back on his word. Remember, that's part of dharma, about your duty to do the right thing; and kings, when they give promises, they're not allowed to go back on them, to do so would be to defy the duty of a king. Rama was exiled, but he was fairly happy to accept his homeless exile and demotion rather than see his father proven untruthful; he had this dharma that he had to follow as well in being obedient to his father. Sita and Lakshmana, not being able to bear life without Rama, accompanied him into the wilderness. Here we see several examples of dharma in action: Rama is the perfect son, who sets aside his own feelings and ambitions to obey his father; and Sita shows herself to be the perfect Hindu wife, completely devoted to her husband; and I suppose Lakshmana shows the dharma of being the ideal brother as well, faithful and loyal to the end.

But there's trouble ahead for the ideal couple of Rama and Sita. An ogress tries to seduce Rama and Lakshmana, and when she's rebuffed she complains to her brother Ravana, the 10-headed demon king of the island kingdom of Lanka. Ravana sends a golden deer to lure Rama and Lakshmana away, and in their absence he swoops in and kidnaps Sita, taking her back to Lanka on his flying chariot. Rama is devastated when he goes back home and finds Sita missing, and then he learns from a valiant vulture that had seen all of this the identity of her captor. Rama soon teams up with Hanuman, the monkey hero, and the search parties they send out hear reports that Sita is being held in Lanka.

The story goes on and on, right? We'll continue: Hanuman takes a great leap over the ocean to the island of Lanka—this is traditionally thought of as Sri Lanka today—and there Hanuman finds Sita. He offers to carry her back because he can jump across, but she refuses, saying that she'd prefer to be rescued by her husband. The ideal of modesty, the dharma of the perfect wife, requires that she only be touched by her husband. Hanuman causes all sorts of havoc in Lanka: He sets fire to the city with his tail, which has been set on fire by Ravana's guards, and then he runs through and everything goes ablaze; and then Hanuman leaps back to the mainland to tell Rama that he's found Sita. Next comes a long account of the war between Rama and Ravana, complete with a causeway across the sea built by monkeys—Hanuman is the minister of the king of the monkeys—and they have a panoply of supernatural weapons that they use in this fight. In the end, Ravana is defeated and killed.

At this point Ravana is defeated, Sita is free, and you might expect a happy reunion between Rama and Sita; but then there's an unexpected twist where Rama accuses Sita of having been unfaithful to him with Ravana. How could she have lived in his palace for nearly a year without having yielded to his force and charisma? Rama tells her that he's fulfilled his duty by avenging her kidnapping and killing Ravana, but that their marriage is over. Sita protests that she's innocent and offers to undergo public ordeal by fire to prove that. When she's vindicated, Rama welcomes her as his wife, explaining that he himself had never doubted her virtue, but he had to put her to the test to prove her innocence to others, otherwise people in the kingdom would be spreading rumors or talking about this. So, with all of that past them, the couple returns in triumph to Ayodhya, the capital, where Rama's brother has agreed to step aside as king in favor of Rama, and they live happily ever after.

Or at least it seems like they should. Some versions of the *Ramayana* end here, but Valmiki's Sanskrit version has one more chapter. A few years later, Rama hears that there are rumors among his people doubting Sita's chastity when she was with Ravana—this was the problem he'd anticipated before—and, uncomfortable with the uncertainty, Sita decides that she's going to leave, even though she's pregnant. She takes refuge with the poet Valmiki—he's the author of the epic—and she gives birth to twins who grow up to become disciples of Valmiki, and who are (wait for it) none other than Lava and Kusha; so Rama's own lost sons are now reciting to him the story of his own life. Rama is joyfully reunited with his boys, and he invites Sita to return to the palace. Sita, however, calls upon her mother, the goddess Earth, to witness her longstanding devotion and purity, and then Sita descends into the earth as it opens to receive her. Sita may be a devoted Hindu wife, but she can insist upon her dignity when she's been wrongfully accused. Rama is heartbroken until the god Brahma reminds him that he's an incarnation of Vishnu, and that he'll once again be with his beloved wife in heaven at some point.

There's much, much more, but this is at least the basic outline; keep in mind that the epic is about as long as the Bible. The *Ramayana* has a lot to say about dharma with regard to gender roles, and kingship, and how kings ought to organize their kingdoms and protect their people; it says a lot about family relationships, about honor, interactions with the gods; and the place of sacrifice, violence, and even poetry within a well-ordered, harmonious life. But what I want to point out is how integral this story is to Indian culture. Not many Hindus have read the Vedas, but hundreds of millions have read the *Ramayana* in vernacular languages such as Tamil in South India, or Bengali in Northeast India, or Hindi; or they've heard versions of the *Ramayana* in storytelling, radio, and TV; they've seen illustrations and reenactments. Indeed, Rama is widely worshipped in India—remember, he's an avatar of Vishnu, so he belongs to the category of gods—and his influence is not confined to India. Robert and Sally Goldman at UC Berkeley have noted that, "Although it is little known to the average, educated Westerner, the *Valmiki Ramayana* is arguably one of the three or four most important and most widely influential texts ever written." They put it at the level of the Bible and the Qur'an, in part because its impact upon art, literature, and social thought has crossed national and even religious borders.

The story of Rama has been transformed into beloved national epics in Indonesia, Malaysia, the Philippines, Thailand, Burma, and Cambodia. You may have heard Muslim countries there and Buddhist countries; so there are Buddhist and Jain versions of this tale, as well as Muslim versions of the tale. It can be found throughout South Asia and Southeast Asia in temple architecture, in some of the statuary and the images in temples, in dance, and in drama. In Thailand, food dishes are named for characters in the *Ramayana*; in Indonesia, the *Ramayana* is one of the staples of Javanese shadow puppet theater; and the most popular Hindu holiday, Diwali, or the Festival of Lights, in part commemorates the lighting of palace lamps when Rama and Sita returned from exile to Ayodhya. On a less happy note, there have been violent disputes in Ayodhya over a plot of land thought to have been the birthplace of Rama and also the site of a later Muslim mosque that was thought to have been built on a temple on that site. In the 1990s, over 2,000 people were killed in rioting over the issue. As with other sacred texts, the stories and characters of Smriti, "what is remembered," matter deeply to many, many people.

I suspect that one of the reasons for the astounding popularity of the *Ramayana* is that it's a fairly straightforward narrative with clear moral meaning: Good triumphs over evil and it ends with peace, prosperity, and love, particularly if you conclude the story at the end of Book Six, with Rama and Sita's return to Ayodhya. But there is another ancient Sanskrit epic, also considered Smriti, that's much longer, more complicated, and more morally ambiguous. For these reasons, the *Mahabharata* is probably even more impressive as a work of literature. The name of that epic, the *Mahabharata*, means "The Great Epic of the Bharata War." It's the longest poem in the world, weighing in at 75,000–100,000 verses depending on the version, and it's divided into 18 books. It's commonly said to be seven times the length of the *Iliad* and the *Odyssey* combined, or about four times longer than the Bible. It's ascribed to the poet Vyasa, who like Valmiki is both the author of the epic and is also a character within it.

The *Mahabharata* has a similar setting to the *Ramayana*, and it was composed at about the same time—so between 300 B.C.E. and 300 C.E.—but it's much darker in tone. Where Rama and his brothers show self-sacrifice and deference to preserve harmony in their family, with conflict coming from mostly outside forces, the *Mahabharata* is a story of a family that tears itself apart and in the process bring ruin upon the whole country.

There was once a king with two sons. The oldest son, Dhritarashtra, should have been the next ruler, but because he was born blind, the kingdom was given to a younger son, Pandu. That may seem unfair to us that a disability from birth would disqualify one, but remember that the law of karma works here; so disabilities or illnesses are something that comes from previous lives, so this king is probably not fit for the kingship, so it goes to Pandu. Pandu had five sons, or that's what people thought at the time; their actual fathers turned out to be gods, as we learn in the epic. The sons are Yudhisthira, the son of Dharma personified (dharma becomes a god); Bhima, who's the strongest of the brothers; Arjuna, the great archer; and then the twins, Nakula and Sahadeva. These are the five Pandava brothers—they're all sons of Pandu—and they're all married to the same woman, the remarkable Draupadi. They grew up with their cousins, who were the hundred sons of Dhritarashtra, and they're described as demons in human form; so even though this epic is going to recount earthly battles between two forces coming from different sides of the family, it represents a conflict between gods (or these sons of gods) and demons.

When Pandu dies (he's the king), the blind Dhritarashtra (he's the older son who couldn't become king) becomes the regent, so he's holding the throne for the next ruler. Naturally, Dhritarashtra's eldest son, Duryodhana, is the one who expects to inherit the kingdom; though Yudhisthira, the oldest son of the Pandu, the former king—and he's the oldest of all the cousins—has a stronger claim. I know there's a lot of confusing names in there, but try to keep those straight and I'll repeat them as we go along here. The blind regent divides the realm in two so that his sons can have some and their cousins, his brother's sons, can have some of this; but this doesn't satisfy Duryodhana, who tries to kill the Pandava brothers by arson (by burning down their house) and he eventually challenges Yudhisthira, the oldest of the Pandava brothers, to a game of dice with the winner taking all. (Spoiler alert: The game is rigged; it's not going to go so well for the Pandava brothers.)

Yudhisthira, whose dharma doesn't allow him to back down from a challenge—he has this dharma of a king, and he needs to be forthright and stand up to challenges—is also not perfect (in this epic, there really aren't any perfect characters), and he has a weakness for gambling. He goes into the dice game and he loses everything, round after round. He loses his brothers and their freedom, so they're going to become servants or slaves to their cousins; and he even loses their shared wife, Draupadi. Draupadi is publicly humiliated when the cousins treat her as a slave and they try to strip off her clothes, but the god Krishna miraculously saves her from such indignity; he actually gives her layers and layers of clothing, so as they pull off clothes there's more that appears there, so they finally figure out that she must be protected here. Dhritarashtra (he's the blind regent) cancels the match, but the cousins play one more round, with the losers promising to go into exile in the forest for 12 years and then remain in disguise for yet another year, and after those 13 years the winners of the dice game will hand over the kingdom and they'll switch places. One more round, the Pandavas lose yet again, and then after fulfilling the terms of their agreement—so 12 years in exile, a year in disguise—they're ready to go back and claim the kingdom; but as you might expect, the cousins refuse to give up their rule. There are some attempts at negotiations, but Duryodhana refuses to give the Pandava brothers even five villages; it's impossible to negotiate, and here's where dharma starts to break down. There's just no way of fulfilling duty, and the brothers who control the kingdom, the cousins, are clearly going against dharma. There seems to be no way out, no alternative, but war.

On the eve of the battle, Arjuna—one of the five Pandava brothers; the one who wields the bow, the great archer—doesn't want to fight, since he knows that in the battle the next day he'll be killing relatives, teachers, and friends. But the god Krishna, who's acting as his chariot driver, explains that doing one's duty is required by dharma; and Arjuna's duty as a warrior, a ruler, is to fight when called upon. This famous episode where Krishna is telling Arjuna why he needs to do his duty even though it's unpleasant or something he doesn't want to do is known as the Bhagavad Gita, and it's an 18-chapter part of the *Mahabharata* that's often read separately from the epic as a whole, and we'll talk about that in the next lecture. In the 18-day war that follows, nearly everyone on both sides dies; the account of the battle goes on and on and on.

The Pandavas are victorious, but peace still doesn't come. Several years later, most of their chief allies are slaughtered in a drunken brawl, and Krishna himself is accidentally killed by a hunter (Krishna is an avatar of Vishnu; he comes into sort of like a human form, not exactly, but he himself will return to heaven). With a heavy heart, Yudhisthira abdicates the throne, leaving the kingdom to a younger kinsman while he, his four brothers, and Draupadi try to reach Indra's heaven in the Himalayas. Along the way, everyone dies—

all of his family members die—except for Yudhisthira and his devoted dog, who in the end turns out to be the god Dharma, and they both are taken into Indra's heaven. However, Yudhisthira is surprised and shocked to discover his arch enemy Duryodhana (the head of the evil cousins) in heaven, while his own four brothers and Draupadi are in hell. Yudhisthira chooses to go to hell to be with his family, and when he makes that choice, the vision dissolves and he's told that he's passed the final test. He's put his dharma, duty toward family above all else, above even the desire for heaven; and because of that, the five Pandava brothers, and Dharma, and I assume the dog as well, are all reunited in heaven.

I'm afraid that at this point you might be rolling your eyes at all the strange names and the odd situations and saying to yourself, "Why exactly should I care about this?" Believe me, you should care. My summary doesn't even begin to touch on the poignancy and the richness of this narrative, which includes framing stories, hundreds of subplots and digressions, sacred vows and terrifying curses, interactions with the gods, and the effects of karma from previous lives. The ideal of dharma is constantly sought for and questioned, even as the heroes make terrible mistakes, and the gods themselves encourage humans to act in ways that might seem ethically troubling; Krishna kind of keeps things stirred up a little bit for his own reasons that are perhaps beyond the capacity of humans to understand. The *Mahabharata* offers plenty of material for thinking about the deepest questions of life. One of its constant refrains is "Dharma is subtle."

I have time to introduce just two favorite characters. Pandu's first wife, Kunti, had a child with the Sun god before she was married, and that boy, his name is Karna (so it's different from karma), was raised by lower-caste foster parents; he was found, and then he was the child of a chariot driver. When Duryodhana, the chief of the evil cousins, recognizes Karna's abilities, he befriends him and then he makes him a king—he elevates him and he gives him a position—so that he can compete on equal terms with men from the warrior caste. Karna is grateful for that trust shown to him and grace, and he never betrays that trust. He fights with Duryodhana to the bitter end, keeping his word to Duryodhana, even when Krishna informs Karna that he's actually the oldest of the Pandava brothers—he didn't even know what his own background was—and urges him to change sides (he doesn't), even when Kunti finally reveals herself as his true mother, his birth mother. But by that time, it's too late; Karna is still committed to the side that he's chosen. After the last great battle, in a book entirely devoted to the women mourning the loss of their loved ones—imagine a whole book about mourning the victims of battle—Kunti finally tells the five brothers that Karna was the sixth brother, the same Karna that they've killed. Imagine when they realize that one of their greatest enemies was actually one of them, was actually their oldest brother.

A second character that I really, really like is Draupadi. She's the wife of the five Pandava brothers. As usual, the *Mahabharata* gives multiple explanations for this unusual domestic arrangement. In one story, Arjuna won her as a bride in an archery contest, and when he returned home and told his mother that he'd won a prize, without knowing what it was she said, "You should share it with your brothers," and then it turned out to be a wife. In another version of the story, we learn that in a previous life Draupadi had asked the god Shiva to send her a fine husband; but then she got impatient and asked five more times, so in her next incarnation Shiva gave her five husbands. Draupadi is more headstrong and strong-willed than Sita. When Draupadi is lost in the game of dice, she berates Yudhisthira with keen logic; and then finally, as she's arguing there, the blind regent Dhritarashtra grants her a wish. "What would you like?" She says, "That Yudhisthira be freed." "You deserve a second wish," he says. "That my other husbands be free as well," she replies. Then Draupadi is offered yet a third wish, but she turns him down, saying "Greed destroys Dharma." It's sort of an odd twist; how many stories have you heard about somebody gets three wishes? But in this one, she takes two and then she says, "I don't want the third one." Karna in turn marvels, "When [the five brothers] were sinking and drowning ... [Draupadi] became the boat that brought the Pandavas to land."

There's a whole lot more; in fact, the *Mahabharata* declares that "whatever is written here may be found elsewhere; but what is not found here, cannot be anywhere else either." In other words, the *Mahabharata* contains all the stories in the world, in some form or another. Actually, even the story of the *Ramayana* is retold in Book Three of the *Mahabharata*.

I'm going to make an unusual recommendation here: start with a film. My first introduction to the *Mahabharata* come in a five-hour TV version directed in 1989 by Peter Brook (and that five-hour version was actually reduced from a nine-hour stage version). My library (the public library) only the second videotape, so I began in the middle with no idea what was going on, especially since Brook used an international cast of various races and ethnicities to represent the Pandava brothers. But I was captivated by the calm, graceful movements of the actors, the strong emotions, and the expressiveness of the words and music; I'd never seen anything like it, and I still watch it regularly. I'm not the only one to be impressed by a television production, though. At the same time that Brook was filming his version, a 94-episode Hindi *Mahabharata* was being broadcast on Indian TV. John Smith, a translator of the *Mahabharata*, reports that "the serial brought the gods themselves into viewers' homes, and they responded accordingly, burning incense sticks and sprinkling water before their television sets as they would have done in front of any more traditional shrine." Both the *Mahabharata* and an earlier 78-episode serialization of the *Ramayana* were enormously popular. It's reported that during the weekly broadcasts, trains and buses stopped running and entire villages gathered around a single TV set to watch the latest exploits of the gods, heroes, and heroines.

If the *Ramayana* is the more beloved of the two epics, the *Mahabharata* is similarly well-known and pervasive throughout India; indeed, Bharat is what Indians call their own county. The *Mahabharata* is a national epic and also a work of profound religious devotion and insight. It's not surprising that it's often referred to as "the Fifth Veda."

Laws of Manu and Bhagavad Gita
Lecture 5

In the sacred texts of Hinduism, the status of the Vedas (including both Samhitas and Upanishads) as Shruti is clear, as is the significance of the epics as Smriti. Then we face hundreds of texts that would probably be classified as Smriti ("What Is Remembered") but are seen as more or less authoritative by different Hindus. Many of these writings are used in a sectarian fashion by the devotees of various gods and goddesses or by the followers of particular philosophical schools. In this lecture, we'll get a sense of what's in the vast Hindu canon, and then we'll focus on two of the most prominent, influential texts: *The Laws of Manu* and the Bhagavad Gita.

The Hindu Canon
- At about the time the Upanishads were composed (700 B.C.E.–300 C.E.), other texts attempted to synthesize Vedic lore in a systematic fashion. These become known as Vedanga ("limbs of the Vedas"), and they covered six topics: etymology, grammar, phonetics, meter, astronomy, and ritual. Often, these texts took the form of sutras—series of short aphorisms that were meant to be memorized and that could sometimes be cryptic without the guidance of a teacher or commentary.

- Somewhat later texts known as shastras were also treatises devoted to specialized topics. Thus, the Dharma-sutras (rules for moral, appropriate behavior) of 300 to 100 B.C.E. were followed by Dharma-shastras, beginning about 100 C.E. Dharma was considered one of the three aims of life appropriate for Hindus, along with *artha* (worldly success) and *kama* (enjoyments).

- Later still came the Puranas ("ancient texts"), which are lengthy collections of myth and legends about the gods and ancient sages. There are 18 major Puranas and dozens of minor ones, written from about 400 to 1000 C.E. The Puranas are especially known as manifestations of *bhakti*, or devotion; they advocate an intense, emotional, passionate faith in particular deities, which in turn promises salvation to all, regardless of caste.

- After the Puranas, there are even later, more sectarian texts that are held to be sacred by some Hindus but not by others. These include devotional poetry from the 6th to the 16th centuries written in vernacular languages, as well as a whole genre of Sanskrit texts known as Tantra (8th–11th centuries).

- Hinduism is more like a family of related religions than a single monolithic tradition, and it is less defined by a fixed scriptural canon than Judaism, Christianity, or Islam. Hindus generally accept the authority of the Vedas (even if they encounter them only rarely), and they feel connected to the great epics, but there is a great deal of variation in their use of other sacred texts.

The Laws of Manu

- *The Laws of Manu*, dated to about 200 C.E., has had a tremendous impact on everyday life in India. This relatively short text outlines rules, customs, and expectations for the four major castes. It is attributed to Manu, the legendary progenitor of the human race, and it purports to record his words to a group of sages when they asked about the laws by which society could be harmoniously organized.

- The four major castes (*varnas*) in India are the Brahmans (priests/teachers), Kshatriyas (warriors/rulers), Vaishyas (farmers/merchants), and Shudras (laborers/servants).
    o All four castes were thought to have been descended from the Indo-European Aryans who migrated into India about 1500 B.C.E. and brought with them the Vedas and the Vedic religion. Only the upper three castes, however, could participate fully in Vedic rituals or receive an initiation known as being "twice-born." Outside the system were outcastes, now referred to as Dalits, who were descendants of indigenous peoples.

    o For twice-born males, life was divided into four stages: student, householder, forest dweller, and wandering ascetic. A man became a forest dweller when he retired from a career, divesting himself of possessions and moving to a hut in the forest, perhaps with his wife. As a wandering ascetic, he became homeless and left everything behind, even his wife, so that he could devote himself to meditation, asceticism, and spiritual pursuits.

- *The Laws of Manu* is composed of 2,684 verses divided into 12 chapter-length books. It starts with the creation of the world, including an account of the origins of the four *varnas*. Then, chapters 2–6 outline the rules for the different life stages of a Brahman male.
  - *The Laws* specifies appropriate teacher/student relations and, for householders, provides guidelines for marriage, sacrifices, hospitality, offerings to ancestors, and so on.
  - Generally, people were expected to stay within their own castes for marriages, meals, and other social interactions. There are also warnings about polluting influences that would compromise one's purity, including coming into contact with forbidden foods, death, members of lower castes, and menstruating women. Chapter 6 provides regulations for forest dwellers and wandering ascetics.

- Chapters 7 to 9 turn their attention to the dharma of Kshatriyas, with rules for kingship, diplomacy, and war and guidelines for the legal system.

- *The Laws* concludes with a chapter on problematic situations, such as children born of mixed-caste parents, a chapter on penance for sins, and a chapter on the workings of karma that explains why people are reborn into different castes.

Implications of *The Laws*
- In India, *The Laws of Manu* has historical value and may provide insights into some of the traditional values that are still part of Indian society. Caste regulations have weakened over time, but they

still play an important role in politics and marriage arrangements. As in Judaism, some of the expectations for priests have spread throughout society, so that education is a higher priority for many Indian women and lower castes, not just for Brahman males.

- But reading *The Laws of Manu* also gives us a chance to reconsider some of our own cultural assumptions. For example, the idea that "all men are created equal" is, in reality, a fiction. It's a fact that some people are smarter than others, or better looking, or were born into more prosperous families—and remember, Hinduism's law of karma provides an explanation for those differences that satisfies our sense of justice. Doesn't it make sense to have different expectations for those of varying abilities? Perhaps there isn't a single standard of achievement by which we can measure everyone.

- As much as we may recoil at the notion of social class fixed by caste, we in the West tend to determine social class by wealth, whereas in India, people could still belong to the Brahman caste even if they were poor. And though we like to think that anyone can succeed through hard work and ability, in actuality, there seems to be less social mobility in the United States than in many other modernized countries.

- It is also striking that for most of its history, India's social stability came from the kind of dharma advocated by *The Laws of Manu* rather than from strict law codes. People had a defined place in society and acted accordingly because of pressure from family, neighbors, and especially, *jati* (local, self-governing subcastes). What does it say about our society that we depend on laws, contracts, and a somewhat intrusive government to keep things running smoothly?

- Although we might enjoy living in a secular society characterized by relative equality and informality, do we lose something when we jettison notions of sacred and profane? Should certain people, places, or activities be regarded as particularly holy or sacred? Are there aspects of your life that are specifically oriented toward the divine or the spiritual?

- Finally, some bits of wisdom from *The Laws* might be worth adopting in our modern lives. For example, the idea that different modes of spirituality might be appropriate at different stages of life seems valuable.

Bhagavad Gita

- The Bhagavad Gita ("Song of the Lord") is a scripture of just 700 verses. As an excerpt from the *Mahabharata*, it qualifies as Smriti, but its philosophical content and dialogue form make it sound like an Upanishad, and it is often treated as if it were Shruti. Further, it speaks to Hindus of all castes, combining discussions of spiritual insight with advice for worldly success and intense devotionalism.

In suggesting that the way of devotion is open to everyone, Krishna tells Arjuna: "No one who is devoted to me is ever lost."

- As we saw in the last lecture, on the eve of the great war between the Pandava brothers and their evil cousins, Arjuna rides in his chariot between the two opposing armies and sees family and friends on both sides. Realizing the enormity of the slaughter to come, he drops his bow and tells his chariot driver, Krishna, that he does not want to fight; kingship and victory are not worth the terrible cost.

- Arjuna is caught in an impossible situation. As a Kshatriya, his caste duty or dharma is to protect the world and punish wrongdoers.

Yet if he kills relatives in the process, he is sure to bring bad karma to everyone.

- Krishna offers multiple reasons why Arjuna should fight. These justifications can be organized into three broad categories: *jnana-yoga*, "the way of wisdom"; *karma-yoga*, "the way of action"; and *bhakti-yoga*, "the way of devotion."
    o The first, the way of wisdom, draws on the insights of the Upanishads, in particular, the ideas of reincarnation and the oneness of all life. The meditations here are probably most appropriate for educated Brahmans.

    o The way of action, in contrast, is perhaps best suited for Kshatriyas. Krishna tells Arjuna that he must perform his caste duty, no matter how unpleasant, because to do otherwise would bring shame upon him and disorder to the world. For a warrior, action is preferable to the inaction or renunciation of a Brahman, but the secret is to act dispassionately. In this way, one can live calmly and peacefully, free from the distractions of fear or anger.

    o In the third path, the way of devotion, bad karma can be avoided if one surrenders one's deeds to Krishna. A little further on, Krishna suggests that the way of devotion is open to everyone, not just noble priests or warriors.

- Over the course of the Gita, Krishna gradually reveals himself, until in chapter 11, Arjuna asks to see Krishna's true form.
    o There follows a terrifying theophany as Arjuna beholds an infinite being who encompasses the entire universe, with innumerable arms, bellies, and faces. Krishna is both creator and destroyer, and Arjuna is shocked to see the chief warriors in both armies hastening into his open mouths.

    o Arjuna begs Krishna to return to human form, but clearly any debate is over, just as when God's voice speaks from the whirlwind in the Hebrew Bible's book of Job.

- The Bhagavad Gita offers an attractive counter to the notion in the Upanishads that salvation comes only to those who leave behind all worldly responsibilities. Instead, the Gita demonstrates how spiritual attainment can be won while still honoring the social obligations of family, caste, and community. For this reason, the Gita has long been chanted in homes and temples, recited at festivals, and quoted by ordinary Hindus throughout India.

Suggested Reading

Dimmitt and Van Buitenen, eds. and trans., *Classical Hindu Mythology*.

Flood, ed., *The Blackwell Companion to Hinduism*.

Flood and Martin, trans., *The Bhagavad Gita: A New Translation*.

Goodall, ed. and trans., *Hindu Scriptures*.

Miller, trans., *The Bhagavad-Gita: Krishna's Counsel in Time of War*.

Mittal and Thursby, eds., *The Hindu World*.

O'Flaherty, ed. and trans., *Textual Sources for the Study of Hinduism*.

Olivelle, trans., *The Law Code of Manu*.

Patton, trans., *The Bhagavad Gita*.

Schweig, *Dance of Divine Love*.

Questions to Consider

1. How has the idea of dharma affected Indian life in the past and in the present?

2. Why is the Bhagavad Gita nearly universally beloved in India, even though it consists of just a few chapters from the *Mahabharata*?

Laws of Manu and Bhagavad Gita
Lecture 5—Transcript

Hello again. In the sacred texts of Hinduism, the status of the Vedas, including both the Samhitas and the Upanishads, is clear since they're Shruti; and the significance of the Epics as Smriti is pretty clear as well. But then we face hundreds of texts that would probably be classified as Smriti, "what is remembered," but that are seen as more or less authoritative by different Hindus. Many of these writings are used in a sectarian fashion by the devotees of various gods and goddesses, or by the followers of particular philosophical schools. In this lecture, I'll try to give you a sense of what's in the vast Hindu canon, and then we'll focus on two of the most prominent, influential texts: *The Laws of Manu* and the Bhagavad Gita.

At about the time the Upanishads were composed—so that's 700 B.C.E.–300 C.E.—there were other texts that attempted to synthesize Vedic lore in a systematic fashion. These become known as the Vendanga, and that means the "limbs of the Vedas." They covered six topics: etymology, grammar, phonetics, meter, astronomy, and ritual. Often these took the form of sutras; those are texts that are composed of short aphorisms that were meant to be memorized and could sometimes be cryptic without the guidance of a teacher or commentary, they're seen as perhaps aids to memorization. The word *sutra* refers to a thread that ties things together and is related to the English word *suture*. Other sutras became the basis for the six orthodox schools of Hindu philosophy. For instance, the Brahma Sutra was a key text of Vedanta, and that was the school that focuses on the identity of *atman* and *brahman*; and there's also a Yoga Sutra as well, which provides a clear outline of the Yoga School. We'll see the word *sutra* in later lectures when we talk about Buddhism, but in that tradition it refers to the words of the Buddha rather than systematic treatises written by experts, followers, in particular fields.

The sutras were thought to have been composed by specific individuals, so they're considered Smriti; remember that the Shruti are revelations or they're sort of eternal texts that are heard by *rishis*, or seers. These are written in prose generally, they're composed by individuals. Then there are somewhat later texts known as the shastras—so the sutras, and then later the shastras—that were also treatises devoted to specialized topics, but the shastras were frequently in verse. So the Dharma-sutras—those are basically rules for moral, appropriate behavior written about 300–100 B.C.E.—were followed by the Dharma-shastras, beginning about 100 C.E. *The Laws of Manu*, which I'll return to in a few minutes, is the earliest and most famous of the Dharma-shastras; so it's written in verse.

Dharma was considered one of the Three Aims of Life appropriate for Hindus, along with *artha* (worldly success), and *kama* (enjoyments); or, for alliteration you get all three of those: piety, profit, and pleasure. Sometimes Hindus talked about a fourth aim in life that was Moksha, or liberation from the cycle of reincarnation. You may have heard of the Arthashastra, a book devoted to kingship, statecraft, and military policy written maybe 200 C.E.; and the Kama Sutra, which outlines the principles of marriage and family life including sexuality (despite its name, the Kama Sutra is actually a shastra treatise); and then later still came the Puranas—and the word means "ancient texts"—which are lengthy collections of myth and legend about the gods and ancient sages. There are 18 major Puranas and dozens of minor ones written from about 400–1000 C.E. These Puranas are associated with the major gods and goddesses of Hinduism, such as Vishnu, including his avatars or incarnations of Rama and Krishna, Shiva, and Shakti, a female divinity manifest as the goddesses Lakshmi, Parvati, or Kali. These gods of the Puranas are different from the primary gods of Vedic rituals or ancient Brahmanism, people like Indra and Agni. The 18 major Puranas together comprise about 400,000 verses of Sanskrit poetry, so maybe four times the length of the Mahabharata.

This huge body of texts covers a little of everything: stories, philosophy, moral teachings, medical advice, information about architecture and veterinary science (especially with regard to elephants), even recipes. This ever-growing body of sacred literature—endlessly recited, adapted, and transformed—was one of the primary ways that Hinduism was able to retain its vitality. The Puranas are especially known as manifestations of *bhakti*, or devotion. They advocate an intense, emotional, passionate faith in a particular deity, and that deity may in turn promise salvation to all, regardless of caste. One of the most important of these texts is the Bhagavata Purana, which tells of various avatars of Vishnu, especially Krishna. His life story is narrated at great length, including his escapades as the irresistible lover of cow-herding women. Their overwhelming desire for Krishna represents the devotion of all his devotees, and their despair at his absence or separation is similarly interpreted as spiritual allegory. Hinduism is more comfortable with religious eroticism than the major monotheistic traditions, though we'll see a bit of this later in the Hebrew Song of Songs and Muslim Sufi poetry.

In the vast category of Smriti literature, we have sutras, shastras, and Puranas; and then, after Puranas, there are even later, more sectarian texts that are held to be sacred by some Hindus but not by others. These include devotional poetry from the 6th to the 16th centuries written in vernacular languages such as Tamil, Marathi, and Hindi, as well as a whole genre of Sanskrit texts known as Tantra; those were written from the 8th to the 11th centuries. The Tantra, which are usually presented as dialogues between the god Shiva and his consort, include secret spells, incantations, gestures, and taboo-defying rituals for initiates that were thought to unlock the powers of the cosmos, or to reveal the divine nature of the body, or hasten liberation from the cycle of reincarnation (to get that Moksha that I talked about earlier). We'll see some Tantric forms of Buddhism in Lecture 18. Hinduism is more like a family of related religions than a single monolithic tradition, and it's less defined by a fixed scriptural canon than Judaism, Christianity, or Islam. Hindus generally accept the authority of the Vedas—even if they encounter them only rarely; remember, sort of life cycle rituals and such—and they feel connected to the great Epics, but there's a great deal of variation in their use of other sacred texts.

Still, whether they've read it or not, *The Laws of Manu*, dated to about 200 C.E., has a tremendous impact on everyday life in India. This relatively short, straightforward text outlines rules, customs, and expectations for the four major castes. It's attributed to Manu, the legendary progenitor of the human race, and it purports to reveal his words to a group of sages when they ask him about the laws by which society could be harmoniously organized; it's all about dharma, about duty. In Sanskrit, the text is often referred to by the title Manu-smriti, so it's easy to remember which category it goes in. *The Laws of Manu* was actually one of the first Sanskrit texts to be translated into English by Sir William Jones in 1794. The English were just at that time trying to set up laws and a legal system, and they hoped in that text that they'd find some legal precedent in Hinduism. It's actually not exactly laws so much as, as I said, expectations and norms; but it's a valuable text nonetheless, and one that's had a tremendous impact on everyday life.

But before we talk about specifically what's in the texts, a quick refresher here. There are four major castes in India called *varnas*: There are the Brahmans, those are the priests and the teachers; and then Kshatriyas, warriors and rulers; the Vaishyas who are farmers and merchants; and finally Shudras, the laborers or servants. All four castes were thought to have been descended from the Indo-European Aryans who migrated into India about 1500 B.C.E. and brought with them the Vedas and the Vedic religion, though only the three upper castes could participate fully in Vedic rituals or receive an initiation known as being "twice-born." Outside the system were outcastes, now referred to as Dalits, who were descendants of indigenous peoples in the Indian subcontinent. One of the late Vedas memorably describes the four *varnas* as those who were born from a primordial giant's mouth (the Brahman), from his arms (the Kshatriyas, the warriors), his thighs (the Vaishyas, the merchants and farmers), and then his feet (those are the Shudras, the servants).

For twice-born males (males who belonged to those three upper castes), life was divided into four stages or ashrams: a student, a householder, a forest dweller, and a wandering ascetic. A man became a forest dweller when he retired from a career after becoming a grandfather and he divested himself of possessions, giving up social connections and responsibilities, and then moved to a hut in the forest, perhaps with his wife. In the last stage, as a wandering ascetic, he becomes homeless and leaves everything behind, even his wife, so that he can devote himself fulltime to meditation, asceticism, and spiritual pursuits, endeavoring to achieve liberation from reincarnation (Moksha) by renouncing all desires and attachments. Actually a person beginning his life as a wandering ascetic renounces everything and even performs his own funeral rites; after he's dead, he's thrown into the River Ganges rather than cremated. These four stages of life—the first two, student and householder pretty clear, right; and then forest dweller and wandering ascetic—represented the ideal, even though it was probably beyond the capacity or even the aspirations of most people. Most people simply want to be reborn into a better life the next go round in reincarnation rather than trying to achieve liberation all in one go, all in this life.

Okay, we're ready now to talk about *The Laws of Manu*. That text is comprised of 2,684 verses divided into 12 chapter-length books. It starts with the creation of the world, including an account of the origins of the four *varnas*, the four major castes; then chapters two through six outline the rules for the different life stages of a Brahman male. For instance, students should "avoid honey, meat, perfumes, garlands, savory foods, women, all foods that have turned sour, causing injury to living beings," and so forth; so lots of rules for students. *The Laws of Manu* specify appropriate teacher/student relations; and then for householders, there are guidelines for marriage, sacrifices, hospitality, offerings to ancestors, proper clothing, hygiene, food, social interactions, and study. For example, it was considered improper to recite Vedic verses when on a horse, in a tree, on a ship, during a fight, soon after eating, or in the presence of a Shudra, the lowest of the four castes. By the way, one of the advantages of the Epics and the Puranas was that anyone could enjoy and learn from these stories, even women and those of lower caste; they were open to everyone. Generally, people were expected to stay within their own castes for marriages, for meals, and other social interactions. There are also warnings about polluting influences that would compromise one's purity, including coming into contact with forbidden foods, death, members of the lower castes, menstruating women, ejaculation, childbirth, defecation, etc. Chapter Six provides regulations for forest dwellers and for wandering ascetics, those last two stages of the ideal life.

The Laws of Manu are certainly written from a male perspective, though they also specify guidelines for women, usually in a supportive or dependent relationship, as they transition from daughters to wives, to mothers, and then widows. Women are sometimes regarded as deficient or dangerous; but on the other hand, occasionally we read verses that praise and honor them. It says: "Where women are revered, there the gods rejoice; but where they are not, no rite bears any fruit. Where female relatives grieve, that family soon comes to ruin; but where they do not grieve, it always prospers." Chapters Seven through Nine of *The Laws of Manu* turn their attention to the dharma of Kshatriyas, with rules for kingship, regarding administration, diplomacy and war, and guidelines for the legal system, and that includes witnesses, contracts, assault and theft, and domestic issues such as marriage, divorce, and inheritance. *The Laws of Manu* conclude with a chapter on problematic situations; so this might include children born of mixed-caste parents, and what occupations are allowable for those who can't find work within their traditional caste duties. There's a chapter on the penance for sins, and a chapter on the workings of karma, which explains why people are reborn into different castes.

Now a tough question: Why should those of us living in a postmodern world care about a pre-modern text like *The Laws of Manu*? Clearly there's a great deal here that doesn't make sense in contemporary society, or might even be offensive. I'd imagine that most of us are uncomfortable with the notion of social status being fixed by birth rather than by merit; by the general exclusion of women from study, professional life, and spiritual endeavors; and by certain things or people being pronounced impure or unholy. We'll revisit this challenge when we take a look at law codes in the Hebrew Bible, where just being born an Israelite gave one certain advantages, and various foods, substances, or people were considered unclean. We'll talk about why ritual impurity isn't quite the same thing as sin.

Back in India, *The Laws of Manu* have historical value, and they may provide insights into some of the traditional values that are still part of Indian society. Caste regulations have weakened over time, particularly in urban areas, but they still play an important role in politics and marriage arrangements; so personal ads in the newspapers or online still usually indicate one's caste. As in Judaism, some of the expectations for priests have spread throughout society so that education is a high priority for many Indian women and lower castes, not just for Brahman males. But reading a sacred text like *The Laws of Manu* also gives us a chance to reconsider some of our own cultural assumptions. I like the idea that "all men are created equal"—that's one of our Western values—but a moment's worth of reflection reveals that to be a convenient fiction. Some people are smarter than others, or better looking, or were born into more prosperous families; and remember, Hinduism's law of karma provides an explanation for those differences that satisfies our human need for justice. But doesn't it make sense to have different expectations for those of varying abilities? It may not make so much sense to treat everyone exactly the same, and perhaps there isn't a single standard of achievement by which we can measure everyone. As much as we may recoil at the notion of social class fixed by caste, in the West we tend to determine social class by wealth, whereas in India you can still be a high-caste Brahman even if you're poor; and though we like to think that anyone can succeed through hard work and ability, in actuality there seems to be less social mobility in the United States than in many other modernized countries. If you're successful enough to have bought a course from the Great Courses, chances are that your parents were successful as well. The advantages bestowed by wealth, upbringing, education, and social connections are pervasive and highly determinative, even if it seems a bit unfair.

It's also striking that for most of its history, India's social stability came from the kind of dharma advocated by *The Laws of Manu* rather than from strict law codes. People had a defined place in society and they acted accordingly because of pressure from family, neighbors, and especially *jati*. *Jati* are the thousands of local, self-governing subcastes, mostly based on occupation and ethnicity, within the *varna* system; so four major *varnas*, and then within those lots and lots of *jati* that may be people who are potters, or people who are farmers in a certain region, or people who deal with certain kinds of building construction materials and such. There's no doubt that there was a great deal of oppression and the squelching of individuality within the caste system, but people also enjoyed the benefits of strong, cohesive, local communities of the sort beloved by conservative thinkers. What does it say about our society that we depend mostly on laws, contracts, and a somewhat intrusive government to keep things running smoothly?

Although I certainly enjoy living in a secular society characterized by relative equality and informality, I wonder if we haven't lost something when we jettison notions of sacred and profane. Indeed, questions about purity now seem foreign or even quaint. But are there any people, places, or activities that you might regard as particularly holy or sacred? Should there be events or buildings that are off limits to outsiders? Are there aspects of your life that are specifically oriented toward the divine or the spiritual? I know that some people find an almost religious awe in contemplating the cosmos scientifically. Is that reasonable? Is it enough? If it's a valuable sentiment, how would we pass it on to the next generation? Finally, there may be some bits of wisdom from a text like *The Laws of Manu* that might be worth adopting in our modern lives. For instance, I like to share with my students Manu's prohibition against mimicking the walk, speech, or mannerisms of one's teacher (don't do that), and I'm quite taken with the idea that different modes of spirituality might be appropriate at different stages of life, even if those life-stages for Americans aren't as stringently prescribed as in *The Laws of Manu*.

But if you only have the time or inclination to read just one of the sacred texts of Hinduism of the hundreds and hundreds that are out there, the one you should read ought to be the Bhagavad Gita, and the title means "the Song of the Lord." It's a short scripture, just 700 verses, which has it all. As an excerpt from the Mahabharata—so it's an 18-chapter segment from the Mahabharata—it obviously qualifies as Smriti; but its philosophical content and dialogue form make it sound like an Upanishad, and it's often treated as if it were Shruti, oftentimes memorized and recited. Furthermore, it speaks to Hindus of all castes, combining discussions of spiritual insight with advice for worldly success and intense devotionalism. No wonder it's become the best known, most beloved work of Hindu scripture; and it's not surprising that it was the first Sanskrit book to be translated into English, way back in 1785. Since that time, there have been more than 300 additional English translations.

You may recall the backstory from the previous lecture: On the eve of the great war between the five Pandava brothers and their evil cousins, Arjuna rides in his chariot between the two opposing armies and sees family and friends on both sides. Realizing the enormity of the slaughter to come, he drops his bow, slumps down, and tells his chariot driver Krishna that he doesn't want to fight; that kingship and victory aren't worth the terrible cost. Arjuna is caught in an impossible situation between his dharma as a warrior and his dharma as a friend, as a family man, as a relative. As a Kshatriya—remember, this is the ruler-warrior—his caste duty is to protect the world and to punish wrongdoers; you can read about that sort of duty for Kshatriya in *The Laws of Manu*. Yet if he kills relatives in the process, he's sure to bring bad karma upon everyone. As the text says: "When the family is ruined, the timeless laws of family duty perish; and when duty is lost, chaos overwhelms the family … the sins of men who violate the family create disorder in society that undermines the constant laws of caste and family duty." Remember, dharma is subtle; sometimes it's hard to figure out exactly what you ought to do.

Krishna thereupon speaks up and he offers multiple reasons why Arjuna should fight. These justifications can be organized into three broad categories: *jnana-yoga*, the way of wisdom; *karma-yoga*, the way of action; and *bhakti-yoga*, the way of devotion. The first, the way of wisdom, draws upon the insights of the Upanishads, in particular the ideas of reincarnation and the oneness of all life. The Bhagavad Gita says: "Know it as indestructible, that by which all is pervaded; no one may cause the destruction of the imperishable one ... This man believes the one may kill; that man believes it may be killed; both of them lack understanding: it can neither kill nor be killed." He's talking about *atman* or ultimately *brahman*; it can't really come in and out of existence, it can just be transformed. Such meditations are probably most appropriate for educated Brahmans. The Way of Action, or *karma-yoga*, by contrast is perhaps best suited for Kshatriyas. Krishna tells Arjuna that he must perform his caste duty no matter how unpleasant because to do otherwise would bring shame upon him and disorder to the world. For a warrior, action is preferable to the inaction or renunciation of a Brahman, but the secret is to act dispassionately; to do what one has to do without being attached to the fruits of one's actions, without worrying about successes or failure, without being overly consumed by the consequences. In this way, a person can live calmly and peacefully doing whatever he or she needs to do, but free from the distractions of fear or anger. It's not necessary to renounce the world or withdraw from it in pursuit of spiritual meaning. That was sort of the plan of Hindu ascetics, sometimes of Brahmans, the forest dwellers; and we'll later see that for Buddhists the highest calling is to give up home, family, and occupation and become a homeless wandering monk or nun.

In the third path, the way of devotion, *bhakti-yoga*, bad karma can be avoided if one surrenders one's deeds to Krishna. The text says: "When you have entrusted all actions to me [Krishna is speaking], with thought on the highest self, when you have become free from desire, free from the idea of 'mine,' then [go ahead and] fight, with grief gone." A little further on, Krishna suggests that the way of devotion is open to everyone, not just to noble priests or warriors. Krishna says: "If one who does evil honors me and not another, that one is thought to be good. That one has begun in the right way. ... No one who is devoted to me is ever lost. ... Those who seek refuge in me, even those who come from evil wombs, women, Vaishyas, even Shudras, they too go on the highest path."

Over the course of the Gita, Krishna gradually reveals himself, until in Chapter 11 Arjuna asks to see Krishna in his true form; and then follows a terrifying theophany as Arjuna is permitted to behold an infinite being, brighter than a thousand suns it says, who encompasses the entire universe with innumerable arms, bellies, and faces. Krishna is both creator and destroyer, and Arjuna is shocked to see the chief warriors in both armies hastening into his open mouths, as it says, "as so many currents of water in a river might run towards the ocean." Arjuna begs Krishna to return to human form, but clearly any debate is over, just as when God's voice speaks from the whirlwind in the Hebrew Bible's book of Job.

The Bhagavad Gita offers an attractive counter to the notion in the Upanishads that salvation comes only to individual renunciants who leave behind all worldly responsibilities. Instead, the Gita demonstrates how spiritual attainment can be won while still honoring the social obligations of family, caste, and community (dharma). This is the reason the Gita has long been chanted in homes and temples, recited at festivals, and it's quoted constantly by ordinary Hindus throughout India.

Not coincidentally, one of the greatest advocates of the Gita in the 20th century was a man who was intensely involved in politics, though in a singularly selfless way. I'm talking about Mahatma Gandhi, who once said, "For me the Gita became an infallible guide of conduct. It became my dictionary of daily reference." As a sacred text, the Gita resists simplistic interpretations. Gandhi recognized that taken at face value, the Gita urges men to go into battle; but Gandhi also saw how the Mahabharata as a whole lavishly illustrates the futility of violence and war, and Gandhi reinterpreted the Gita as a book of peace, as an allegory for how we must fight against our own selfish passions. The battle that Krishna tells Arjuna he can't escape from is like the battle within each of us as individuals as we attempt to overcome our weaknesses, as we struggle with our own inadequacies. Gandhi loved the self-discipline described at the end of Chapter Two of the Gita. It says there: "He whose mind is not agitated in calamities and who has no longing for pleasure, free from attachment, fear, and anger, he indeed is said to be a saint of steady wisdom." For both the ancient Kshatriyas and the modern Gandhi, giving into desire is a manifestation of weakness.

In closing, I'll just note that in the 21st century, the first Hindu elected to the US Congress, Tulsi Gabbard of Hawaii, chose to take her oath of office on her personal copy of the Bhagavad Gita. When an interviewer asked about what the book had meant to her in her own military service (she was deployed twice to the Middle East with the Hawaiian National Guard):

> She initially said that the Gita isn't really about war. The central topics of the Gita are, she said, "enlightenment, love for God, selfless service, and how each of us can succeed in our struggle on the 'battlefields' of life." She then added that during wartime [literal war], she "found great comfort and shelter in the Bhagavad Gita's message of the eternality of the soul and God's unconditional love."

Related Traditions—Sikh Scriptures
Lecture 6

From the ancient, massive, continuously expanding canon of Hinduism, we now jump to a related tradition that is nearly its opposite, at least with regard to scripture. Sikhism is one of the youngest global religions. It began in the 15th century in the Punjab region of India, now divided between India and Pakistan, and today, it claims nearly 30 million believers scattered around the world. Yet wherever they go, Sikhs show reverence for a particular sacred text whose form is exactly fixed: the Adi Granth ("First Scripture"). In this lecture, we'll explore the development and content of this text and the Sikhs' unique relationship to it.

Overview of Sikhism
- Sikhism is a religious tradition that comes out of Hinduism, though it has elements in common with Islam, as well.
  - Like Hindus, Sikhs believe in reincarnation and karma, and they see salvation as an escape from the cycle of rebirth and redeath, a liberation whereby they merge with God.
  - Yet like Muslims, they are monotheistic; their temples have no images or idols; and they reject the caste system, believing that all people are equal. In fact, one of the primary acts of charity associated with Sikh temples is free communal meals, where everyone, regardless of caste, social status, or even religion, eats together.

- Sikhs stress the importance of good works rather than rituals; they value ordinary life over asceticism or renunciation; and they strive to keep God in mind at all times, living lives of honest labor and generosity toward those in need.

- They also have one of the most distinctive relationships with scripture of any major world religion. Many faiths show great respect for their sacred texts, but Sikhs take this to an extraordinary level, treating the Adi Granth as if it were a living person.

The 10 Gurus

- Sikhism began with revelations to Nanak, the first Guru (1469–1539). At about the age of 30, Nanak had a vision in which he was taken up to God's heavenly court and commanded to rejoice in God's name and to teach others to do the same. Over the next quarter century, he went on four long journeys to spread his message of reverence for God's name.

    o According to Nanak, there is one God, eternal and unchanging, beyond form and gender. We are separated from God by ignorance and sin, but he is manifest throughout the cosmos, in our individual souls, and in the divine word that comes through the Gurus.

    o This concept of the "word" is closely associated with God's name, which is not a specific title—he can be called many things—but, rather, an expression of divine reality, and God himself is considered the true Guru.

    o God's grace can bring humans into mystical union with himself and free them from reincarnation, particularly if they meditate on his name and live wholesome, productive lives.

- Nanak spread his message through singing hymns that he had written himself, and eventually, some 974 of his poems became part of the Adi Granth. Unlike the *Mahabharata* or the Bible, the most sacred text of Sikhism does not include narrative; it is focused on timeless, eternal truths rather than the mundane facts of history, and these spiritual insights are often expressed in beautiful, poignant images.

- Over the course of two centuries, Punjabi Sikhs gradually became more distinct from other Hindu religious movements. The second Guru standardized a new script of 35 letters called Gurmukhi ("from the mouth of the Guru") to write down the sacred hymns of

Nanak. The third Guru established new birth, marriage, and death ceremonies and emphasized the importance of the *langar* (free kitchens) of the Sikh temples.

- The fifth Guru, Arjan, is a key figure in the story of Sikh scripture. Not only did he build the Golden Temple in Amritsar, but he also selected nearly 6,000 hymns, written by his four predecessors and himself, for inclusion in the Adi Granth, which he formally established as the sacred text of the Sikhs in 1604. Somewhat surprisingly, the Adi Granth also included songs that had been composed by 15 Muslim Sufis and Hindu Sants, or holy men, that the fifth Guru felt were in tune with Sikh principles.

- Two years after editing the Adi Granth, Guru Arjan came into conflict with the Muslim Mughal emperor and was arrested and tortured to death, according to tradition, when Arjan refused to remove Hindu and Muslim references from the Sikh holy book. Tensions continued, and the seventh Guru disowned his own son when the young man offered to change a line from the Adi Granth to please another Mughal emperor.

- After the ninth Guru was executed when he refused to convert to Islam, his son, Gobind Singh, the final Guru, militarized the movement in 1699 by introducing the Khalsa, an order of soldier-saints, including both men and women, who would always protect and defend the faith.

- Gobind Singh added a few hymns to the Adi Granth that had been composed by his late father, the ninth Guru, and then in 1708, shortly before his death, he announced that there would be no more Gurus after himself. Instead, the perpetual Guru of the Sikhs would be their holy book, the Adi Granth, or as it was now to be known, the Guru Granth Sahib ("Revered Teacher Scripture").

The Guru Granth Sahib
- The Guru Granth Sahib is composed of three sections of unequal length. It begins with an introductory collection of prayers, starting

with the Japji, which was written by Nanak and is recited every morning by devout Sikhs, followed by two evening prayers and a bedtime prayer.

- The second, quite long section consists of hymns or poems that are meant to be sung. They are organized by the melodic modes of classical Indian music called *ragas*, which are combinations of notes associated with different moods, times of the day, and seasons.
  - There are 31 *ragas* in the Adi Granth, and within each *raga* section, the hymns are subdivided into six categories based on length or meter. The poems within each subcategory are arranged by the order of the Gurus who wrote them.
  - Finally, at the end of each of the 31 *raga* sections are the songs of the 15 Hindu Sants and Muslim Sufis that Arjan thought worthy of inclusion in the sacred text of the Sikhs.

- The third part of the Guru Granth Sahib is made up of 77 pages of miscellaneous poems written by the Sikh Gurus, earlier Sants and Sufis, and 17 court poets.

- The language is mostly early-modern Punjabi, sometimes mixed with other northern Indian dialects, along with words from Sanskrit, Persian, and Arabic. It can be difficult for contemporary Sikhs to understand, yet the beauty and sacredness of the words as they are chanted or sung conveys profound religious emotion.

- As in many religious traditions, the opening verses of Sikh scripture are given particular attention, and they are thought to be the epitome of Sikh beliefs. The Guru Granth Sahib begins with the first composition of Nanak, the Mul Mantar ("root mantra").
  - The beginning of the first verse is *Ik Onkar*, "the one creator," referring to God. It is written by combining the numeral 1 with the first letter of the word *onkar*, which is also the first letter of the Gurmukhi alphabet. The combination of the number 1 and the first Gurmukhi letter is often used as a symbol of Sikhism.

- The Japji, the first prayer that is recited every morning by Sikhs, goes on to praise the one God, who is beyond human understanding, language, and the sacred texts of the world.

- The hymns of the Adi Granth proclaim the oneness of God and the equality of all human beings, and they offer some general guidelines for living. Mostly, however, the Adi Granth has thousands of devotional hymns praising God, many of which offer lovely phrases and striking images.

Reverence for the Guru Granth Sahib

- The Guru Granth Sahib is at the center of all Sikh ceremonies, and Sikhs treat their sacred text as a living Guru. In a Sikh house of worship, or *gurdwara* ("doorway to the Guru"), a copy of the Guru Granth Sahib takes the central place. It is brought out every morning and placed on a throne. When people come into a *gurdwara*, they cover their heads, remove their shoes, and bow to the Guru Granth Sahib. They sit on the floor, listening as the Adi Granth is read, sung, or interpreted.

- The Guru Granth Sahib speaks to worshippers directly through a practice called *vak* ("reading"). In the morning, the book is opened at random and the passage at the top of the left-hand page is read, which is considered a *hukam* ("order") for the day. This may happen in a home for an individual or a family or in a *gurdwara* for an entire congregation.

- It is the Guru Granth Sahib that makes the *gurdwara*; wherever the text is, that place is holy. Some homes have a special room for the text, or it can be taken outside the home, but it is always treated with the utmost respect. Whenever the Adi Granth is transported, it is wrapped up and carried on top of someone's head, and it is often accompanied by a procession.

- Like a beloved friend or teacher, the Guru Granth Sahib is present at all the important milestones of a Sikh's life: when a child is born, when Sikhs are initiated into the Khalsa, and at marriage ceremonies.

The daily order from the Guru Granth Sahib in the Golden Temple in Amritsar is made known electronically to Sikhs all over the world.

- At times of celebration and sorrow, it is customary for friends and family to read the entire Adi Granth aloud nonstop, day and night, in shifts. Any Sikh who can pronounce the Gurmukhi script, male or female, old or young, is allowed to participate as a reader, and it usually takes about 48 hours to get through the text.

- Celebrations at the *gurdwara* are often marked by nonstop singing of the entire Adi Granth.

• Sikh families and individuals often read the Adi Granth at a slower pace, though the sacredness of the book means that not all families have a copy. To show proper reverence, the Guru Granth Sahib must be taken out from a special resting place every morning and returned every evening. Because not everyone has an extra room, most Sikhs make do with smaller volumes of daily prayers and hymns from the Adi Granth, which don't require the same level of care.

- In fact, a complete copy of the Guru Granth Sahib, even in translation, is a bit difficult to come by. Probably the easiest way to gain access to the entire Adi Granth is through translations that have been posted online, such as the Khalsa Consensus Translation.

Suggested Reading

Dass, Nirmal, trans., *Songs of Kabir from the Adi Granth*.

———, trans., *Songs of the Saints from the Adi Granth*.

Holm, ed., *Sacred Writings*.

Guru Granth Sahib, Khalsa Consensus Translation.

Mann, *The Making of Sikh Scripture*.

McLeod, trans., *Textual Sources for the Study of Sikhism*.

Nesbitt, *Sikhism: A Very Short Introduction*.

Shackle and Mandair, eds. and trans., *Teachings of the Sikh Gurus*.

Singh, Nikky-Gurinder Kaur, *Sikhism: An Introduction*.

Questions to Consider

1. Why do Sikhs treat their holy book, the Adi Granth, with such extraordinary reverence?

2. What has made the Adi Granth the most successful new scripture of the last several centuries?

Related Traditions—Sikh Scriptures
Lecture 6—Transcript

Hello, are you ready for some more sacred texts? The way this course is organized, I'll do several lectures on major religious traditions; and then in between I'll do a lecture on something that might be a smaller religious tradition, but one that's still interesting in different sorts of ways.

From the ancient, massive, continuously expanding canon of Hinduism, we're going to jump to a related tradition that's nearly its opposite, at least with regard to scripture. Sikhism is one of the youngest global religions. In English, we sometimes say "Sickism" and sometimes "Sikhism." I know "Sick" or "Sickism" sounds a little strange in English, but that's the way Sikhs themselves pronounce their religion, so we'll go with that. Sikhism began in the 15th century in the Punjab region of India, now divided between India and Pakistan, and today it claims nearly 30 million believers, scattered around the world. Yet wherever they go, Sikhs show reverence for a particular sacred text whose form is exactly fixed. In fact, every official copy of the Adi Granth (and that means the "First Scripture") has exactly the same page numbering, so there's no need to cite its contents by chapter and verse.

Sikhism is a religious tradition that comes out of Hinduism, though it has elements in common with Islam as well. Like Hindus, Sikhs believe in reincarnation and karma, and they see salvation as an escape from the cycle of rebirth and re-death; a liberation whereby they merge with God. Yet like Muslims, they're monotheistic. Their temples, called *gurdwaras*, have no images or idols; and they reject the caste system, believing that all people are equal. In fact, one of the primary acts of charity associated with Sikh temples is free communal meals, where everyone, regardless of caste, social status, or even religion can eat together. Sikhs stress the importance of good works rather than rituals, they value ordinary life over asceticism or renunciation, and they strive to keep God in mind at all times, living lives of honest labor and generosity toward those in need. One of their slogans is "Pray, work, and give." They also have one of the most distinctive relationships with scripture of any major world religion. Many faiths show great respect for their sacred texts, but Sikhs take this to an extraordinary level, treating the Adi Granth as if it were a living person.

The religion began with revelations to Nanak, the first Guru, who lived from 1469–1539; it makes him a contemporary of Martin Luther. At about the age of 30, Nanak had a vision in which he was taken up to God's heavenly court and commanded to rejoice in God's name and to teach others to do the same. Upon his return, Nanak announced that "God is neither Hindu nor Muslim, and the path which I follow is God's." Over the next quarter-century, Nanak went on four long journeys throughout India and its surrounding lands, accompanied by a Muslim musician named Mardana, to spread his message of reverence for God's name.

According to Nanak, there's one God, eternal and unchanging, beyond form and gender. We're separated from this one God by ignorance and sin, but He's manifest throughout the cosmos, in our individual souls and in the divine word that comes through the gurus. The concept of "Word" is closely associated with God's Name, which isn't a specific title—he can be many things—but the name is rather an expression of divine reality, and God himself is considered the true Guru (remember *Guru* means "a teacher"). God's grace can bring humans into mystical union with himself—I say "himself," but God isn't exactly male—and he can free them from reincarnation, particularly if they meditate upon his name and live wholesome, productive lives.

Nanak spread his message through singing hymns that he'd written himself, and eventually some 974 of his poems became part of the Adi Granth, though only 4 of them refer to contemporary events; most of the time they refer to God in sort of generalized, universal ways. Unlike the Mahabharata or the Bible, the most sacred text of Sikhism doesn't include narrative; it's focused on timeless, eternal truths rather than on the mundane facts of history, and these spiritual insights are often expressed in beautiful, poignant images. For instance, Nanak once sang to God:

> You are the ocean, all-knowing, all-seeing
> How can I, a fish, perceive your limits?
> Wherever I look, there you are.
> If I leave you I burst and die.

Before his death, Nanak appointed as his successor a follower and fellow poet named Angad—strikingly, Angad wasn't one of his own sons—and then this pattern continued through 10 Gurus, although several of the later gurus were related to one another. Over the course of two centuries, Punjabi Sikhs gradually became more and more distinct from other Hindu religious movements (remember, Hinduism encompasses a wide variety of movements). The second Guru standardized a new script of 35 letters called Gurmukhi, and it means "from the mouth of the guru"; and he used that script of 35 letters to write down the sacred hymns of Nanak. Imagine a text so sacred that it needs its own alphabet.

Today, Gurmukhi is used to write all sorts of things in the Punjabi language. The third Guru established new birth, marriage, and death ceremonies and emphasized the importance of the *langar* (the free kitchens) in the Sikh temples. The fifth guru, Arjan, is a key figure in the story of Sikh scripture. Not only did he build the Golden Temple in Amritsar, which is the holiest site of Sikhism, he also selected nearly 6,000 hymns written by four of his predecessors and himself for inclusion in the Adi Granth, which he formally established as the sacred text of the Sikhs in 1604.

Somewhat surprisingly, the Adi Granth also included songs that had been composed by 15 Muslim Sufis and Hindu Sants. *Sant* is sometimes translated as "saint," but the words are actually distinct. The Punjabi word *sant* comes from *sat*, or "truth." These holy men, like Kabir and Ravidas, had preceded Nanak; so they weren't Sikhs, but the fifth guru he felt that their teachings were in tune with Sikh principles. These Sants and Sufis preached *bhakti-yoga*, or loving devotion to God, though they stressed inward spirituality rather than outward religious practices such as Vedic rituals, Muslim religious rules, temple worship, pilgrimages, or caste restrictions. They seemed to be earlier thinkers or religious figures in India who transcended these religious boundaries, and so Sikhs adopted them as their own.

Two years after editing the Adi Granth, Guru Arjan came into conflict with the Muslim Mughal emperor and was arrested and tortured to death, according to tradition, when Arjan refused to remove Hindu and Muslim references from the Sikh holy book (those references to God being neither Hindu nor Muslim). Tensions continued, and the 7th Guru disowned his own son when the young man offered to change a line from the Adi Granth to please another Mughal emperor who felt that the line insulted Muslims. After the 9th Guru was executed when he refused to convert to Islam, his son, Gobind Singh, the 10th and final guru, militarized the movement in 1699 by introducing the Khalsa. This is an order of soldier-saints that includes both men and women that made a vow that they would protect and defend the faith at all times. Today, members of the Khalsa undergo a ritual initiation and thereafter are known by their adoption of the Five K's: Kesh for uncut hair; Kara, a steel bracelet; Kangha, a wooden comb; Kaccha, cotton underwear; and Kirpan, a short dagger.

Gobind Singh added a few hymns to the Adi Granth that had been composed by his late father, the ninth guru, and then in 1708, shortly before his death, he announced that there would be no more gurus after himself; the line would come to an end with him, almost. Instead of another human guru, the perpetual guru of the Sikhs would now be their holy book, the Adi Granth, or as it was now to be known, the Guru Granth Sahib, which means the "Revered Teacher Scripture." Today, these are interchangeable titles; you might hear Guru Granth Sahib, or you might hear Adi Granth. I'll use both in the remainder of this lecture.

More than 2,000 years earlier, when the Buddha was on his deathbed, he realized that his disciples were anxious about who their next teacher would be; and he told them that the Vinaya (those are rules for monks) and the Dharma (meaning his teachings; the meaning is a little bit different in Buddhism than it is in Hinduism, so *Dharma* is "Buddhist teachings") would hereafter be the guide for later generations of Buddhists. But as we shall see in later lectures, the texts claiming to have recorded the teaching of the Buddha multiplied at an alarming rate (or maybe an exciting rate for some Buddhists). By contrast, Gobind Singh indicated that what Sikhs needed to follow was a very specific book of 1,430 pages, no more, no less, and that book is going to remain unchanged.

The Guru Granth Sahib is comprised of three sections of very unequal length. It begins with an introductory collection of prayers starting with the Japji, which was written by Nanak and is recited every morning by devout Sikhs, followed by two evening prayers, and a bedtime prayer; those are in that first introductory section. That takes us through page 13. Pages 14–1,353 consist of hymns or poems that are meant to be sung. They're organized by the melodic modes of Classical Indian music called *ragas*, which are somewhat like musical scales or combinations of notes associated with different moods, different times of the day, and seasons.

There are 31 *ragas* within the Adi Granth, and within each *raga* section, the hymns are subdivided into six categories based on the length or the meter. The poems within each subcategory are arranged by the order of the gurus; so each section begins with the poems of Nanak, and then those of the second guru, and on through the fifth guru. Finally, at the end of each of those 31 *raga* sections are the songs of the 15 Hindu Sants and Muslim Sufis that Arjan, the fifth guru, thought worthy of inclusion in the sacred text of the Sikhs. The third and final part of the Guru Granth Sahib is made up of 77 pages of miscellaneous poems written by the Sikh gurus, earlier Sants and Sufis, and 17 court poets. These weren't given a musical setting.

Altogether, there are 5,894 poems: 974 by Guru Nanak, 2,218 by Guru Arjan, 1,763 by four of the other Sikh gurus, and 939 by poets other than the gurus. It's rather astounding that we can give those exact numbers in this kind of way; the Hindu canon by contrast is much more fluid, it's hard to know exactly what's in there. The 10th guru, Gobind Singh, was a prolific poet himself, but out of modesty he didn't include any of his own verses in the final version of the Guru Granth Sahib. Many of his own compositions were collected in a book called the Dasam Granth. That means the "Tenth Scripture"; so it's different than the Adi Granth, the "First Scripture," which is based on Nanak. The Dasam Granth is also considered sacred by Sikhs and is sometimes read in *gurdwaras*, but it doesn't have the same prominence and reverence as that given to the Guru Granth Sahib. The Dasam Granth includes not just prayers and hymns, but also long legendary narratives that sound a little like the Hindu Puranas, and they're narrative stories about Vishnu, Krishna, Brahma, and the goddess Chandi.

The language of the Adi Granth is mostly early-modern Punjabi, the kind used by Hindu Sants, sometimes mixed with other Northern Indian dialects, along with words from Sanskrit, Persian, and Arabic. The language can be difficult for contemporary Sikhs to understand, yet the beauty and sacredness of the words as they're chanted or as they're sung conveys profound religious emotion. It's not as unintelligible as the Sanskrit Vedas are to modern speakers of Hindi, but the sound of the sacred words in the Adi Granth does matter. Another contrast, though, is that the Guru Granth Sahib, the Adi Granth, was always meant to be read and heard by everyone, regardless of caste or gender.

As in many religious traditions, the opening verses of Sikh scriptures are given particular attention, and they're thought to be the epitome of Sikh beliefs. The Guru Granth Sahib begins with the first composition of Nanak, the Mul Mantar, which is translated as the "root mantra." One respected translation renders it as "There is but one God. True is His Name, creative His personality and immortal His form. He is without fear, sans enmity, unborn and self-illumined. By the Guru's grace (He is obtained)." But you may recall that Sikhs believe that God is without gender, so there's perhaps too "his" and "he's" in that translation. A more recent translation does the same verse in this way; it says: "One Universal Creator God. The Name is Truth. Creative Being Personified. No Fear. No Hatred. Image Of The Undying, Beyond Birth, Self-Existent, By Guru's Grace."

The beginning of the beginning verse is *Ik Onkar*, "the one creator," referring to God. It's written by combining the number "1" with the first letter of the word *onkar*, which is also the first letter of the Gurmukhi alphabet; so it's almost as if the Bible began with "number 1 Alef" in Hebrew or "1 Alpha," if we're using Greek for the Septuagint. The combination of the number "1" and the first Gurmukhi letter is often used together as a symbol of Sikhism. The Japji—remember that's the first prayer by Nanak in 38 stanzas that's recited every morning by Sikhs—goes on to praise the One God, who's beyond human understanding and language:

> By thinking I cannot obtain a conception of Him, even though I think hundreds of thousands of times. Though I be silent and keep my attention firmly fixed on Him, I cannot preserve silence. The hunger of the hungry for God does not subside, though they obtain [loads of worldly goods].

We can only meditate upon his name; it goes on to say:

> By listening to the Word, the seeker becomes equal to Shiva, Brahma, and Indra; By listening to the Word, the seeker becomes praiseworthy; By listening to the Word, one learns the secrets of Yoga; By listening to the Word, one learns the wisdom of the Shastra, the Smriti, and the Veda; Nanak says: Devotees find bliss, By listening to the Word, sorrow and sin are destroyed.

You can see how Sikh comes into a religious context where people are familiar with Hindu scriptures, and Sikhism says, Nanak says, the name of God that we're contemplating is beyond these scriptures that were already familiar to Hindus. Indeed, the Supreme Being is beyond all of the sacred texts of the world. It says: "the thousands of Puranas and Muslim books tell that in reality there is but one principle. If God can be described by writing, then describe Him; but such description is impossible. O Nanak, call Him great; only God Himself knows how great He is!" It's all a quote from the Adi Granth; Nanak sometimes refers to himself in the third person.

The hymns of the Adi Granth proclaim the oneness of God and the equality of all human beings, and they offer some general guidelines for living. For instance, on page 1,083, the Fifth Guru proclaims that purifying one's heart is as good as a pilgrimage to Mecca; that good conduct is as good as circumcision; and that the "five most sublime daily prayers" are praising God, contentment, humility, giving to charities, and holding one's desires in restraint. It sort of is a counterpoint to the five daily prayers that Muslims say. Several poems in the Guru Granth Sahib list the five vices to be avoided, and those include: lust, anger, greed, materialism, and pride. But mostly the Adi Granth has hundreds—actually thousands—of devotional hymns praising God, many of which offer lovely phrases and striking images. For instance, the fourth Guru, Ram Das, sang: "You are the River of Life, O Lord; in you all beings dwell. You are the One, no other exists, your presence encompassing all. This world where we live is your realm of delight, here where you revel and play. Here the bereft can be summoned again, restored to your loving embrace." Or take this Adi Granth hymn from the Hindu Sant Kabir, which combines religious doubt with deep trust and devotion:

> Those who say they know Him who is beyond thought and conception, hope to go to heaven by merely saying so. I don't know where heaven is. Everyone says, "I'm going there, I'm going there." There is no comfort in saying this. Your heart can only be happy when pride leaves you. As long as you yearn for heaven, you cannot live near His feet. Kabir says, "How can I understand it enough to explain: Heaven is found in the company of sages."

When I say those words from the Adi Granth, it's not quite the same as hearing them sung or chanted, I'm afraid, in the original; but it'll have to do for this course.

One of the striking features of Sikhism is the importance that believers give to the gurus. One hymn from the Adi Granth says, "To reach Nam [this is the name of God] the Guru is ladder, boat, and raft. The Guru is the ship to cross the ocean of the world. The Guru is place of pilgrimage and sacred stream." But what happens when that new guru is a book rather than a person, as was announced by the 10th guru Gobind Singh?

When we're looking at religious texts, we're interested in the content, what they actually say; but there are other ways to approach texts as well, and part of it comes from how texts are used or the role that they play in communal worship or communal relations. In this case, the Adi Granth takes a remarkable place in the lives of Sikhs around the world. In fact, The Guru Granth Sahib is the center of all Sikh ceremonies, and Sikhs treat their sacred text as a living guru. In a Sikh house of worship, or *gurdwara*—the day means a "doorway to the Guru"—a copy of the Guru Granth Sahib takes a very central place. It's brought out every morning and placed up on a throne with a canopy over the top, and then it's draped with richly embroidered cloths; sort of treated like you treat a king maybe. It's opened up with great ceremony, and it's fanned throughout the day with a whisk. When people come into a *gurdwara*, they cover their heads, they remove their shoes, and they bow to the Guru Granth Sahib. Then they sit on the floor, listening as the Adi Granth is read, sung, or interpreted, and this goes on all day long. People can come and go as they wish. In the evening, the book is ceremoniously closed and then taken to its resting place until the next morning.

The Guru Granth Sahib speaks to worshippers directly through a practice called *vak* (the word means "reading"). In the morning, the book is opened at random and then the passage at the top of the left-hand page is read, which is considered a *hukam*, an order for the day. This may happen in a home when a family does this, for an individual or for a family; it may happen in a *gurdwara*, where it provides sort of a verse of the day, a thought of the day, or an order of the day for an entire congregation; and the daily order from the Guru Granth Sahib in the Golden Temple in Amritsar is made known electronically to Sikhs all over the world every morning (there's actually an app for that).

It's the Guru Granth Sahib that makes the *gurdwara*; anyplace the text is, that place is rendered holy by its presence. Some homes have a special room for the text, or it can be taken to less spacious homes, hotels, or other hired halls for weddings or other ceremonies, but it's always treated with the utmost respect. Whenever the Adi Granth is transported, it's wrapped up and carried on top of someone's head, and it's often accompanied by a procession with people singing hymns or sprinkling water before it, or waving a whisk to keep it cool and ward off insects.

Like a beloved friend or teacher, the Guru Granth Sahib is there at all the important milestones of a Sikh's life. When a child is born, a closed copy of the Adi Granth is allowed to fall opened at random, and then the child is given a name that begins with the first letter that appears on the top of the left-hand page. The Adi Granth is present and its verses are recited at the ceremony when Sikhs are initiated into the Khalsa—remember, this order that protects the religion—and that initiation is sort of like a baptism, with initiates drinking and being sprinkled with water that's been made holy by stirring sugar into it with a sword. Sikhs are married when the bride and groom walk around the Guru Granth Sahib four times in a clockwise direction as specific hymns from that text are recited. Sets of hymns from the Adi Granth are recited every morning and evening, and the last evening hymn is also sung at the death of a Sikh as he or she is cremated (sort of a lovely imagery there). In addition, at times of celebration and sorrow—when a child is born, or moving into a new house, or getting a new job, birthdays, engagements, or on the other side of things sickness or at times of death—it's customary for friends and family to read the entire Adi Granth aloud nonstop, day and night, in shifts. Any Sikh who can pronounce the Gurmukhi script, male or female, old or young, is allowed to participate as a reader, and it usually takes about 48 hours to get through the text from beginning to end. Celebrations at the *gurdwara* are often marked by nonstop singing of the entire Adi Granth, and those are sometimes shared with the neighbors through loudspeakers. It's now possible to download audio files from the Internet of the Guru Granth Sahib being read or sung so that Sikhs can listen to their holy scripture, their sacred book, continuously. I'd recommend giving this a try. What you'll want to do is you'll want to go to YouTube or the internet and type in the word *kirtan*—*kirtan* means "devotional singing" and it's specifically for Sikh ceremonies—and then you can hear what it sounds like for the Adi Granth to be recited or sung in this sort of lovely, continuous musical performance.

Sikhs families and individuals often read the Adi Granth at a slower pace, though the sacredness of book means that not all families have their own copy; so it's not really like the Bible. To show proper reverence, the Guru Granth Sahib needs to be taken from a special resting place, preferably its own room, every morning and then returned every evening. Not everybody has an extra room in their house, so most Sikhs make do with smaller volumes of daily prayers and hymns from the Adi Granth, which don't require the same level of care and devotion. In fact, a complete copy of the Guru Granth Sahib, even in translation, is a little hard to come by. Sikhs don't mass produce them the way that Buddhists, Christians, or Muslims do with their holy books. Probably the easiest way to gain access to the entire Adi Granth is through translations that have been posted online, such as the Khalsa Consensus Translation.

With this continual reading, reciting, and singing of the Adi Granth from beginning to end, you might imagine the joy and satisfaction that Sikhs feel whenever they come to the beautiful hymn by the fifth Guru that concludes the book; so the book ends by saying:

> Three things have been put into this dish: truth, contentment, and deep reflection. With them has been mixed the name of the Lord, its sweet nectar sustaining all. He who eats and enjoys it shall be set free. He who tastes this food will make it his own, for evermore. By

clinging to God's holy feet, we cross the ocean of existence and out of the world's darkness come to the light which pervades all.

Then the Adi Granth comes to a close; and, of course, Sikhs would want to start reading it again.

I should note in my own conclusion that Sikhs don't worship the Adi Granth, though they do give it the reverence appropriate to a beloved guru through whom the One God speaks. Their remarkable connection to a sacred text is similar in some ways to other religions, but it's also rather distinct. For instance, Hindus revere gurus, as we saw with the Upanishads, but their most sacred compositions didn't go easily or quickly into written form, they stayed oral for a long time in teacher to student transmission. We'll see in future lectures how Mahayana Buddhists sometimes thought of scripture as an embodiment of the Buddha, and they treated such texts as they would sacred relics; but they didn't exactly treat it like a living Buddha, and in any case there were lots and lots of scriptures rather than one single book. We'll see also in future lectures how Muslims show great respect for their own holy book, the Qur'an; and that Muslim respect for the Qur'an may have influenced Sikhism, but Islam's attitudes toward scripture in turn were influenced by Christian and Jewish precedents.

In the next lecture, we'll examine the case of Judaism, which was perhaps the first faith to define itself by a strictly limited, written canon. It was a revolution in world religions, which came about in part because of the Roman destruction of the Jerusalem Temple in 70 C.E. We'll talk about that next.

Judaism—People of the Book
Lecture 7

In the next few lectures, we'll explore the contents and origins of the Hebrew Bible and the role it has played in Judaism over the centuries. We'll see how the Hebrew Bible is connected to other texts that some Jews have regarded as sacred at different times and places, and we'll compare it to the scriptures of other religions. But we'll start in the middle, with the story of one particular copy of the Hebrew Bible: the Aleppo Codex. Many scholars consider this to be the oldest (c. 930 C.E.), most complete, and most accurate text of the Hebrew Bible, even though a large portion of it has been mysteriously missing since the 1940s.

Production of the Aleppo Codex

- The Aleppo Codex was produced in a workshop overseen by one of the great masters of Jewish scripture production, Aaron ben Asher. He was a Masorete, that is, part of a group of scribes and scholars active in the 7th to the 11th centuries and dedicated to preserving the text of the Hebrew Bible as accurately as possible.

- These scholars faced two challenges, the first of which was the inevitability of errors in hand copying and the replication of errors in subsequent copies. The Masoretes came up with various techniques of quality control designed to detect such errors, such as counting the exact number of verses, words, and letters in biblical manuscripts.

- The second challenge was trying to establish the correct pronunciation of the text, which was more difficult than we might assume because Hebrew is written with consonants only. There were centuries of tradition in reading the Hebrew Bible, of course, but the Masoretes tried to fix exact pronunciations by adding marks to indicate vowels, accents, and pauses.

Later History of the Codex

- About a century after it was first created, the Aleppo Codex was bought by the Karaite community at Jerusalem (c. 1050). The Karaites were Jews who rejected the oral Torah of the rabbis (the Talmud), instead focusing exclusively on what was written in the Hebrew Bible. Naturally, they were interested in using the most accurate text possible.

- In 1099, the codex was taken away from Jerusalem as plunder by Christians in the First Crusade and held for ransom. Karaites in Ashkelon borrowed money from Jews in Egypt to rescue the codex.

The Aleppo Codex, now housed in the Shrine of the Book in the Israel Museum, has been at the center of an international mystery since the 1940s.

- Eventually, the book ended up in Cairo, in the care of rabbinical Jews, where it became known for its meticulous accuracy. Many scholars, including the great Maimonides, consulted it.

- In the last half of the 14th century, the great-great-great grandson of Maimonides took the codex to Aleppo, Syria, where it remained for 600 years, locked away in the central synagogue. In 1943, concerned Jews in Jerusalem sent a Hebrew University lecturer to Aleppo to gain permission to take the codex to a safer location or, if need be, even to steal it. Unfortunately, he did neither.

- In November 1947, the day after the UN voted to establish the state of Israel, there was rioting in Aleppo, and a mob broke into and burned the synagogue. Someone, however, managed to save part of the codex. It was smuggled out of Syria and taken to Israel in 1958; today, most of the codex is in the Shrine of the Book at the Israel Museum.

- The codex is missing a few pages here and there, and most disappointingly, nearly the entire Torah has been torn out. There is, however, the tantalizing possibility that the missing pages might someday turn up. One page came to light in 1982, and another fragment was identified in 1988.

Origins of the Torah

- The sacred text contained in the Aleppo Codex is not the Old Testament. As we will see in a later lecture, early Christians regarded the Jewish scriptures as sacred, and they adopted a Greek translation called the Septuagint as part of their own canon. But there are differences in the number and order of the books in the Septuagint compared to the Hebrew scriptures. Further, some of the "Hebrew" Bible is written in the later language of Aramaic.

- Probably the best name for this sacred text is the one used by Jews themselves: Tanakh, which is an acronym consisting of the first letters of the three major divisions: Torah (the first five books, ascribed to Moses), Nevi'im (the Prophets), and Ketuvim (the Writings). Together, these constitute a library of Hebrew texts in many different genres, written over a 1,000-year period.

- For a long time, these writings circulated separately, with some books being regarded as authoritative in some communities but not others. Eventually, a core group of documents was recognized by all Jews as sacred, though this worked out differently for each of the three biblical divisions of Tanakh.

- The oldest compositions of the ancient Hebrews were originally passed down orally. Starting around the 10th century B.C.E., perhaps at the court of King David, various oral traditions were combined and recorded. Over the next few centuries, during the time of the divided kingdoms of Israel and Judah and the destruction of Israel by the Assyrians in 722 B.C.E., the texts were further revised. By the time of the Babylonian Conquest in 586 B.C.E., it appears that the Torah as we know it today had taken shape.

- When Judah was conquered and its leading citizens were taken captive to Babylon, it seemed as if the Jews would lose their identity as a distinct people. But the Babylonians were themselves conquered by the Persians in 539 B.C.E., and the new king, Cyrus the Great, agreed to let the Jews return to Jerusalem and rebuild the Temple.

- The return did not go smoothly; there was conflict with the Jews who had remained in Judea, and it took two waves of immigration and more than 20 years to rebuild the Temple, which was dedicated in 515 B.C.E. (This is the beginning of the Second Temple period.) In 458 B.C.E, another group of Jews from Babylon returned to Judea under the leadership of Ezra the scribe, and they were joined in 445 by more Jewish immigrants led by Nehemiah.

- Ezra and Nehemiah were appalled at the corruption and laxity they found among their coreligionists in Judea. In an attempt to reform and unify the community, Ezra gathered the people together and read aloud "the book of the Law of Moses." Modern scholars believe that this "book of the Law" was the Torah. Thereafter, the people began to try to live their lives in accordance with the Torah; thus, Ezra started the transformation of the Jews into "the people of the book."

Origins of the Prophets and Writings

- If the Torah was canonized around 400 B.C.E., the process took a bit longer for the second section of the Tanakh, the Prophets.

    o In Jewish Bibles, there are two subdivisions of this section: the Former Prophets (Joshua through Kings) and the Latter Prophets (Isaiah, Jeremiah, Ezekiel, and the 12 Minor Prophets).

    o It appears that an early version of the history of the Hebrews was written shortly before the Exile and then revised by Jews in Babylon. There were also extensive revisions and additions made to the books of the so-called writing prophets during the Exile, though these books probably circulated separately. Eventually, a standard collection came to be accepted as canonical around 200 B.C.E.

- But the third section of the Tanakh, the Writings, was still open-ended in the 1st century C.E. Today, the Writings include Psalms, Proverbs, Job, Daniel, Ezra-Nehemiah, Chronicles, and the Five Scrolls that are associated with Jewish festivals. This list of works wasn't agreed on until the 2nd or 3rd century C.E., and even then, it wasn't decided by a specific leader or a council. Rather, over time, the rabbis gradually came into agreement.

- Earlier Jewish communities, however, had larger collections of sacred texts. By the late Second Temple period, that is, before the Jerusalem Temple was destroyed by the Romans in 70 C.E., many Jews were living far from Judea, across the Roman Empire. Not all of these Roman Jews were fluent in Hebrew or even in Aramaic; thus, they needed translations of their sacred texts. One of the most prominent of these was a Greek rendition called the Septuagint ("the Seventy").

- A Greek rendition of the remainder of the Hebrew Bible eventually rounded out the Septuagint, but where the Greek Torah and the Prophets had the same books as the Tanakh, the rest of the Septuagint included additional books. The first Christians adopted the Greek version of the Hebrew scriptures, and that tradition has continued into Catholic Bibles today. Early Protestants, however, relegated biblical books that were in Greek but not Hebrew to a separate section called the Apocrypha, and after some time, they stopped publishing them as part of their Bibles.

- Why weren't the extra books in the Septuagint accepted by later Jews as scripture? When the rabbis were arguing over which texts belonged in the Writings section of the Tanakh, they had two basic criteria: The books had to be in Hebrew, and they had to be at least as old as Ezra. These criteria eliminated some books for which the

Hebrew originals had been lost (or had never existed) and some later books.

- But several Jewish groups in the late Second Temple period thought that even more books should be accepted as scripture. Among these groups was the dissident community of Qumran, producers of the Dead Sea Scrolls.

- Other Jews at the time wrote and treasured additional texts, known as pseudepigrapha, none of which was included in the Tanakh.

A Text-Centered Religion

- In many ways, the Jews became "the people of the book" through a series of losses. The ancient Israelites were connected to their God through the land he had promised them, the prophets who spoke in his name, the temple where he received sacrifices, and the kingly line he had established (the Davidic dynasty).
  - During the Exile, the Judeans in Babylon lost all four of these connections.

  - When the Jews returned to their land, the Davidic kings and the prophets were gone; thus, they compensated by consolidating their national histories and the writings of the prophets, starting with the five books of the Torah that were ascribed to the greatest of the prophets, Moses.

- After the Great Revolt in 66–70, the holy city of Jerusalem was leveled by the Romans, The Second Temple was destroyed, and the dispersion of the Jews was accelerated. The Jews needed something to bind them as a people.
  - The rabbis took their lead from Ezra the scribe and created a community that would be centered on a specific text. This innovation would eventually affect most of the world's population through the influence of Christianity and Islam.

- Once the focus of Jewish identity became the Tanakh, it became more important than ever to carefully define its contents and the exact form the text would take forever after.

Suggested Reading

Coogan, *The Old Testament*.

Friedman, *The Aleppo Codex*.

Halbertal, *People of the Book*.

Rogerson, ed., *The Oxford Illustrated History of the Bible*.

Silver, *The Story of Scripture*.

Questions to Consider

1. What are the three major divisions of Jewish scripture, and why is the Hebrew Bible often called the Tanakh?

2. How did Jews ensure the accurate transmission of their sacred texts?

Judaism—People of the Book
Lecture 7—Transcript

Hello, welcome back. This lecture is an introduction to the sacred texts of Judaism. I know that there are hundreds of detailed introductions to the Old Testament, or more accurately the Hebrew Bible; there's even an entire Great Courses lecture series devoted to the subject. But in the next few lectures, I'll briefly explain what's in the Hebrew Bible, where it comes from, and the role that it's played in Judaism over the centuries. I'll also show how it's connected to other texts that at least some Jews have regarded as sacred at different times and at different places, and I'll make comparisons to the scriptures of other religious traditions. But I'm going to start in the middle, with the story of one particular copy of the Hebrew Bible.

This copy is called the Aleppo Codex. Aleppo is a city in Syria where this manuscript resided for some 600 years, and it's called a "codex" because it's a handwritten manuscript with two-sided pages bound along one edge; so it's like a modern book as opposed to a rolled-up scroll. It's often referred to as "the crown of Aleppo," one of the great treasures of that part of the world. Many scholars consider it the oldest, most complete, most accurate text of the Hebrew Bible, even though a good-sized chunk has been missing since the 1940s in sort of an international Bible mystery.

The Aleppo Codex was produced about 930 C.E. in the city of Tiberius on the western shore of the Sea of Galilee in a workshop overseen by one of the great masters of Jewish scripture production. His name was Aaron ben Asher, and his family had been in the business for many generations, in the business of copying biblical manuscripts. Like all Bibles at the time, it was copied by hand from earlier manuscripts that have since been lost, and it was copied onto pages that were made of animal skin; this is before the discovery of paper in the West, or actually the invention of paper in China that then made its way to the West in the late Middle Ages. The Aleppo Codex was beautifully written on nearly 500 parchment leaves—each leave is made of tanned skin, not paper—and each of those pages has three columns of 28 lines each. Just the materials and the labor that went into its production must've made it very, very valuable—think of all of those animals that would've had to have been killed and then their skins processed for it—but this particular copy was also extraordinarily accurate.

Aaron ben Asher was a Masorete; that is, part of a group of scribes and scholars active from the 7th to the 11th centuries that were dedicated to preserving the text of the Hebrew Bible as accurately as possible. They faced two big challenges: The first was that copying by hand, even if done carefully, always produces mistakes as the writer looks back and forth from the source manuscript to the new copy, and then back to the source, and back to the copy. So sometimes they'd misread things, letters that look similar or words that look similar; or they'd mishear similar-sounding words because they may have actually spoken it out loud, or even in your mind you tend to vocalize things there; or they might transpose letters as they're copying it down; or accidentally repeat letters or words (that's called dittography); add they might add things that were written in the margins, they might accidentally add those into the text itself; or they might unintentionally omit words or phrases as they look back and forth (it's called haplography), especially at the ends of lines (it's called homeoteleuton), so you look and you see a similar word, and then you look and you write, and then you look again and it might be a similar word that's a couple of lines down, and then you might miss the lines in between. Once a mistake gets made in one copy, every manuscript that's made from that copy will perpetuate the error; you're copying the entire manuscript with all the mistakes there as well. It's kind of like DNA: Textual critics can arrange manuscripts into family trees, trying to figure out which was the original, how they fit together, and such. In general, no two manuscripts are exactly alike; and then once scribes start trying to correct mistakes—or what they assume are mistakes in the example that they're copied from—then things get really messy or really complicated.

The Jewish Masoretes came up with various techniques of quality control designed to detect such errors. They determined the exact number of verses, words, and letters in the Bible, and then counted and recounted for every new manuscript to make sure that they'd missed nothing. They also noted the middle word of each book so they could count on both sides, and they noted the exact middle word of the Bible as a whole. They put notations in the margins indicating unique or rare forms of particular words, some of which appear only once or twice in the entire Bible, and they'll note that. The Masoretes even included notes saying that mysterious dots over some letters or obvious misspellings should be preserved as is; they're trying to copy things exactly, even down to the mistakes they see in the manuscript. By the way, Hindu Brahman priests also developed elaborate memorization techniques for ensuring that the oral Vedas were passed on exactly. Memorization matters; and in this case, exact copying matters to Jewish scribes.

The first challenge is mistakes get made as copies are done. The second major challenge was trying to establish the exact pronunciation of the text, which was more difficult that you might guess since Hebrew is a language that's written with consonants only. If English were written without vowels, imagine how you might read the word "bt," and it might be "bat," or "bet," or "bit," or "bite," and so forth. There were centuries of tradition in reading the Hebrew Bible, of course, but the Masoretes tried to nail down the exact pronunciation by adding small dots and lines under and over the consonant letters to indicate what vowels should be in those words. They also added some hooks over some letters that told readers where to put accents and pauses when the text was chanted; these are known as cantillation marks. At the time the Aleppo Codex was written, this elaborate system of vocalization and cantillation was fairly new, and the codex is a magnificent example. In fact, Aaron ben Asher himself added the vocal pointing, the accents, and the Masoretic notes to the consonantal text that would've been written out by a scribe in his employ earlier. You should actually check out the Aleppo Codex yourself. There's a website with photographs at www.aleppocodex.org.

About a century after it was created, the Aleppo Codex was bought by a Karaite Jewish community at Jerusalem. We'll see the Karaites again in a later lecture. They were Jews who rejected the oral Torah of the Rabbis, or the Talmud, and instead they wanted to focus exclusively on what was written in the Hebrew Bible; so they naturally were very interested in getting the most accurate biblical text possible. Today, nearly all Jews follow the rabbinical tradition; they look to the Talmud for guidance. There are only about 40,000 Karaites left, though they were once a major division of Judaism.

Around 1050 C.E., the Codex went to Jerusalem, where it remained for some 50 years, serving as an authoritative Bible for both Karaites and rabbinical

Jews. In 1099, however, it was carried off as plunder by Christians in the First Crusade. The book was held for ransom, along with some other copies of the Jewish scriptures and a few actual people. The Karaite community in Ashkelon, on the Mediterranean coast, borrowed some money from Jews in Egypt to pay a hefty price to rescue the Aleppo Codex. Eventually it ended up in Cairo in the care of rabbinical Jews, where it became known for its meticulous accuracy; and many scholars, including the great Maimonides, consulted it regularly. Indeed, Maimonides pronounced it a model text that ought to be followed by everyone making copies of the Bible.

In the last half of the 14th century, Maimonides's great-great-great grandson took that codex from Cairo to Aleppo, Syria, where it remained for about 600 years, locked away in the basement of the Central Synagogue. In an effort to keep the treasured manuscript safe, the authorities in the synagogue restricted access to it, so that, for instance, they turned down requests to photograph it in the 1920s for a scholarly edition of the Hebrew Bible; the editors of that edition had to use a somewhat later Masoretic text called the Leningrad Codex as the base text instead of the Aleppo Codex. In 1943, concerned Jews in Jerusalem sent a Hebrew University lecturer to Aleppo to gain permission to take the codex to a safer location—in the 1940s, there was a lot of turmoil at the time—and even, they said, if need be, to steal it to protect it. The lecturer did neither, and upon his return someone lamented, "It's too bad we sent an honest man."

In retrospect, it's indeed unfortunate that the synagogue didn't allow the text to go or permit more scholars to take notes or photographs because in November, 1947—that was, in fact, the day after the U.N. voted to establish the state of Israel—there was rioting in Aleppo and a mob broke into and burned the synagogue. After more than a thousand years, it looked like the Crown of Aleppo had been lost forever. But someone, undoubtedly at great risk, managed to grab what they could of the Codex; and then it was passed secretly from hand to hand until it was smuggled out of Syria and taken to Israel in 1958, apparently with quite a bit of conniving and double crossing. Today, most of the Aleppo Codex is in the Shrine of the Book at the Israel Museum, where it can be seen alongside some of the Dead Sea Scrolls. It's missing a few pages here and there; but most disappointingly, nearly the entire Torah—remember, the first five books of the Bible, which Jews regard as the most sacred part of the Bible—has been torn out and is missing; that's about 40 percent of the codex, some 200 pages. That might be the end of the story, but there's a tantalizing possibility that those missing pages might someday turn up. One page came to light in 1982, and another fragment was identified in 1988. You can read a fine account of all of this in Matti Friedman's book, *The Aleppo Codex*.

Okay, clearly a lot of people cared a great deal about this particular manuscript, because it's a nearly perfect copy of the Hebrew Bible. But what exactly is that sacred text, and where did it come from? First of all, it's not the Old Testament. As we'll see in a later lecture, early Christians regarded the Jewish scriptures as sacred, and they adopted a Greek translation called the Septuagint as part of their own canon. But the number and the order of the books were different from the Septuagint and the Hebrew texts, the Masoretic texts, and Christians reinterpreted the text in ways that aligned with their own beliefs. Second, even though I've been calling it the Hebrew Bible, that name doesn't exactly fit either, since some of it's written in the later language of Aramaic rather than Hebrew; not a lot of it, but a few chapters in the books of Daniel and Ezra that seem to be some of the latest books that were included within the Hebrew Bible.

Probably the best name, however, is the one used by Jews themselves. They call it Tanakh, which is an acronym consisting of the first letters of the three major divisions: Torah, which is the five books ascribed to Moses; Nevi'im, the Prophets; and Kethuvim, the Writings. So together it's "T-N-K" with English letters, but "Tanakh." Together these constitute not a single book, but a library of Hebrew texts in many different genres, written over a thousand-year period. For a long, long time, these writings circulated separately, with some books being regarded as authoritative in some communities but they weren't thought of as authoritative in other communities; so they circulate separately as individual scrolls. Keep in mind, too, that literacy was quite limited in the ancient world; religious texts tended to be the concern of a few educated specialists. Eventually, however, a core group of documents was recognized by all Jews as sacred, though this worked out differently for each of the three biblical divisions of Tanakh.

The oldest compositions of the ancient Hebrews, like those of India, were originally passed down orally, by word of mouth. Starting perhaps as early as the 10th century B.C.E., maybe at the court of King David, various oral traditions were combined, they were edited, and then written down. Over the next few centuries, during the time of the divided kingdoms of Israel up in the north and Judah in the south, and them the destruction of Israel by the Assyrians in 722, those texts were further revised and augmented until the Babylonian Conquest in 586 B.C.E. when it appears that the Torah as we know it today had basically taken shape; so it's Genesis, Exodus, Numbers, Leviticus, and Deuteronomy. I should note that scholars argue vigorously about nearly everything that I'm going to be telling you, but I'll keep to a general consensus.

When Judah was conquered in 587 B.C.E. and its leading citizens were taken captive to Babylon, it seemed as if the Jews would lose their identity as a distinct people, much like the Israelites under the Assyrians a century later or like innumerable other ancient peoples and ethnic groups. But the Babylonians themselves were conquered by the Persians in 539 B.C.E., not long after the conquest of Jerusalem, and miraculously, the new king of Persia, Cyrus the Great, agreed to let the Jews in Babylon return to Jerusalem and rebuild their temple after an exile that lasted for only about half a century.

The return to Jerusalem didn't go particularly smoothly. There was conflict with Jews who'd remained Judea, and it took two waves of immigration and more than 20 years to rebuild the temple, which was dedicated in 515 B.C.E. This is the beginning of what we call the Second Temple period; so the First Temple was Solomon's Temple destroyed by the Babylonians, and then the Second Temple was dedicated in 515 and that will remain in Jerusalem being continuously used (pretty much) until the romans destroy it in 70 C.E.

Nearly 60 years after the dedication of the temple, in 458 B.C.E., another group of Jews from Babylon returned to Judea under the leadership of Ezra the scribe, and they were joined in 445 by more Jewish immigrants led by Nehemiah. Ezra and Nehemiah were appalled at the corruption and the laxness that they found among their co-religionists in Judea; and in an attempt to reform and to unify the community, to bring it together, Ezra gathered the people, both men and women, he ascended a high wooden platform, and he read them, as it says in the Hebrew Bible, "the book of the law of Moses" from early morning till noon. Modern scholars believe this "book of the law" was the Torah. The people wept—we're not sure whether it was from grief or from joy—and the next day, as it says in Nehemiah 8:13, "the heads of the ancestral houses of all the people, with the priests and the Levites, came together to the scribe Ezra in order to study the words of the law." Thereafter, Jews in Judea began to try to live their lives in accordance with the Torah, and thus Ezra began to transform the Jews into "the people of the book"; that phrase actually comes from the Qur'an, but it's particularly apt for Judaism. To this day, Jews read the Torah aloud together every week in synagogue.

If the Torah was canonized around 400 B.C.E.—that is, if it was put in a fixed form generally accepted as authoritative—the process took a bit longer for the second section of the Tanakh, the Prophets. In Jewish Bibles, there are two subdivisions: the Former Prophets, so those are the books of Joshua through Kings, which contain many stories about figures such as Samuel and Elijah, some early prophets who seem not to have written things themselves; and then the second division is the Latter Prophets, Isaiah, Jeremiah, and Ezekiel, and the 12 Minor Prophets, who include Hosea through Malachi. It appears that an early version of the history of the Hebrews, or of the Israelites, in the Promised Land, from Joshua's conquest to the fall of the kingdom of Judah, was written shortly before the Exile and then revised by Jews in Babylon; so that's the so-called Deuteronomistic history, because it uses concepts and themes from Deuteronomy but basically goes from Joshua to the end of 2 Kings. There were also extensive revisions and additions made to the books of the so-called "writing prophets" during the Exile, though these books probably circulated separately. Eventually, however, a standard collection came to be accepted as canonical around 200 B.C.E. In the New Testament, when Jesus talks about "the law and the prophets," he's referring to the first two of those three divisions of the Tanakh that were generally acknowledged in his day. It's always good to remember that Jesus himself was a 1st-century Jew.

But the matter wasn't quite settled, even in the 1st century. The third section of the Tanakh, the Writings, was still open-ended, still kind of fluid. Today, the Writings include Psalms, Proverbs, Job, Daniel, Ezra-Nehemiah (in Jewish Bibles that's one book), Chronicles, and the Five Scrolls that are associated with Jewish festivals. The Five Scrolls are the Song of Solomon, Ruth, Lamentations, Ecclesiastes, and Esther. It's quite an eclectic collection; but as we'll see Lecture 9, but this specific list of works wasn't really agreed upon until the second or maybe even the 3rd century C.E., and even then it wasn't decided by a specific leader or a council. Rather, it appears that over time and with lots of arguments, the rabbis gradually came into agreement.

Earlier Jewish communities, however, had larger collections of sacred texts. By the late Second Temple period—that is, before the Jerusalem Temple was destroyed by the Romans in 70 C.E.—many Jews were living far from Judea, all over the Roman Empire. It's actually rather remarkable that Jews seem to have made up about 10 percent of the population of the Roman Empire. Today, despite their profound influence in modern culture, there are only about 14 million Jews in world, or maybe one-fifth of one percent of the world's population. Back in the Roman Empire, not all of these far-flung Roman Jews were fluent in Hebrew or even in Aramaic— which was the everyday language spoken by Jews in Palestine; Aramaic is fairly closely related to Hebrew—so these Jews, scattered elsewhere in the Roman Empire, needed translations of their sacred texts. One of the most prominent of these translations was a Greek rendition called the Septuagint; the name means "the Seventy." That name comes from a legend that around 250 B.C.E., the Greek king in Egypt asked for a translation of the Torah for the library at Alexandria—he was apparently collecting books from all over the world; a terrific lover of books—and so he commissioned a translation. They appointed 70 or 72 scholars (sources sort of vary on that) who were working for about 70 days, but they were working independently. At the end of that time period, they all came up with exactly the same translation, which would've been miraculous indeed. I've done translations. There's no single right outcome for the process; everyone will put things in slightly different words to try to catch the meaning. The story that the Septuagint was agreed upon by everyone made it seem like it was really a gift from God.

A Greek rendition of the remainder of the Hebrew Bible eventually rounded out the Septuagint; but where the Greek Torah and the Prophets had the same books as in the Tanakh, the rest of the Septuagint included extra writings such as the books of Judith, Tobit, Baruch, 1-2 Maccabees, the Wisdom of Solomon, and Sirach, which is sometimes called Ecclesiasticus. Actually this is another problem with the story about the Septuagint: The whole thing wasn't complete in 350 B.C.E.; they were still waiting to add more books into that translation. The names that I've just given you—Tobit, Baruch, and Maccabees—those names may be familiar to Catholic listeners. The first Christians adopted the Greek version of the Hebrew scriptures as their own, and that tradition has continued into Catholic Bibles today. Early Protestants, by contrast, relegated biblical books that were in Greek but not in Hebrew, not in the Hebrew Masoretic text. Those books went into a separate section called the Apocrypha—Martin Luther put them in between the Old and New Testaments—and after a while, Protestants quit publishing those smaller, in-between books as part of the their Bibles.

Why weren't the extra books in the Septuagint accepted by later Jews as scripture? When the rabbis were arguing over which texts belonged in the Writings section of the Tanakh, they had two basic criteria: The books had to be in Hebrew; for several of the books in the Greek Septuagint, the Hebrew originals had been lost, or they may have been written in Greek to begin with. Then the second criteria is the rabbis wanted books that they thought were at least as old as Ezra, whom they believed had brought the time of the prophets to a close. So 1 Maccabees, which is the story of the successful Jewish revolt in the 2nd century B.C.E.—this is the book that gives us Hanukah; actually, the revolt gives us Hanukkah, the book of Maccabees doesn't talk about that celebration at all—that whole book is out. On the other hand, some books that really were written after Ezra, like Daniel and Esther, claimed to be older and thus they were accepted through this complicated, long, drawn out process of canonization that explains why Daniel is in the Writings section of the Tanakh rather than the Prophets, where we might expect him.

But that's still not the whole story. Several Jewish groups in the late Second Temple period thought that there were even more books that should be accepted as scripture; that they regarded as binding and authoritative. I'm sure that you've heard of the Dead Sea Scrolls. These ancient documents, discovered in caves in 1947, were produced by a dissident group of Jews living in a desert community of Qumran from about 250 B.C.E.–68 C.E. The clay jars, hidden away for centuries, yielded more than 220 biblical manuscripts in Hebrew, Aramaic, and Greek, most of them just fragments, but among them was a nearly complete copy of Isaiah. Pieces of every book in the Tanakh have been found in the Dead Sea Scrolls, except for Esther. We're not exactly sure whether the people in that community didn't accept it as scripture, or maybe it just got lost; we're not sure. Yet there were also other, non-biblical texts among the fragments, such as 1 Enoch and Jubilees, which is a reworking and expansion of the book of Genesis; as well as books that were specific to the Qumran community like the Community Rule, the Temple Scroll, the War Scroll, and the Thanksgiving Hymns. I'll talk more about these texts in Lecture 10. Other Jews at that time wrote and treasured additional texts known as pseudepigrapha, which means that they were ascribed to famous figures from earlier ages. These included the Testaments of the Twelve Patriarchs and the Psalms of Solomon. None of these texts made the cut for acceptance into the Tanakh.

In many ways, the Jews became "the people of the book" through a series of losses. The Ancient Israelites were connected to their God through the land that he'd promised them, through the prophets that had spoken in his name, the temple where he received sacrifices, and the kingly line God had established, the Davidic Dynasty. During the Exile, the inhabitants of Judea (who were known as Jews) were carried away to Babylon and they lost all four of those. Amazingly, after a generation or two they were allowed to return. They again enjoyed the land and the temple, but the Davidic kings and the prophets were gone; so they compensated by gathering up and consolidating their national histories—all the stories about the prophets and the kings that had been descended from the line of David—and they started with the five books of the Torah that were ascribed to the greatest of all the prophets, Moses.

After the Great Revolt in 66–70 C.E., the holy city of Jerusalem was leveled by the Romans, the Second Temple was destroyed, and the dispersion of the Jews accelerated. What would become of them? I like Matti Friedman's summary; he says:

> There was no precedent for a scattered people's remaining a people; dispersion meant disappearance. If the Jews were to be an exception, instead of being bound by a king, a temple, or geography,

they needed to be bound by something else, something portable. What emerged was the idea that people could be held together by words.

That is to say, the rabbis took their lead from Ezra the scribe so many centuries earlier and created a community that would be centered on a specific text. That innovative idea would eventually affect most of the world's population through the influence of Christianity and Islam, not to mention other religions like Sikhism. Once the focus of Jewish identity became the Tanakh, it became more important than ever to carefully define its contents; and through the work of the Masoretic scholars like Aaron ben Asher, the creator of the Aleppo Codex, the exact form of that text would stay the same, forever after. In the next lecture, we'll look at the contents of the Torah in more detail, followed by a lecture on the Prophets and the Writings.

There's certainly more to the story of Jewish sacred texts after the closing of the canon; and in coming lectures, we'll talk about the Talmud, a little bit about Jewish mysticism, and the rise of textual scholarship that attempted to correct the standard Masoretic Text on the basis of other versions such as the Septuagint and the Dead Sea Scrolls. But it's fascinating to trace the development of a faith where religious authority belongs to scholars rather than to prophets or priests; and the extreme reliance on a sacred text makes the inscription on the Aleppo Codex rather poignant. It says there—it's sort of written on the margins or before it—the Aleppo Codex has an inscription that says: "Blessed [is] he who preserves it, and cursed be he who steals it. … It may not be sold and it may not be defiled forever." The book is everything.

Five Books of Torah
Lecture 8

The word *Torah* is often translated as "Law," but "Instruction" or "Teaching" might be a better rendition. The word sometimes refers to the first five books of the Bible, but it can also mean the Tanakh as a whole or the Talmud. To be more specific, we can talk of the Chumash (derived from the Hebrew word for "five") or the Pentateuch (Greek for "five books"). Whatever we call it, this section includes Genesis, Exodus, Leviticus, Numbers, and Deuteronomy. After a brief overview of its contents, we'll look at two responses to the Torah, one from those who accept it as the word of God and another from those who try to understand it by reading it critically.

Influences of the Torah

- Even those who are not religious have had their lives shaped to some extent by the Torah. For example, we owe the practice of taking a break from our labors every seven days—the weekend—to the Torah, not to mention innumerable other aspects of art, literature, music, law, politics, history, ethics, and science. The Torah is one of the foundations of Western civilization.

- Early Christian missionaries to China were shocked to discover that the Chinese did not have any ancient creation myths; they simply believed that the cosmos had always been running as it was in the present. How could intelligent people not crave the sorts of explanations found in Genesis? This reaction on the part of the missionaries was also a subtle influence of the Torah.

- On a related note, when historians try to explain why China did not develop Western-style science, despite a long lead over Europe in technological advances, one possible factor that arises is the absence in China of the idea of a supreme lawgiver or creator god who established the rules of the universe. Because the Chinese never expected to find a coherent set of causes and effects underlying the natural world, they didn't look for one.

- In addition to its historical significance, the Torah also serves as a source of guidance and comfort for large numbers of people, despite the fact that the world is quite different today than it was 2,500 years ago. One reason this ancient text remains relevant is that its meaning and application have been continuously debated and reevaluated.

Contents of the Torah

- The book of Genesis opens with 11 chapters about the early history of the world and humanity. In chapter 12, however, the focus shifts to the story of one particular family, starting with Abraham and extending to his descendants, the Hebrews or Israelites (named after Abraham's grandson, Israel).

    o God chooses Abraham and promises him land, numerous offspring, fame, and a key role in human history. He makes a covenant with Abraham and, in return, requires circumcision of the male members of the clan as a sign of that covenant.

    o There are complications along the way—barrenness, political conflict, family squabbles, and a test of Abraham's faithfulness—but God makes good on his promises to Abraham, his son Isaac, his grandson Jacob (renamed Israel), and Israel's 12 sons.

- In Exodus, we read that the Israelites were reduced to slavery in Egypt and that God appointed Moses to rescue them. Leading the people through the desert to Mount Sinai, Moses received commandments from God—not only the Ten Commandments but also laws regarding personal injuries, property rights, festivals, and so on. At Sinai, God makes a new, conditional covenant with his people: He will bless and protect them as long as they keep his commandments and worship only him.

- Leviticus consists almost entirely of religious regulations for the Israelites: instructions concerning offerings and sacrifices, the ordination of priests, festivals, permissible foods, and how to deal with sin.

- Numbers gets its name from a census of the Israelites in its first chapters. God had intended to give them the Promised Land of Canaan (later called Judea or Palestine) shortly after the revelation at Sinai, but they rebelled when they learned they would have to fight to take possession of it.
    - God then condemned the Israelites to wander for 40 years in the wilderness, until every adult had died except Caleb and Joshua. Not even Moses makes it into the Promised Land.

    - Still, God keeps his people alive by providing the miraculous food manna, and he blesses them so that their clothes and sandals don't wear out (Deut. 29:5). There are stories of travels, apostasy, warfare, divine healing, and even a talking donkey.

- The last book of the Torah, Deuteronomy ("Second Law") consists of three speeches given by Moses to the Israelites on the plains of Moab shortly before his death and their long-awaited entry into the Promised Land. Moses reaffirms the covenant, reiterates its requirements, and pronounces blessings and curses upon the people, depending on their faithfulness.

- The God of the ancient Israelites seems similar in many ways to the gods of other nations at the time, yet there were important differences, as well, highlighted in the term *ethical monotheism*. The Hebrew God insisted that his people worship him alone, and he cared not just about rituals and sacrifices but also about how the Israelites treated one another.

Religious Perspectives
- For more than 2,000 years, Jews assumed that the Torah was revealed by God to Moses, who then wrote it all down. As we saw in the last lecture, the Masoretes developed one standard form of

the text between 600 and 1000 C.E. The Torah was divided into 54 weekly sections to be read over the course of a year in Sabbath services. In the 2nd century B.C.E., Antiochus Epiphanes, an anti-Semitic ruler, banned the public reading of the Torah, and Jews substituted 54 selections from the Prophets. Today, both are chanted every week in synagogue.

- The most prized possession in any synagogue is the Torah scroll. Even today, these scrolls must be handwritten to exacting specifications. When the members of the congregation hear the words of the Torah, it is as if they, too, were at Sinai or on the plains of Moab, receiving and renewing the covenant given to their ancestors.

- The Torah was not only encountered in ritual and worship, but it was also studied intensely. The main messages of covenant and ethical monotheism came through clearly, but the rabbis also noticed gaps, redundancies, and contradictions, which they sought to explain and harmonize in quite sophisticated ways.
  o The Torah depicts God as righteous and compassionate, yet he can also be difficult to understand. His commandment to Abraham to sacrifice his son Isaac is a famous and troubling example. Further, God's commandments sometimes make perfect sense, while at other times, the regulations seem arbitrary.

  o In their Torah study, the rabbis were particularly concerned with the application of its precepts. The point was to live in accordance with the laws of Moses to sustain the covenant.

- Christians, who adopted the Torah as part of their own sacred text, saw the law of Moses as superseded in Christ; thus, they mostly ignore the regulations of Exodus, Leviticus, and Deuteronomy, or they apply them selectively, focusing on the Ten Commandments. Christians often criticize the hundreds of detailed rules as overly legalistic or ritualized, yet from a Jewish perspective, the effort required to live in accordance with Torah is a way to make one's whole life sacred.

- Debates about how best to adapt an ancient text to the modern world still continue among both Jews and Christians. The stories told in the Torah are still inspiring to many, but perhaps we need to read those narratives in different ways in light of contemporary notions of gender roles, racial equality, democracy, science, and religious pluralism.

Scholarly Perspectives
- At about the time of the Enlightenment, scholars of ancient languages and documents began to apply the methods they used in studying these other ancient texts to the Bible. From this perspective, the redundancies and repetitions found in the Bible could be seen as clues to the origins of the text.
  - These scholars noticed, for instance, that some passages referred to God as Elohim, rendered into English as "God," while others used the name Yahweh, written with the consonants YHWH and usually translated as "Lord." Some passages differed in other ways related to characteristic vocabulary and themes.

  - It occurred to scholars that the Torah might not have been written all at once by Moses but might be a composite of different sources assembled over time. This view may challenge traditional assumptions, but it is not necessarily dismissive of the Torah as scripture. In fact, many anomalies in the Bible start to make sense when we recognize that the text came into being through a long and complicated process.

- In addition, as scholars deciphered long-lost languages and archaeologists unearthed ancient artifacts, it became easier to understand the Torah in its original historical context. Its narratives could be compared to other creation stories, flood narratives, and national epics.

- By the late 20th century, scholars had arrived at a conception of the Torah as a combination of four basic sources.

- o The first is J, which stands for the Yahwist. This scribe, working in the 10th century B.C.E., uses the term Yahweh, called the sacred mountain Sinai, and portrays God in a somewhat anthropomorphic fashion as a deity who communicates directly with humans.

- o The second source is E, the Elohist, who uses the term Elohim for God, refers to the sacred mountain as Horeb, and most often shows God working through dreams and angels. This source is dated to the 8th century B.C.E.

- o At some point, the J and E sources were combined and augmented by D, the Deuteronomist. This source, dated from the late 7th century, is mostly concerned with the book of Deuteronomy, with its emphasis on centralizing worship and sacrifice at the Jerusalem Temple.

- o Finally, P, the priestly source, was a product of the Exile in the 6th century and is characterized by an interest in order, boundaries, priests, and the tabernacle. Parts of P are interspersed throughout the first five books of the Torah.

- In recent decades, this neat scheme has been disputed. Perhaps E was an oral tradition rather than a written document. Perhaps the four major sources were the products of different scribal

A mezuzah is a piece of handwritten parchment with verses from Deuteronomy 6 and 11, rolled up and placed in a small case, and affixed to the doorpost of a Jewish home.

schools rather than individuals. The various strands of the Torah have proven difficult to disentangle and to date, but nearly all scholars now accept that the text had a long and complicated editorial history.

- The insights of the historical-critical method have been challenging for some believers because they complicate the traditional story, but scholarship has helped us to understand the text more clearly than ever before. And reading the Torah as carefully as possible, with all the scholarly tools available, can be seen as an act of devotion.

Suggested Reading

Alter, trans., *The Five Books of Moses*.

Berlin and Brettler, eds., *The Jewish Study Bible*.

Blenkinsopp, *The Pentateuch*.

Coogan, ed., *The New Oxford Annotated Bible*.

Friedman, *Who Wrote the Bible?*

Jewish Publication Society, *JPS Torah Commentary*.

Robinson, *Essential Judaism*.

Questions to Consider

1. What are the main genres contained in the Torah?

2. Why did this collection of books become the most sacred part of Jewish scripture, and what are its origins, according to scholars?

Five Books of Torah
Lecture 8—Transcript

Hi, it's good to be with you again. This lecture will be devoted to the first section of the Tanakh: the Torah.

The word *Torah* is often translated as "law," but a better rendition might be a more general term such as "instruction" or "teaching." When Jews speak of Torah, they sometimes mean the first five books of the Bible, but Torah can also refer to the Tanakh as a whole (the entire Hebrew Bible) or even the Talmud. To be more specific, we can talk of the Chumash, derived from the Hebrew word for "five," or the Pentateuch, which is Greek for "five books." Whatever we call it, we'll be talking about the books of Genesis, Exodus, Leviticus, Numbers, and Deuteronomy. These are some of the most familiar parts of the Bible, with stories like Adam and Eve, the Flood, the Exodus, and the Ten Commandments; and they're closely associated with Moses, who plays a starring role in four of the five books. The Torah is revered as scripture by both Jews and Christians; and even in the Qur'an, Moses is mentioned more than any other human, even more than Muhammad. Muslims care about these books as well.

One of the characteristics of sacred texts is that they are constantly read, consulted, and reinterpreted over time; and today, even those who aren't religious have had their lives shaped, at least to some extent, by the Torah. Just as a quick example: There's nothing in nature that requires people to take a break from their labors every seven days. We owe the whole concept of "weekend" to the Torah; not to mention other innumerable other aspects of art, literature, music, law, politics, history, ethics, and science. The Torah is one of the foundations of Western civilization.

Let me give you two more examples of how it's influenced our assumptions of how things are. I mentioned in a previous lecture that early Christian missionaries to China were shocked to discover that the Chinese didn't have any ancient creation myths; that they simply believed that the cosmos has always been running pretty much the way it does now. How could intelligent people not crave the sorts of explanations found in Genesis, we might ask? How could people not be curious about where they came from? But the

Chinese just aren't; not in the same way. On a related note, when historians try to explain why China didn't develop Western-style science despite a long lead over Europe in technological advances, one possible factor that comes up is the absence in China of the idea of a Supreme Lawgiver, of a Creator God who established the rules by which the universe operates. The Chinese never expected to find a coherent set of laws of cause and effect underlying the natural world, so they didn't look for those.

In addition to its historical significance, large numbers of people still turn to the Torah for guidance and for comfort, despite the fact that the world is very different today than it was 2,500 years ago. How can an ancient text remain relevant for so long? One answer is that the meaning and the application of the Torah has been continuously reevaluated, debated, and updated. After a brief overview of its contents, we'll look at two kinds of responses to the Torah, one from those who accept it as the word of God, as a repository of eternal truths, and another response from those who want to make sense of it by taking it apart and reading the Torah critically, much as we might any other book from antiquity. But I should point out that the latter approach isn't necessarily irreligious; it's another way of taking the text seriously.

Interestingly, Max Müller originally wanted to include the Old and New Testaments in his Sacred Books of the East series; but in the late 19th century, Oxford University Press was afraid that some people would find that offensive. You know: Other people have sacred texts, but we have holy scripture. In today's pluralistic society, however, and especially in an academic setting, that sort of special treatment for some books isn't really fair; so in what follows, imagine what you might think if you were a Buddhist hearing about the Torah for the first time. Müller once observed that "the warning not to do unto others what we do not wish others to do unto us [is] shared by nearly all the great religions of the world." Most of us are familiar with the Golden Rule from the New Testament, but an early variant is found in Leviticus 19:18: "Love your neighbor as yourself." Now would be a good time to put that particular bit of advice from the Torah into practice.

The book of Genesis opens with 11 chapters about the early history of the world and humanity, from the Creation and Adam and Eve, to Noah's Ark and the Tower of Babel. In Chapter 12, however, the focus shifts to the story of one particular family, or one family line, which starts with Abraham and then extends to his descendants, who were called the Hebrews or the Israelites (when they're called Israelites, this is when they're named after Abraham's grandson, Israel). Seemingly out of the blue, God chooses Abraham and promises him land, numerous offspring, fame, and a key role in human history. God says to Abraham: "In you all the families of the earth shall be blessed." He makes a covenant with Abraham, and in return he requires circumcision of the males in the clan ever after as a sign of that covenant. There are complications along the way—there's barrenness of some of the women who are supposed to be ancestresses of this lineage, there are political conflicts and family squabbles, there's even a test to see if Abraham's faithfulness to God extends to killing his own son—but God makes good on his promises to Abraham, his son Isaac, and his grandson Jacob (he's the one who gets renamed Israel later on), and also in turn to Israel's 12 sons. Despite the patriarchal nature of the story, the women in the family also have crucial roles, and sometimes act independently or even defiantly; think of women such as Sarah, Rebekah, Rachel, Tamar, and Miriam.

The narrative of Joseph, the second to the youngest of Israel's sons, is a masterpiece of world literature. Sold into slavery by his jealous older brothers, Joseph rose to a position of prominence in Egypt and was able to save his family at a time of famine. That tale is wonderfully told, with all sorts of poignant details: how Joseph, meeting his brothers but in disguise, nearly gives himself away with tears when he overhears them blaming their current misfortunes on how poorly they'd treated him so many years before. They don't realize who he is, they don't realize that he can understand Hebrew, and as they're talking amongst themselves he overhears this and is nearly overcome when he realizes how guilty they still feel. Another detail that I like is how they pass the test that Joseph sets for them and then he urges them to return home and to bring their aged father back to Egypt. As this all takes place, his last words as he's sending them out are "Don't quarrel on the way"; he knows these brothers pretty well.

In the book of Exodus, the second of the Pentateuch or the Chumash, we read how the Israelites were eventually reduced to slavery in Egypt; how God appointed Moses to rescue them through the plagues, the Passover, and the parting of the Red Sea. Leading the people through the desert to Mount Sinai, Moses there received commandments from God; not only the 10 commandments that are so familiar to many of us, but also laws regarding personal injuries, property rights, festivals, priests, and the furnishing of a portable tent-temple called the tabernacle. At Sinai, God makes a new, conditional covenant with his people: He'll bless and protect them so long as they keep his commandments and worship only him.

Leviticus consists nearly entirely of religious regulations for the Israelites. So in this third book, we get explicit instructions concerning offerings and sacrifices; how to ordain priests, the regulations for that; festivals; what foods the Israelites were and weren't allowed to eat; how to deal with skin diseases; how to deal with mildew, bodily discharges, and other impurities, as well as out and out sin. Leviticus may not be quite as detailed as the Hindu Brahmanas, but it's in the same league.

The fourth book of the Pentateuch, Numbers, gets its name from a census of the Israelites in its first chapters. God had intended to give them the promised land of Canaan, later called Judea or Palestine, shortly after that revelation at Sinai to Moses; but then the Israelites rebelled when they learned that they were going to have to fight to take possession of the Promised Land—they weren't just going to be able to walk in there; there were already people that were there—and when they hesitated, when they didn't want to go in and do that, God then angrily condemned them to wander for 40 years in the wilderness, around and around, until every adult had died except for Caleb and Joshua. Not even Moses himself makes it into the Promised Land. On the other hand, God kept the Israelites alive by providing the miraculous food called manna, and he blessed them so that even their clothes and their sandals didn't wear out. There are stories in this book of Numbers about travels and apostasy, about warfare and divine healing, and even a talking donkey.

The last book of the Torah, Deuteronomy, which is the Greek word for "second law," has very little narrative. Instead, it consists of three speeches given by Moses to the Israelites on the plains of Moab shortly before his death and their long-awaited entry into the Promised Land. Moses reaffirms the covenant, he reiterates its requirements, and pronounces blessings and curses upon the people, depending on their faithfulness; actually, there are more curses than blessings, but they kind of balance each other out. Moses said: "I have set before you life and death, blessings and curses. Choose life so that you and your descendants may live, loving the Lord your God, obeying him, and holding fast to him." Deuteronomy is also the source of the Shema, a prayer that's recited morning and evening by Jews around the world that begins: "Hear O Israel, the Lord our God, the Lord is One"; or in another translation, "Hear O Israel, the Lord is our God, the Lord alone."

The God of the ancient Israelites seems similar in some ways to the gods of other nations at the time: He was a warrior deity who protected his people in battle in return for animal sacrifices and loyalty. Yet there are important differences as well; differences highlighted in the term "ethical monotheism." The Hebrew God insisted that his people worship only him (that's the monotheism part, one god); and he cared not just about rituals and sacrifices, but also about how the Israelites treated each other, how they treated their neighbors, especially the weak and the vulnerable, and even their animals (that's the ethical part of all this).

I assume that at some point you're going to want to read the Torah yourself, so a quick word on translations. There are many fine Bibles available today, and if you come from a Christian background you're likely to know some of them already: Evangelicals often use the New International Version or the English Revised Version; Catholics might turn to the New American Bible or to the New Jerusalem Bible. I have three particular recommendations, though: First, the New Revised Standard Version is used across denominational boundaries and is the standard academic translation. It's accepted by Catholics, Protestants, and by Jews as well. My second recommendation is the Jewish Publication Society Tanakh, which is the gold standard in Judaism. If you go to synagogue, this is the translation that you'll find in the pews there. Third, I'm also quite partial to Robert Alter's *Five Books of Moses*, which tries to bring some of the literary qualities of the Hebrew into English.

For more than 2,000 years, Jews assumed that the Torah was revealed by God to Moses, who wrote it all down before he died. Actually, it's a little odd because the last bit of the book of Deuteronomy talks about his death, so that might seem a little bit strange; but some of the rabbis said, "No, Moses even wrote down the account of his own death with tears in his eyes." Eventually, there was one standard form of the text that developed, as we saw in the last lecture, with the help of Masoretes between 600 and 1000 C.E. The Torah was divided into 54 weekly sections so that over the course of a year, the entire Torah was read in Sabbath services; there are 52 weeks, of course, but there are a couple of extra sections, and there are some times when there will be more Saturdays than 52 in a single year. In the 2nd century B.C.E., an anti-Semitic ruler named Antiochus Epiphanes banned the public reading of the Torah—he banned a lot of other Jewish practices—so the Jews instead substituted 54 sections from the Prophets, each of which had some connection to that week's Torah reading, so that they could read a selection from the Prophets and then be reminded of the Torah reading that they were supposed to do that week but weren't allowed to. Today, both the readings from the Prophets and the readings from the Torah are chanted every week in synagogue.

The most prized possession in any synagogue is the Torah Scroll. These scrolls, which even today have to be handwritten to exacting specifications on animal skin parchment, are regarded as particularly holy and they're kept in an ark; that is, in a special cabinet built into the wall of the synagogue that's closest to Jerusalem. Unlike the Aleppo Codex—which, as you recall, was is in book form with pages written on both sides and then a spine, and it also had the vowel pointings and cantillation marks—a Torah scroll, which is unwound from one stick or roller to the other, has only the consonantal text, no marks for vowels. During worship services, the Torah Scroll is taken out of the ark and then carried around the room to the accompaniment of hymns, and members of the congregation bow or kiss it as it passes by, or they might touch it with the edge of a prayer shawl or with a prayer book and then kiss those. It's a remarkable show of devotion to this text, and respect for it. Then, the prescribed weekly passage is read in Hebrew. When the congregation hears the words of the Torah, especially in Hebrew, it's as if they, too, were at Sinai or on the plains of Moab, receiving and renewing the covenant that had been given to their ancestors.

The Torah wasn't only encountered in ritual and worship, it was also studied intensely. The main messages of the covenant and ethical monotheism came through clearly enough, but the rabbis also noticed gaps, redundancies, and contradictions, which they sought to explain and to harmonize, often in quite sophisticated ways. The Torah depicts God as righteous and compassionate—for instance, he requires that kindness be shown to the unfortunate; that is, to widows and orphans, to slaves, to the poor, and to resident aliens—yet he can also be hard to figure out at times. God's commandment to Abraham to sacrifice his son Isaac is a famous and troubling example. At one point, God wanted to kill all of the Israelites, he was just kind of fed up with them in the desert, until Moses talked him out of it. In another somewhat mysterious episode, God wanted to kill Moses; and he most certainly didn't want any images made of himself. Sometimes he acts in kind of surprising ways; God's ways aren't always human ways apparently.

Sometimes God's commandments make perfect sense, while other regulations might just seem arbitrary. For example, observant Jews can eat carp but not catfish, because the latter doesn't have scales. There are, in fact, many rules about taboos; and though pronouncing menstruating women or diseased people as unclean might strike many as unfair, it's important to remember that those restrictions had to do with ritual purity or holiness, not with sin. Childbirth and coming into contact with a corpse made a person ritually impure, though giving birth was an occasion to be celebrated, of course, and touching the dead might sometimes be the right thing to do. It's morally appropriate to touch the dead, but as you do so you become ritually impure and then you have to go through certain ceremonies to purify yourself. Sin and impurity aren't necessarily the identical thing.

In their Torah study, the rabbis were particularly concerned with the application of its precepts. Their point was to live in accordance with the laws of Moses so as to keep the covenant going from generation to generation. Rather than just 10 commandments, there were said to be 613 commandments in the Torah, especially as they were listed by Maimonides, the medieval scholar who, as you recall from the last lecture, established rules for copying the Torah based on the Aleppo Codex. The 248 positive commandments (those are the "thou shalt" do something's) were combined with the 365 negative commandments (the "thou shalt not's"), and together those provide detailed guidelines for all aspects of Jewish life, from prayer, worship, and the Sabbath, to what to wear and what to eat, to social interactions, then contracts, sexual relations, and civil and criminal law.

Christians, who adopted the Torah as part of their own sacred text, nevertheless saw the Law of Moses as superseded in Jesus Christ; and so they mostly ignore the regulations of Exodus, Leviticus, and Deuteronomy, or they might apply them rather selectively, focusing on the Ten Commandments, perhaps the prohibitions against homosexuality. They often criticize the hundreds of detailed rules as being overly legalistic or ritualized, yet things look different from a Jewish perspective. The effort required to live in strict accordance with Torah is a way to make one's whole life sacred. God is present in every moment and in every action, from the time a person wakes up in the morning to when he or she goes to bed; and to many Jews, that's a blessed life.

Debates about how best to adapt an ancient text to the modern world still continue among both Jews and Christians. What do the rules for temple worship mean at a time when there hasn't been a temple since the 1st century? What about laws concerning slavery, or those forbidding the charging of interest? The stories told in the Torah are still inspiring to many—think about the importance of the Exodus to the African American community—but perhaps we need to read those narratives in different ways in light of contemporary notions of gender roles, racial equality, democracy, science, or religious pluralism. A 2,500-year-old conversation continues; but in the last couple of centuries, there's been a fascinating, sometimes controversial development, called the historical-critical method.

We've talked about the response of religious people to the Torah; and now we're going to talk about the response of still oftentimes religious people, but people who are looking at it a little more critically. At about the time of the Enlightenment, scholars who were reading ancient languages and analyzing ancient documents started to turn their attention to the Bible. "What if we read the Bible as if it were one of the Greek or Latin Classics?" they asked. From that perspective, the redundancies and the repetitions could be seen as clues to the origins of the text. Scholars noticed, for instance, that some passages referred to God as Elohim, which is rendered into English as just "God," while others used the name Yahweh, which is written with the consonants "YHWH" and is usually translated as "Lord." The name was regarded by many Jews as too sacred to pronounce, and this is where we get the English term *Jehovah*.

These passages differed not just in the name they used for God, but in other subtle, regular ways having to do with characteristic vocabulary and themes. It occurred to scholars that the Torah might not have been written all at once by Moses, but it might be a composite of different sources that had been put together over time. That would explain, for example, why there seem to be two creation accounts in Genesis. You may recall the familiar account in Chapter One when God creates the whole cosmos in a series of seven days. On the sixth day, God creates humans, both male and female, after the animals, and then on the seventh day he rests. But then in Chapter Two, the story seems to start over again, with the deity this time being referred to as the Lord God, as Yahweh Elohim, and man comes first; and then God creates the animals, brings them to the man, to Adam, and asks what he'll name them. None of them is a good match for him, and then God creates a woman for Adam by creating her out of his rib. In the story of Noah and the flood, there are two accounts, identifiable by their different names for God, which seem to have been interwoven into a single story. If you take that story and then you separate out the verses where God is referred to with one name and to another one, and then you put those together, they make two complete accounts.

This scholarly approach may challenge traditional assumptions, but it's not necessarily dismissive of the Torah as scripture. Many readers have noticed that after Noah saved two of every kind of animal in the ark, he then made sacrifices when the waters receded. "That would be a quick end to those species," they might've said, dismissing the biblical account as so much nonsense. But a closer examination shows that in one of those two accounts, Noah saves seven pairs of the clean animals and then two pairs of the unclean animals; and it's that account, that version, which tells of his thanksgiving sacrifice, so there are some extra clean animals that are sacrificeable that he can work with. So also there are important differences between the rules regulating slavery in Exodus, Leviticus, and Deuteronomy. These make much more sense if we see them as the products of different eras. In fact, a lot of anomalies in the Bible start to make sense when we recognize the text came into being though a long and complicated process.

In addition, as scholars deciphered long-lost languages such as Egyptian, Assyrian, and Ugaritic, and as archaeologists started digging up artifacts from those civilizations, it became easier to understand the Torah in its original historical context. They could compare it to other creation stories, or to flood narratives and national epics, noting what was similar and what was distinct about Hebrew culture. One of the great discoveries was how much the blessings and the curses of Deuteronomy resemble those of Assyrian vassal treaties of the 7th century B.C.E., which were composed long after Moses and make his authorship of Deuteronomy unlikely.

By the late 20th century, scholars thought they'd pretty much figured things out. The Torah, they said, was a combination of four basic sources. The first is J, which stands for the Yahwist; the J gives away the German origins of the theory because a "j" is pronounced with a "y" sound in German. This scribe, J, working in the 10th century B.C.E., uses the term *Yahweh*, called the sacred mountain Sinai that Moses received the commandments at, and he portrays God in a somewhat anthropomorphic fashion as a deity who communicates directly with humans. The second source is E, which stands for the Elohist, and uses the term *Elohim* for God. It refers to the sacred mountain in the desert as Horeb, and most often shows God working through dreams and angels. This source is dated to the 8th century B.C.E. At some point J and E were combined, and then they were augmented by D, the third source, which stands for the Deuteronomist, which, as you might guess, consists mostly of the book of Deuteronomy with its distinctive emphasis on centralizing worship and sacrifice at the Jerusalem temple; though it also takes pains to emphasize that God doesn't actually live in the temple like pagan gods did, only his name resides there. This source, D, is from the late 7th century, and many have seen it as the text that was found by King Josiah during the renovation of the temple in 622 B.C.E. Lastly came P, or the priestly source, which was thought to be a product of the Exile in the 6th century B.C.E. and is characterized by its interest in order, boundaries, priests, and the tabernacle. Parts of P were interspersed throughout the first five books of the Torah.

In recent decades, this neat scheme has been disputed. Perhaps E was just an oral tradition rather than a written document; or could P have been composed before rather than during the Exile? What about the three different legal codes; and could the four major sources have been the product of different scribal schools rather than individuals? The various strands of the Torah have proven hard to disentangle and hard to date, but nearly all scholars now accept that the text, the Torah, is an amalgamation of different sources, with a long and convoluted editorial history.

The insights of the historical-critical method have been challenging for some believers because they complicate the traditional story. The same thing happened as scholars have begun to apply such methods to the study of other sacred texts, such as the Qur'an or the Adi Granth. But the keen eyes of scholars have helped us to understand the text more clearly than ever before; and reading the Torah as carefully as possible, with all of the scholarly tools available, can be seen as an act of devotion.

I'll conclude by noting another, more popular form of Jewish devotion. Several years ago, my inlaws bought a house in Connecticut and discovered that the previous owners had left a mezuzah on the upper right-hand side of the doorframe of the front door. A mezuzah is a piece of handwritten parchment with verses from Deuteronomy Chapters 6 and 11, rolled up and placed in a small case, and then affixed to the doorpost. The verses begin with the Shema: "Hear O Israel, the Lord our God, the Lord is One. You shall love the Lord your God with all your heart, and with all your soul, and with all your might." The two passages continue with a command to teach these words to your children, to talk about them at home and away, and to write them on the doorposts of your house. A mezuzah is a very literal sign of keeping that commandment, and many Jews reach up and touch the mezuzah whenever they enter or leave their home. My in-laws aren't Jewish, but they nevertheless kept the mezuzah as a reminder of their own religious obligations, and as a way to honor people who show such devotion to their sacred texts.

Prophets and Writings
Lecture 9

There is a tremendous variety of material in the Prophets and the Writings, from histories of ancient Israel to the words of the prophets, from wisdom literature to charming narratives, from philosophical disputations to ancient hymns. Regardless of your religious background, you already know some of these texts because they constitute one of the foundations of Western culture; still, you may be surprised at how gritty or earthy some of these writings are. At the center of all of them is the God of Israel, a terrifying and unpredictable being, yet one who is nevertheless devoted to his people Israel and to all of humankind.

Overview of the Prophets and Writings
- As mentioned earlier, the Hebrew Bible is similar but not identical to the Christian Old Testament. Christians have a few extra books (at least in the Catholic and Eastern Orthodox traditions) because their versions were originally derived from the Greek Septuagint rather than the Hebrew Masoretic text. In the 4th century, there was a turn toward Hebrew by Catholics following the example of Jerome, but Orthodox Christians have continued to use the Septuagint.

- Another noticeable difference is in the arrangement of the books. The Torah ends with Moses on the plains of Moab, giving his last words to the Israelites before they move into the Promised Land.
  - In Christian Bibles, the Torah is followed by a series of historical books, then poetical and wisdom books, and ending with the Prophets.

  - In the Tanakh, the order is somewhat different. Joshua is regarded as the first book of the Former Prophets (Joshua through Kings). Next come the Latter Prophets and then the Writings.

- The Christian ordering puts emphasis on genres, but the Jewish arrangement makes more sense in terms of the canonization of these particular documents. As we have seen, the Writings were the last books to be accepted as canonical, and some of them were among the last to be written.

The Prophets
- The Prophets section begins with Joshua and what appears to be a strikingly successful conquest of the Promised Land by the Israelites. In Judges, however, we discover that the Israelites are not well organized, and a good deal of fighting takes place with other ethnic groups still left in the land and even between different tribes of Israel.

- The books of Samuel and Kings narrate the rise and fall of the monarchy, starting with Saul and moving to David and Solomon. The united kingdom lasts only three generations, and after the death of Solomon, the Israelites split into the northern kingdom of Israel and the southern kingdom of Judah.
    o Israel has a tumultuous history, replete with coups and assassinations as different families vie for power. In 722 B.C.E., the Israelites are conquered by the Assyrians.

    o Judah, on the other hand, is ruled by a single dynasty, the house of David. But in 586 B.C.E., it, too, succumbs to foreign invasion, when the Babylonians take over and exile many of the most prominent and wealthy Jews to Babylon. At this point, the Jews have lost their land, their nation, their monarchy, and their temple, all because, according to the biblical historians, they have been unfaithful to the covenant.

- The Prophets section of the Tanakh continues with the writings of the Latter Prophets, all of whom spell out in detail what was expected of the Israelites by God and where they fell short.
    o It begins with the 8th-century-B.C.E. prophet Isaiah (probably more than one author, writing over about two centuries), then moves to Jeremiah (writing at the time of the fall of Judah),

and Ezekiel (writing from Babylon during the Exile). The 12 Minor Prophets come in roughly chronological order, from Hosea in the 8th century to Malachi in the 5th.

- Frequently writing in poetic form, the prophets combine condemnations of wickedness and idolatry with promises of hope and national restoration—that God will not forget his wayward people, even in exile.

- In the Prophets, we see the work of a number of writers and later editors trying to make sense of the political and social catastrophe of Jewish history.
    - Since the 1940s, scholars have referred to the sequence of books from Joshua to Kings as the Deuteronomistic History because they narrate the story of the Israelites using the language and theology of the book of Deuteronomy. Israel's disregard of God's commands brought on the curses pronounced by Moses at Moab. God is faithful to his promises, even if Israel was not.

    - The writings of the Prophets reinforce this message, but they also hold out hope that God will still have mercy on his people—that someday he will gather them together again and usher in the messianic age of peace, good will, and prosperity.

- It is striking that the Jews believed God's personality and will could be ascertained through the study of history, and this perspective continued with Christians and Muslims. By contrast, there was never quite the same emphasis in India on the accurate recording of the reigns of specific kings, and as a result, the history of early India is much more difficult to recover.

The Writings
- If the Prophets section tends to be focused on the political and religious history of Israel, the Writings are more diverse and broad-reaching. The Writings include the stories of Job and Ruth, who were foreigners rather than Hebrews, and Proverbs, which offers universal wisdom that crosses religious and ethnic boundaries.

- The Writings also include books that seem to break all rules. The Song of Songs is erotic love poetry; the author of Ecclesiastes wonders if life is pointless; and after the famous tale of the lion's den, the book of Daniel veers into strange apocalyptic prophecies. The Psalms praise God and his creation, yet they also express frustration and bewilderment at his inaction. And Job offers one of the most powerful theological explorations in world literature, asking why God allows the righteous to suffer while the evil prosper.

- The Hebrew Bible is a sacred text in conversation with itself, and it's a striking reminder that religious faith is not necessarily opposed to doubt and questioning. Indeed, another take on the challenge of how different religions and cultures can get along is the Hebrew Bible's implicit suggestion that one should be wary of people who claim to have all the answers. The Tanakh may be a closed canon, but the reticence of biblical narratives and the abundance of prophetic perspectives can lead to deeper analysis and more fervent seeking.

- The Writings conclude with some historical books—Ezra-Nehemiah and Chronicles—that narrate the story of Israel down to about 400 B.C.E. The Tanakh ends on a note of hope: In the last verses of Chronicles, the Persian king Cyrus fulfills a prophecy of Jeremiah by charging the Jews to return to Jerusalem and rebuild the Temple.

Themes in the Prophets and Writings
- Obviously, there is a great deal of material here, written over many centuries and incorporating different genres and perspectives, but we can identify at least four themes. The first of these is ethical monotheism, a radical idea in the ancient world but one that becomes emphatic in the Prophets.
  o References in the Torah might be seen as henotheism, that is, the worship of a single god while accepting the existence of other deities. Thus, Israel should worship only Yahweh, even if other nations have their own gods.

- Isaiah, however, stresses that there is only one God in the universe and that any others are fakes or figments of human imagination. This one universal God cares not just about receiving offerings of meat and grain but about how we treat one another, particularly the most vulnerable among us. There are elements of social justice in most major religions, but the declarations along these lines of the prophets are particularly powerful.

- A second theme concerns the mission and destiny of Israel. At first, Yahweh seems similar to a tribal God, concerned mostly with his own people, and the Former Prophets constitutes a national history. But the Prophets once again expands that vision and argues that even though God has his chosen people, that people has been chosen as a means to bless the entire world. Isaiah, for example, quotes God as saying, "I will also make you a light of nations, That My salvation may reach the ends of the earth'" (Isa. 49:6, Jewish Publication Society Tanakh).

- A third theme is God's faithfulness and loving kindness. In numerous places in the Hebrew Bible, God seems like a vengeful destroyer of the wicked, yet it is also clear that he is a compassionate, merciful deity, a loving father figure who enters into covenantal relations with his children and has their best interests at heart, even when they do not reciprocate his devotion. The prophet Hosea

Ruth makes a brave promise to stand by her mother-in-law, Naomi, but the two women have no food and no means of support.

captures this idea in a beautiful verse in which God speaks of Israel as a parent might speak of a toddler.

- A final theme in the last two sections of the Tanakh is a deep sense of humanity, seen in the stories of Job and Ruth.
  - Job is a lengthy philosophical examination, in poetry, of one of the most difficult questions in religion: If God is loving and powerful, why do bad things happen to good people? In the end, God speaks out of whirlwind, but he doesn't explain why he has taken everything from Job. For his part, Job ultimately acknowledges his limited perspective compared with God's majesty and power. Even if clear-cut answers are not forthcoming, it still makes sense to trust God.

  - On the other end of the spectrum is the story of Ruth, a tale of kindness and grace that is short and simple yet profoundly moving. The story of Ruth's self-sacrifice for her mother-in-law, Naomi, is one in which terrible misfortunes are overcome and barriers of nationality, ethnicity, class, and generations are transcended—all through kindness.

Suggested Reading

Alter and Kermode, eds., *The Literary Guide to the Bible*.

Brettler, *How to Read the Bible*.

Coogan, *The Old Testament: A Historical and Literary Introduction to the Hebrew Scriptures*.

Harris and Platzner, *The Old Testament: An Introduction to the Hebrew Bible*.

Kugel, *How to Read the Bible: A Guide to Scripture, Then and Now*.

Rosenberg, ed., *Congregation*.

Questions to Consider

1. What are some of the most important stories and themes in the last two sections of the Hebrew Bible?

2. Why did it take longer for theses writings to be accepted as scripture?

Prophets and Writings
Lecture 9—Transcript

Hello, thanks for spending some more time with me. In the last lecture, we talked about the Torah, the first of the three divisions in the Tanakh; and in this lecture, we'll cover the last two of those three divisions: the Prophets and the Writings. There's a tremendous variety of material here, from histories of ancient Israel to prophets like Isaiah and Jeremiah, from wisdom literature such as Proverbs and Ecclesiastes to charming narratives like Ruth and Esther, to philosophical disputations that we might see in Job and ancient hymns in the Psalms.

If you're familiar with these writings, you may wonder what I could possibly say in a half-hour lecture that would do them justice. I've been worried about this myself, but keep in mind that the same problem applies to most of the lectures in this course. Here, in this lecture, we're only discussing 34 documents that take up about 600 pages or so. By contrast, our half-hour lecture on the Buddhist Mahayana Sutras in Lecture 16 will have to cover 627 texts, comprising some 13,000 pages, and that's only if we only count those in the Chinese canon.

But back to the Prophets and the Writings of Judaism: Regardless of your religious background, you already know some of what's in these texts, because they constitute one of the foundations of Western Culture. There are stories such as Joshua and the walls of Jericho, Samson and Delilah, David and Goliath, Daniel in the lions' den, and Jonah and the whale, as well as familiar sayings like "to everything there's a season," or "turning swords into plowshares," and "pride goes before the fall." Actually, except for that last one: Proverbs actually says "Pride goes before destruction and a haughty spirit before the fall," but it gets shortened in popular usage to "Pride goes before the fall"; and perhaps this just goes to show that it may be worthwhile to read these texts yourself, rather than simply relying on paraphrases or common assumptions about them. For instance, you may be a bit surprised at how gritty or earthy some of these writings are. Much of the Hebrew Bible is inspiring and uplifting, yet there are also enough stories of murder, rape, warfare, and destruction to get a solid "R" rating for a movie version. These 34 books include erotic love poetry, fierce denunciations of the wealthy and powerful, and even expressions of bitter religious skepticism, and those are the sorts of things that sometimes get skipped over in Sunday school. At the center of all this is the God of Israel, a being who can be terrifying and unpredictable, and yet is nevertheless devoted to his people Israel and to all of humankind.

I mentioned earlier that the Hebrew Bible is similar to but not identical to the Christian Old Testament. Christians have a few extra books, at least in the Catholic and Eastern Orthodox traditions, since their versions were originally derived from the Greek Septuagint rather than the Hebrew Masoretic Text. In the 4th century, however, there was a turn toward Hebrew by Catholics when Jerome used the Hebrew manuscripts wherever he could for his Latin translation called the Vulgate. Orthodox Christians have continued to use the Septuagint—Orthodox Christians are the Greek-speaking Christians of Eastern Orthodox tradition—and they have a few more books than even the Catholics, such as 1 Esdras and 3 Maccabees.

Another noticeable difference is in the arrangement of the books. The Torah ends with Moses on the plains of Moab giving his last words to the Israelites before they move into the Promised Land. In Christian Bibles, the Torah is followed by a series of historical books (those include Joshua through Esther, or 2 Maccabees, if you're Catholic); and then a section of poetical and wisdom books (that's Job, Psalms, Proverbs, Ecclesiastes, and Song of Solomon, plus a couple more for Catholics); and then it ends with the prophets (from Isaiah to Malachi). In the Tanakh, in the Jewish scriptures, the order is a little different. The book of Joshua still follows the Torah, but it's regarded as the first book of the former prophets (that's Joshua through Kings); next comes the latter prophets (Isaiah, Jeremiah, and Ezekiel, plus the 12 minor prophets); and then the Writings (Psalms, Proverbs, Job, the Five Scrolls, which are the Song of Solomon, Ruth, Lamentations, Ecclesiastes, and Esther, and then finally it concludes with Daniel, Ezra-Nehemiah, and Chronicles). The Christian ordering puts emphasis on genres—so you get history books, then poetry, then prophecy—but the Jewish arrangement makes more sense in terms of the canonization of these particular documents. As we've seen, the Writings were the last books to be accepted as canonical, and some of the Writings were among the last books to be written.

That's the basic roadmap; let's start our tour, following the arrangement in the Tanakh. The Prophets begin with Joshua and what appears to be at first glance a strikingly successful conquest of the Promised Land by the Israelites. In the next book, in Judges, however, we discover that the Israelites are not well organized and there's a lot of fighting going on with other ethnic groups still left in the land, and there's even conflict between different tribes of Israel. This is an era that's memorably described as a time when "there was no king in Israel, but every man did that which was right in his own eyes"; in general, not a happy time.

The books of Samuel and Kings narrate the rise and fall of the monarchy, starting with Saul and then moving on to David, and then his son Solomon, who was famous for his wisdom and for building the temple in Jerusalem. The united kingdom lasts only three generations; and after the death of Solomon, the Israelites split into the northern kingdom of Israel and the southern kingdom of Judah. Israel has a tumultuous history full of coups and assassinations as different families vie for power, and then in 722 B.C.E. Israel is conquered by the Assyrians. The deportation of that population gives rise to legends later on of the Lost Ten Tribes. The Israelites up in the north seem to have assimilated or disappeared into the grand sweep of history. Judah, on the other hand, is ruled by a single dynasty, a single family, the house of David; but it, too, in the end succumbs to foreign invasion a century and a half later in 586 B.C.E. when the Babylonians take over and carry off many of the most prominent and wealthy Jews to Babylon. At this point, the Jews have lost their land, their nation, their monarchy, and their temple, all because, according to biblical historians, they've been unfaithful to the covenant. Things look very, very bleak. The idea there is that God will protect Israel—or Judah in this case—as long as they keep the commandments; and when they break those commandments, when they ignore God, when they turn to other deities, other gods, then they lose that protection from God and then they're overcome by their enemies. These books seem to be the result of Jews looking back to their history and then trying to explain: What went wrong? How did we end up where we are now?

The Prophets section of the Tanakh continues with the writings of the Latter Prophets, all of whom spell out in detail what was expected of the Israelites by God and where they fell short. It begins with the 8th-century B.C.E.

prophet Isaiah, though the book now ascribed to him appears to have been written by several individuals over the course of a couple of centuries. We also see Jeremiah, who was writing about the time of the fall of Judah, and Ezekiel, who wrote from Babylon during the Exile. The 12 Minor Prophets who follow all have their say, in roughly chronological order, from Hosea in the 8th century B.C.E. to Malachi in the fifth. Frequently writing in poetic forms, the prophets combine condemnations of wickedness and idolatry with hope-filled promises of a national restoration: that God won't forget his wayward people, even in exile. In the Prophets, we see the work of a number of writers and later editors trying to make sense of the political and social catastrophe of Jewish history. What went wrong, and how did we get here? What can we expect in the future? The historian Robert Seltzer has memorably described this part of the Bible as "a national epic of self-criticism."

Since the 1940s, scholars have referred to the sequence of books from Joshua to Kings as the Deuteronomistic History, since they narrate the story of the Israelites using the language and theology of the book of Deuteronomy. That is to say, Israel's idolatry, oppression of the poor and the vulnerable, and the general disregard of God's commands brought upon them the curses pronounced by Moses at Moab. God is faithful to his promises, even if Israel wasn't. The writings of the prophets reinforce this message. As Isaiah says (Isaiah's going to quote God here in this case): "If only you would heed My commands! Then your prosperity would be like a river, Your triumph like the waves of the sea." Isaiah's speaking at a time when this has most surely not been the case; Israel hasn't been at a time of triumph. Nevertheless, the prophets hold out hope that God will still have mercy on his people; that someday he'll gather them together again and usher in the messianic age of peace, goodwill, and prosperity.

It's striking that the Jews believed that God's personality and will could be ascertained through the study of history; and this perspective continued with Christians and Muslims. All three religious traditions look towards records of the past to understand God, and who he was, and his relationships with human beings. By contrast, there was never quite the same emphasis in India on the accurate recording of the reigns of specific kings; and as a result, the history of early India is much more difficult to recover. I guess if your basic understanding of the world is samsara—remember, reincarnation—where everything happens again and again, the details of who did what when are perhaps less significant.

If the Prophets section tends to be focused on the political and religious history of Israel, the Writings are more diverse and more broad-reaching. They include the stories of Job and Ruth, who were foreigners rather than Hebrews; it includes the book of Proverbs, which offers universal wisdom that crosses religious and ethnic boundaries. For example, a favorite proverb of mine is: "a soft answer turns away wrath, but a harsh word stirs up anger"; that's the kind of truth that might be applicable in many times, in many places. In fact, some of the proverbs that appear in the Hebrew book of Proverbs were originally borrowed from an Egyptian collection of aphorisms called the Book of Amenemope.

Then there are books that seem to break the rules. The Song of Songs, for example, is erotic love poetry, sometimes rather explicit, which has often been interpreted metaphorically; sort of like the stories of Krishna and the cowherds in the Hindu Puranas. The author of Ecclesiastes, another book, wonders if life in the end isn't just pointless, which seems to go against a lot of what the Bible says. After the famous tale of the lion's den, the book of Daniel veers into strange apocalyptic prophecies of the end of times. The book of Esther tells of a courageous young Jewish woman living at a time when Jews were a vulnerable minority who saves her people by marrying a Gentile king, which is a little strange because that goes against some other commandments in the Hebrew Bible not to marry Gentiles; and even more notoriously in the book of Ester, God is never mentioned. This apparently bothered some people in antiquity. The Greek version of Ester in the Septuagint had six added sections of more than a hundred verses that give the story a much more religious cast with prayers, references to ritual purity, and more than 50 invocations of God's name. The Psalms praise God and his creation, yet they also regularly express frustration and bewilderment at his inaction. The psalmist says, "I've tried to be true to you, oh Lord, why are my enemies prospering?" Then the book of Job offers one of the most powerful theological explorations in world literature, which tackles head on the difficult question of why, if God is watching over all, the righteous so often suffer while the evil prosper.

The Hebrew Bible is a sacred text in conversation with itself, sometimes even arguing with itself; and it's a striking reminder that religious faith isn't necessarily opposed to doubt and questioning. Indeed, another take on the challenge of how different religions and cultures can get along with each other is the Hebrew Bible's implicit suggestion that one should be wary of people who claim to have all the answers, sort of like Job's friends (we'll be talking about them in just a few minutes). Things are rarely so simple, and sometimes all it takes is a closer look at the scriptures themselves. The Tanakh may be a closed canon, but the reticence of biblical narratives and the multiplicity of perspectives within the Tanakh can lead to deeper analysis, to more fervent seeking, and to endless discussions. For example, Chronicles is a reworking of the books of Samuel and Kings from a different theological viewpoint; and as we'll see in a later lecture, the Talmud is full of vigorous, faithful disputations about the meaning of the Tanakh.

The Writings conclude with some historical books—Ezra-Nehemiah and Chronicles—and these books narrate the story of Israel a little further after the Exile, down to about 400 B.C.E. In this way, the Tanakh ends on a note of hope, with the last verses of Chronicles in which the Persian king Cyrus fulfills a prophecy of Jeremiah long before by charging the Jews to return to Jerusalem and rebuild the temple; so the end of the Hebrew Bible is the Jews are commanded by Cyrus to return to Jerusalem and rebuild the temple. By contrast, the Christian Old Testament places Chronicles after Kings with the other historical books and puts all the Prophets together thus ending with a very different sort of hope: with the book of Malachi, and with Malachi's prophecy of the return of the prophet Elijah, which early Christians associated with John the Baptist.

Obviously, there's a great deal of material here, written over many centuries and incorporating different genres and perspectives. Still, we can ask whether there are any themes that bring all of this together. I'm going to suggest four themes, and I'm going to provide illustrative examples of each. The first theme is ethical monotheism. In the last lecture, I introduced that concept, which was a radical idea in the ancient world: the idea that there was one God, and that God cared about how people treated their neighbors. In the Prophets, however, the notion of that single god gets even more emphatic. References in the Torah might be seen as henotheism, which is a term popularized by our old friend Max Müller; that is, the worship of a single god while accepting the existence of other deities. So that's to say that there are many gods, but Israel should only worship Yahweh, even if other nations have their own gods. Isaiah, however, stresses that there's in actuality only one God in the whole universe, and that any others are just fakes or figments of human imagination. This one universal God cares not just about receiving offerings of meat and grain in a sort of "You give sacrifices to me and I'll bless you" sort of quid pro quo arrangement, but this one God cares about how we treat each other, and in particular the most vulnerable amongst us: the poor and the defenseless.

There are elements of social justice in most major religions—in Hinduism, Buddhism, Christianity, and Islam—but the declarations of the Prophets in the Tanakh are particularly powerful. Take, for example, Amos, who's an early prophet, a native of Judah who denounced injustice in the northern kingdom of Israel in the early 8th century B.C.E.; in fact, he's one of the earliest of the writing prophets. Reporting the words of God, who speaks in Hebraic poetic couplets, Amos writes (this is God's words now):

> I hate, I despise your religious festivals; your assemblies are a stench to me. Even though you bring me burnt offerings and grain offerings, I will not accept them. Though you bring choice fellowship offerings, I will have no regard for them. Away with the noise of your songs! I will not listen to the music of your harps. But [and then here's the key point; this is what God really wants] let justice roll on like a river, righteousness like a never-failing stream.

You may remember that analogy; it was used by Martin Luther King in his famous "I Have a Dream" speech.

This emphasis on economic and social justice continues through the last of the prophets, Malachi, who says (also quoting God): "'So I will come to put you on trial. I will be quick to testify against sorcerers, adulterers and perjurers, against those who defraud laborers of their wages, who oppress the widows and the fatherless, and deprive the foreigners among you of justice, but do not fear me,' says the Lord Almighty."

One other thing that I like about this ethical monotheism is its social justice not just for human beings, but also for animals. In those 613 commandments, there's a requirement that if you have an ox that's harnessed to a grindstone who walks around all day long in a circle, you're not allowed to muzzle that ox so the ox every so often can put its head down and pick up some of the grain that's fallen on the floor. A god that cares about animals as well as human beings is a remarkable god in the ancient world.

The second theme that I want to talk about is the mission and destiny of Israel. At first, Yahweh seems like a tribal God, concerned mostly with his own people; and the former prophets—remember, all those historical books of from Joshua through Kings—constitute a national history. Why should people who aren't Jewish care about that national tribal history? But the prophets once again expand that vision and argue that even though God has his chosen people, that people have been chosen as a means to bless the entire world. But Isaiah says it better in the second of the four servant songs that appear in his book. There are disputes about who exactly this servant might be—some people say maybe Isaiah, or Moses, or Cyrus the Great, or Jesus—but in Isaiah 49, the servant is explicitly the people of Israel. It says there:

> And He said to me, "You are My servant, Israel in whom I glory." I thought, "I have labored in vain, I have spent my strength for empty breath." But my case rested with the Lord, My recompense was in the hands of my God. ... For He has said: "It is too little that you should be My servant In that I raise up the tribes of Jacob and restore the survivors of Israel: I will also make you a light of nations, That My salvation may reach the ends of the earth."

The idea there is that Israel has a special relationship with God, and that relationship includes being appointed by God as a light to the nations.

An argument can be made that Jews have indeed elevated the understanding and thought of the entire world. Take, for example, the number of Nobel Prize winners. Since 1901, these prestigious annual awards have recognized the greatest achievements in physics, chemistry, physiology or medicine, literature, and peace, and beginning in 1969, prizes have also been given in economics. Over 20 percent of Nobel Prizes have gone to Jews, even though they make up only about one-fifth of 1 percent of the world's population. That's sort of amazing: 20 percent goes to one-fifth of 1 percent of the world's population. It's not my job here to evaluate religious claims to say who's right and who's wrong; but objectively, from a strictly historical perspective, that's remarkable. It might be taken as empirical evidence of God's favor; or at the very least, this could be seen as a result of a people believing that they had a special mission, one that put a premium on intellectual ability and accomplishment.

God's faithfulness and loving kindness is my third theme that I'm drawing out of the Writings and the Prophets. There are plenty of places in the Hebrew Bible that might make modern readers wince, where God seems like a vengeful destroyer of the wicked, yet it's also clear that God is a compassionate, merciful deity; a loving father figure who enters into covenantal relations with his children and who has their best interests at heart, even when they don't reciprocate his devotion. Another early prophet, Hosea, captures this idea in beautiful verse, where God speaks of Israel like a parent might speak of a toddler. God says:

> When Israel was a child, I loved him, and out of Egypt I called my son.
> The more I called them, the more they went away from me;
> They kept sacrificing to the Baals and offering incense to idols.
> Yet it was I who taught Ephraim to walk, I took them up in my arms;
> but they did not know that I healed them.
> I led them with cords of human kindness, with bands of love.
> I was to them like those who lift infants to their cheeks.
> I bent down to them and fed them.

It's just a lovely image of picking up a toddler and sort of being sort of cheek to cheek there.

My fourth theme is a deep sense of humanity. The Hebrew Bible includes some of the world's great literature; works that keenly observe human relationships and hearts, as we saw in the last lecture with the story of Joseph.

So far, my examples have been from the Prophets; but I want to conclude with two books from the Writings that are nearly opposite from each other in form and style. The book of Job is a lengthy philosophical examination in poetry of one of the most difficult questions in religion: If God is loving and powerful, why do bad things happen to good people? On the other end of the spectrum is the book of Ruth, a tale of kindness and grace that's short, simple, and yet profoundly moving.

It's not clear when the story of Job is supposed to have happened, but Job himself was a non-Israelite who nevertheless worshipped the Hebrew God and who's described as blameless and upright in every way. The book begins with two chapters of prose in which we learn how Job's children, his possessions, and his health are all suddenly taken from him at the behest of Satan. Satan in the book of Job isn't exactly the later Christian devil; in the Hebrew Bible, Satan, which means "the accuser," is a member of the divine council and works for God, sort of like his prosecutor or a spy that he has.

After those first two chapters that set up the situation, there come three dozen chapters of poetry in which Job's friends arrive at his home to console him. But they're not very effective; they're actually not all that great of friends. They've accepted the theology of Deuteronomy—this is the notion that God blesses the righteous and punishes the wicked—and since they see what looks like punishment in the case of Job, they argue that he must've sinned. Job pushes back against this assumption, declaring his innocence and even challenging God to meet in him in court so that he can argue his case. (I'm not sure that's a great idea.) Finally, God himself speaks out of a whirlwind; but he doesn't give any explanations, and he certainly doesn't talk about how he gave Satan permission to tempt Job. Instead, God reminds Job just who exactly he's dealing with. God asks: "Who is this that darkens counsel by words without knowledge [meaning Job]? ... Where were you when I laid the foundation of the earth. Tell me, if you have understanding." Then there are a whole lot more similar questions; these are rhetorical questions that sort of point out the difference between God and human beings, and his infinite knowledge as opposed to limited human perspectives and understanding. In the end, Job acknowledges that his understanding is quite limited compared to God's power and majesty. Even if clear-cut answers aren't forthcoming for all of our doubts and concerns, it still makes sense to trust in God, according to the book of Job.

In contrast with the difficult, magnificent poetry of Job, the book of Ruth tells a simple story of ordinary villagers long ago in just 85 verses. It begins with a series of untimely deaths that leaves Naomi and her two daughters-in-law widowed in the land of Moab; so all three widows living together. Naomi, who's an Israelite, wants to return to her homeland and she urges her daughters-in-law to stay in their native land and marry again; but Ruth refuses, telling Naomi: "Where you go, I will go ... your people shall be my people, and your God my God." It's a brave, noble gesture, but the two women still have no food and no means of support. The Law of Moses allowed the destitute to follow behind harvesters and pick up what had been overlooked or dropped. Ruth does this in a field and so meets Boaz, a kindly older farmer who has heard of her self-sacrifice on Naomi's behalf. There are some complications along the way having to do with a near kinsman who had a legal responsibility to marry Ruth but then decided against it because he didn't want to complicate his family or jeopardize the inheritances of his children by taking a new wife who might have additional children, etc.; and so the way was cleared for Ruth and Boaz to wed and have children. Eventually this Moabite woman, Ruth, became one the ancestors of David and of the royal line of Judah.

It's a lovely story, in which terrible misfortunes are overcome and barriers of nationality, ethnicity, class, and generations are transcended, all through kindness. But the real attraction of the narrative is in the details that have been analyzed and discussed for more than 2,000 years. Here's how the novelist Cynthia Ozick describes the nearest, cautious kinsman. She says: "He has only the usual order of courage. He avoids risk. ... He thinks of what he has, not of what he might do." Boaz, on the other hand, does have the strength of imagination to start a new life that he couldn't have dreamed of when he first heard of the impoverished young foreigner out gleaning in his fields. It all leads to a new beginning, and "the beginning is of course a baby," according to Cynthia Ozick.

It's hard to express what I feel when I reread these words today. I first came across them many years ago, when my wife read Ozick's essay. At that time, we'd just been asked, very unexpectedly, if we'd consider adopting a baby who was due to be born in a month or so. At first we wavered—it would be a tremendous responsibility with a lot of unknowns, and we felt like we were a happy family already—but we read this essay about Ruth and decided that we, too, would follow Boaz and take the path of courage and kindness, thinking not of what we already had but what we might do. The boy that entered our family shortly thereafter, the baby boy, has been one of the great blessings of our lives. You never know what might happen if you start reading sacred texts seriously.

Apocrypha and Dead Sea Scrolls
Lecture 10

One of the more colorful figures in 1st-century Judaism was a historian named Josephus, who wrote several books in Greek to explain and defend Judaism to a Gentile audience. In one of them, he described the Jewish scriptures as containing 22 books and said that no one would venture "to alter a syllable." Of course, we know that the Tanakh today has 24 books, that many versions of Jewish scriptures were circulating in the 1st century, and that the gradual process of canonization was still underway in the time of Josephus. In this lecture, we'll discuss two collections of sacred texts that didn't make it into the Hebrew Bible: the Apocrypha and the Dead Sea Scrolls.

The Apocrypha and Pseudepigrapha
- The Apocrypha are the books in the Greek Septuagint that weren't included in the later Masoretic text of the Hebrew Bible. They were considered scripture by Greek-speaking Jews in the Roman Empire and by Christians at least until the time of Martin Luther. Roman Catholics and Eastern Orthodox Christians still include the Apocrypha in their Bibles, but Protestants and Jews today regard these texts as extracanonical.

- The major works in the Apocrypha are Tobit, Judith, the Wisdom of Solomon, Sirach (also known as Ecclesiasticus), Baruch, 1 and 2 Maccabees, and expanded versions of Esther and Daniel. All date from the Hellenistic period, that is, the 4th through 1st centuries B.C.E.
    o The book of Tobit is about a God-fearing Jew living in Nineveh, who becomes blind and prays to die. At the same time, a young woman named Sarah also prays to die because each of her seven husbands has been killed by an evil demon on their wedding night. But God sends an angel in disguise to accompany Tobit's son Tobias on a journey, during which he catches a magic fish whose entrails can be used to both drive

away demons and cure blindness. Tobias marries Sarah and returns home to heal his father.

- The Book of Judith is supposedly set during the time that Nebuchadnezzar was king of Assyria, although Nebuchadnezzar was, in fact, a Babylonian ruler. It tells the story of the pious and beautiful widow Judith, who, when her town was besieged by the Assyrians, devised a plan to win the trust of the Assyrian commander and cut off his head. When the Assyrian soldiers saw their leader's headless body, they fled in panic.

- The Wisdom of Solomon consists of moral exhortations, praise of wisdom (personified as a woman), and a retelling of the Exodus story. Sirach offers proverbs and advice for living happily and ethically. Baruch is a reflection on the meaning of the Babylonian Conquest, supposedly written in the early 6th century, although it's actually a later work.

- The books of Esther and Daniel are expanded with additional stories that, in the case of Esther, make the tale more explicitly religions, and for Daniel, add some colorful details about his life, including the story of his rescue of Susanna, a woman falsely accused of adultery.

- The book of 1 Maccabees is a historical account of the years 175 to 135 B.C.E., when Jews under the leadership of the Maccabee brothers revolted against their Seleucid overlord, Antiochus IV. The Jews defeated their oppressors and rededicated the Temple in an eight-day celebration, which was memorialized as Hanukkah. The Jews succeeded in establishing an independent kingdom, which lasted for a century, until they were conquered by the Romans in 63 B.C.E.

- The book of 2 Maccabees is a more explicitly religious retelling of the early events of 1 Maccabees. It is also the only book in the Old Testament, aside from Daniel, that speaks directly of a resurrection, a controversial doctrine among 1st-century Jews.

- The pseudepigrapha ("false writings") were texts written in the late centuries B.C.E. or early centuries C.E. and attributed to major figures from the Bible, such as Enoch or Moses. There are dozens of such works. Although some Jews at the time seem to have accepted them as sacred texts, they fell out of favor and, like the Apocrypha, were preserved by Christians.
  - One example is 1 Enoch, which tells of visions that Enoch had about the end of times, along with a great deal of lore about angels and astronomy.

  - Another prominent book of the pseudepigrapha is Jubilees, an extensive rewriting of Genesis and Exodus that emphasizes calendar issues, the rules of ritual purity, and the importance of the Torah.

- Scholars learned more about the Apocrypha when the *genizah* ("book repository") at the Ben Ezra Synagogue in Old Cairo was discovered in 1896. Some pages of text found in the synagogue made their way to Solomon Schechter, a professor of Jewish studies at Cambridge. Recognizing their value, he arranged for an expedition and discovered that the *genizah* contained more than 200,000 manuscript fragments, dating from the 9th to the 19th centuries.
  - The *genizah* yielded a treasure trove of biblical and rabbinical manuscripts, as well as new sources about medieval Jewish life.

  - Schechter was particularly interested in a few lines in Hebrew of the apocryphal book of Sirach, a book scholars thought had survived only in Greek. Schechter also noticed several large fragments of a previously unknown text that he hypothesized had been written by an early Jewish dissident group. He was later proven right about this text, which he called the Zadokite Document.

The Dead Sea Scrolls

- The traditional story of the discovery of the Dead Sea Scrolls is that they were found by a Bedouin boy near the ruins of Qumran in 1947. Eventually, fragments of nearly 900 manuscripts were discovered in 11 caves at Qumran, dating from the 3rd century B.C.E. to the 1st century C.E., when the documents were apparently hidden to preserve them from the Romans during the Great Revolt. There is still debate about who exactly wrote these documents, but the best guess is a community of Essenes living at Qumran.

- According to Josephus, the Essenes were Jews who were critical of the authorities at Jerusalem and had gone into the desert to live in devotion, asceticism, and celibacy until the end of the world, which they expected to come soon. Josephus reported that they lived in communal settings without money or personal property, ate common meals, performed daily ritual baths, refused to participate in temple sacrifices at Jerusalem, and observed strict Sabbath restrictions.

Aside from a nearly complete scroll of Isaiah and half a dozen other large scrolls, the Dead Sea Scrolls were found mostly in pieces—some 25,000 fragments in all.

- The Zadokite Document described a similar sort of community that had been founded by a mysterious "preacher of righteousness" who urged his followers to avoid the "three nets of Belial": fornication, riches, and profanation of the temple. Several longer copies of this same text were found among the Dead Sea Scrolls, and because it mentions the city of Damascus several times, it has been renamed the Damascus Document.

- Other distinctive texts from the Qumran community include the Community Rule, which sets forth procedures for those who wish to join and for a governing council; the Temple Scroll, which provides a blueprint for how the Temple should be rebuilt and how its rituals should be carried out; and the War Scroll, which summarizes the coming 40-year conflict between the "sons of light" and the "sons of darkness." The Copper Scroll purports to reveal the locations of some 60 places in the land where treasures were buried.

- About two-thirds of the nearly 900 scrolls that were hidden by the members of the Qumran community were writings that were specific to their particular type of Judaism or other similar movements, but 222 were copies of books from the Bible, with another 10 scrolls from the Apocrypha and several dozen from the pseudepigrapha.

Comparing the Dead Sea Scrolls and the Bible

- Biblical scholars faced a monumental task in piecing together and deciphering the scrolls, but it was incredibly exciting to work with copies of biblical texts that were 1,000 years older than what they had previously had access to. Scholars had long compared the Hebrew Bible with the Greek Septuagint, guessing at what the underlying Hebrew might have been, but the Dead Sea Scrolls predated even the Septuagint by centuries.

- Further, because the scrolls were in Hebrew, scholars didn't have to wonder about the accuracy of the translation, and they found that the Masoretes had generally been correct in preserving these sacred texts; most of the differences were minor.

- It soon became clear that the biblical books did not have a fixed form in the 1st century. Some copies seemed to be the ancestors of the Masoretic text, while others appeared to be more like the Hebrew originals of the Septuagint. For instance, the Greek version of Jeremiah is about 13 percent shorter than the Masoretic version. Of the six Hebrew copies recovered from the caves, we can determine from the surviving fragments that several are of the longer Masoretic type and one is clearly related to the shorter Septuagint version.

- Readings from the Dead Sea Scrolls are frequently incorporated in footnotes to modern translations of the Bible, such as the New International Version (NIV) or New Revised Standard Version (NRSV).
    - For example, at Isaiah 53:11, the Jewish Publication Society Tanakh (NJPS) has "Out of his anguish he shall see it," while the NRSV reads: "Out of his anguish he shall see light."

    - The difference is that the word *light* appears in the Dead Sea Scrolls version of Isaiah, but not in the Masoretic text. Such variants may seem inconsequential to some, but many believers feel that every word in a sacred text is important.

- In the century or two after the Dead Sea Scrolls were written, when the rabbis were still debating which books belonged in the Writings section of the Tanakh, they developed the notion of "texts that defile the hands." This was their working definition of *canon*; a book belonged in the Hebrew Bible if coming into contact with it made people ritually impure, forcing them to wash their hands afterward.
    - This concept is counterintuitive. How could something sacred make someone unclean? The idea may be related to the famous story in 2 Samuel of an Israelite who reached out to steady the Ark of the Covenant when it was being transported and looked like it might topple. Despite his good intentions, he was struck dead on the spot. Some objects can be so awesomely holy that they become dangerous to ordinary mortals.

- Today, when the Torah Scroll is read in a synagogue, the reader follows along in the text with a *yad*, or Torah pointer, so that he or she doesn't actually touch the scroll. Perhaps this tradition is for the reader's protection as much as for that of the Torah Scroll.

Suggested Reading

Attridge, ed., *Harper Collins Study Bible.*

Charlesworth, ed., *The Old Testament Pseudepigrapha.*

Collins, *The Dead Sea Scrolls: A Biography.*

Coogan, ed.. *The New Oxford Annotated Bible.*

Hoffman and Cole, *Sacred Trash.*

The Israel Museum, *The Digital Dead Sea Scrolls* (http://dss.collections/imj.org.il/).

Nickelsburg, *Jewish Literature between the Bible and the Mishnah.*

Rogerson and Lieu, eds., *The Oxford Handbook of Biblical Studies.*

VanderKam, *The Dead Sea Scrolls Today.*

Vermes, trans., *The Complete Dead Sea Scrolls in English.*

Questions to Consider

1. Why were the books of the Apocrypha excluded from the Hebrew Bible, even though some Jews anciently regarded them as scripture (and Catholics still do to this day)?

2. What is the significance of the Dead Sea Scrolls for biblical scholarship?

Apocrypha and Dead Sea Scrolls
Lecture 10—Transcript

Hello, thanks for spending some more time with me. One of the more colorful figures in 1st-century Judaism was a historian named Josephus. He'd originally fought against the Romans as the commander of forces in Galilee during the great revolt of 66–70 C.E.; but when Josephus and his men were trapped in a cave, surrounded on all sides by the enemy, they made a pact with each other to die rather than to surrender. They drew lots, agreeing that according to the lots some would kill the others, and then the last would commit suicide. Somehow Josephus managed to be the last one alive—there may've been some quick mathematical figuring on his part to make that work out, we're not sure—and then Josephus walked out of the cave and surrendered to the Romans. As a prisoner of war, Josephus claimed to have had a revelation from God that Vespasian would be the next emperor; and when that came true, he was freed and then taken into imperial service as a scholar and a translator. And so it was that Josephus, the former general in Galilee, was in Jerusalem at the destruction of the Temple in 70 C.E., but on the Roman side.

Josephus did, however, remain loyal to the traditions of his ancestors; and he wrote several books in Greek defending and explaining Judaism to a Gentile audience. In one of those books, he described the Jewish scriptures as follows: "Our books, those which are justly accredited, are but two and twenty, and contain the record of all time. Then he continued, "no one has ventured to add, or to remove, or to alter a syllable; and it is an instinct with every Jew, from the day of his birth, to regard them as decrees of God, to abide by them, and, if need be, cheerfully to die for them." "Greeks," said Josephus, "on the other hand would never do this for their national writings." Josephus is an apologist; not in terms of being sorry or giving an apology, but someone who wants to defend Judaism and the tradition that he came from.

This description of the Jewish scriptures is a stirring celebration of the Jewish devotion to sacred texts, even if it wasn't quite accurate, at least not in the 1st century. To begin with, the Tanakh—and remember, we used that term from before, it's Torah, Nevi'im (the Prophets), and Ketuvim (the Writings)—today has 24 books, not 22; so either someone has added something, or Josephus was looking at a copy with a somewhat different division of books. Second, there were a lot of versions of Jewish scripture circulating in the 1st century. The desire to produce a single, definitive text in which even a syllable couldn't be changed didn't come to fruition until the work of the Masoretic scribes in the 9th and the 10th centuries. Third, as we've seen, the Torah was regarded from the 5th century B.C.E. as the most holy and authoritative text in Judaism, while the Prophets and the Writings followed in a gradual process of canonization that was still underway at the time of Josephus. Not all the Jews in his day would've agreed about what should've been included in the canon. In this lecture, we'll be talking about two collections of sacred texts that didn't make it into the Hebrew Bible. Those two collections are the Apocrypha and the Dead Sea Scrolls.

The Apocrypha—the name there means "hidden away"—is defined as the books in the Greek Septuagint that weren't included in the later Masoretic texts of the Hebrew Bible. They were considered scripture by Greek-speaking Jews in the Roman Empire and later by Christians as well, at least until the time of Martin Luther, who decided that only books in Hebrew should be included in the Old Testament. Roman Catholics and Eastern Orthodox Christians still include the Apocrypha in their Bibles because their Bibles come from the Septuagint, but Protestants and Jews today regard these texts as extracanonical; that is, they're interesting from a historical point of view, they may be inspiring, but they're not authoritative. Catholics sometimes refer to these books as deuterocanonical, which means they're in Greek but not in Hebrew; both parts of that, the Greek scriptures and the Hebrew scriptures, are thought to be of equal authority. The major works in the Apocrypha are Tobit, Judith, the Wisdom of Solomon, Sirach (which is also known as Ecclesiasticus), Baruch, 1 and 2 Maccabees, as well as expanded versions of the books of Esther and Daniel. All of these writings date from the Hellenistic Period; that is, from the fourth to the 1st centuries B.C.E. Since these books aren't always familiar to non-Catholics, I can give you some idea of what to expect when you open up a Catholic Bible and want to read these.

We'll start with the book of Tobit. Tobit is a God-fearing Jew living in Nineveh—this is the capital of Assyria—who often risks his life to keep the

Law of Moses. Nevertheless, he becomes blind and prays to die; he's just had enough of his life. At the same time, there's a young woman named Sarah, who also prays to die since she's been married to seven men, each of whom was killed by an evil demon on their wedding night. But God sends an angel in disguise to accompany Tobit's son, Tobias, on a journey, during which he catches a magic fish whose entrails can be used to both drive away demons and also to cure blindness (you can sense a happy ending coming here probably). Tobias marries Sarah and then returns home to heal his father, accompanied the whole way not just by the angel but also by his faithful dog (sort of like that devoted canine that went with Yudhisthira to Indra's heaven at the end of the Mahabharata).

Next is the book of Judith. This is supposedly set during a time when Nebuchadnezzar was a king of Assyria; and there are already some historical problems, because Nebuchadnezzar was actually a Babylonian ruler rather than an Assyrian ruler. But this is a story of the pious and beautiful widow Judith, who when her town was besieged by the Assyrians and the town elders were helpless not knowing what to do, she devised a plan to walk into the Assyrian camp unarmed, actually with a handmaid, and she'd win the trust of the Assyrian commander Holofernes, and then get him drunk and cut off his head. The plan worked great; and when the Assyrian army saw their leader's headless body, they fled in panic; there are actually some graphic depictions of Judith's exploits in Renaissance art.

The Wisdom of Solomon consists of moral exhortations and praise of Wisdom—who's often personified as a woman—and, in addition, a retelling of the Exodus story. Sirach offers proverbs, and advice for living happily, epically, and successfully. Baruch is a reflection on the meaning of the Babylonian conquest, supposedly written in the early 6th century B.C.E. by Jeremiah's scribe named Baruch. It's actually a later work that reinterprets those events for its contemporaries with an emphasis on confessing sins and turning to God.

The books of Esther and Daniel are familiar to readers of the Old Testament, Protestant and Catholic; but in the Catholic version, in the Septuagint version, they're expanded with some additional details and stories that in the case of Esther make the tale much more explicitly religious, and for Daniel they add some colorful details about his life, such as the story of Susanna. Here's the story: Two wicked elders were attempting to force Susanna into having sex with them by threatening to accuse her of adultery if she doesn't comply. When she refuses, they have her arrested and claim that they've caught her in the act with a young man in her husband's garden. It looks like Susanna will be put to death on the testimony of these wicked elders, but she prays to God, who hears her cries and then sends the young Daniel. When Daniel comes into the situation, he hears what's going on and then he separates the two false witnesses and asks each separately under which tree did they see her adulterating (if that's the word)? When their stories don't match up, then the deception is uncovered and they themselves are executed.

Next we'll turn to 1 Maccabees, which is a historical account of the years 175–135 B.C.E. when the Jews, under the leadership of the Maccabee brothers, revolted against their Seleucid overlord Antiochus IV, who'd attempted to force the inhabitants of Judea to accept Greek culture by desecrating the Jerusalem Temple and banning Jewish sacrifices, Torah studies, circumcision, Sabbath observance, and Kosher dietary restrictions; so he wanted to pretty much get rid of traditional Jewish culture. The Jews rose up in revolt under the Maccabees, they defeated their oppressors, and they rededicated the temple that had been desecrated in an eight-day celebration, which was ever after memorialized as Hanukkah (though the miracle of the self-replenishing lamp oil isn't in the book; the miracle that's probably familiar to you from Hanukkah celebrations to this day). Amazingly, the Jews succeeded in establishing an independent kingdom, which lasted for about a century until they were conquered by the Romans in 63 B.C.E. Ironically, a text that was so defiantly against Hellenization was preserved in Greek, rather than in Hebrew.

2 Maccabees you might expect to be a sequel, but it's not. It's rather a more an explicitly religious retelling of the early events of 1 Maccabee, which had adopted a fairly secular tone and didn't mention God much, despite the fact that the revolt was over religious principles. 2 Maccabees takes a more religious perspective on those events, and it's also the only book in the Old Testament, aside from Daniel, which speaks directly of a resurrection. Resurrection was a controversial doctrine among [1]st-century Jews. It was rejected by the Sadducees, who were the elite upper class who were

associated with the Temple and believed only what was contained in the Torah; they weren't so keen on the Prophets and the Writings. Resurrection, on the other hand, was embraced by the Pharisees, who we'll talk about more in the next lecture. Eventually, the doctrine of resurrection was listed by Maimonides, the great 12th-century Jewish scholar, as one of the fundamental tenets of Judaism; but it wasn't central to the earliest forms of the religion. For those coming from a Christian background, in which resurrection is a given—it's at the heart of the Christian message—it might be worth thinking about what it would mean to be devoted to God and obedient to his commandments with no clear conception of an afterlife; that is, without the hope of Heaven or the fear of Hell. Would there still be enough motivation to keep all the commandments and be true to God if there wasn't a clear notion of the afterlife, it was just for this life? There were many Jews in earlier times who believed that the covenant required obedience to commandments without any promise of Heaven or threat of Hell.

As we've seen, some of the themes of the Apocrypha include new emphases on women (there are many striking women in these stories like Esther and Judith), an emphasis on prayer, and on the challenges that Jews face in staying true to their traditions either as inhabitants of foreign lands or in Judea, in their own homeland, but under the political and cultural domination of occupying armies.

The Apocrypha is pretty easy to find, since it was preserved by Christians and is included in many Christian bibles and commentaries. There's another category of Second Temple Jewish writings, however, that you might have to dig a bit for, and this is the pseudepigrapha. *Pseudepigrapha* means "false writings"; and these are texts that were written in the late centuries B.C.E. or the early centuries of the C.E. and attributed to major figures of the Bible such as Enoch or Moses. There are dozens of these kinds of pseudepigraphal texts. Although some Jews at the time seem to have accepted them as sacred and authoritative, these writings fell out of favor and like the Apocrypha tended to be preserved by Christians rather than Jews.

One example is 1 Enoch, which tells of visions that Enoch had about the end of times, along with a great deal of lore about angels and astronomy. You may recall that Enoch is a major figure from the first chapters of Genesis. This book, 1 Enoch, was cited as scripture in the New Testament book of Jude. Another prominent book of Second Temple pseudepigrapha is Jubilees, an extensive rewriting of Genesis and Exodus that emphasizes calendar issues, the rules of ritual purity, and the importance of the Torah; and it portrays Adam and Abraham as living the Law of Moses even though Moses hadn't yet been born when Adam and Abraham lived. Interesting, both 1 Enoch and Jubilees are still in the bible of the Ethiopian Orthodox Church; and indeed, the only full texts of each that have survived aren't in Hebrew or Greek, but rather in the Ge'ez language of Ethiopia.

Scholars learned more about the Apocrypha when the Cairo *genizah* was discovered in 1896. The Jewish reverence for books is such that many hesitated to throw away old or dilapidated volumes, particularly if they were religious texts, or if they were written in the sacred language of Hebrew, or if they might contain the name of God. Rather than throwing them out or burning them, synagogues had an old book repository called a *genizah* where volumes and stray pages could be stored away, and then eventually they'd be given a formal burial in a cemetery. In 1896, Agnes Lewis and Margaret Gibson, two Scottish twin sisters, visited the *genizah* at the Ben Ezra Synagogue in Old Cairo and brought back a few pages to show Solomon Schechter, a professor of Jewish studies at Cambridge. (So in this *genizah*, they never actually got around to burying these; they just had these stacks of fragments and old books that were lying around for a long time.) When Professor Schechter saw these, he recognized their value and he arranged for an expedition to Cairo and discovered that the *genizah* contained more than 200,000 manuscript fragments dating from the 9th to the 19th centuries. It was a spectacular find; a treasure trove of biblical and rabbinical manuscripts, as well as a trove of new sources about medieval Jewish life. (In Lecture 13, we'll hear about a similar earlier 20th-century discovery of thousands of Chinese Buddhist manuscripts that had been walled up in cave shrines at Dunhuang on the Silk Road.) In the Cairo *genizah*, there were two letters about the Aleppo Codex that we heard of before, and even fragments of Maimonides's own handwriting. But the document that first caught Professor Schechter's attention was a few lines of the apocryphal book of Sirach in Hebrew, a book that scholars thought had only survived in Greek. Schechter also noticed several large fragments of a previously unknown text that he hypothesized had been written by an early Jewish dissident group spelling out the rules for their community; and this is a text that he titled the Zadokite Document.

Schechter died in 1915. I'm sure that he would've been thrilled to have been proven right some 30 years later by another manuscript find in the Judean Desert on the shores of the Dead Sea. Once again, there's an entire Great Courses lecture series on the Dead Sea Scrolls, but I can give you a quick preview here. The traditional story of the discovery of the Dead Sea Scrolls is that in 1947, a Bedouin boy herding goats near the ruins of Qumran threw a stone in a cave up in some cliffs nearby, he heard a crash, and then he scrambled up the cliff to take a look; and there, he discovered clay jars that contained scrolls. Eventually fragments of nearly 900 manuscripts were discovered in 11 different caves dating from the 3rd century B.C.E. to the 1st century C.E., when the documents were apparently hidden away during the Great Revolt to preserve them from the Romans. There's still debate about who exactly wrote these scrolls, but the best guess is that there was a community of Essenes living at Qumran who had both a library and a scriptorium where they wrote out new copies of manuscripts.

According to our friend Josephus—remember, the 1st-century historian—the Essenes were Jews who were critical of the authorities at Jerusalem, and they'd gone into the countryside or the desert to live more pure lives of devotion, asceticism, and celibacy until the end of the world, which they expected would be coming pretty soon. Josephus reported that they lived in communal settings without money and without personal property; they ate common meals together, they performed daily ritual baths, and they refused to participate in the temple sacrifices at Jerusalem; and in addition, they observed very strict Sabbath restrictions. Some of the inhabitants of Qumran were apparently not celibate, but otherwise most of the clues match. You may be wondering: How do we know if people were celibate or not from archaeological data? In this case, there are over 1,000 people who have been buried in this old cemetery at Qumran; a few of these graves have been exhumed, and they include not just of men but also of women and children. Those bodies are on sort of the outskirts of the main cemetery, and so there must've been women and children in the settlements. Perhaps there were some Essenes who went with full celibacy and other who were more secular, who were still living with families; it's still kind of a mystery about who lived there and why. Lots and lots have been written about the Qumran community and its relationship with the Dead Sea Scrolls.

We're going to go back to that document that Professor Schechter had found in the Cairo *genizah* that he called the Zadokite Document. In that text, there was a description of a similar sort of community that had been founded by a mysterious preacher of righteousness who urged his followers to avoid the three nets of Belial (that's the name of a demon); the three nets that will catch you up are fornication, riches, and profanation of the temple. Several longer copies of this same text were found among the Dead Sea Scrolls; and because it mentions the city of Damascus several times, it's been renamed the Damascus Document.

Other distinctive texts from the Qumran community, all of which were previously unknown before this discovery of the manuscripts in the desert, new texts include the Community Rule, which sets forth procedures for those who wish to join the group and for a governing council; the Temple Scroll, which offers a blueprint for how the temple should be rebuild and its rituals carried out, assuming that the right people were someday put in charge (remember that the Essenes weren't thrilled with the way that the Sadducees were running the temple in Jerusalem); and there was also a new text, previously unknown, called the War Scroll, which summarizes how the coming 40-year conflict will go between the Sons of Light and the Sons of Darkness. This is the sort of text that we now describe as apocalyptic; that is, it sees the present age as a time of conflict between the forces of good and the forces of evil, and then it looks forward to the day when judgment will come: God's judgment will overtake the wicked while the righteous enjoy a new messianic age under the rule of a king from the lineage of David. Remember, a messiah is originally thought of as an early king, and then later as a future king descended from David. An apocalyptic perspective can also be seen in one of the latest books to make it into the Tanakh, the book of Daniel.

There are many fragments from dozens of distinctive Qumran texts dealing with liturgy, the calendar, various regulations, thanksgiving hymns and psalms, and unique commentaries on the scriptures. There's also the Copper Scroll, written not on parchment but etched into copper, which purports to reveal the locations of some 60 places in the Holy Land where treasures have been buried. (Yes, people have looked for those and have come up with nothing.)

These are all the sacred texts of a religious group that no longer exists. We'll pick up that general topic in Lecture 34; that is, how we might respond to other people's scriptures when there aren't any more of those people alive.

About two-thirds of the nearly 900 scrolls that were hidden by the Qumran community were writings that were specific to their particular type of Judaism, or other similar marginal texts. But 222 of those were copies from books of the Bible, with another 10 scrolls from the Apocrypha, from Tobit, Sirach, and Baruch, and then several dozen texts from the pseudepigrapha. The Qumran community especially liked 1 Enoch and Jubilees. Remember, we just have fragments from most of these scrolls; but there's at least a bit from every book in the Bible except for Esther. We're not sure if maybe there's something that's since has been lost, or was decayed or destroyed by time, or if the inhabitants of Qumran didn't view Esther as being authoritative, we're not sure; but that's the only book that's missing from the Qumran scrolls.

It's clear that the community of the inhabitants of Qumran cared more about some books than other, starting with the Torah (as you might guess). Texts from the Dead Sea Scrolls, of which there are more than 10 separate copies—we just have bits from these copies, but we can tell that there are different copies, so more than 10—include, in descending order: Psalms, there are 39 copies of that; Deuteronomy, with 33 copies; 1 Enoch from the Apocrypha with 25 copies; Genesis, 24 copies; Isaiah, 22 copies, including an almost complete copy of the book of Isaiah that's just magnificent; then Jubilees, 21 copies; the book of Exodus, 18 copies; Leviticus, 17 copies; and Numbers, 11. You can hear the first five books of the Chumash, of the Pentateuch, in that list.

We can talk a bit about what the Dead Sea Scrolls means for biblical studies; but first, let's pause for a moment to admire, and to feel sorry for, those scholars who worked with these materials. Aside from that nearly complete scroll of Isaiah that I just mentioned, and half a dozen other large scrolls that had generally held together, scholars mostly are faced with bits and pieces of text, some 25,000 fragments in all; and their task was to fit together what they could. It would be like mixing up 800 jigsaw puzzles—remember, there are 800 different scrolls—and then discarding most of the pieces, and then trying to put together what remains, with little idea of the borders, or what was missing, or even what the picture on the box was. Most of the scrolls were in Hebrew, so it's relatively easy to pick out the few fragments of scrolls that are in Aramaic or Greek, and it was also helpful when scholars could recognize a few familiar words from the Bible—they might know what they were dealing with—or when they night match up the handwriting of a particular scribe; so if you have different fragments and they have the same handwriting, those might belong to the same text, though some of the longer texts were copied by more than one scribe, so a single scroll might have different handwriting on it (just so that it's not too easy).

Putting together the Dead Sea Scrolls from these fragments that had survived was an incredible feat of scholarship; but even now, most of the translations are of disjointed passages, or there are a few lines from this text and a few lines from that text. On the other hand, it was incredibly exciting for scholars to be working with copies of biblical texts that were a thousand years older than what they'd previously had access to; so the oldest Hebrew manuscripts before this time would've been those 10th- and 11th-century Masoretic manuscripts like the Aleppo Codex. Scholars have also been able to compare the Hebrew Bible with the Greek Septuagint, guessing what the underlying Hebrew might've been; but the oldest copies of the Greek version of the Old Testament were two 4th-century manuscripts, the Codex Sinaiticus and the Codex Vaticanus. We'll meet those particular codices again in the lectures on Christian scriptures. The Dead Sea Scrolls predated even the Septuagint by centuries; and they were in Hebrew, so scholars didn't have to worry about the accuracy of the translation.

The question was: How accurate had the Masoretes been in preserving their sacred texts? You're comparing texts that are written 1,000 years apart; how accurate are those going to be? In general, the answer is: Pretty accurate. There were many differences, but most of them were fairly minor; just a word or a phrase different every so often. It soon became clear, though, that there wasn't a fixed form for biblical books in the 1st century; it wasn't exactly what it was a thousand years later. Some of those early copies from the Dead Sea Scrolls looked like the ancestors of the Masoretic texts; others appeared to be more like the Hebrew originals of the Septuagint translation. For example, the Greek version of Jeremiah is about 13 percent shorter than the Masoretic version. Of the six Hebrew copies of the book of Jeremiah recovered from the caves, we can determine from the surviving fragments that several are of the longer Masoretic type and one is clearly related to the shorter Septuagint version; so there seem to be somewhat different versions of some of these scrolls that were circulating at about the same time, in the 1st century.

If you look at the footnotes to modern translations of the Bible, such as the New International Version or the New Revised Standard Version, you'll see dozens and dozens of verses where the editors have incorporated readings from the Dead Sea Scrolls into the text. The Jewish Publication Society's Tanakh translates the Masoretic text, but it has readings from the Dead Sea Scrolls in the footnotes so you can compare those. For example, the standard text of 1 Samuel 17:4 gives Goliath's height as six cubits and a span; this is the Goliath of David and Goliath. Six cubits and a span works out to be about nine feet, nine inches tall. A fragment from the Dead Sea Scrolls' Samuel, however, has four cubits and a span, or six feet, nine inches tall; perhaps a little easier to believe, and it matches up with the Septuagint reading as well. Elsewhere in Samuel, the Dead Sea Scrolls provide an entire paragraph that was somehow lost from the Masoretic text. At Isaiah 53:11, a chapter beloved by Christians, the Jewish Publication Society Tanakh has "Out of his anguish he shall see it." Compare that with the New Revised Standard Version, which says "Out of his anguish he shall see light." The difference is the word *light*, which appears in the Dead Sea Scrolls' Isaiah but not in the Masoretic text. These sorts of variants may seem rather inconsequential to you; but remember, when it comes to sacred texts, many believers feel that every word matters.

In the century or two after the Dead Sea Scrolls were written—when the rabbis were still debating which books belonged in the Writings sections of the Tanakh and ultimately deciding against the Apocrypha and the pseudepigrapha—they developed a notion of texts that defile the hands. This was their working definition of a canon. A book belonged in the Hebrew Bible if coming into contact with it made a person ritually impure; so they had to wash their hands afterwards. The concept may be a bit counterintuitive; how could something sacred make someone unclean? You'd expect that these texts, you'd have to wash your hands before instead of afterwards. But this idea of texts that defile the hands may be related to the famous story in 2 Samuel of an Israelite who reached out to steady the Ark of the Covenant when it was being transported and looked like it might topple. Despite his good intentions, he was struck dead on the spot. Some objects can be so awesomely holy that they become dangerous to ordinary mortals. Today, when the Torah scroll is read in a synagogue, the reader follows along in the text with a *yad*, or a Torah pointer, which is a six- to eight-inch piece of thin silver than ends in the shape of a tiny hand. This is so the reader doesn't actually touch the scroll with his finger; remember that the Torah scroll is thought of as being particularly holy, it's copied with great care and precision, it needs to be taken care of, and it's given a lot of reverence. But also, this idea of not touching it may be as much for the protection of the reader as for the Torah scroll.

But who are the rabbis? Where do they get the authority to decide which texts are in the Bible and which aren't, when you have to wash your hands, how you need to treat these texts, and what you need to do? Where do they come from; and what about that marvelous text that they themselves produced, the Talmud? That will be the subject of our next lecture.

Oral Torah—Mishnah and Talmud
Lecture 11

The process by which Jews became "the people of the book" began after the destruction of the First Temple by the Babylonians in 586 B.C.E. and reached its culmination a few centuries after the Romans leveled the Second Temple in 70 C.E. In the absence of kings, prophets, and priests, a new group arose to help Jews scattered around the world fashion a new identity and preserve their traditions. These were the rabbis, or teachers of Torah. Unlike the priesthood or kingship, the position of rabbi was not a hereditary one; it came through individual effort and study. In this lecture, we'll explore the results of that study found in the Mishnah and the Talmud.

Philosophical Groups among the Jews

- The historian Josephus described three philosophical groups or parties among the Jews in the 2nd and 1st centuries B.C.E.: the Essenes, who rejected the authority of the Temple priesthood and withdrew from society to practice purity and asceticism; the Sadducees, the wealthy, aristocratic priestly authorities associated with the Temple; and the Pharisees, who were devoted to the study and application of the Mosaic Law. Josephus tells us that the Pharisees were better liked than the Sadducees, who were seen as collaborators with the Romans.

- One of the main points of contention between the Pharisees and the Sadducees was the Torah.
  - The Pharisees claimed that when God had given Moses his five books at Mount Sinai, he had also revealed to Moses an oral Torah of explanations and interpretations, which was passed down to later generations.

  - This was, the Pharisees claimed, the origin of their distinctive beliefs and interpretations, such as their belief in the immortality of the soul and the resurrection of the dead.

- Only one author from the Second Temple period—the apostle Paul—explicitly states, "I was a Pharisee." Nevertheless, from what we can piece together about their beliefs from later sources, the Pharisees were sometimes strict, but they could also be humanely lenient.

- After the Great Revolt of 66–70 C.E., when the Essenes were wiped out and the Temple (the power base of the Sadducees) was destroyed, the Pharisees, led by rabbis, became dominant. Their emphasis on studying Torah became even more pronounced after the Bar Kokhba Revolt (132–136 C.E.).

    o Some had seen Simon bar Kokhba as a messiah who would restore Jewish independence, but the rebellion was brutally suppressed, the dispersal of Jews from the Holy Land was accelerated, and the rabbis began to regard apocalypticism and political aspirations as dead ends.

    o Judaism became a text-centered religion, with a focus on adherence to the moral and ritual requirements of the law.

The Pharisees claimed that the oral Torah God had given Moses at Mount Sinai had been passed down by word of mouth through generations until it reached them.

The Mishnah

- The rabbis looked to the Torah, both written and oral, as the key to the survival of Judaism, but there were concerns about the accuracy and transmission of the oral Torah. Thus, about 200 C.E., Rabbi Judah Ha-Nasi ("Judah the Patriarch") wrote down the first part of the oral Torah, the Mishnah ("repetition" or "oral instruction"). It's not exactly a law code but more a collection of legal judgments, some attributed to specific rabbis; frequently, more than one opinion is recorded.

- The Mishnah is a fairly lengthy book, organized into six parts or orders: (1) Seeds—agriculture and prayers; (2) Appointed Seasons—Sabbath, festivals, and fast days; (3) Women—marriage, divorce, and vows; (4) Damages—business relations, law courts, and punishments; (5) Holy Things—dietary laws, the temple, and sacrifices; and (6) Purities—ritual purity and purification. Each of the six orders has between 7 and 12 subsections called tractates, for a total of 63.

- The judgments are terse and orderly, as if designed for memorization or teaching. The first paragraph, for example, concerns rules for reciting the daily evening prayer, the Shema. The passage also includes an argument between the followers of two great rabbis, Shammai and Hillel, about whether people had to lie down to say the evening prayer.

- The Mishnah is, obviously, an unusual law code. Multiple opinions are offered, often with none being pronounced correct. Rabbis quote scripture, cite precedents from defunct temple practices, offer varying perspectives, and tell stories. Rather than simply providing the correct answer, the Mishnah is a tool for teaching students how to think through difficult issues and arrive at reasonable opinions themselves.

The Talmud
- Of course, the conversations continued, with rabbis and students debating the meaning of the Mishnah, particularly in academies in Palestine and Babylonia. Out of those debates came the Talmud—also considered part of the oral Torah—which includes learned disputations, detailed legal analyses, folktales, stories of famous teachers, aphorisms, scriptural interpretation, and much more.
    - The oral traditions in Palestine were edited and written down about 400 C.E. in what is commonly referred to as the Jerusalem Talmud ("teaching" or "learning").

- o The discussions in Babylonia were similarly put into writing about 100 years later. The Babylonian Talmud, about three times longer than the Jerusalem version, has long been considered more eloquent, subtle, and complete. It is second only to the Tanakh in the library of the sacred texts of Judaism.

- The Talmud is a massive work that reproduces the Mishnah in Hebrew and adds a commentary in Aramaic called the Gemara. This commentary is an edited transcript of the debates of the rabbis and their students as they investigated, explained, and elaborated on the Mishnah and the principles they deduced from its rulings. Since early modern times, the Talmud has been printed with multiple commentaries surrounding the Mishnah and Gemara on each page.

- There are many great stories in the Talmud, but what we usually see on display is detailed legal reasoning, often backed up by quotations from the Tanakh.
  - o In long, complicated arguments, with frequent digressions, the rabbis work their way through all aspects of Jewish life and lore with an astonishing level of psychological and philosophical nuance.

  - o Different scriptural interpretations and legal rulings from several generations are set side by side and given equal weight. When there was a practical need, one could be chosen as more authoritative (usually by consensus), but dissenting opinions were preserved for possible reevaluation and use in future debates.

- It's impossible to overstate the importance of the Talmud in Judaism. Students can spend their entire lives exploring its contents, and indeed, Orthodox Jews probably spend more time with the Talmud than with the Tanakh. But the Talmud is not just another commentary; it's Torah, the oral counterpart to the written Torah given to Moses at Sinai. Many Jews believe that, even today, Talmud study should be done aloud with a partner, reading in turns and discussing its meaning line by line.

- Although rabbis were not prophets, the oral Torah provided access to continuing revelation. The will of God in new eras and situations could be ascertained through the discussions of the rabbis in the Talmud—and this was God's preferred mode of communication. One of the most famous stories in the Talmud has God laughing when the rabbis point out that even he can't intervene in the system of the two Torahs and the proper procedures for their interpretation.

- The idea of a sacred oral text might remind us of the Hindu Vedas, but there are important differences. The Vedas were used primarily in rituals, where they were valued more for their sacred sounds than their meaning, and they always remained the possession of priests. The Talmud, in contrast, didn't have a role in public worship services, its meaning was endlessly investigated and debated, and Jews from all walks of life were encouraged to study it.

- Today, tens of thousands of Jews all over the world participate in the Daf Yomi program ("page of the day"), which was started in Poland in the 1920s. The idea is that one can read through the entire Talmud in 7.5 years, reading one page (two sides) every day. The specified page for the day is the same for everyone, and there are celebrations at the end of each cycle.

Judaism's Sacred Texts
- The sacred texts of Judaism, in order of authority and holiness, are the Torah (Pentateuch), the Tanakh, and the Talmud (including the Mishnah), but the library of Judaism includes much more. There is an extensive supplement to the Mishnah called the Tosefta that predates the Talmud. There are rather free commentaries on the Tanakh called Midrash that were written by rabbinic sages before the year 1000. From the medieval period, there are voluminous commentaries to the Hebrew Bible, as well as works of Jewish philosophy and attempts to codify the rulings of the Talmud.

- But in the midst of all this learning and study, there were also Jews who were looking for more direct ways to connect with God through mystical practices. Jewish mysticism, or Kabbalah, is a huge, fascinating topic. Its masterpiece is the *Zohar* ("*Book of Splendor*"), a text that many Jews have considered sacred. Indeed, from about 1500 to 1800, the *Zohar* was regarded by some as a source of doctrine and revelation almost equal in authority to the Torah and the Talmud.

- The *Zohar* first appeared in 13th-century Spain, published by Rabbi Moses De León, who claimed that he had found an ancient Aramaic text dating back to the 2nd-century Palestinian master Simeon ben Yohai and his disciples. The *Zohar* is composed of several separate treatises, including spiritual commentary and mystical stories. Modern scholars have determined that it was probably written by Moses De León, but that hasn't dampened the enthusiasm of many for this remarkable text.

- When Jews use the term *Torah*, they sometimes have in mind the Five Books of Moses, which they regard as the most authoritative part of the Tanakh. But just as often, *Torah* refers to both the written and oral traditions that were thought to have been received by Moses, particularly as the latter were embodied in the discussions in the Talmud.

- There are several forms of Judaism in the world today—Orthodox, Conservative, Reform, and Reconstructionism—that differ in their degree of observance of traditional rules and their engagement with the modern world, but they all come out of rabbinical Judaism and its concern for the oral Law.
  o It is interesting to imagine how different Judaism would be today if it had not closed its canon with the Tanakh and, instead, had continued to produce new scriptures of equal or greater authority.

  o Certainly, the tradition of textual analysis, interpretation, and commentary was decisive in creating a community of close readers and tireless debaters, who expressed their devotion to God through study.

Suggested Reading

Alexander, ed. and trans., *Textual Sources for the Study of Judaism*.

Bokser, ed. and trans., *The Talmud: Selected Writings*.

Cohen, *Everyman's Talmud*.

Giller, *Reading the Zohar*.

Holtz, *Back to the Sources*.

Jacob, *The Talmudic Argument*.

Matt, trans., *Zohar: The Book of Enlightenment*.

Neusner, *Making God's Word Work*.

———, trans., *The Mishnah: A New Translation*.

Scholem, ed., *Zohar: The Book of Splendor*.

Solomon, ed. and trans., *The Talmud: A Selection*.

Steinsaltz, *The Essential Talmud*.

Questions to Consider

1. How did rabbinical Judaism become the dominant form of the religion after the destruction of the Jerusalem Temple?

2. How does the Talmud combine creativity and tradition?

3. What is the *Zohar*?

Oral Torah—Mishnah and Talmud
Lecture 11—Transcript

Hello, again. This lecture will complete our overview of the sacred texts of Judaism. The process by which Jews became the "people of the book" began after the destruction of the First Temple by the Babylonians in 586 B.C.E., and then it reached its culmination a few centuries after the Romans leveled the Second Temple in 70 C.E. In the absence of kings, prophets, and priests, a new group arose to help Jews scattered all over the world fashion a new identity and preserve their traditions. These were the rabbis, or teachers of Torah; the word *rabbi* means "my master." Unlike priests or kings, being a rabbi wasn't a hereditary position; it came through individual effort and study. Although there are no rabbis mentioned in the Hebrew Bible, the profession had its roots in the Second Temple era with the Pharisees.

The historian Josephus described three philosophical groups or parties among the Jews in the 2nd to the 1st centuries B.C.E. The first group was the Essenes. These Jews rejected the authority of the temple priesthood, and they withdrew from society to live lives of purity and asceticism. Remember, this was probably the group that was responsible for the Dead Sea Scrolls. The second group in the 1st century B.C.E. was the Sadducees. These were wealthy, aristocratic, priestly authorities who were associated with the temple. Third were the Pharisees, who were devoted to the study and application of the Mosaic Law. Although the Pharisees kept their jobs and their families, they nevertheless tried to maintain a level of ritual purity in their homes that would've been appropriate to the temple. Josephus tells us that the Pharisees were respected in better light than the Sadducees, whom the common people saw as collaborators with the Romans.

The Pharisees and Sadducees didn't get along very well, and one of the main points of contention between them was the Torah. The Pharisees claimed that when God had given Moses the five books at Mount Sinai, he'd also revealed to Moses an oral Torah of explanations and interpretations; and this oral Torah was passed down by word of mouth to later generations all the way to the Pharisees. This was, they claimed, the origin of their distinctive beliefs and interpretations, such as how a monetary fine could be substituted for actual mutilation when Leviticus spoke of an eye for an eye and a tooth for a tooth; or their belief in the immortality of the soul and the resurrection of the dead. Those were two doctrines that had been rejected by the Sadducees because they weren't taught clearly in the written Torah.

Sometimes English speakers today use the word *Pharisee* to criticize someone as a self-righteous rule keeper, but that betrays a Christian bias. Jesus was often critical of the Pharisees in the New Testament; there are stories of confrontations between Jesus and the Pharisees. Our firsthand knowledge of the Pharisees, however, is rather limited. There's only one author from the Second Temple period who explicitly states "I was a Pharisee," and that one author was Paul, the apostle, who's hardly an unbiased witness. Nevertheless, from what we can piece together of their beliefs from later sources, the Pharisees were sometimes strict, but they could also be humanely lenient. For instance, the Mosaic Law forbids carrying certain objects outside of one's home on the Sabbath, which would've made it impossible for someone to take a meal to share with friends, or to use a cane, or even to carry a baby outdoors. The Pharisees, however, weren't just strictly rules for the sake of rules; they made a decision that if houses were surrounded by a common fence, they could be counted as a single domicile, so within that area people could carry a cane or so some of these other things. This rabbinical ruling is why there's a thin wire called an eruv that encircles many neighborhoods with large Jewish populations; it's usually strung up by telephone wires. With that enclosure, it allows all of the Jews who live in houses in that area to regard themselves as living in one greater domicile, and it provides a ritual enclosure that allows for mobility on the Sabbath.

After the Great Revolt of 66–70 C.E., when the Essenes were wiped out— this is when the Dead Sea Scrolls were hidden away and the Temple was destroyed; remember the Temple is the power base of the Sadducees—the Pharisees, led by rabbis, became dominant. Their emphasis on studying Torah even became more pronounced after the Bar Kokhba revolt of 132–136 C.E. Some Jews had seen Simon bar Kokhba as a messiah who would restore Jewish political independence; but the rebellion was brutally repressed by the Romans, and the dispersal of Jews from the Holy Land accelerated, and the rabbis began to regard apocalypticism and political aspirations as dead ends. They'd gone that way looking for a political messiah; it ended in disaster. Judaism then became more of a text-centered religion, with a focus on adherence to the moral and ritual requirements of the law. Modern Judaism is rabbinical Judaism.

By contrast, Christianity, which also had its origins as a Jewish offshoot in the aftermath of the Great Revolt, continued its apocalyptic expectations of the end of the world—you may remember that the book of Revelation is what concludes the New Testament and looks forward to that final destruction—Jews eagerly sought for power, spiritual and otherwise. It's important to observe that modern Judaism and Christianity don't have a mother-daughter relationship; they're sister religions that took place at about the same time.

The Jewish rabbis look to the Torah, both written and oral, as the key to the survival of the religion. But there were concerns about the accuracy and transmission of the oral Torah; so about 200 C.E., Rabbi Judah ha-Nasi (it means "Judah the Patriarch") wrote down the first part of the oral Torah, the Mishnah (I guess it sort of makes a contradiction that you have now a written form of the oral Torah). The Mishnah means "repetition" or "oral instruction." It's not exactly a law code; it's more like a collection of legal judgments, some of which are attributed to specific rabbis—in the Mishnah there are 128 named rabbis—and frequently more than one opinion is recorded. The Mishnah is a fairly lengthy book; it's organized into six parts or orders: The first part is called "Seeds," and it has regulations and rules about agriculture and prayers; the second part is appointed "Seasons," Sabbath, festivals, fast days; the third is "Women," and it has regulations concerning marriage, divorce, and vows; the fourth is called "Damages," and that includes business relations, law courts, and punishments; the fifth is "Holy Things," so there are dietary laws, and rules about the temple and sacrifices (but remember this is being written down about 100 years after the destruction of the Temple, so they're trying to retain these traditions that really don't have much practical application anymore); and the sixth and final part of the Mishnah is called "Purities," and it deals with, as you might imagine, rules about ritual purity and purification. Each of these six orders has between 7 and 12 subsections called tractates, for a total of 63.

The judgments within the Mishnah are terse and orderly, as if the texts were designed for memorization or teaching; and in this way it's similar perhaps to Hindu sutras like the Yoga Sutra. We can see how the Mishnah operates by reading the first paragraph, which concerns rules for reciting daily, evening prayer, the Shema; and remember, this is the prayer that begins "Hear, O Israel, the Lord is our God, the Lord is One." The Mishnah starts out by asking a question:

> From what time may people recite the evening Shema?
>
> [The answer:] From the hour that the priests come in to eat of their heave-offering.
>
> Until the end of the first watch – these are Rabbi Eliezer's words.
>
> But the Sages say: Until midnight.
>
> Rabbi Gamaliel says: Until the first light of dawn.
>
> There was a case when his sons came back from a feast.
>
> They said to him: "We have not recited Shema."
>
> He said to them: "If dawn light of dawn has not appeared, you are obligated to recite."
>
> "And not only in this case; but in every case where the Sages have said until midnight — the commandment applies until the first light of dawn.
>
> "The burning of fat parts and prescribed limbs on the altar [these are the old temple sacrifices] — the commandment to do so applies until the first light of dawn.
>
> "All [sacrifices] which are to be eaten for only one day — the commandment to do so applies until the first light of dawn.
>
> If so, why did the Sages say, "until midnight"?
>
> In order to keep a man away from transgression.

That was a long quotation, but you can the way that this thought unfolds is if it says midnight, why is it really allowed to go until dawn? The idea there seems to be that that gap will allow people some buffer time. It's natural for human beings to forget; if you don't say the evening prayers or do things that you need to do in the evening by midnight, you still have until dawn to get those important tasks accomplished.

The passage then goes on to other aspects of evening and morning prayers, including an argument between the followers of Shammai and those of Hillel as to whether you had to actually lie down to say the evening prayer. Shammai and Hillel were two of the great rabbis, and their disputations were legendary, with Shammai generally taking the stricter side. He answered, "Yes, Deuteronomy says, 'When you lie down and when you rise up,' so you have to lie down," that's what Shammai says; very strict interpretation. Hillel said, "No, it's not required, it's just customary." Then a later rabbi tells a story—this is still in the Mishnah—of how once when traveling he laid down to pray as Shammai demanded and nearly lost his life to robbers; and other rabbis respond, "Well, that's what you get when you go against the opinions of Hillel." So there are these disputations that go back and forth; both sides are arguing; rabbis line up on one side or the other. But then again, another part of the Mishnah says, "Any dispute which is for the sake of Heaven will in the end yield results"; and what's a dispute for the sake of Heaven? This is the sort of dispute between Hillel and Shammai. Somehow it's important that we get both of these perspectives; that the arguments go back and forth, on and on; and that sort of critical thinking and of argumentation is something that's pleasing to God, it keeps the tradition going, and it's put within the Mishnah.

This is a very unusual sort of law code. Multiple opinions are offered, often with no single one being pronounced right; and it's not comprehensive. There's nothing in the Mishnah about mezuzahs, or the handling of the Torah scrolls, for instance. Rabbis, when they're arguing with each other, quote scripture; they cite precedents from now-defunct temple practices; they say, "Yes, but from this perspective things could be different"; and they tell stories. Rather than just providing a correct answer, the Mishnah is a tool for teaching students how to think through difficult issues; how to come up with reasonable opinions themselves, and how to defend those opinions.

I want to draw your attention to one of the most famous of the Mishnah's subsections. The Tractate Avot, which means "fathers," is unusual in that it doesn't have any legal rulings. Instead, it consists entirely of ethical maxims of 60 rabbis who lived between 200 B.C.E. and 200 C.E. It's one of the most beloved and quoted parts of the Mishnah, well worth your time for a quick look. You may have already heard the saying that attributes to Rabbi Hillel, who says in the Avot Tractate, "If I am not for myself, who will be for me? And if I am only for myself, who am I? And if not now, when?" I also particularly like these two quotations: "Do not say when I have time I shall study, for you may never have time." Then a second favorite of mine: "It's not your job to finish the work, but you're not free to walk away from it."

Of course, the conversations between rabbis continued, with rabbis and their students debating the meaning of the Mishnah, particularly in the academies in Palestine and Babylonia. Out of these debates about the Mishnah comes the Talmud, also considered part of the oral Torah, which goes even further with learned disputations, detailed legal analysis, folk tales, stories of famous teachers, aphorisms, scriptural interpretations, and so much more. The oral traditions in Palestine were edited and written down about 400 C.E. in what's commonly referred to as the Jerusalem Talmud (the word *Talmud* means "teaching" or "learning"). The discussions in Babylonia were similarly put into writing about 100 years later. The Babylonian Talmud, about three times longer than the Jerusalem version, has long been considered more eloquent, more subtle, and more complete. It's second only to the Tanakh in the library of sacred texts of Judaism.

The Talmud—and by that term we usually mean the Babylonian Talmud, sometimes known as the Bavli—is a massive work consisting of some 2.5 million words; so it's four times the length of the Tanakh, the Hebrew Bible, and about a third longer than the Mahabharata, that Indian epic. The Talmud reproduced the Mishnah, so it's there in Hebrew, and then it adds a commentary in Aramaic called the Gemara. This commentary is an edited transcript of the debates of the rabbis and their students as they investigated, explained, and elaborated on the Mishnah and the principles they deduced from its rulings. Since early modern times, the Talmud has been printed with multiple commentaries surrounding the Mishnah and the Gemara on each page, starting with the commentary of Rashi, the 11th-century French scholar who also wrote one of the most popular commentaries on the Torah. When you open up the Torah in Hebrew, you'll see the Hebrew part and then an Aramaic part with the same Hebrew letters, and then surrounding it are various commentaries in little boxes on the sides. It's a very complicated text to look at; it's a complicated text to read through. In modern English translations, the Neusner Talmud is 22 volumes and the Soncino Talmud, which includes the Hebrew and Aramaic texts on facing pages, comes in at about 30 oversize volumes; it's huge.

Fortunately, there are a number of edited selections from the Talmud that can give you some sense of things. Here's one story, out of thousands; and I like this story in part because in it a rabbi's wife sets him straight. The story says:

> There were some lawless men living in the neighborhood of Rabbi Meir and they used to vex him sorely. Once Rabbi Meir prayed for their death. His wife, Beruriah, thereupon exclaimed: "What do you take as the sanction for your prayer? Is it because it is written, Let sinners cease out of the earth? [That's a quotation from Psalms.] But [she continues, still quoting from the Talmud] the verse may also be rendered to mean, Let sin cease out of the earth. Consider, moreover, the conclusion of the verse: And let the wicked be no more. When sins shall cease, the wicked shall be no more [this is the wife still talking]. Rather should you pray that they repent and be no more wicked." Rabbi Meir offered prayer on their behalf and they repented.

There are lots of great stories in the Talmud, but what you'll usually see on display is detailed legal reasoning, often backed up by quotations from the Tanakh. Rabbi Louis Jacobs, the 20th-century founder of Conservative Judaism in Britain, wrote a book called *The Talmudic Argument* in which he describes the Talmud as follows:

> Theories are advanced and then contradicted. They are examined from many points of view and qualified where necessary. One argument leads to another when logic demands it. The claims of conflicting theories are investigated with great thoroughness

and much subtlety. Fine distinctions abound between apparently similar concepts.

The chapter titles in Rabbi Jacobs's book may be enough to capture the imagination of the legally inclined. The titles of these chapters include things like "Unconscious Abandonment of Property," or "Conveyance of a Thing Not Yet in Existence," or "Indiscernible Damage to Property," and "Admission of Part of a Testimony Even Though Another Part of the Same Testimony is Rejected." There are some impressive mental gymnastics going on here, but it's all within a sacred texts.

In long, complicated arguments with frequent digressions and stories, the rabbis worked their way through all aspects of Jewish life and lore with an astonishing level of psychological and philosophical nuance. Different scriptural interpretations and legal rulings from several generations are set side by side and given equal weight. When there's a practical need, one could be chosen as more authoritative—when you actually have to do something and decide what you're going to do—and usually they take consensus as being the more authoritative position; but dissenting opinions were nevertheless preserved within the Talmud, for possible reevaluation and for use in future debates.

The Talmud is a marvel in world literature, and it's impossible to overstate its importance in Judaism. Students can spend their entire lives exploring its contents; and, indeed, Orthodox Jews probably spend more time with a Talmud than with a Tanakh. It's said that the Talmud contains so many verses from the Hebrew Bible that the commandment to study scripture could be accomplished by studying the Talmud. But the Talmud isn't just another commentary—there are plenty of those in Judaism—it's Torah; it's the oral counterpart to the written Torah that was given to Moses at Mount Sinai. Many Jews believe that even today Talmud study should be done aloud with a partner, taking turns in reading and then discussing its meaning line by line, page by page, as they work through it together.

Although the rabbis weren't prophets, the oral Torah provided access to continuing revelation. The will of God in new eras, in new situations, could be ascertained through discussions of the rabbis in the Talmud; and this indeed was God's preferred mode of communication. One of the most famous stories in the Talmud tells of a heated debate about whether a certain kind of oven could be pronounced unclean if it were taken apart and then put back together again. Rabbi Eleazar said no, everybody else said yes. When Rabbi Eleazar failed to persuade his colleagues with arguments, he said, "If I'm right, let this tree be uprooted and thrown 100 feet," and then he said, "If I'm right, let this stream flow backwards." Both of those things happened, but the other rabbis wouldn't budge; they still weren't persuaded. Rabbi Eleazar said, "Let the walls of the school prove it," and the walls leaned in dangerously. Finally, he said, "If I'm right, let Heaven prove it," and a voice came from Heaven saying basically, "Rabbi Eleazar is always right." But then Rabbi Joshua rejected the heavenly voice, citing a voice from Deuteronomy stating, "It's not in Heaven." The other rabbis agreed, stating, "The Torah has already been given from Mount Sinai, so we do not pay attention to echoes. The rule from Exodus is 'Follow the majority.'"

How did God, the voice from Heaven, react to this defiance? The other rabbis aren't going to be persuaded that Rabbi Eleazar is right even when a voice comes from Heaven. According to the Talmud, God laughed and said, "My children have overcome me. My children have overcome me." In other words, once God has set up the system of the two Torahs, the written and the oral Torah, and then set up the proper procedures for their interpretation, even he can't intervene; and he was delighted when the rabbis pointed this out to him. It's a tale that might remind us of Abraham challenging God's decision to destroy Sodom and Gomorrah, negotiated until God agrees to spare the cities if he can find just 10 righteous people in them. Remember he doesn't, and that he destroys it, but it's that sort of debate; it's people sort of giving God their best understanding and using their best evidence, and the God of Israel respects human intelligence and agency.

The idea of a sacred oral text might remind us of the Hindu Vedas, but there are important differences. The Vedas, as you'll recall, were used primarily in rituals, where they were valued more for their sacred sounds than for their meanings—at least with regard to the Samhitas, the hymns that were used in those sacrifices—and the Vedas always remained the prized possession of priests. The Talmud, by contrast, didn't have a role in public worship services; its meaning was endlessly investigated and debated, and Jews from all walks of life were encouraged to study it. The Mishnah recommended combining Torah study with a profession; and in modern times, women, too, have been encouraged to take part in Talmud study (today, most forms of Judaism have female rabbis).

Tens of thousands of Jews all over the world participate in the Daf Yomi program (it means "page of the day") that was started in Poland in the 1920s. The idea is that you can read through the entire Talmud in seven-and-a-half years if you read just one page a day (two sides every day). The specified page for the day is the same for everyone, and you can download that page in Hebrew or in translation to your phone. There are celebrations at the end of each cycle of seven-and-a-half years; and why not? The Talmud says that God himself studies Torah three hours a day.

The sacred texts of Judaism, in order of authority and holiness are: the Torah first, the Pentateuch; and then the Tanakh, including the Prophets and the Writings; and then the Talmud, which includes the Mishnah. But the library of Judaism goes much, much further. There's an extensive supplement to the Mishnah called the Tosefta that predates the Talmud, and it's similarly discussions by rabbis about the meaning of the Mishnah. There are rather free commentaries on the Tanakh called Midrash that were written by rabbinic sages before the year 1000; and in those commentaries, they explain the text, they sometimes elaborate or enlarge the text, but most especially they make applications of the text to contemporary issues and questions. In the medieval period, there were voluminous commentaries to the Hebrew Bible, as well as works of Jewish philosophy and attempts to codify the rulings of the Talmud; so Maimonides wrote major books in both of those latter categories.

But in the midst of all this learning and studying, there were also Jews who were looking for more direct ways to connect with God through mystical practices. Jewish mysticism, or Kabbalah, is a large, fascinating topic, and I won't do much with it here. There are a number of introductions that you can consult, including a Great Courses lecture series that compares the mystical traditions of Judaism, Christianity, and Islam. But I want to mention briefly just one text that many Jews have considered sacred, the Zohar; the title means "The Book of Splendor." Indeed, from about 1500–1800, this masterpiece of Kabbalah was regarding by some as a source of doctrine and revelation almost equal in authority to the Torah and the Talmud. The Zohar first appeared in 13th-century Spain, published by Rabbi Moses De León who claimed that he'd found an ancient Aramaic text dating back to the 2nd century, a text that was written by the Palestinian master Simeon ben Yohai and his disciples. The Zohar is composed of several separate treatises, including a spiritual commentary on the weekly synagogue readings from the Five Books of Moses; a story of an encounter with a great mystic who's disguised as a donkey driver; a narrative of a visionary journey to the Garden of Eden; and a report of a gathering of Simeon ben Yohai and his companions as they speak about the esoteric hidden meanings of the Torah, particularly with regard to the 10 emanations of God. Modern scholars have determined that the entire Zohar was probably written by Moses De León himself; but that hasn't dampened the enthusiasm of many for this remarkable text.

When Jews today use the term *Torah*, they sometimes have in mind the five books of Moses, which they regard first among equals, the most authoritative part of the Tanakh; but just as often, the Torah refers to both the written and the oral traditions that were thought to have been received by Moses, the written traditions in the Tanakh and the oral traditions particularly as they were embodied in the discussions in the Talmud.

There are several forms of Judaism in the world today—Orthodox Judaism, Conservative Judaism, Reformed Judaism, and Reconstructionism—that differ in their degree of observance of traditional rules in their engagement with the modern world; but they all come out of rabbinical Judaism and its concern for the oral law. By contrast, the Karaites, who were a major Jewish group in the latter half of the first millennium and who rejected the teachings of the rabbis and the whole notion of oral Torah—much like the earlier Sadducees—have nearly died out; there are only a few thousand of them left.

The centrality of the Talmud to Judaism is such that it was often banned or even burned by Jewish authorities in the medieval period in various times of anti-Semitic activities; yet the Talmud was also one of the first Jewish books, after the Bible, to be published with the new technology of the printing press, with a complete edition coming out in 1520, within about 70 years of the publication of the Guttenberg Bible.

It's interesting to imagine how different Judaism would be today if it hadn't closed its canon with the Tanakh and instead continued to produce new scriptures with equal or greater authority, much as was done in Hinduism or Buddhism. Certainly the tradition of detailed textual analysis, rigorous interpretation, and voluminous commentary (especially as practiced in the Mishnah and the Talmud) was decisive in creating a community of close readers and tireless debaters who expressed their devotion to God through study.

One last famous story: In the 1st century B.C.E., a non-Jew approached the great Rabbi Hillel and challenged him, saying, "I will convert if you teach me the whole Torah while I stand on one foot"; so he's looking for "Give me the essence of that massive Talmudic argumentation and discourse; I just want a little bit because you can't stand on your foot for very long." Hillel replied: "What is hateful to you, do not do to your neighbor: that is the whole Torah; all the rest is commentary; now go and study." We often use that tale and we focus on the Golden Rule part of the story, which can be found in most major religions; but it's the "go and study" that makes this version particularly Jewish, and it's an appropriate reminder of the way that Jews are and have been the "people of the book."

Related Traditions—Zoroastrian Scriptures
Lecture 12

In this course, we discuss scriptures of the world's major religious traditions in roughly the order that their earliest sacred texts appeared; thus, we first covered Hinduism, then Judaism, Buddhism, and so on. At the end of our discussion of each of the major religions, we will also devote a lecture to the scriptures of a smaller, related tradition. Most of the time, these are later faiths, such as Sikhism, Mormonism, and Baha'i, but following our lectures on Judaism, we will take a brief look at Zoroastrianism, which has scriptures that are nearly as old as the Vedas. Although there are relatively few Zoroastrians today, the religion has a long and rich history, with important connections to Judaism.

Zoroaster, Founder of the Faith
- Zoroastrianism is an ancient religion of Iran, though it's difficult to know just how ancient.
  - The earliest literary references are from the Greeks and Persians in the 5th century B.C.E. They traced the roots of the faith to priest named Zoroaster (the Greek transliteration of Zarathustra), and both scholars and believers long assumed that he lived sometime in the 6th century B.C.E.

  - However, nearly everything we know of Zoroaster's life comes from 17 hymns he wrote that have been preserved in the Avesta, the most important sacred text of the religion. The language of these texts suggests that Zoroaster probably lived between 1500 and 1200 B.C.E., perhaps about the time of Moses.

- As a priest, Zoroaster mastered the rituals dedicated to the various gods, but at the age of 30, he saw a vision of Ahura Mazda ("Wise Lord"), whom he perceived to be the creator, the most powerful god, and the only one worthy of worship. The god of evil was Angra Mainyu, also known as Ahriman. Zoroastrianism seems to be the earliest religion to explain the world in dualistic terms, with humans caught in a cosmic conflict between the forces of good and the forces of evil.

History of Zoroastrianism

- The Avesta is the most revered scripture of Zoroastrianism. It is about 1,000 pages and is divided into four major parts.
    - The Yasna consists of 72 hymns that are recited in sequence at the *yasna* ceremony, where praises and offerings are directed to various divinities and the sacred hoama plant. It also includes the 17 Gathas, which were thought to have been composed by Zoroaster himself. The language of the Yasna is Old Avestan and seems to date back to the 2nd millennium B.C.E.

    - The second major section of the Avesta is known as the Yashts—21 prose hymns and prayers to various divinities, written in Younger Avestan. These may date to the time of the Persian (Achaemenid) Empire (550–330 B.C.E.).

    - Even later are the Visperad—24 hymns that are chanted in conjunction with the Yasna—and the Vendidad—22 chapters of myths and codes of religious regulations, put in the form of conversations between Zoroaster and Ahura Mazda. The Vendidad includes two creation myths and the story of how Angra Mainyu once tried to kill Zoroaster, along with criminal and civil laws and rules about purification.

- As with Hindu scriptures, these texts were originally oral compositions, and they continued as such for a long time. If Zoroaster lived sometime around 1500–1200 B.C.E., Zoroastrianism as a religion seems to have become popular only during the Achaemenid Empire.

- According to later Zoroastrian sources, when Alexander the Great conquered the Persians in 330 B.C.E., he killed many Zoroastrian priests and, thus, destroyed most of their memorized scriptures. For this reason, the Avesta we have today is perhaps only a quarter of its original length.

- After Alexander, Persia was ruled by the Greek Seleucids, but with the Arsacid (Parthian) Empire (247 B.C.E.–224 C.E.), Zoroastrianism made a comeback. The next rulers of Persia, the Sassanids (224–651), declared Zoroastrianism their official religion. Under the Sassanids, the Avesta was first transcribed into written form, in a specially created alphabet called Avestan, in the 4th or 5th centuries. Our oldest extant manuscripts of Zoroastrian scripture date to the 14th century.

- When Muslim armies conquered Persia in the 7th century, they treated Zoroastrians with a measure of tolerance as one of the peoples of the book, like Jews and Christians. Even though Zoroaster is never mentioned in the Qur'an, many Muslims believed that he was one of the prophets who preceded Muhammad.
    - Under Muslim rule, in the 9th and 10th centuries, a series of Zoroastrian texts was composed in the language of Pahlavi, or Middle Persian.
    - The Pahlavi books are not considered scripture, but they are nevertheless sacred literature and are some of our major sources for understanding Zoroastrianism.

- Over the centuries of Muslim rule in Iran, pressure to convert to Islam increased, and at some point, in the 8th or perhaps the 10th century, a group of Zoroastrians migrated to the west coast of India, near modern Mumbai. They became known as the Parsis, and today, most of the Zoroastrians in the world are Indian Parsis.

Contents of the Avesta
- In 1771, the French scholar Abraham Anquetil-Duperron published the first Western translation of what he called the Zend-Avesta, which is the Avesta as interpreted in Pahlavi.
    - As Western scholars started to decipher Sanskrit, they discovered that the Old Avestan language was closer to Sanskrit than it was to Pahlavi, and as they made progress in understanding the Vedas, they also found that they could make sense of the Avesta.

- o A three-volume translation of the Avesta was published as part of Max Müller's Sacred Books of the East, and the series also included five volumes of translations from the later Pahlavi literature of Zoroastrianism.

- What attracted the most attention were the Gathas—the 17 oldest hymns in the Avesta that went back to Zoroaster himself. These sacred texts are difficult to understand and interpret. Avestan is such an old language that translations are often only tentative, the language can be cryptic, and the theology is quite foreign.

- The 17 hymns of the Gathas are organized into five sections. In the first, Zoroaster praises Ahura Mazda and the six *amesha spenta* ("bounteous immortals"). He then pleads to the ox soul for help against the cruelty of the wicked. Mazda appoints Zoroaster as the ox's guardian, but the ox soul complains that Zoroaster is powerless. Zoroaster himself then pleads for aid in fulfilling his assignment; he desires divine knowledge.

- The hymn describes the dualistic world: "The primeval spirits as a pair combined their opposite strivings [Ahura Mazda and Angra Mainyu], yet each is independent in his action. ... One is better, the other worse, in thought, in word, and in deed" (Mills, trans.). In the conflict between good and evil, humans can freely choose a side, and eventually, heaven or hell will be their reward. The phrase "good thoughts, good words, good deeds" eventually became a popular summary of Zoroastrian ethics.

- Many of the Gathas consist of dialogues between Zoroaster and Ahura Mazda, and they tend to stay on a rather abstract, spiritual plane. In later Zoroastrian texts, many of the ideas from the Gathas are developed further, such as the concept of a bridge over which souls must cross to enter the world of the dead.

Two-Way Influence
- Scholars debate exactly what sort of influence Zoroastrianism had on other religions, but the basic ideas of Zoroaster certainly appear to have had an impact on Judaism, Christianity, and Islam.
    - For instance, it is not clear from the Torah what exactly awaits us after death. This is why the Sadducees, in the 1st century B.C.E., denied the doctrines of the immortality of the soul and the resurrection, while other Jewish groups, such as the Pharisees, developed more detailed teachings. The fact that Jews had lived under Persian rule for two centuries and, thus, had been in contact with Zoroastrians may have spurred such thinking.

    - Zoroastrian dualism and apocalypticism also made their way into the Dead Sea Scrolls and Christianity. The wise men who followed the star to Bethlehem, according to the Gospel of Matthew, were magi, that is, Zoroastrian priests. The word *paradise* comes from ancient Iran, where it meant "an enclosed garden," and both the word and the concept of a garden-like heaven were incorporated into Christianity and Islam.

    - Two Zoroastrian deities appear in the Qur'an as fallen angels, and Islam has a concept of a bridge that is as thin as a hair and as sharp as a knife by which souls enter paradise.

- Even though today Zoroastrianism is a religion in danger of extinction, it has nevertheless left its mark on the majority of the world's population. But the influence goes both ways.
    - By the time Zoroastrians put the Avesta into written form, after centuries of oral transmission, Jews and Christians had created their canons and become peoples of the book. Having a written sacred text that could be preserved and copied seemed like an integral part of a religious tradition.

    - During the Sassanid era, there was an offshoot of Zoroastrianism called Zurvanism that looked more like monotheism than dualism, and in later centuries, Zoroastrians

Zoroastrians believed that burial would pollute the earth; thus, they built towers of silence where corpses were exposed to be eaten by vultures.

developed the notion of a Saoshyant, a savior-like figure who would come at the end of the world to usher in a new age.

- Frequently, religions influence one another through challenge and competition. In the 1830s, John Wilson, a Christian missionary from Scotland, arrived in Bombay (now Mumbai) and began to criticize Parsi beliefs and scriptures. Wilson's criticism inspired a reform movement, in which some Parsis attempted to make their religion look more like Western models.

- The 20th century saw strong disagreements between reform and orthodox Parsis. Traditionalists had long seen the essence of the faith as keeping ritual purity and participating in initiation rituals, daily prayers, seasonal festivals, and temple worship. Theology was of lesser significance; the religion was more like an ethnicity than a set of doctrines.

- Earlier, we mentioned the term *Protestant bias*, and we can see it on display in our own discussion of Zoroastrianism: a focus on the founder of the faith, the notion that the earliest scriptures are the purest expression of the faith, and so on. But this perspective is not the only way to understand Zoroastrianism. Religions tend to be rich, multifaceted phenomena; they are often ways of life rather than simply lists of beliefs. And one of the benefits of studying varied religions is their ability to make us aware of our own assumptions.

Suggested Reading

Boyce, ed. and trans., *Textual Sources for the Study of Zoroastrianism*.

———, *Zoroastrians*.

Darmsteter, trans., *The Zend-Avesta*.

Duchesne-Guillemin, trans., *The Hymns of Zarathustra*.

Rose, *Zoroastrianism*.

Skjærvø, trans. and ed., *The Spirit of Zoroastrianism*.

Stausberg, *Zarathustra and Zoroastrianism*.

West, trans., *Pahlavi Texts*.

Questions to Consider

1. What influence has Zoroastrianism had on major religions of the West?

2. What is the story of the survival and translation of the Avesta—one of the oldest sacred texts in the world?

Related Traditions—Zoroastrian Scriptures
Lecture 12—Transcript

Welcome back. In this course, we discuss scriptures of the world's major religious traditions in roughly the order that their earliest sacred texts appeared; so first Hinduism, then Judaism, Buddhism, and so on. At the end of our discussion of each of the major religions, which usually takes several lectures, there's one lecture devoted to the scriptures of a smaller, related tradition. Most of the time, these are later faiths such as Sikhism, Mormonism, and Baha'i. But following our lectures on Judaism, we're now going to take a quick look at Zoroastrianism, which has scriptures that are nearly as old as the Vedas. Although there are relatively few Zoroastrians today, probably less than 150,000, the religion has a long, rich history with important connections to Judaism.

Zoroastrianism is an ancient religion of Iran, though it's hard to know just how ancient. The earliest literary references are from the Greeks and Persians in the 5th century B.C.E. They trace the roots of the faith to a priest named Zoroaster—that's the Greek transliteration of Zarathustra—and both scholars and believers long assumed that Zoroaster lived sometime in the 6th century B.C.E. But nearly everything that we know of Zoroaster's life comes through 17 hymns that he wrote that have been preserved in the Avesta, the most important sacred text of the religion. The people of ancient Iran, or ancient Persia, were closely related to the Aryans, who migrated into India and then composed the Vedas. The language of old Avestan is similar to the Sanskrit of the Vedas, which suggests that Zoroaster probably lived between 1500 and 1200 B.C.E., perhaps about the time of Moses, so about 1,000 years earlier than what scholars had previously assumed.

As a priest, Zoroaster mastered the rituals dedicated to the various gods; but at the age of 30, he saw a vision of Ahura Mazda, the Wise Lord, who he perceived to be the creator, the most powerful god and the only one worthy of worship. Zoroastrianism has also sometimes been called Mazdaism after that god, Ahura Mazda; and where all good things come from Ahura Mazda, the bad can be attributed to Angra Mainyu, also known as Ahriman, the god of evil. In this way, Zoroastrianism seems to be the earliest religion to explain the world in dualistic terms; that is to say, that humans are caught in a cosmic conflict between the forces of good on the one hand and the forces of evil on the other, and each of us are caught in the middle and we have to choose which side we're going to follow. Eventually there will be a resurrection and a day of judgment, after which each person will receive either eternal punishments or eternal rewards, like Heaven or Hell, depending on the choices that they made during their lifetime.

If that basic religious scenario strikes you as sounding somewhat like Judaism, Christianity, or Islam, you're not alone. Many scholars have suggested that Zoroastrianism was very influential on the monotheistic religions, the Abrahamic religions; and, in fact, in the 19th century, Western observers thought that Zoroastrianism itself was monotheistic, that it believed in one god. Nevertheless, it appears that Zoroastrist beliefs are more accurately described as dualistic. In Christianity and Islam, the devil isn't equal to God; despite his adversarial role, he was created by the One God and is somehow subordinate to him. In Zoroastrianism, by contrast, Ahura Mazda and Angra Mainyu are independent beings with equal status; although Zoroaster prophesied that Ahura Mazda in the end would prove victorious.

This is a very simplified version of what's actually a rather complicated theology; but before we dive in, it might be useful to give an overview of Zoroastrian history and its sacred texts. The Avesta is the most revered scripture of Zoroastrianism. It contains about 1,000 pages or so, and it's divided into four major parts: The Yasna consists of 72 hymns that are recited in sequence at the *yasna* ceremony, where praises and offerings are directed to various divinities, and the sacred haoma plant, which is related to the Hindu soma (remember, it's that sort of mysterious intoxicating substance that was deified in the Vedic religion). The *yasna* is one of the principal rituals in the religion, and it's performed daily in temples. A priest should be able to recite all 72 hymns in the Yasna from memory in two or three hours. The Yasna also includes the 17 Gathas, which were thought to have been composed by Zoroaster himself. The language of the Yasna is Old Avestan, and it appears to date back to the second millennium B.C.E.

The second major section of the Avesta is known as the Yashts. These are 21 prose hymns and prayers to various divinities written in Younger Avestan—

that's a slightly newer language—and these may date to time of the Persian Empire (that's sometimes known as the Achaemenid Empire) of 550–330 B.C.E. Even later—and this is part three—are the Visperad. Those are 24 hymns that are chanted in conjunction with the Yasna. Then fourth and finally the Vendidad: Those are 22 chapters of myths and codes of religious regulations that are put in the form of conversations between Zoroaster and his god Ahura Mazda. This last section also includes two creation myths and the story of how Angra Mainyu once tried to kill Zoroaster. It includes criminal and civil laws; some rules about purification, including the proper disposal of corpses and fingernail clippings; and the proper treatment of dogs; lots of miscellaneous stuff in there. Aside from those four major sections, there are also a few more prayers and fragments that make up the whole of the Avesta.

As with the Hindu scriptures, all of these were originally oral compositions; and they were continued as being passed on from priest to priest for a very long time, perhaps 1,500 years or more. If Zoroaster lived around 1500–1200 B.C.E., Zoroastrianism as a religion only seems to have become popular during the Achaemenid or Persian Empire (remember 550–330 B.C.E.); and there are Persian inscriptions indicating that King Darius worshipped Ahura Mazda. Later Zoroastrian sources say that when Alexander the Great conquered the Persian Empire in 330 B.C.E., he killed many of the Zoroastrian priests and thus destroyed many of their memorized scriptures; so the Avesta that we have today is perhaps only a quarter of its original length, although much may have actually been lost centuries after Alexander. What's survived into the present is mostly liturgy—so those are hymns used in worship ceremonies and rituals—but there were apparently other sections that were lost that dealt with cosmogony, eschatology, law, medicine, astronomy, and more details about the life of Zoroaster.

After Alexander's conquest, Persia was ruled by the Greek Seleucids; and with the coming of the Arsacid Empire (those were the Parthians) in 247 B.C.E–224 C.E., so about 500 years, in that period Zoroastrianism makes a comeback in Persia. The next rulers of Persia, the Sassanids—and they rule from 224–651 C.E.—they declared Zoroastrianism to be their official religion, and then they discriminated against nonbelievers. It was under the Sassanids that the Avesta was first transcribed into written form in a specially created alphabet called Avestan; it was created in the 4th or the 5th centuries. Our earliest extant manuscripts of Zoroastrian scripture date to the 14th century; so it's a situation similar to what we've seen in other religious traditions: Our oldest manuscripts are themselves copies of copies of copies of oral traditions that were passed on by word of mouth for a long time before that even.

When Muslim armies conquered Persia in the 7th century, they treated Zoroastrians with a measure of tolerance as one of the peoples of the book, like Jews and Christians, because Zoroastrians had a sacred text, the Avesta. Even though Zoroaster is never mentioned in the Qur'an, many Muslims believe that he was one of the prophets that preceded Muhammad. Under Muslim rule in the 9th and the 10th centuries, a whole series of Zoroastrian text was composed in the language of Pahlavi, or Middle Persian. These books contained extensive quotations and paraphrases from lost books of the Avesta; that's one of the ways that we know that some things were lost and what they might've been. It also included commentaries and even a sort of encyclopedia of Zoroastrian belief called the *Denkard*. The Pahlavi books aren't considered scripture, but they're nevertheless sacred literature and are some of our major sources for understanding Zoroastrianism.

Over the centuries of Muslim rule in Iran, pressure to convert to Islam increased; and at some point in the 8th or perhaps the 10th century, a group of Zoroastrians migrated to the western coast of India, near modern Mumbai. There they became known as Parsis, and the word *Parsi* means "Persians" in the Gujarati language. Today, most of the Zoroastrians in the world are Indian Parsis.

At this point, you know more about Zoroastrian scriptures than just about any Westerner in the 18th century. In 1723, the Bodleian Library at Oxford acquired a partial manuscript of the Avesta, which they put on display for many years—the book was hanging from the wall by an iron chain—but it was more of a curiosity than a source of historical or religious knowledge since people could come by and look at it, but no one could read its archaic language. However, in 1754, a young French scholar in Paris named Abraham Anquetil-Duperron saw a few pages that had been copied from that manuscript. He looked at that and decided that he wanted to go to India to sort of figure out what was going on with this. In time, he won the trust of the Parsi priests there who taught him a bit of Avestan, this old archaic language, and they explained the meaning of the text to him in modern Persian. Anquetil-Duperron did a French translation from the Persian; and then he returned to France in 1762 with 180 manuscripts, some that were in Avestan, and then the Middle Persian language of Pahlavi, and then Sanskrit. He continued to work with his manuscripts and about 10 years later, in 1771, he published the first Western translation of what he called the Zend-Avesta, which is the Avesta interpreted in Pahlavi. You may recall the name Anquetil-Duperron: A few decades later, he produced the first Western translation of the Upanishads in Latin, relying on an early Persian version.

As Western scholars started to decipher Sanskrit, they discovered that the old Avestan language was closer to Sanskrit than it was to Pahlavi, that Middle Persian language; and as the made progress in understanding the Vedas, they also found that they could make sense of the Avesta. A three-volume translation of the Avesta was published as part of Max Müller's Sacred Books of the East, and the series also included five volumes of translations from the later Pahlavi literature of Zoroastrianism.

Of course, what attracted the most attention were the Gathas. Remember, those are the 17 oldest hymns in the Avesta that went back to Zoroaster himself; they were part of the Yasna. As we take a look ourselves, I should first warn you that these are among the most difficult of the sacred texts we'll encounter in this course. Avestan is such an old language that translations are often only tentative. The language can be cryptic, and the theology is quite foreign. For instance, even though Ahura Mazda and Angra Mainyu are the main gods and they're locked in this cosmic conflict that seems sort of familiar, there are nevertheless numerous angelic beings called Ahuras and false gods or demons called Devas. In particular, there are six divinities that are referred to as *amesha spenta* (that means "the bounteous immortals"), and these deities are considered emanations of Ahura Mazda, or perhaps aspects of his personality. These aspects of his personality are good mind, righteousness (which is Asha, which is a key term in Zoroastrianism that also means "truth" and "order"), dominion, devotion, wholeness, and immortality; all aspects of Ahura Mazda or emanations coming from him.

The 17 hymns of the Gathas are organized into five sections, the first of which begins like this: "With hands outstretched in prayer towards the support, I will first ask you all O Wise One [he's talking to Ahura Mazda] with Righteousness the acts of the holy spirit, to satisfy the will of the Good Mind and the Ox-soul" (and you may say "What is an Ox-Soul?"; we'll come to that in a minute). Zoroaster continues to praise Ahura Mazda and the six *amesha spenta*, and then in the next hymn the Ox-Soul pleads for help against the cruelty of the wicked. The early Indo-Aryans were nomadic herders, and the wellbeing of their animals was a primary concern; so here's this notion of an Ox-Soul. Mazda appoints Zoroaster as the ox's guardian, and the Ox-Soul complains that Zoroaster's powerless. Then Zoroaster himself pleads for aid in fulfilling his assignment, this guardianship. He says, "Where are Righteousness, Good Mind, Dominion, O Immortal Ones [some of those emanations of Ahura Mazda]? Admit me to the great sacrament, O Wise One, that I may achieve knowledge."

The desire for divine knowledge and help may be nearly universal, but the setting is very archaic; we're sort of back in the world of the Rig Veda. Nevertheless, familiar ideas appear regularly. Another quote:

> The primeval spirits as a pair combined their opposite strivings [this is talking about Ahura Mazda and Angra Mainyu], yet each is independent in his action. They have long been famous. One is better, the other worse, in thought, in word, and in deed. [Keep in mind that phrase.] [And then continuing the quote] Let those who act wisely choose correctly between these two. Do not choose as evil-doers choose!

> When the two spirits came together at first, they made life and life's absence. They decided how the world shall be ordered at its end. The wicked receive hell, the worst life; the holy receive heaven, the Best Mental State.

I know it's a little complex, but did you catch what's going on there? In the conflict between good and evil, humans can freely choose a side, and then eventually heaven or hell will be their reward. The phrase "good thoughts, good words, good deeds" eventually became a popular summary of Zoroastrian ethics; that's the one I want you to keep in mind.

Many of the Gathas consist of dialogues between Zoroaster and his god Ahura Mazda, and they tend to stay on a rather abstract spiritual plain, though every so often the concerns of this world break through. Here's an example, Zoroaster says:

> To what land to flee? Whither shall I go to flee? They thrust me from my family and clan. The community with which I have kept company has not shown me hospitality, nor those who are the wicked rulers of the land. [He seems to be talking in sort of vague terms about some difficulties he's had and being caste out or having to flee.] [He continues in this prayer] How shall I then propitiate Thee, Lord Mazda? I know why I am powerless, Mazda: I possess few cattle and few men. I lament to Thee. Take heed of it Lord, granting the support which friend should give to friend.

In this case, he says, "I'm in trouble here, could you help me out with some cattle, some followers, some sort of blessings in this world, not just heaven and hell in the distant hereafter?" No wonder, at elsewhere Zoroaster inquires: "This I ask thee, tell me truly, Ahura—whether I shall indeed, O Righteousness, earn that reward, even ten mares with a stallion and a camel, which was promised to me, O Mazda, as well as through thee the future gift of Welfare and Immortality." So we're looking at a religion that promises rewards in the hereafter, but also there might be the hope of something like mares and a camel in this life.

In later Zoroastrian texts, many of the ideas from the Gathas are developed further. For instance, Yasna 51, speaking of the fate of the wicked, says, "His soul shall surely vex him at the Chinvat Bridge, for he has strayed from the path of Truth by his acts and (the words) of his tongue." One of the Pahlavi texts, remember those are those later Middle Persian texts, explains that after death the soul stays by the body for three days, and then on the fourth day it crosses over into the world of the dead via the Chinvat Bridge, driven forward by demons and guided by angels. For the righteous, that bridge will be wide and easy to cross, and he will be greeted by all of his good deeds in the form of a beautiful woman. Then, with his first step, he enters into the heaven of good thoughts, with his second the heaven of good words, and with his third step he enters into the heaven of good deeds (remember that trilogy that we talked about before); and then with his fourth, he reaches the endless light where all is bliss. For the wicked, by contrast, the trip over the bridge is terrifying since a wicked person is greeted by an ugly woman who represents his bad actions, and the bridge is so narrow that he falls off into the torments of hell, where he stays at least until the time of the resurrection.

Mary Boyce, one of the world's experts on the religion, has asserted that Zoroastrianism is the oldest of the revealed creedal religions, and it's probably had more influence on mankind, directly and indirectly, than any other single faith. Scholars debate exactly what sort of influence it had, but the basic ideas of Zoroaster certainly appear to have had some impact on Judaism, Christianity, and Islam. For instance, it's not exactly clear from the Torah what awaits us after death; remember, that's why the Sadducees in the 1st century B.C.E. denied the doctrines of the immortality of the soul and the resurrection while other Jewish groups, like the Pharisees, developed more detailed teachings. The fact that the Jews had lived under Persian rules for two centuries, from 550–330 B.C.E., and thus had been in contact with Zoroastrians may have spurred thinking about the afterlife, about resurrection. The Second Temple period is also a time when Judaism developed a stronger interest in angels and demons; so the spirit in the book of Tobit, who killed seven of Sarah's husbands in succession on their wedding nights, was named Asmodeus, a name that was derived from one of the Zoroastrian chief demons, Aeshma (Daeva).

Similarly, Zoroastrian dualism and apocalypticism made their way into the Dead Sea Scrolls in Christianity; and the wise men who followed the star to Bethlehem, according to the gospel of Matthew, at the birth of Jesus were identified in the gospel of Matthew as magi, Zoroastrian priests. The word *paradise* comes from ancient Iran where it meant an "enclosed garden," and both the word and the concept of the well-watered gardenlike heaven were incorporated into Christianity and Islam. Some more similarities or points of contact: Two Zoroastrian deities appear in the Qur'an as fallen angels; and Islam as well has a concept of a bridge by which souls enter into paradise. In

Islamic thought, this bridge is as thin as a hair and as sharp as a knife, so it's something rather similar to the Chinvat Bridge of the Avesta.

Even though today Zoroastrianism is a religion in danger of extinction, it's nevertheless left its mark on the majority of the world's population. But the influence goes both ways. By the time Zoroastrians put the Avesta into written form after many, many centuries of oral transmission, Jews and Christians had already created their canons and become peoples of the book. Having a written sacred text that could be preserved and copied seemed like an integral part of a religious tradition. During the Sassanid Empire, there was an offshoot of Zoroastrianism called Zurvanism that looked more like monotheism than dualism. In later centuries, Zoroastrians developed their notion of a Saoshyant, which is a savior-like figured who'd come at the end of the world and the resurrection to usher in the new age; and that belief may have some similarities to messianism in Shia Islam, where they believe there's a figure, the Mahdi, who'll someday come and usher in the new age.

Frequently, religions influence each other through challenge and competition. In the 1830s, John Wilson, a Scottish missionary from Scotland, showed up in Bombay (the city now known as Mumbai) and he began to criticize Parsi beliefs and scriptures. Wilson wasn't entirely a bad guy. He established schools and a university, and he was an early advocate of girls' education; indeed, he admired the moral uprightness of the Parsi community. But his plan for converting them to Christianity was to demonstrate the deficiencies of their beliefs; so he read Anquetil-Duperron's translation of the Avesta and then gave sermons, and he wrote articles and books about how the Parsi dualism and polytheism were more primitive than monotheism. He treated their rituals as so much superstition; Wilson disparaged Zoroaster's claims of revelation; and he ridiculed the purity laws in the Vendidad (apparently he didn't have a whole lot to say about the book of Leviticus in his own Bible). The Parsis were shocked, in part because most of them didn't know themselves what was in the Avesta. The Avesta, in its ancient language, was recited as a memorized accompaniment for worship and for sacrifice; but it wasn't studied or meditated upon, and it wasn't used to formulate doctrine or to teach. Parsis at the time used the Avesta much as Hindus used the Vedas: It was the traditional ceremonies and the sacred sounds that mattered, rather than the meaning of the words.

Wilson's aggressive, proselyting tactics didn't win him many converts, but they did inspire a Parsi reform movement whereby some Parsis attempted to make their religion look more like Western models. They adopted an interpretation of their tradition in which Ahura Mazda was indeed a monotheistic deity. They studied the Gathas and they made those 17 hymns the center of their faith. They demoted the Vendidad—with lots of regulations about ordinary life and taboos and such—to secondary importance, and that allowed them to set aside some of the purity rules that it included; and they regarded the Pahlavi texts as corruptions of Zoroaster's original teachings. In addition, they downplayed the myths and the miracles, and they encouraged the use of modern languages in their worship services. (By the way, similar reform movements occurred in the 19th century within Hinduism and within Judaism as well.)

As you might imagine, the 20th century saw strong disagreements between Reform Parsis and Orthodox Parsis. What does it mean to be a Zoroastrian? Is it adherence to certain rituals and practices that have been handed on through the ages, or is it a belief in a set of doctrines derived from a sacred text? Traditionalists have long seen the essence of the faith as keeping ritual purity and participating in initiation rituals, daily prayers, seasonal festivals, and temple worship where the ceremonial fires were continually kept burning. Zoroastrians had their own dialect, their own sacred clothing; they had distinctive marriage practices and funeral customs. For example, they believed that burial would pollute the earth and cremation would pollute fire (which they also thought was holy), so instead of those two means of disposing of the dead they built towers of silence, where corpses would be exposed and then eaten by vultures. So they had distinct ceremonies, rituals, and dress and that was what made them a people, a religious community. Theology was of lesser importance. The religion was more like an ethnicity than a set of doctrines and that has important implications for this lecture.

You may recall that in the second lecture, I mentioned something called "Protestant bias," and you can see it on display in my treatment of Zoroastrianism. Protestant bias indicates a focus on the founder of the faith and his initial revelations; the notion that the earliest scriptures (the Gathas in this case) are the purest expression of its essence; an emphasis on doctrine rather than practice; and an assumption that texts and ceremonies that came later are less authentic. You can see how these attitudes were connected to a rejection of Catholic traditions by Protestant reformers.

Who's to say whether changes in Christianity over the centuries are best described as a decline from some sort of initial perfection or whether they're a development, whether they represent progress; but it's telling that we often speak of religions as a system of belief rather than a system of ritual. We'll see some similar concerns in a later lecture when I talk about Shintoism, which seems to be characterized more by its rituals than by its beliefs, and sacred texts have sort of an ambiguous position within that religious tradition of Japan.

I don't regret organizing this lecture as I did. I think that I've presented Zoroastrianism in a way that will make sense to many listens—remember that focus on the founder, and on scriptural texts, and on doctrines—but I want to point out that this isn't the only way to understand the tradition. Religions tend to be rich, multifaceted phenomena. They're often ways of life rather than simply lists of beliefs. One of the benefits of studying a religion like Zoroastrianism is its ability to make us aware of our own assumptions, and sometimes to challenge those assumptions, whether they come from Protestantism or wherever.

Let me give you just one more example: It's easy to imagine how shocked Christians and Muslims were when they encountered statues of deities in Indian temples. After all, one of the major tenets of the monotheistic religions is the evil of idolatry. On the other hand, it takes a little more effort to imagine the reactions of Hindus and Zoroastrians to Westerners, who carried around written copies of their most sacred texts, often translated into everyday language. From an Indian perspective—from Hinduism or Zoroastrianism—how could those people, those foreigners, those Westerners, not see that it's the sacred sounds that matter; that holy words have to be spoken around to be actualized; that only by memorization can those sacred texts truly become part of believers, and that putting them into a book form makes those revered syllables common or ordinary and accessible to the ignorant and disrespectful outsiders. Writing and translation make a travesty of what's most sacred, or at least that might be what it seems to do from an Indian perspective.

After more than 3,000 years, it appears that Zoroastrianism is an endangered religion; 150,000 believers aren't very many people, and there are more deaths than births and conversions within the Parsi community. But if the faith does die out in the 21st century, the world will become a poorer place religiously.

The Three Baskets of Buddhism
Lecture 13

There are about 400 million Buddhists in the world, mostly in Southeast Asia and East Asia but also in Europe and North America. The Buddhist canon of scripture is huge, running to more than 100,000 pages. Buddhists call their canon the Tripitaka, which means "Three Baskets." These are the Vinaya (rules for monks and nuns), the Sutras (discourses of the Buddha), and the Abhidharma ("higher teachings," that is, works of systematic philosophy). Buddhism also has several well-defined sets of texts: the Pali canon, Chinese canon, and Tibetan canon. In this lecture, we'll learn the basic divisions and origins of the Buddhist canon, then take a closer look at specific texts in the four lectures that follow.

Oral Origins of the Buddhist Canon

- Siddhartha Gautama, the northern Indian prince who became the Buddha, lived in the 5th century B.C.E. After his enlightenment under a bodhi tree, he wandered about for 45 years, preaching the Four Noble Truths and related doctrines about the nature of reality, causation and interconnectedness, and the workings of the human mind.

- The Buddha never wrote anything down, but he gathered around him disciples, who gave up ordinary life to become monks and nuns; they listened intently and memorized the sermons they heard him teach.

- When the Buddha died, around 480 B.C.E., he didn't appoint a successor; instead, he indicated that the movement should follow the dharma and the Vinaya. Thus, the word of the Buddha became paramount. But there were difficulties almost immediately. For example, shortly before his death, the Buddha had told Ananda, one of his chief disciples, that the minor rules for monks could be eliminated, but because he didn't specify which rules were the minor ones, the disciples hesitated to change anything.

- At the first three-month retreat season after the Buddha's death, his followers held their initial council. Some 500 enlightened monks gathered together for a communal recitation of the Buddha's words. The Vinaya were first recited by Upali, a former barber. Then, Ananda recited the Sutras—tens of thousands of words—without missing a syllable. Even now, all the Buddhist sutras begin "Thus have I heard," connecting each one with Ananda's firsthand account.

The Pali Canon
- The oral transmission of the Buddha's teachings continued for several centuries. During that time, there arose 18 different schools of Buddhism, each with a somewhat different set of memorized, authoritative texts.
  - Eventually, all the early schools disappeared, with the exception of the Theravada school ("Teachings of the Elders").

  - Perhaps one of the reasons for the survival of this particular form of early Buddhism was the fact that these believers managed to preserve their scriptures in written form, although not in India but on the island of Sri Lanka.

- The Buddhist scriptures were first brought to Sri Lanka in the 3rd century B.C.E. by monks who had memorized them. Two centuries later, in 29 B.C.E., a king in Sri Lanka, fearing that too many monks would die in political turmoil and famine, called for a council of Theravada monks. Five hundred scribes wrote down the scriptures they recited in Pali, an old Indian language that was closely related to the dialect in which the Buddha had originally taught.

- The Pali canon is the oldest surviving set of Buddhist scriptures. It included six volumes of the Vinaya, with rules for monks and nuns and commentaries on the rules. The second basket consisted of the Sutras in 36 volumes. These are arranged in five collections (*nikayas*), mostly by length. The last section, the Little Texts, contains some of the most popular Buddhist texts, including the Dhammapada and the Jataka, stories of the Buddha's previous lives.

- The Pali canon was rounded out by six volumes of the Abhidharma, in seven texts. These "higher teachings" include analysis and commentary on various lists in the Vinaya and Sutras, with no stories, illustrations, or anecdotes. This basket systematizes Buddhist teachings about psychology and philosophy, constituent elements of reality or the mind, and causation. For the most part, the Abhidharma was developed in the centuries after the Buddha's death.

- The Pali canon, with its numerous lists and repetitions, appears to have been shaped for memorization. The sounds of the Pali texts were eventually transcribed into various Southeast Asian regional scripts, such as Sinhalese, Burmese, Thai, and Khmer. There is even a transliteration of the Pali canon into Roman letters, accompanied by an English translation—a project that was begun in 1881 and is still ongoing.

Chinese and Tibetan Canons
- In the 1st century B.C.E., new Buddhist sutras began to circulate. These texts were written in Sanskrit, the classical language of India, and offered a somewhat different view of Buddhism.
    - The Buddha was now considered a god to be worshipped rather than a man who had found enlightenment and then passed from this existence into nirvana; there was more emphasis on bodhisattvas; and salvation was thought to be available to anyone, not just monks and nuns. This was Mahayana Buddhism, or the "Greater Vehicle."

    - These sutras were longer and more philosophically sophisticated, with even more miraculous elements than those of the Theravada school. They also originated as written literature rather than oral teachings.

- In the 1st and 2nd centuries C.E., Buddhist missionaries began to travel from India to China, and they took with them some of these new scriptures, along with older scriptures from the Theravada and other early schools. Efforts to translate these scriptures into Chinese started in about the 2nd century and continued for 800 years. The

Chinese canon eventually stabilized in about the 10th century, when printed copies began to become available.

- In the standard, punctuated edition of the Chinese canon, published in Japan in the 1920s, there are 55 volumes of the Tripitaka, plus another 45 supplementary volumes.
    - The Chinese canon includes Chinese translations of five versions of the Vinaya from schools other than the Theravada, a version of the Abhidharma, many Mahayana sutras, Tantras (esoteric texts), commentaries, treatises, encyclopedias, dictionaries, histories, and even some non-Buddhist texts from Hinduism and Nestorian Christianity.

    - We often have Chinese translations of Indian Buddhist scriptures for which the originals have completely disappeared.

- From the 7th to the 13th centuries, there were translations of Buddhist scripture into Tibetan, and eventually, a separate Tibetan canon was established in the 14th century, with two major divisions: the Kangyur, which consists of texts attributed to the Buddha and translated from Sanskrit originals (98 volumes), and the Tengyur, 224 volumes of commentaries and treatises. Most of these were also translated from Sanskrit.

Effects of an Extensive Canon
- Obviously, the sacred texts of Buddhism play a different role in that religion than the Bible does in Judaism or Christianity. Ordinary believers are not expected to be familiar with the entire canon, and even monks and nuns—some of whom devote their lives to scriptural scholarship—can master only a small portion of the whole.

- For many centuries, Buddhists had an open canon, to which new books and perspectives could be added. This sense of continuing revelation and deepening understanding was exhilarating to many, but the profusion of Buddhist scripture could also be confusing. Different schools of Buddhism focused on particular texts, and there was a realization that the canon was full of inconsistencies.

- Buddhism, like most other religious traditions, also encompasses a number of paradoxes or contradictions. These do not discredit or delegitimize the faith; rather, they function as creative tensions that impel believers toward greater searching and dedication.

The Significance of Sacred Texts

- Despite the size of the Buddhist canon, any discussion of it is pervaded by a sense of impermanence and loss. The scriptures were originally written on dried palm leafs that were quite fragile, particularly in the tropical climates of South and Southeast Asia. The Theravada Pali canon survived in such manuscripts, but the scriptures of other early schools have not.
  - For example, in 1994, the British Library acquired 80 Buddhist manuscript fragments, dating to the 1st century C.E. These are the oldest surviving Buddhists writings in the world.

  - They are not Theravada texts but seem to be a tiny fraction of the canon of the Dharmaguptaka school. Such discoveries are a poignant reminder of how much has been lost.

- Some Buddhists, concerned about the perishability of palm leaf manuscripts and paper, turned to more durable substances. In caves in Fangshan County, 45 miles southwest of Beijing, there are more than 14,000 stone slabs inscribed with texts from the Chinese Buddhist canon. This massive project was begun by monks and laypersons in the 7th century and eventually gained governmental support in the 11th and 12th centuries.

- Similarly, the world's largest book is written, not on paper, but on 730 marble tablets, each tablet

The Kuthodaw Pagoda in Mandalay, Burma houses the world's largest book, text from the Pali canon inscribed on marble tablets.

housed in a pagoda in a massive array at the Kuthodaw Pagoda in Mandalay, Burma. These tablets represent a copy of the Pali canon commissioned by the king of Burma in 1860.

- Buddhists in East Asia, seeking to preserve and propagate their scriptures, were the first to adopt the new technology of printing. In 764, the Japanese Empress Kōken commissioned the printing of 1 million copies of a brief Buddhist chant, each housed in a portable wooden pagoda, some of which have survived to this day.

- The world's earliest printed book, produced in 868, is a copy of the Diamond Sutra found at Dunhuang, a way station on the ancient Silk Road in northwest China. It had been walled up in a secret vault in a cave temple, along with thousands of other manuscripts, around the year 1000 and was rediscovered in 1900. The 16-foot-long scroll predated Gutenberg's Bible by almost 600 years and is today housed in the British Library.

- These printing projects, like the many Chinese, Korean, Japanese, and Tibetan editions of the Buddhist canon that followed, were motivated by a desire to preserve the scriptures, to make them more widely available, to show compassion to others, and to gain merit for the next life. Yet in good Buddhist fashion, this merit was not always for oneself. The Diamond Sutra from Dunhuang ends with a colophon noting that it was made in memory of a believer's parents. Often, the significance of sacred texts lies not just in the contents of the books but also in what they meant to the people who created and used them.

Suggested Reading

Denny and Taylor, eds., *The Holy Book in Comparative Perspective*.

Harvey, *An Introduction to Buddhism*.

Holm, ed., *Sacred Writings*.

Mitchell, *Buddhism*.

Questions to Consider

1. How do the Three Baskets of Buddhist scripture differ from the three Buddhist canons?

2. Why would a religion so focused on the impermanence of all things put so much effort into the preservation of sacred texts?

The Three Baskets of Buddhism
Lecture 13—Transcript

There are about 400 million Buddhists in the world today, mostly in Southeast Asia and East Asia, but also there are many adherents in Europe and North America. This lecture will introduce you to the Buddhist canon of scripture. I'll explain its basic divisions and origins, and then we can take a closer look at some specific texts in the four lectures that follow; but right now, we'll start with an overview.

The first thing that you should know is that the Buddhist canon is big; it's huge. Many Christians, despite their deep commitment to the Bible, have had a hard time reading their sacred book from cover to cover. It's about 1,000 pages of small print, so it's a serious undertaking. But the Buddhist canon can run to over 100,000 pages; it's a sacred library, rather than a sacred book. I know I described the Bible before as a sacred library because it's made up of writings that were done by different authors over a long period of time, but still, you can print it in a single volume. The Buddhist canon would take many shelves to put together. The second thing to remember is that the library has three basic divisions. Buddhists call their canon the Tripitaka, which means the "three baskets." The three baskets are the Vinaya, those are rules for monks and nuns; the Sutras, discourses of the Buddha; and the Abhidharma, which are higher teachings, works of systematic philosophy. I'll try not to pile on too many foreign terms, but these three words are important; and we'll get more details later on.

Unlike in Hinduism where there's a large body of religious literature with some rather fluid boundaries as to what counts as scripture, Buddhism has a well-defined set of sacred texts; or rather, several well-defined sets: There's a Pali canon, a Chinese canon, and a Tibetan canon. But let's start our story at the beginning: Siddhartha Gautama, the northern Indian prince who became the Buddha, lived in the 5th century B.C.E. After his enlightenment or awakening under a Bodhi tree, he wandered about for maybe 45 years, preaching the Four Noble Truths and related doctrines about the nature of reality, about causation and interconnectedness, and the workings of the human mind. The Four Noble Truths are, as you may recall are first that all life is suffering; second that suffering comes from desire; third that if you stop desire you can stop suffering; and then the fourth Noble Truth is that you can stop desire by following the Eightfold Path, which is right view, right intention, right speech, right action, right livelihood, right effort, right mindfulness, and right concentration. Of course, Buddhists have lots of commentaries and explanations for each of those parts of their basic story of salvation.

The Buddha's basic worldview was similar to that of the Hindus. There are four parts to that: There's samsara, which is reincarnation; and then karma, which is cosmic justice; dharma, which is moral behavior; and then finally moksha, which is enlightenment, it's an escape from the cycle of birth and rebirth and death (it's sometimes referred to as nirvana), and that's attained through meditation. The metaphysics is basically the same as in Hinduism, but Buddhism has two important differences: The first is that Buddhists reject the authority of the Vedas and the Brahman priests and the rituals that they perform; and the second major difference is the Buddha taught that there's no such thing as the soul. You may remember from the lecture on Hinduism there's *atman*, but in Buddhism there's no self, there's no soul. Instead there are five aggregates: We're made up of form (like a body), sensation, perception, mental formations, and consciousness; and each of those is changed at any time and then those are together in a temporary combination that we might regard as our self, but that self has no eternal existence, it has no independent identity.

But the Buddha never wrote any of this down. In fact, he was like Socrates or Jesus in that the scriptures are going to come from his followers rather than from his own writing. Indeed, he gathered around him disciples who gave up ordinary life to become monks and nuns, and they listened intently and memorized the sermons that they heard him teach. Perhaps this wasn't entirely surprising. There's a long history of oral teaching and memorization in India; you remember the Brahmans who memorized the Vedas. There's something to be said for the oral transmission of spiritual truths; that you're always learning directly from a master, from somebody who already has a good grasp of that, who can explain it. By contrast, when we read sacred texts, we're just eavesdroppers on a conversation that would've been between individuals long ago.

When the Buddha died around 480 B.C.E., he didn't appoint a successor. Instead, he indicated that the movement should follow the Dharma and the Vinaya; those are going to be the two things that Buddhists can follow, and remember that the Vinaya are the teachings and rules for monastic disciplines. So the word of the Buddha became paramount instead of focusing on a particular leader or person. But there were difficulties almost immediately. For example, shortly before his death, the Buddha had told Ananda, one of his chief disciples, that the minor rules for monks could be eliminated. But then Ananda forgot to ask which rules were the minor ones, so they hesitated to change anything at all.

At the first three-month retreat season after the Buddha's death, his followers held their first council. Some 500 enlightened monks gathered together for a communal recitation of the Buddha's words to make sure that everyone had gotten those oral teachings right. The Vinaya—and those are 227 rules for monks and then 311 rules for nuns—were first recited by Upali. He was a barber before he became a monk; and because he had that skill he was in charge of shaving the heads of the new monks, and so he heard all of those sermons of the Buddha about how monks should act and the regulations that should guide their lives. After Upali recited the Vinaya, Ananda recited the Sutras. Ananda apparently had a prodigious memory; he was able to recite tens of thousands of words without missing a syllable, and these are words that he'd heard the Buddha speak at various times and in various places. Even now, all Buddha sutras begin, "Thus have I heard, at one time the lord was saying at such and such a place," and then it goes on. The "Thus have I heard," the "I" there is going to be Ananda—it's his firsthand account— even though some sutras present the words of the Buddha's disciples or other sages in heavenly deeds. But in general, the idea is that all of these came through Ananda.

The oral transmission of the Buddhist teachings continued for several centuries. During that time, there arose 18 different schools of Buddhism, each of which had a somewhat different set of memorized, authoritative texts. Eventually, all 18 schools disappeared with the exception of the Theravada school, and the word *Theravada* means "the teaching of the elders." Perhaps one of the reasons for the survival of this particular form of early Buddhism was the fact that Theravada monks managed to preserve the scriptures in written form. But not in India; rather, it took place on the island of Sri Lanka, off India's southeast coast. The Buddhist scriptures were first brought to Sri Lanka in the 3rd century B.C.E. in heads of monks; they're still oral compositions. Two centuries later, the king there, Vattagamani, fearing that too many monks would die in political turmoil and in a famine, called for a council of Theravada monks in 29 B.C.E.; so they gathered together the monks and then 500 scribes to write down the scriptures that they recited in Pali. Pali is an old Indian language that was closely related to the dialect that the Buddha had originally taught in.

The Pali canon is the oldest surviving set of Buddhist scriptures, and it's called the Tripitaka or Tipitika; Tripitaka is the Sanskrit pronunciation and Tipitika is the Pali pronunciation. The Tripitaka includes six volumes of the Vinaya; that's the first basket, the rules for monks and nuns (the whole idea of baskets here is that the texts were first written down on palm leaf pages and then were piled in baskets.) The Vinaya by this time included not only a list of rules but also commentaries on those rules; on the stories and the situations that first made a particular rule necessary and descriptions of exceptional cases where the rules might not apply. The second basket of the Tripitaka consists of Sutras in 36 volumes. The word *sutra* refers to a thread that holds things together; the word *sutra* is related to our English word *suture*. The Sutras are arranged into five collections, or *nikayas*, mostly by length. There are 34 long discourses; 150 middle-length discourses; 7,762 connected discourses, which are arranged by subject; then 9,550 enumerated discourses, and those are arranged by the number of items of discussed (there are 1's, and then texts that talk about 2 things, and 3 things, and 4 things, up to 11 things within a single text); and then, finally, there are 15 little texts, though some of these little texts are quite long. This last section, the little texts, is comprised of miscellaneous materials, many in poetic form, and it contains some of the most popular Buddhist texts, including the Dhammapada and the Jataka. The Jataka are stories of the Buddha's previous lives, and we'll be talking about those in the next lecture.

The Pali canon was rounded out by six volumes of the Abhidharma in seven texts. The Abhidharma are higher teachings; they're an analysis and commentary on various lists in the Vinaya and Sutras with no illustrations or anecdotes. They try to systemize Buddhist teachings about psychology and philosophy; about the constituent elements of reality or the mind, about causation. Perhaps a few lists were recited by Ananda at that first Buddhist council way back in 480 B.C.E.; but this basket, the Abhidharma, was greatly developed in the centuries after Buddha's death. In this lecture series, I won't do too much with the Abhidharma, which is rather dry and specialized; but just to give you a flavor of what's going on: In one text, called the *Enumeration of Dharmas*, there's a list of 10 mental states, all arising from good thought, which can result in right concentration; that's the eighth step in the Eightfold Path. Here's the list: When a good thought concerning the sense-desire realm has arisen, accompanied by gladness and knowledge, and has as its object a visible form, or sound, or smell, or touch, or mental state, or whatever, whatever the object of the thought might be, then there's first contact, second sensation, third perception, fourth volition, fifth thought (you may recognize the five aggregates there), then sixth there's an application of the thought, and then seven sustained thought, eight zest, nine ease, and tenth self-collectedness. Each of those 10 mental states is defined in turn by a paragraph, and then the discussion moves on to other wholesome states of mind that can follow right concentration, and so forth; so it's lists of lists with terse explanations for all of those.

That's the Abhidharma; and you can see there, and in other parts of the Buddhist canon, that the Pali canon appears to have been shaped from memorization; there are lots of lists and lots of repetitions. Different monks specialized in different subsections of the canon; we'll see some specific examples of stories and teachings from the Theravada sutras in Lecture 15.

This is the Buddhism of Southeast Asia, and the sounds of the Pali texts were eventually transcribed into various regional scripts such as Sinhalese from Sri Lanka, into Burmese, Thai, and Khmer. There's even a transliteration of the Pali canon into Roman letters; so it's the English alphabet, but it's the English alphabet that spells out the canon in the Pali language, and then it's accompanied by an English translation. This was a huge project that was undertaken by the Pali Text Society started in 1881 by T. W. Rhys Davids, a British civil servant stationed in Sri Lanka. That project of the Pali canon into English is still ongoing, because it's not just the canon itself but also commentaries, histories, and dictionaries.

Have you got your head around the Pali canon? So 48 volumes; and there are three major divisions or baskets: Vinaya, Sutras, and Abhidharmas. Good, because things get much more complicated from here. In the 1st century B.C.E., there were new Buddhist Sutras that began to circulate. These texts were written not in Pali but in Sanskrit, the Classical language of India that had been used for the Hindu scriptures; and these new scriptures offered a somewhat different view of Buddhism. The Buddha was now considered as a god to be worshiped rather than as a man who'd found enlightenment and then passed from this existence into nirvana. There was more of an emphasis on bodhisattvas; and in these new scriptures, salvation was thought to be available to anyone, not just monks and nuns. These new scriptures become the basis for Mahayana, or the Buddhism of the Greater Vehicle. These sutras are longer, they're more philosophically sophisticated with even more miraculous elements than those of the Theravada school, and they originated as a written literature rather than as oral teachings. You might ask, though: How can they be newer and still be more authoritative? The answer is that these were thought to be secret teachings that the Buddha had given to some of his most advanced disciples; while the ordinary listeners got the Theravada scriptures, the disciples who were ready to hear deeper forms of the doctrine received the Mahayana teachings, and then those were hidden away for centuries until they were recovered (but we'll talk more about this in Lecture 16).

In the 1st and 2nd centuries C.E., Buddhist missionaries began to travel from India to China; and they took with them some of these new scriptures, along with the older scriptures from the Theravada and other early schools. All of these needed to be translated into Chinese, and this turned out to be a difficult task; Chinese is a very different language from Pali or Sanskrit. These translation projects began in about the 2nd century, and they continued for maybe 800 years. It's important that they had imperial sponsorship—they're expensive to undertake—and there are stories of heroic scholars and monks traveling back to India for authoritative texts. But Buddhist scriptures in Chinese made these texts accessible to scholars not just in China, but also in Korea, Japan, and Vietnam. In East Asia, Classical Chinese was a little like Latin in the medieval West; it was the universal language of scholars.

The Chinese canon eventually stabilized in about the 10th century when the Chinese began to print copies of the entire canon. One of the most noteworthy printings of the Chinese canon occurred in Korea in the 13th century. That involved over 81,000 carved printing blocks with 52 million characters on them. By comparison, the Bible has about 750,000 words, and Classical Chinese is a much more concise language than English; so imagine how large that canon is at 52 million words. These printing blocks have survived still to this day in a temple in South Korea.

In the standard punctuated edition of the Chinese canon, which was published in Japan in the 1920s, there are 55 volumes of the Tripitaka, plus another 45 supplemental volumes, and each of those volumes has about 1,000 pages. The Chinese canon includes Chinese translations of five versions of the Vinaya from schools other than the Theravada, a version of the Abhidharma from the Sarvastivada school, and many Mahayana sutras, sometimes with multiple translations of the same one. There are also tantras (those are esoteric texts), and there are commentaries, treatises, encyclopedias, dictionaries, and histories. There are even some non-Buddhist texts from Hinduism and Nestorian Christianity that made their way into this Chinese Buddhist canon. We often have Chinese translations of Indian Buddhist scriptures for which the originals have complete disappeared; all we have is the Chinese translation.

But that's not all; there's even more to the Chinese canon. From the 7th to the 13th centuries, there were translations of Buddhist scriptures into Tibetan; and eventually a separate Tibetan canon was established in the 14th century with two major divisions: the Kangyur, which consists of texts attributed to the Buddha and then translated from Sanskrit originals, those are 98 volumes; and the Tengyur, which are commentaries and treatises, and that's 224 volumes, and most of these were also translated from Sanskrit. The Kangyur includes more than 600 texts, including Vinaya, sutras, and tantras, three-quarters of which are Mahayana, and a quarter from maybe Theravada and other early schools; so perhaps 25 million words. The Tengyur is even longer, over 3,600 texts at 48 million words. We'll come back to the Tibetan canon in Lecture 18.

Obviously, the sacred texts of Buddhism play a different role in that religion than the Bible does in Judaism or Christianity; it has to play a different role just because of the size of this canon. Ordinary believers aren't expected to be familiar with the entire canon; and even monks and nuns, some of whom devote their entire lives to scriptural scholarship, can still master only a small portion of the whole. For many centuries, Buddhists had an open canon, where new books and new perspectives could be added to the library of sacred texts and they'd have equal authority to what had been there before. This sense of continuing revelation and deepened understanding was exhilarating to many; it might've been something like the oral Torah of the Jewish Talmud. But the astonishing profusion of Buddhist scripture could also be confusing. Different schools of Buddhism focused on particular texts, and there was a realization that the canon was full of inconsistencies; it was just so large. Nevertheless, the divisions within Buddhism generally didn't lead to persecution and violence, as they did so often between Catholics and Protestants in Christianity, or between Sunni and Shia Muslims. In the next few lectures, we'll explore why Buddhism, despite tremendous doctrinal diversity, has generally been a religion of peaceful coexistence.

Finally, we can note that Buddhism, like most other religious traditions, encompasses a number of paradoxes and contradictions. These don't discredit or delegitimize the faith; rather, they function as creative tensions that impel believers toward greater searching and greater dedication. For instance, how can one desire to attain nirvana if desire itself is the problem according to the Four Noble Truths? How can there be a reincarnation if there's no such thing as a soul (remember there are just the Five Aggregates)? There are answers to these questions, but not simple answers. More to the point in this lecture: Why is there such devotion to the scriptures—in memorizing, in translating, in editing, in printing them—if the scriptures themselves have no ultimate value? In a well-known simile from the Lankavatara-sutra, the scriptures are like a finger pointing at the moon; what's important aren't the texts but the reality that they point toward. At some stage in their spiritual progress, Buddhists leave the scriptures behind; Gaining nirvana has to be an experiential kind of thing, it can't be done through books. For a religion based on the realization of impermanence—that all things change and eventually disappear; that even Buddhism itself will someday come to an end (which is Buddhist doctrine)—what might explain those immense efforts to preserve sacred texts?

I'll say it again: The Buddhist canon is huge; yet even so, there's a sense of impermanence and loss that pervades any discussion of it. The scriptures were originally written on dried palm leaves that were quite fragile, particularly in tropical climates of South and Southeast Asia. Typically these palm leaves would be maybe 2 inches by 10 inches, or maybe 20 inches, and then they're bound together with string; and then they needed to be recopied after a certain period because after a while they started to fall apart and decay. Most of the Buddhist scriptures that are written on these palm leaves that we have, the physical artifacts, are mostly from the 18th and 19th centuries; they're copies of copies of copies of copies.

The Theravada Pali canon survived in palm leaf manuscripts, but the scriptures of other early schools haven't survived. For example, in 1994, the British Library acquired 80 Buddhist manuscript fragments written on birch bark in the ancient Gandhari language of Central Asia and dating to the 1st century C.E. These are the oldest surviving Buddhist writings in the world and preserved in clay jars in monasteries in Afghanistan. They're not Theravada texts, but instead they seem to be just a tiny fraction of the canon of the Dharmaguptaka school. It's kind of a poignant reminder of how much has been lost, despite the vast canon that survives.

Some Buddhists, concerned about the perishability of palm leaf manuscripts and paper, turned to more durable substances. In caves in Fangshan County, about 40 miles southwest of Beijing, there are more than 14,000 stone slabs inscribed with texts from the Buddhist canon; there are over 22 million characters that have been carved into these stone steles. This massive project was begun by monks and laypersons in the 7th century, and eventually it gained governmental support in the 11th and 12th centuries. Similarly, the world's largest book is written not on paper but on marble tablets: 730 leaves (so that makes 1,460 pages front and back), and each page is 3.5 feet wide, and 5 feet high, and maybe 5 or 6 inches thick. Each has its own little pagoda—it sits under a little pagoda—in a massive array at the Kuthodaw Pagoda in Mandalay, Burma. If you stacked up this marble book, all of these pages, it would be more than 300 feet tall. It's a copy of the Pali canon that was commissioned by King Mindon of Burma in 1860 when he was worried about the cultural effects of the British invasion of southern Burma; he was anxious to preserve this sort of precious Buddhist text that was so important to the Burmese people.

Buddhists in East Asia seeking to preserve and propagate their scriptures pioneered a new tactic as well: They were the first to adopt the new technology of printing. In 764, the Japanese Empress Kōken commissioned the printing of a million copies of a brief Buddhist chant, and each of those copies was housed in a small wooden, portable pagoda about eight inches tall; and some of those pagodas, with the printed text inside, have survived to this day. The world's earliest printed book, produced in 868, is a copy of the Diamond Sutra that was found at Dunhuang, a way station on the ancient Silk Road in northwest China. It had been walled up in a secret vault in a cave temple along with thousands of other manuscripts around 1000, and then it was rediscovered in 1900. This copy of the Diamond Sutra is a scroll that's 16 feet long, and it was made from seven printed sheets of paper that were pasted end to end—so they used a big block printing, they printed seven different blocks, and then they pasted this together—and this scroll, the Diamond Sutra, this particular copy, predated Gutenberg's Bible by almost 600 years. Today it's in the British Library.

These printing projects—like the many Chinese, Korean, Japanese, and Tibetan editions of the Buddhist canon that followed—were motivated by a desire to preserve the scriptures, to make them more widely available, to show compassion to others, and to gain merit for the next life. Yet in good Buddhist fashion, this merit wasn't always for oneself. The Diamond Sutra from Dunhuang that I just talked about ends with a colophon, an inscription at the very end, which reads: "Reverently made for universal free distribution by Wang Jie on behalf of his two parents on the 15th day of the 4th month of the 9th year of Xiantong rain period," so that works out to the 11th of May, 868. In this case, Wang Jie has paid for the printing of this manuscript, which was undoubtedly quite expensive, and he gets merit for that, this is a good action. But rather than keep that for himself, he's dedicated that merit on behalf of his parents who have since passed on to the other side to benefit their souls (or not-souls, as Buddhism would have it).

The Diamond Sutra is a rather abstruse, philosophical text with lots of reference to nonbeing and nonattachment; yet here we see the importance of Buddhist scripture in dealing with a very particular sort of loss: the death of one's parents. In this way, Buddhists could show the traditional Chinese value of filial piety. Oftentimes the significance of sacred texts from around the world lies not just in the contents of those books, but also what they meant to the people who created and used them for various purposes.

One last example comes from a funeral epitaph written in 1619 by a Chinese father for Shen Azhen, the eldest of two small daughters he'd lost to smallpox within a week. As Azhen's mother chanted scriptures daily in hope of gaining merit for the girl, her father wrote a brief account of her life, which included the following. He says, in this written account:

> When you were born I was not pleased. A man over thirty wants a son, not a daughter. But you won me over before you had completed your first year. Even then you would respond with giggles each time I made a face at you. ...
>
> Sometimes you recited the Great Learning while bowing to Amit'ofo. [The Great Learning is one of the Confucian Four Books; we'll hear about that in a later lecture.] Sometimes you would play a guessing game with me and the winner would chase the loser around the house. When you finally caught me you laughed jubilantly and clapped your hands. Who would have believed that not quite half a month later you would breathe your last? ...
>
> I have been thinking of you all the time. If you know how much I miss you you will come back, again and again, in my dreams. If fate permits, be reborn as my next child [it's actually a very sweet thing that's possible in reincarnation; the idea that a deceased child might be able to come back as another child]. For such hopes I am sending you a copy of the Diamond Sutra [and what he means is he'd take a copy of this scripture and then he'd burn it, and the smoke of that would go up to the afterlife, sort of like incense]...

> When you see the King of the Underworld, kneel down with raised hands and plead for mercy. ...
>
> Just say the words to him and don't cry or be noisy. You must not forget that the underworld is different from home. ...
>
> Azhen, your sad father is mourning you.

Over the next four lectures, we'll be looking at the contents of some of the most famous sacred texts in the Buddhist canon. But to truly appreciate the capacity of these writings to shape and even transform lives, we'll need to keep in mind Azhen's sad father and how he turned to the Diamond Sutra for help.

Vinaya and Jataka
Lecture 14

In a religious tradition with a large canon, some texts naturally get more attention than others. In this lecture, we'll discuss two types of Buddhist scriptures that are used with great frequency but in different ways. The first type, Pratimoksha, the rules of the order, in the Vinaya basket, is used nearly exclusively by monks and nuns. The second type, Jataka, or birth stories, has been beloved by ordinary believers for centuries and constitutes a subsection within the Sutra basket. We'll also look for details of the Buddha's life that can be gleaned from various sacred compositions.

The Vinaya
- In its early centuries, Buddhism was not a religion based on its founder. Siddhartha Gautama, the Indian prince who would become the Buddha, was thought to have discovered and shown to others the path to spiritual freedom and nonsuffering, but he wasn't the path himself. As a result, the first biographies of the Buddha were not written until the 1st century C.E., some 500 years after his death.

- Bits and pieces of the Buddha's life were recorded in various sacred compositions within a specific teaching context. Some of the earliest of these oral scriptures eventually became the Vinaya, the regulations for the sangha, that is, the community of Buddhist monks and nuns. There is a long list of rules, as well as texts that describe how the behavioral guidelines and ceremonies came about.

- One particular composition, the Mahavagga, begins by describing the origins of the sangha, with a story that begins shortly after the Buddha's enlightenment under a bodhi tree.
    o The Buddha decided to share his newfound knowledge with the five men who had been his companions earlier. He saw in vision that they were living in a deer park near Benares (now known as Varanasi); thus, he traveled 150 miles to seek them out.

- He announced to these men that he had discovered the middle way between a life of self-indulgence and self-mortification. Then, in this first sermon, he taught the Four Noble Truths.

- The first truth is that the "fivefold clinging" to existence is suffering. The second truth is that the cause of suffering is desire. The third is that the cessation of suffering comes from stopping desire. And the fourth truth is that the path to the cessation of suffering is the Eightfold Path—right view, right intention, right speech, right action, right livelihood, right effort, right mindfulness, and right concentration.

- The Buddha goes on to explain that "fivefold clinging" refers to the Buddhist idea that there is no self or *atman*; instead, all sentient beings are composed of five *skandhas*, or aggregates—body, sensations, perceptions, psychic dispositions, and consciousness—which are temporarily connected and constantly changing. There is no eternal, unchanging soul.

• This is a wonderfully concise restatement of the basic message of Buddhism, but the point of this particular text is not just doctrine; it's about the origins of the community of monks, which is as essential to Buddhism as any specific beliefs. The Mahavagga goes on to report that each of the five ascetics became enlightened upon hearing the words of the Buddha and was immediately ordained by him. From then on, monks ordained by the Buddha ordained other monks, who in turn, ordained others in an unbroken succession that has continued for more than 2,500 years.

• All Buddhists strive to live by the Five Precepts: no killing, no stealing, no sexual misconduct, no lying, and no intoxicants. Buddhist monks and nuns, beginning as novices, adopt five additional restrictions (in addition to celibacy): no eating after noon; no singing, dancing, or attending shows; no perfumes, cosmetics, or decorative accessories; no sleeping in luxurious beds; and no accepting money. Eventually, these rules became elaborated into a lengthy code called the Pratimoksha.

The Pratimoksha

- Buddhist monks and nuns give up home, family, and possessions and wander about or reside in a monastery, begging for the basic necessities of life while devoting themselves to spiritual matters. They are supported by donations from ordinary believers, and in return, they preach the dharma, that is, the principles of Buddhism. Without the oversight and responsibilities that come with family life, they are a vulnerable group, subject to temptations and difficulties.

- The Buddha, recognizing their special needs, mandated that twice a month, monks and nuns would gather (separately) to recite the Pratimoksha, which is a list of rules regulating their behavior. The idea is that this is a time to confess any sins or mistakes; silence is taken as a sign of continuing purity.

- There are eight sections to the Pratimoksha, and at the end of each, the monks recite the words of the Buddha: "In respect to [these rules] I ask the venerable ones, 'Are you pure in this matter?' A second time I ask the venerable ones, 'Are you pure in this matter?' A third time I ask the venerable ones, 'Are you pure in this matter?' The venerable ones are pure herein. Therefore do they keep silence."

- The eight categories of offenses are arranged according to severity, from those that require expulsion (sexual intercourse, theft, killing of humans, and false claims of supernatural powers), through probation, forfeiture, and so on.

- As with many sacred texts, it's not just the words that are important but also the ceremony.
    - For monks, the ceremony serves as a reaffirmation of their values and commitment, a check on one another, and an aid to mindfulness; it also increases awareness of the Three Poisons: greed, hatred, and delusion. Finally, the ceremony and the rules preserve the harmony of the sangha and enable spiritual progress.

- For laypersons, the ceremony assures them that the monks are worthy of donations, that they are self-disciplined and trustworthy in every way, and that they are following tradition. The Pratimoksha requires regular contact between the sangha and laity, but these interactions are carefully regulated. The sangha is dependent on the lay community and vice versa.

- For outsiders, it's remarkable to note the success of the sangha—a self-perpetuating social organization with no leader—and the practicality of the Pratimoksha. These rules don't seem to include any arbitrary taboos, as can be found in other religious traditions, and there's no notion that the regulations were revealed from on high. Rather, they were developed over the course of the Buddha's lifetime in response to various situations and questions.

Unlike Christianity, where celibate priests and nuns are not part of every branch of the faith, in Buddhism, the sangha—the community of monks and nuns—is at the core.

Buddhist Nuns

- Three versions of the Vinaya are in use today, one for each of the major Buddhist traditions, and the Pratimoksha in each is slightly different, although in all three versions, there are more rules for nuns.
  - The Buddha was originally reluctant to allow women to leave their homes and families and join the sangha, but he was persuaded to do so on the condition that nuns accept eight rules that subordinated them to monks.

  - His foster mother, Maha Pajapati, accepted these constraints and was ordained, along with 500 other devout women.

- There was never any doubt that women could progress spiritually and even achieve full enlightenment, but the Buddha seems to have worried about the vulnerability and respectability of females living independently at a time when it was thought that women needed male protection and guidance. He was also concerned that the common people might be suspicious of a celibate monastic community that included both men and women. Nevertheless, he gradually granted nuns the right to recite the Pratimoksha apart from monks and confess their wrongdoings to other nuns rather than to monks.

- The order of nuns continues to thrive in the Mahayana countries of East Asia, but the order in Theravada Buddhism mostly died out between the 11th and 13th centuries. Still, there are devout, celibate women in Theravada Buddhism who leave their families, shave their heads, and live by the Ten Precepts but aren't full nuns.

Jataka Stories

- The Jataka stories appear in the Little Texts subsection of the Sutra basket. According to tradition, as the Buddha sat under the bodhi tree seeking enlightenment, he went through a series of ever-deepening meditative states, one of which allowed him to view his past lives. In his post-enlightenment preaching, the Buddha sometimes drew on these recovered memories to make moral points, talking about something that happened when he was a king, a commoner, or even an animal.

- There are 547 Jataka stories in the Theravada canon. The story of the goose with the golden feathers and the greedy wife, told within the frame of a problem caused by a greedy nun, is similar to Aesop's tale of the goose that laid golden eggs. In fact, some scholars have speculated that this story came to Greece from India, along with several other Jataka tales.

- Each of these stories from the Buddha's previous lives teaches a simple lesson in Buddhist morality. The tales include the story of a woodpecker who risked his life to help a lion; an elephant who threw himself off a cliff to feed a group of people who were starving; and a monkey king who stretched out his body like a bridge so that his fellow monkeys, under attack from humans, could scramble across him to safety.

- One of the most inspiring, or perhaps most troubling, of the Jataka stories is the tale of the Buddha's last incarnation before he became Siddhartha Gautama.
    - At that time, the Buddha was born as a prince named Vessantara, who was extraordinarily, even dangerously generous. He gave away a magic rain-making elephant to a neighboring kingdom that was suffering from drought, and his people were so unhappy with him that he was forced to take his family into exile. Before he left, he gave away most of the royal treasury to the poor. On the road, he gave away the four horses that pulled his carriage; then he gave away the carriage.

    - A poor, greedy Brahman asked Vessantara for his two children to be his servants, and though he knew the Brahman would not treat them well, Vessantara nevertheless ignored his own feelings and handed them over.

    - One of the gods, worried that Vessantara would give away his wife next, disguised himself as a beggar and asked for her. Of course, Vessantara agreed, though the god immediately revealed his true nature, returned the wife, and tricked the cruel Brahman into leading the children back to their royal grandparents in the capital.

    - The Brahman was rewarded richly for returning the children, but he died of overeating within a few days. At last, Vessantara was welcomed home to the capital, reunited with his family, and crowned king.

Suggested Reading

Cowell, ed., *The Jataka*.

Gethin, *The Foundations of Buddhism*.

Khoroche, trans., *Once the Buddha Was a Monkey*.

Rhys Davids and Oldenberg, trans., *Vinaya Texts*.

Questions to Consider

1. How has the Vinaya been crucial in making the Buddhist sangha (monks and nuns) the longest continuously existing social organization in the world?

2. Why have stories of the Buddha's previous lives, including times when he took the form of animals, become so important in teaching the principles of Buddhism?

Vinaya and Jataka
Lecture 14—Transcript

Hello, it's good to have you back. In religious traditions with a large canon, some texts are going to get more attention than others. In this lecture, we'll discuss two types of Buddhist scriptures that are employed with great frequency but in very different ways. The first type of text is the Pratimoksha, those are the rules of the order, and those are in the Vinaya basket. The Pratimoksha is used nearly exclusively by monks and nuns. The second type of text, Jataka or birth stories, have been loved by ordinary believers for centuries, and they constitute a subsection within the Sutra basket.

But first, a little background about Buddhism. One of the interesting things about Buddhism is that in the early centuries, it wasn't a religion based on its founder. Siddhartha Gautama, the ancient Indian priest who'd become the Buddha, was thought to have discovered and then to have shown others the path to spiritual freedom and non-suffering; but he wasn't the path himself. As a result, the first biographies of the Buddha weren't written until the 1st century C.E., maybe 500 years after his death. You can contrast that with the Christian gospels that were written maybe 40–50 years after Jesus. Bits and pieces of the Buddha's life were recorded in various sacred compositions—remember, these are still memorized orally, they're not yet written down—and they were always within a specific teaching context; so at this point, there's still no text or biography that's just devoted to the life of the Buddha. Some of the earliest of these oral scriptures eventually became the Vinaya, the regulations for the sangha; that is, the community of monks and nuns. What I mean to say is some of the earliest of these bits and pieces of the Buddhist life are going to be inside the Vinaya.

There's a long list of rules, which we'll come to in a moment; but there are also texts that describe how the behavioral guidelines and the ceremonies came about. One particular composition, the Mahavagga, begins by describing the origins of the sangha, and it begins with a story shortly after the Buddha's enlightenment under a Bodhi tree. The Buddha wonders who he might share his newfound knowledge with, realizing that they'd need to be spiritually advanced enough to understand it; and then he remembers the five men with whom he once wandered about and practiced austerities. He sees in vision that those five men are now living in a deer park near Benares (it's the city now known as Varanasi), so he travels 150 miles from Bodhgaya to seek them out. He announces to them that he's discovered the middle way between a life of self-indulgence on the one hand and self-mortification on the other. Then, in his first sermon, he taught the Four Noble Truths, which begin as follows according to the Mahavagga: "This, o bhikkhus, is the noble truth of suffering: birth is suffering, decay is suffering, illness is suffering, death is suffering; presence of objects we hate is suffering; separation from objects that we love is suffering; not to obtain what we desire is suffering; briefly, the fivefold clinging to existence is suffering."

The Buddha later explains that the fivefold clinging refers to the distinctive idea that there's no self, or *atman*, unlike Hinduism. Instead, all sentient beings are composed of five *skandhas*, or aggregates. There's a body that you have, and then sensations that you can think of as being these nerve signals coming up through your body; and then perceptions, as we recognize and categorize those impulses that are coming. The fourth aggregate is psychic dispositions, sometimes called mental constructs, and that includes habits or disposition to certain kinds of mental states such as anger or passivity; and then the fifth of the aggregates is consciousness, these sorts of deliberate mental processes. These are all temporarily connected, and each of those is itself changing all the time, so there's no eternal, unchanging soul; we're just a bundle of these five temporary changing elements to our personality.

The second Noble Truth is the cause of suffering, which is desire; and then the third Noble Truth is the truth of the sensation of suffering, which comes from stopping desire. It's sort of a logical thing: If desire's the problem and you stop desire, then that will stop suffering. The fourth Noble Truth is the Eightfold Path, and this is often organized into three parts, which makes it easy to memorize. Starting with the parts of the Eightfold Path that have to do with wisdom, there's right view and right intention. Then there's the category of ethical conduct, so right speech, right action, right livelihood. Then finally, in the category of meditation, are right effort, right mindfulness, and right concentration.

This is a wonderfully concise restatement of the basic message of Buddhism; but the point of this particular text, the Mahavagga, isn't just doctrine, it's about the origin of the community of monks, which is as essential to Buddhism as any specific beliefs. The Mahavagga goes on to report that each of the five ascetics became enlightened or awaked upon hearing the words of the Buddha and was immediately ordained by him. From then on, monks ordained by the Buddha in turn ordained other monks, and then they ordained other monks in an unbroken succession that has continued for over 1,500 years. Remember, this story about the Buddha teaching those five ascetics, then teaching them the Four Noble Truths, comes from the Vinaya, which is all about monks and nuns. The word *Vinaya* itself means "that by which one is let out," and the idea is let out from suffering; it's a way of escaping.

All Buddhists strive to live by the five precepts, which are: no killing, no stealing, no sexual misconduct, no lying, and no intoxicants. I guess the first four sound a little bit like the Ten Commandments; it's sort of basic moral principles. The fifth one, no intoxicants, means that it would be a mistake to try to drink and otherwise change your mental consciousness so you could forget about the facts of life and death, and samsara and nirvana and moksha; you need to keep that focus at all times. So intoxicants are out of the way and also for monks and nuns you're not supposed to sleep too much either; you want to be awake and aware at all times that death is ever-present, that suffering is ever-present, that there's a way to escape that.

Buddhist monks and nuns, beginning as novices, adopt five additional restrictions in addition to those first five; and for monks and nuns, the one about no sexual misconduct is going to mean celibacy. The five additional rules for monks and nuns are: No eating after noon; no singing, dancing, or attending shows; no perfumes, cosmetics, or decorative accessories (so they have to shave their heads); no sleeping in luxurious beds; and no accepting money. Eventually these rules became elaborated into a lengthy code called the Pratimoksha in Sanskrit or the Patimoksha in Pali. Just one of those I want you to think about a little more is about the notion that monks and nuns shouldn't eat after their lunch, after noonday, which means that eating in the evening, eating in entertainment, isn't really allowed. You need to eat, you need to keep up your strength, it's important, but you're not allowed to make food a major priority in your life; it's to sort of keep a balance between eating too much and just giving way to all your desires and on the other hand eating nothing, of fasting too much. Remember, Buddhism offers a middle way.

Monks and nuns give up home and family and possessions, and instead they wander about or they reside in a monastery and they beg for the basic necessities of life while devoting themselves to spiritual matters, mostly to scripture study, to meditation, and to preaching the dharma. In this case, dharma doesn't mean caste duty as it did in Hinduism; in the Buddhist context, the word *dharma* means the "teachings of the Buddha." Monks and nuns are supported by donations from ordinary believers, and in return they preach the Dharma, the principles of Buddhism. Without the oversight and responsibilities that come from family life, they're a vulnerable group. Monks and nuns are subject to all sorts of temptations and difficulties, not the least of which come from celibacy. The Buddha, recognizing their special needs, mandated that twice a month, at the full moon and new moon days, monks would gather together to recite the Pratimoksha, which is a list of rules regulating their behavior. The idea is that this is a time to confess any sins or mistakes; so if the monks remain silent, then that's taken as a sign of their continuing purity. You want to confess before you go into the Pratimoksha ceremony. Nuns also gather twice a month to recite the Pratimoksha, but they do so separately from monks.

> There are eight sections to the Pratimoksha, and at the end of these the monks recite the words of the Buddha:
>
> In respect to these rules I ask the venerable ones, "Are you pure in this matter?"
>
> A second time I ask the venerable ones, "Are you pure in this matter?"
>
> A third time I ask the venerable ones, "Are you pure in this matter?"
>
> The venerable ones are pure herein. Therefore do they keep silence.

The venerable ones are the monks, and silence denotes compliance as they recite these passages.

There are eight categories of offenses in this long list of rules. The first category is the most extreme, the most serious offenses, and they can result in expulsion from the order of monks and nuns for four offenses: for sexual intercourse, for theft, for killing humans, or false claims of supernatural powers. If you committed one of those mistakes, that's described as a defeat and you're kicked out of the sangha. Then the second category is offenses that result in probation, generally for as many days as the mistake was concealed. There are 13 offenses: sexual transgressions other than intercourse, building dwellings that are too large or require clearing away trees, false accusations, schisms, refusing to accept discipline, and corrupting families. Then there's a category that will result in variable punishment; there are two rules there prohibiting sitting alone with a woman in a secluded place. Then there are 30 offenses that can result in forfeiture, so they're going to take something away; these are rules regarding robes, alms bowls, rugs, medicines, or the use of money, some kind of contraband goods that the monks have been using.

The next category is 92 offenses, relatively minor transgressions, and you deal with these by confessing your mistake and promising not to do it anymore; and these offenses include things like digging in the ground (so monks aren't allowed to farm at all), sleeping in the same house as a woman, verbal abuse, lying, striking someone, drinking alcohol, interaction with nuns, horsing around in water, tickling anyone, scaring another monk, hiding another monk's robe or bowl as a joke, eating after noon, sleeping in a luxurious bed, attending entertainments, going out to watch an army, and pretending not to know what the rules are. You can imagine the circumstances that might've given rise to those various rules; I'm thinking especially about scaring a monk, hiding his begging bowl, or horsing around in water.

The next category is mistakes that just require acknowledgment to repent for, and these are mistakes such as receiving food from an unrelated nun. Then there's a section of training rules; these are 75 guidelines for manners and calm deportment. It talks about the way you should eat, and walk, and beg; the proper way of accepting donations and wearing robes; of teaching—that is, for example, when you're teaching there shouldn't be any loud laughing or smacking one's lips; don't spit into water; don't teach anyone who has a weapon in their hand—and these are described as "disciplines which ought to be observed." The final section of the Pratimoksha is seven rules for settling disputes.

As with many sacred texts, it's not just the words—those are important—but it's the ceremony that goes with it. I want you to imagine what it means to recite this long list of offenses with all of the penalties for it twice a month as a monk, or to watch the ceremony as a Buddhist layperson. It probably takes 30–60 minutes to go through. For monks and nuns, as they recite this text from the Vinaya portion of the scriptures, this Pratimoksha, it reaffirms their values and commitment; it offers them a chance to check on themselves and on their brothers and sisters; it's an aid to mindfulness. To go through all of these regulations in order is to come up against boundaries. There's a greater awareness of the three poisons, which are described as greed, hatred, and delusion. Remember, this list of rules to keep has to be memorized; so it becomes interiorized, it becomes part of you. It preserves the harmony of the sangha, and it provides for some measure of quality control with regard to people. Remember that Buddhism invites recruits from all social classes; and you want to make sure that those people aren't coming into the sangha under false pretenses, but they're actually keeping the rules and regulations. Reciting the Pratimoksha allows for spiritual progress; their safety and respectability in keeping these rules. Respectability's important, because remember that monks and nuns are dependent on the generosity of laypersons as they beg for food and for clothing; so laypeople are going to be more willing to help you out if they're sure you're actually taking this seriously, if you know the rules and you are abiding by them.

For laypersons who might watch the monks and nuns recite this text, the Pratimoksha, it assures them that the monks are worthy of donations; that they're self-disciplined and trustworthy in every way; that they're following the tradition. The Pratimoksha requires regular contact between the sangha and the laity, but the interactions are carefully regulated; there are rules about where you can stay and who you can take food from and such. The sangha is dependent on the lay community for their means of livelihood; and then the lay community is also dependent on the sangha for teaching about Buddhism, for teaching the dharma.

For outsiders, as people who aren't Buddhists—perhaps for scholars, or those who are interested in Buddhism—it's remarkable how successful this ceremony, this process of self-regulation, has been. The Buddhist sangha is a self-perpetuating social organization. The sangha has no leader; the seniority comes from date of ordination; and then there's due process in how things are done. It's also striking how practical these rules are. They don't seem to be arbitrary; they don't seem to be the kinds of taboos that are found in other religious traditions that seem to have come out of nowhere that are kind of hard to explain; the rules for monks and nuns pretty much make sense. There's no notion that these regulations were revealed from on high; rather, they were developed over the course of the Buddha's lifetime as various situations came up, and then he gave answers to questions or decisions on situations that were confusing to the monks.

Some of the other texts in the Vinaya have the stories behind all of these rules. Once there was a monk who, shortly after ordination, indulged in some bad habits; and when he was confronted about this by his fellow monks, he protested to the Buddha that he'd never asked to be ordained, the ceremony had been done at someone else's initiative. The Buddha said that from now on, only people who request ordination themselves can join the sangha; so that's the kind of rule that would make it into the Pratimoksha. Similar irregularities led the Buddha to decree that ordinations have to be done by 10 or more monks acting together. When a number of first-year monks ordained someone, the Buddha said, "No, it has to be 10 monks who have been serving for at least 10 years." Then when some foolish, ignorant, long-term monks ordained someone unwisely, the Buddha said in that situation, "No, the ordinations have to be done by at least 10 monks of 10-year standing who are competent and experienced," and so on; so you can see how these rules come out of ordinary situations.

Before we move on, let's talk for a minute about nuns. There are three versions of the Vinaya in use today, one for each of the major Buddhist traditions, and the Pratimoksha in each is slightly different. In the Theravada version of the Pratimoksha—so this is the tradition that's in Southeast Asia—there are 227 rules for monks and 311 for nuns. Mahayana Buddhists in East Asia—so in China, Korea, Vietnam, and Taiwan—tend to follow the Dharmaguptaka version of the Pratimoksha, and that has 250 rules for monks, 348 for nuns. In Tibet and Mongolia, where Vajrayana Buddhism is prominent, monks and nuns live by the Mulasarvastivada Vinaya that has 258 rules for monks, 366 for nuns. By the way, schisms in Buddhism tend to occur over the rules rather than because of doctrinal differences. We'll see in a later lecture that sometimes in the same monastery some monks will like Mahayana sutras and others will like Theravada sutras. They can still live together and work together, beg together as long as they keep the same version of the Pratimoksha; when they disagree about the rules, that's when there are splits in the Buddhist community.

In all three versions of the Vinaya, though, you may have noticed that there are more rules for nuns. The Buddha was originally reluctant to allow women to leave their homes and families and to join the sangha, and he was persuaded only by the entreaties of his foster mother, Maha Pajapati, and his favorite disciple Ananda, but only on the condition that nuns accept eight rules that subordinated them to monks. So the Buddha said, "Ok, we can have nuns who are living independently of families, but they have to keep a few more rules; in particular, eight rules." These eight rules include that nuns with decades of experience would have to defer to monks who were ordained only a few days ago; and while monks can reprove nuns, nuns can't correct or reprove monks. Maha Pajapati accepted these constraints and was ordained, along with 500 other devout women; and this story is in the Vinaya.

There was never any doubt that women could progress spiritually just as men, and even achieve full enlightenment; but the Buddha seems to have worried about the vulnerability and the respectability of females living independently at a time when it was thought that women always needed male protection and guidance. He was also concerned that the common people might be suspicious of a celibate monastic community that included both men and women. Nevertheless, he granted nuns the right to recite the Pratimoksha apart from monks; to confess their wrongdoings to other nuns, rather than to monks. The rules of monks and nuns are similar; but, as we've seen, it was thought that nuns needed a few extra.

The order of nuns continues to thrive in Mahayana countries of East Asia. Nuns were never really established in Tibet, but in Southeast Asia there were nuns in the Theravada tradition; but that order of nuns died out in the 11th–13th centuries. The requirement for ordaining nuns was they needed 10 duly ordained nuns to take part in the ordination, in addition to the 10 monks. There are devout, celibate women in Theravada Buddhism who leave their families, they shave their heads, they live by the 10 basic precepts, but they aren't full nuns. There's been a move by some to try to reinstate official nuns within the Theravada tradition, but that would require finding Mahayana nuns who are worthy by Theravada standards in order to witness and take part in the ordination. In the last couple of decades, there have been several controversial ordinations of nuns, with objections coming not only from conservative monks, but also some resistance from women who believe that becoming full nuns would then be more restrictive than what Theravada monastic women now enjoy precisely because of those many, many rules that official nuns would have to keep.

In most religions, it's a challenge to adopt the requirements of ancient sacred texts to the modern world with our contemporary styles of dress, and our ideas of medicine, transportation, economics, education, and gender relations. The questions are compounded in Buddhism because, unlike Christianity where celibate priests and nuns aren't part of every branch of the faith (it's in Catholicism, but not in Protestantism), by contrast in Buddhism the sangha is at the core of the tradition. All Buddhists take refuge in the three treasures—the Buddha, the dharma, and the sangha—and these rules for monks and nuns have been pretty successful. Because of them, the Buddhist sangha is probably the longest-running continuous social organization in the history of the world. Buddhist monks and nuns today can trace their ordination patterns back to the Buddha himself living in the 5th century B.C.E.

We can now turn to a portion of the Buddhist Tripitaka that was used by monks and nuns for teaching purposes and has been long beloved by ordinary Buddhists. Remember that the Pratimoksha is mostly just for monks and nuns, for themselves, sometimes witnessed by outsiders; but now we're going to talk about Jataka stories, which appear in the little texts subsection of the sutra basket. All sorts of Buddhists know these stories, have grown up with these stories, and love them. According to tradition, as the Buddha sat under the Bodhi tree seeking enlightenment, he went through a series of ever-deepening meditative states. One of those states allowed him to view his past lives, and in his post-enlightenment preaching the Buddha sometimes drew on those recovered memories to make moral points: when he was talking about something that happened once when he was a king or a commoner, or even one of his past lives when he was an animal.

In the Theravada canon, there are 547 Jataka stories in poetic form. Here's an example of one of those: Once there was a layperson who had a garlic field, and he allowed the nuns to gather garlic when they needed. When a festival was coming up one nun, named Nanda, went to the field and took much more garlic than was reasonable. That upset the farmer; he thought that he was being generous, and then this nun, Nanda, had taken advantage of his generosity. The other nuns criticized Nanda and complained to the Buddha; and the Buddha, in replying to them, warned against greed and he told a story from one of his past lives: Once, he said, there was a Brahman—remember this is the upper caste of Hinduism—who died and left behind a wife and three daughters. He was reincarnated as a golden swan, and when he remembered his former family that was living in poverty, as a swan he visited them and he gave them one of his feathers to sell. Every so often he would show up and donate another feather of gold, and eventually they became quite prosperous. But his former wife, who was impatient and greedy, worried that the golden swan might stop coming; so on his next visit, she grabbed him and she plucked out all of his feathers. The golden feathers taken by force, however, turned into ordinary feathers; and the swan, unable to fly, was thrown into a barrel. The daughters nursed him back to health and he regrew feathers; but his new feathers were just ordinary feathers, and once he could fly away he did and he never returned. The Buddha then explained that the wife's greed had cost her her supply of golden feathers, just as Nanda's greed had cost the nuns their supply of garlic. In fact, he continued, in a previous existence Nanda was that greedy wife and the other nuns were the daughters, and the Buddha himself had been the Brahma who was reborn as the golden swan.

Does this story sound a little bit familiar? Perhaps you've heard the story of the goose that laid the golden eggs only to have the farmer and his wife—supposing that there was a great amount of gold inside this goose—cut open the bird only to find ordinary goose innards, and thus they lost the future golden eggs that they could've had. This is a tale from the Ancient Greek writer Aesop, and the two stories are similar enough that some scholars have supposed that this story made its way from India to Greece, along with several other Jataka tales.

As I said, there are hundreds of these stories from the Buddha's previous lives, each of which teaches a simple lesson in Buddhist morality. They were popular and well known, as can be seen from the many depictions of them in cave paintings, in temple decorations, and in stone carvings. These pictorial representations of Jataka tales played the same function for illiterate Buddhist peasants as the images of Bible stories in the stained glass windows in European cathedrals, so that people who couldn't read the scriptures themselves could go and see these tales, they could hear the stories read to them or recited to them by priests in the case of Christian cathedrals or Buddhist monks, and then they could be reminded of these stories, and when they'd go into the building or they'd see these images in the temple they'd be reminded of these moral principles. Even today, there are Jataka picture books and animated cartoons for children.

There are lots and lots of stories. There's the story of a woodpecker who risks his life to help a lion with a bone stuck in his throat. There's a story of an elephant who threw himself off a cliff so he could feed a group of people who were starving; sort of committed suicide and then gave them his body to eat. There's a story of a monkey king who stretched out his body like a bridge so that his fellow monkeys, who were under attack from humans, could scramble across him to safety. There's a story of a rabbit who taught his friends, the otter, the jackal, and the monkey, the importance of sharing their food with human travelers, which they did. But then when the rabbit realized that his own food of bitter grass wasn't of any use to people, he jumped into a fire to roast his own flesh for them to eat, to share what he had. By the way, the gods were so impressed by this last action of selfless giving of the rabbit that they put an image of the rabbit on the moon as a constant reminder to everyone; so as you look at the full moon, you don't see a man in the moon if you're living in India or Buddhist countries, you see a rabbit in the moon.

One of the most inspiring—or perhaps most troubling—of the Jataka stories is the tale of the Buddha's last incarnation before he became Siddhartha

Gautama. This is also one of the most famous of these Jataka stories. In that reincarnation, in that life, the Buddha was born as a prince named Vessantara who was extraordinarily, even dangerously generous. He gave away a magic rainmaking elephant to a neighboring kingdom that was suffering from drought; and his people were so unhappy with him for giving away the rainmaking elephant that he was forced to take his family into exile. Before he left, he gave away most of the royal treasury to the poor. On the road, he gave away the four horses that pulled his carriage, and then he gave away the chariot. A poor, greedy Brahman asked Vessantara for his two children to be his servants; and though he knew that the Brahman wasn't going to treat them very well, Vessantara nevertheless ignored his own feelings and he handed his children over. One of the gods at that point, worried that Vessantara would give away his wife next, disguised himself as a beggar and asked for his wife; and sure enough, Vessantara agreed, though the god immediately revealed his true nature as a god, returned the wife, and then he tricked the cruel Brahman in leading the children back to their royal grandparents in the capital. The Brahman was rewarded richly for returning the children back to Vessantara, but he died from overeating a few days later; this is that greedy Brahman. Then at last, Vessantara was welcomed home to the capital, reunited with his family, and then crowned as king.

It's an example of justice; of how extraordinary selflessness catches the attention of the gods and brings good results, even if at first they seem unlikely, while greed inevitably leads to ruin, like the bad Brahman who took the children gets rewarded with the food and then dies shortly after. In Theravada Buddhism, these Jataka stories were used to teach children morality; to provide memorable ideals of virtue. In Mahayana Buddhism, the extreme cases of selfless generosity represent the bodhisattva ideal. In the next two lectures, we'll examine some of the characteristic sutras from both the Theravada and Mahayana traditions.

Theravada Sutras
Lecture 15

In this lecture, we'll discuss some of the most famous and significant sacred texts in the Theravada tradition of Buddhism. Theravada was one of the 18 early schools of Buddhism and the only one to survive to the present day, mostly in Southeast Asia. There are two other major divisions within Buddhism: the Mahayana and Vajrayana. The main differences among the three traditions are in some ways analogous to Catholicism, Protestantism, and Eastern Orthodoxy in Christianity, except the different types of Buddhists have traditionally gotten along much better than Catholics and Protestants. In this lecture and the next two, we'll explore the sacred texts of each of these schools.

Buddhist Traditions

- Theravada ("Teachings of the Elders") is the oldest surviving form of Buddhism, and its followers number about 125 million, mostly in Southeast Asia. They believe that the Buddha was a man who gained enlightenment, then passed into nirvana; thus, there is nothing left of him to worship.
  - Believers must follow the path that the Buddha took, but in practical terms, only monks and nuns are able put in the time necessary for study and meditation or to abandon all earthly attachments in a way that will achieve enlightenment.
  - The characteristic scriptures of Theravada Buddhism are in the Pali language.

- The term *Mahayana* means the "Greater Vehicle," and this form of Buddhism teaches that all believers, not just monks and nuns, are capable of enlightenment. This form of Buddhism dominates East Asia (China, Korea, Taiwan, and Japan) and claims more than 185 million believers.

- o Mahayana Buddhists believe that the Buddha was a god rather than just a spiritually advanced man, and they put a great deal of emphasis on bodhisattvas—beings who achieve enlightenment but choose to remain in the world system rather than entering nirvana. The bodhisattvas vow that they will enter nirvana only after all other sentient beings have been enlightened. These are Buddhist divinities to whom one can pray.

- o Mahayana Buddhism, which began in about the 1st century C.E., includes many schools (similar to Protestant denominations), such as the emptiness school of Madhyamika, the consciousness-only school of Yogacara, and several distinctive schools of Japanese Buddhism, including Zen. The Mahayana scriptures were originally composed in Sanskrit, though they were eventually translated into Chinese and Tibetan.

- Vajrayana ("Thunderbolt") Buddhism is by far the smallest of the three Buddhist traditions, with about 20 million adherents. Nevertheless, its prominence in Tibetan culture, which includes a reverence for the Dalai Lama, has brought it a great deal of attention in the West. This form of Buddhism builds on various Mahayana schools but adds many Tantric texts that introduce various ritual shortcuts for attaining Buddhahood, including mantras, mudras, mandalas, and visualizations.

- There are different versions of the Vinaya for Theravada, Mahayana, and Vajrayana Buddhists, but the differences are minor. The most striking contrasts are to be found in the largest section of the Three Baskets—the Sutras.

Samyutta Nikaya: "Connected Discourses"
- In the Pali canon of the Theravadas, there are five subsections in the Sutra basket: 34 Long Discourses, 150 Middle-Length Discourses, several thousand Connected Discourses and Enumerated Discourses, and 15 Little Texts, which offer a plethora of miscellaneous writings. Most of these sacred texts were intended for monks and nuns.

- In one of the Connected Discourses, for example, the Buddha explains to an ascetic, Kassapa, that suffering is not created by oneself or by others, and it does not simply arise without being created. Kassapa's mistake, according to the Buddha, is to assume that there is a self that is responsible for suffering.

- The Buddha then offers an alternative analysis of causation, in which suffering is the result of the cycle of conditioned arising (sometimes known as dependent origination). The 12 conditions arise from ignorance—the origin of suffering. The Buddha breaks the weak link in the chain—ignorance—by achieving enlightenment.

- There are some profound ideas in this discourse about causation and the elusiveness of individual identity, but the sutra perhaps means more to a devoted Buddhist than to an outsider. However, there are several other texts that have been powerful in the lives of laity and may even mean something to non-Buddhist seekers of wisdom.

The Therigatha

- The Therigatha ("Verses of the Elder Nuns") consists of 73 poems in which nuns recount how they became enlightened. This is the world's earliest known collection of women's literature, with poems supposedly written in the 5th century B.C.E.

- A typical example was composed by Vaddhesi, a woman who was a nurse to Maha Pajapati, the Buddha's foster mother. She speaks of trying and failing—day after day, for 25 years—to calm her mind and overcome desire.

- A more famous nun is Kisa Gotami, whose story has been retold in many versions over the centuries. After the death of her son, half-mad with grief, she asks the Buddha for medicine to make the boy well. He teaches her, however, that her grief is not unique—death is an inescapable part of life. She finally buries her son and asks the Buddha to be ordained a nun. Kisa Gotami became well respected for her spiritual insight and poetry, and in time, she escaped the sorrows of this world and passed into nirvana.

The Dhammapada

- The Dhammapada ("Verse of the Buddha's Teachings") is probably the most famous of all Theravada scriptures, and it also comes from the Little Text section of the Sutra basket. Even though the Pali canon tends to be focused on monks, the Dhammapada has ethical advice and inspiration for all Buddhists.

- The Dhammapada consists of 423 verses, divided into 26 sections, and includes no extended arguments or complicated doctrinal formulations. It has been loved and memorized by both Theravada and Mahayana Buddhists for more than 2,000 years. The prominence of the Dhammapada in Asia made it one of the first Buddhist texts to be translated into English.

- We can get a sense of the book's contents by simply looking over the 26 section headings, which include such titles as "Thought," "The Fool," "The Wise Man," "Old Age," "Self," "The World," "Happiness," "Pleasure," "Anger," and "The Way." In general, its themes concern moral action, the fleeting nature of life, self-mastery, and warnings about desire. Some of its teachings refer to specifically Buddhist doctrines, such as the Four Noble Truths and the Three Refuges, but much of it might be applicable to almost anyone's life.

- The Dhammapada tends to sound like a book of proverbs. Buddhists have long considered each one a saying of the Buddha himself, and later commentators provided collections of anecdotes that gave the story behind each saying. For example, the tale of Kisa Gotami was thought to be the basis for verse 287: "As a great flood carries off a sleeping village, death carries off the person whose mind is distracted, intoxicated by possessions and children" (Wallis).

- Verse 276 on individual effort reads: "It is you who must make the effort. The masters [i.e., the Buddhas] only point the way. But if you meditate and follow the law, you will free yourself from desire" (Byrom).

- One of the things that is most striking about Theravada Buddhism is that it is not a savior religion. The Buddha can't rescue anyone from the consequences of karma or give someone enlightenment. People must do these things for themselves. The Buddha can only show the way.

- There's a tough-minded realism here that may be attractive to some people in our own scientific, skeptical age. Of course, Buddhism is an ancient religion, and in the earliest texts, there is talk of miracles, gods, demons, and superhuman powers, but there is also a streak of practical empiricism that is worth considering.

Discourse to the Kalamas

- The Discourse to the Kalamas begins with Ananda reciting, "Thus have I heard"; he then tells the story of a time when the Buddha, traveling with a large number of monks, arrived at the town of Kesaputta. The inhabitants there, members of the Kalama clan, came out to greet him because they had heard reports of the Buddha's wisdom and spiritual attainments.

- But the Kalamas had a question. Many holy men, ascetics, and sages had come through their town, and each of them had praised his own doctrines while condemning the teachings of others. How, the Kalamas asked, can they tell the difference between truth and falsehood?

- The Buddha tells the Kalamas that it is appropriate to have doubts or to be perplexed. That in itself is worth noting, became some religions put a premium on faith and discourage questioning. The Buddha then continues with these famous words:

Do not accept a thing by recollection [repeated hearing], by tradition, by mere report, because it is based on the authority of scriptures, by mere logic or inference, by reflection on conditions,

Selections from the Dhammapada

The dangers of giving in to desire:
He who lives looking for pleasures only, his senses uncontrolled, immoderate in his food, idle, and weak, Mara (the tempter) will certainly overthrow him, as the wind throws down a weak tree. (7, Muller)

Disciplining one's mind:
The wise man guards his mind which is unruly and ever in search of pleasure. The mind well-guarded brings great happiness. (36, Austin, in Humphries)

Impermanence:
A fool is troubled, thinking, "I have sons; I have wealth"; but even himself doesn't belong to himself—let alone sons, let alone wealth. (62, Roebuck)

Karma:
Whosoever offends a harmless, pure and innocent person, the evil falls back upon that fool, like light dust thrown up against the wind. (125, Babbitt)

How we should treat others:
Conquer anger through gentleness, unkindness through kindness, greed through generosity, and falsehood by truth. (223, Easwaran)

The superiority of Buddhism:
The best of paths is the path of eight. The best of truths, the four sayings. The best of states, freedom from passions [nirvana]. The best of men, the one who sees. (273, Mascaro)

Individual effort:
It is you who must make the effort. The masters [i.e., the Buddhas] only point the way. But if you meditate and follow the law, you will free yourself from desire. (276, Byrom)

because of reflection on or fondness for a certain theory, because it merely seems suitable, nor thinking: "The religious wanderer is respected by us." (Holder)

- The Buddha then tells the Kalamas how they can know not what to accept but what to reject: "But when you know for yourselves: 'These things are unwholesome, blameworthy, reproached by the wise, when undertaken and performed lead to harm and suffering'—these you should reject" (Holder). In other words, he tells them that they should base their beliefs on personal experience and direct observation.

- The Buddha follows up by introducing the Kalamas to the doctrine of the Three Poisons—that suffering and sorrow in this world have three basic roots: greed, hatred, and ignorance. Then he suggests that they can know what to accept by looking for the opposites: things that are wholesome, unblameworthy, commended by the wise, and when put into practice, lead to benefit and happiness. These sorts of things will lead to an untroubled mind, pure and free from hatred.

- In other words, the Buddha says that we don't have to believe his teachings because they are traditional, scriptural, popular, or reasonable or because the Buddha himself is well known. Instead, we should try out the practices he recommends—the Five Precepts, kindness, meditation, self-mastery, detachment—and see if they bring good results. In fact, he goes on to say that whether there is an afterlife or not, this is still a good way to live.

- It seems as if Buddhism is a religion that would be well-suited for our modern Western ideas of individual autonomy—the freedom to choose and to act—but then the Buddha undercuts it all with a paradox. He suggests that there is no self that chooses or acts. Later Buddhists, in the Mahayana tradition, will heighten this contradiction by arguing that there is also no nirvana, no samsara, no salvation, and even no Buddha.

Suggested Reading

Burtt, ed., *The Teachings of the Compassionate Buddha.*

Gethin, *Sayings of the Buddha.*

Holder, trans., *Early Buddhist Discourses.*

Murcott, trans., *The First Buddhist Women.*

Rhys Davids, trans., *Psalms of the Sisters.*

Roebuck, trans., *The Dhammapada.*

Questions to Consider

1. How did the world's earliest anthology of women's literature become part of the Buddhist canon?

2. What has made the Dhammapada the most popular text in Theravada Buddhism, that is, the oldest surviving branch of the religion?

Theravada Sutras
Lecture 15—Transcript

Hello, again. In this lecture, we'll discuss some of the most famous and significant texts in the Theravada tradition of Buddhism. Remember, Theravada was one of the 18 early schools of Buddhism, and the only one of those 18 to survive to the present day; and apparently they were also the first to put their scriptures into written form, about the 1st century B.C.E. Today, Theravada Buddhism is mostly to be found in Southeast Asia. There are two other major divisions within Buddhism, the Mahayana and Vajrayana; I'll be talking out both of these in the next two lectures. For right now, let me outline some of the main differences between these three traditions, which were in some ways analogous to Catholicism, Protestantism, and Eastern Orthodoxy in Christianity; except the different types of Buddhists have traditionally gotten along much better than Catholics and Protestants.

For Theravada—and the name means the "teachings of the elders"—Theravada is the oldest surviving form of Buddhism, and its followers number about 125 million, mostly in southeast Asia in Thailand, Cambodia, Myanmar, and Sri Lanka. They believe that the Buddha was a man who gained enlightenment and then passed into nirvana so that there's nothing left of him to worship. Believers must themselves follow the path that he took, but in practical terms, only monks and nuns are able to put in the time necessary for study and for meditation, or to abandon all earthly attachments in a way that will help them achieve enlightenment. Their characteristic scriptures are in the Pali language.

The term Mahayana, by contrast, means the "greater vehicle"; and this form of Buddhism teaches that all believers, not just monks and nuns, are capable of enlightenment. This is the Buddhism that dominates East Asia—so China, Korea, Taiwan, and Japan—and it claims over 185 million believers. Mahayana Buddhists call themselves the greater vehicle and they contrast themselves with what they call Hinayana, or the smaller vehicle. Sometimes when I talk to students about this I describe it as if Theravada Buddhism is the Buddhism of a raft that can carry you over this life of turmoil to nirvana, Mahayana is like cruise ship Buddhism, all kinds of people can be on that boat. Mahayana Buddhists contrast themselves with Hinayana Buddhists, smaller vehicles, but Hinayana is actually kind of a derogatory term; so we'll say Theravada Buddhists for that earlier school and then Mahayana Buddhists, the great vehicle.

Mahayana Buddhists believe that the Buddha was as god rather than just a spiritually advanced man, and they put a great deal of emphasis on bodhisattvas. These are beings that achieve enlightenment and then choose to stick around in this world system rather than going into nirvana. Indeed, they vow that they will enter into nirvana only after all other sentient beings have been enlightened. So these are Buddhist divinities that one can pray to and ask for help. Mahayana Buddhism, which began in about the 1st century C.E. with new and distinctive sacred texts, includes a great many schools—so they're something like Protestant denominations—and those schools range from the emptiness school of Madhyamika, and the consciousness-only school of Yogacara, and several distinctive schools of Japanese Buddhism, including Zen. The new Mahayana scriptures were originally composed in Sanskrit, though they were eventually translated into Chinese and Tibetan.

The third form of Buddhism is Vajrayana; and Vajrayana means "the thunderbolt." It's by far the smallest of the three Buddhist traditions, with about 20 million adherents; so maybe five percent of Buddhists worldwide are Vajrayana Buddhists. Nevertheless, its prominence in Tibetan culture, which includes reverence for the Dalai Lama, has brought it a great deal of attention in the West. This form of Buddhism builds on various Mahayana schools, but then adds a great number of Tantric texts, which include various ritual shortcuts for attaining Buddhahood including mantras, mudras (which are hand gestures), mandalas (which are schematic diagrams), and visualizations.

There are different versions of the Vinaya for Theravada, Mahayana, and Vajrayana Buddhists, but their differences are rather minor. The most striking contrasts are to be found in the largest section of the three baskets: in the Sutras. Each Sutra is traditionally associated with the Buddha's favorite disciple, Ananda, who'd memorized the teaching that he heard the Buddha proclaim; so each Sutra beings, in Ananda's voice, "Thus have I heard," and then something, something. In the Pali canon of the Theravadas, there are five subsections of the Sutra basket, the first two of which are 34 long discourses and 150 middle-length discourses; then follows several thousands connected discourses and enumerated discourses; and then the largest subsection by far consists of the 15 little texts that offer a plethora of miscellaneous writings such as the Jataka tales that we talked about in a previous lecture—those are the stories about the Buddha in his previous incarnations—along with stories of how early monks and nuns gained enlightenment; there are stories of heavenly or ghostly rebirths, and they include the Dhammapada, which we'll discuss in just a few minutes. Taken together, the Pali Sutras are a large collection of sacred texts, most of which were intended for monks and nuns. Many of these Sutras are rather technical and repetitive, as the Buddha gives instructions or meditation, or he may explain the nonexistence of a permanent self, or he may outline the 12 stages of conditioned arising.

Here, for example, is an excerpt from the connected discourses, the third section of the Sutra basket. Let me set the stage: The sutra beings, of course, with "Thus have I heard," and then it continues with the story of how once, when the Buddha was living in the bamboo grove outside of Rajagaha, he was going into town to beg for alms when a naked ascetic, Kassapa, saw him and asked if he would mind answering a few questions. The Buddha said this isn't a convenient time, I'm going to visit some houses, and Kassapa said, "But just a few questions," and then he began to ask:

> "How is it, Master Gotama: is suffering created by oneself?"
>
> "Not so, Kassapa," the Blessed One said.... [The question concerns the law of karma, where does suffering come from?]
>
> "Then, Master Gotama: is suffering created by another?"
>
> "Not so, Kassapa," the Blessed One said.
>
> "How is it, then, Master Gotama: is suffering created both by oneself and by another?" [The idea is do we suffer in this life because of things that we did ourselves, or because of what other people did?]
>
> "Not so, Kassapa," the Blessed One said.

> "Then, Master Gotama, has suffering arisen fortuitously, being created neither by oneself nor by another?"
>
> "Not so, Kassapa," the Blessed One said.
>
> "How is it then, Master Gotama: is there no suffering?"
>
> [The Buddha responded] "It is not that there is no suffering, Kassapa; there is suffering."

Then the Buddha goes on to explain that Kassapa's mistake is to assume that there's a self that's responsible for suffering. He then offers an alternative analysis of causation, in which suffering is the result of the cycle of conditioned arising, which is sometimes known as dependent origination. Hold on, because things are about to get technical as he breezes through the 12 stages of the cycle; but the point to keep in mind is that a permanent self doesn't show up anywhere in this sequence.

> Conditioned by ignorance are karmic constituents [that is to say, karmic constituents are caused by ignorance; we're going to work backwards here]; conditioned by karmic constituents is consciousness; conditioned by consciousness is individuality [name and form]; conditioned by individuality are the six senses [those are the five regular senses plus the mind; Buddhists thought that the mind was a sense because it could sense mental constructs like dreams]; conditioned by the six senses is contact; conditioned by contact is feeling; conditioned by feeling is desire; conditioned by desire is clinging; conditioned by clinging is becoming; conditioned by becoming is rebirth; conditioned by rebirth are old age, death, sorrow, lamentation, suffering, depression and dismay. In this way the whole great heap of suffering originates.

Oftentimes this is presented in a cyclical form, and then this last one brings us back to ignorance.

All of this comes as a revelation to Kassapa; and once his eyes have been opened by this analysis—it's not that suffering comes from bad karma that was produced by oneself or by someone else, or by neither oneself or someone else, or by both someone and someone else; it's rather this cycle of suffering, those stages in it that all depend on each other—and once he's realized that this is how things are, he becomes a Buddhist monk, eventually gaining enlightenment himself. In this cycle of dependent origination, ignorance is the weak link in the chain; and that's what the Buddha's going to break with his preaching. That's what happens with Kassapa: Once he realizes the truth of this, then he's able to break through this cycle and achieve enlightenment, awakening, and nirvana.

There are some profound ideas here about causation and the elusiveness of individual identity, but perhaps only a devoted Buddha could love a Sutra like this; this is the kind of Sutra that's for monks and nuns. But there are several other texts that have been powerful in the lives of laity and ordinary Buddhists, and perhaps these might even mean something to non-Buddhist seekers of wisdom, or even those who are simply curious about how the world looks to Buddhists. I'll introduce you to three more Theravada texts from the Sutra basket.

The first of these texts is one of the 15 little discourses. It's called the Therigatha, or the "Verses of the Elder Nuns." It consists of 73 poems in which nuns recount how they became enlightened. This is the world's earliest-known collection of women's literature, with poems supposedly written in the 5th century B.C.E. Here's a somewhat typical example, composed by a woman who was a nurse to Maha Pajapati, the Buddha's foster mother, the one who asked him to establish an order of nuns so that women could have an equal chance of enlightenment with monks. When the finally agreed to allow nuns to leave their home and family and to devote themselves fulltime to religion, Maha Pajapati became the first nun and her old nurse Vaddhesi also renounced the world, but with less successful results. This is a poem that her nurse said:

> For five-and-twenty years since I came forth,
> Not for one moment could my heart attain
> The blessedness of calm serenity.
> No peace of mind I found. My every thought
> Was soaked in the fell drug of sense-desire.

> With outstretched arms and shedding futile tears
> I retreated, a wretched woman, to my cell.

This is a sad poem; I'm struck by the sincerity and the poignancy of this woman's spiritual quest. Twenty-five years is a long time to try and fail day after day to calm one's mind and overcome desire. Meditation is hard; and perhaps among the desires that she couldn't quite master was the desire for enlightenment. Fortunately, the poem ends happily. Vaddhesi finally approached a nun whom she trusted and she shared her frustrations; and after being taught the dharma more clearly by this woman, the two of them sat down together to meditate. Over time, Vaddhesi was able to gain the peace and the enlightenment that the Buddha had promised.

A much more famous nun is Kisa Gotami whose story has been told and retold in many versions over the centuries; but it starts in the Therigatha, this collection of women's verse. Kisa Gotami came from a poor family, and because she was thin people made fun of her; they called her "Skinny Gotami." When she was married, people continued to jeer at her and her low origins; but after she gave birth to a son, then they started to treat her with some respect. Unfortunately, just when that son was able to run and play, he died; he became ill, and then passed away. Gotami, remembering how poorly she'd been treated before, suspected that people were plotting against her. Half mad with grief, she put her dead baby on her hip and then went from house to house asking for medicine to make him better. "Are you crazy?" people asked. "The child is dead." Finally, a kindly neighbor realized that Kisa Gotami was too distraught and grief-stricken to think clearly, and he suggested that she go ask the Buddha for medicine.

When Kisa Gotami found the Buddha and asked him for medicine for her sick child, he looked at the little corpse and he understood at once what was going on; and he told her to bring him some mustard seeds, but only from homes where no one had died. Again, she went from house to house, and although there were people who were willing to give her some mustard seeds, every family had lost someone to death; a parent, or an aunt or uncle, a sibling, or a child. At last her frenzy abated and she realized that the death of loved ones is a universal fact of existence; and she understood that that had been the Buddha's point. Her own grief wasn't unique; death is an inescapable part of life. Everyone suffers in this way; so she buried her son and then returned to the Buddha. He asked, "Have you got the mustard seed?" "No," she replied, "that medicine has already done its work," and then she asked to be ordained a nun. Kisa Gotami became a well-respected nun, and she was admired for her spiritual insight and her poetry; and in time she escaped the sorrows of this world and passed into nirvana.

The Dhammapada is the next text that we'll talk about. The title Dhammapada means "Verse of the Buddha's Teachings," and it's probably the most famous of all Theravada scriptures; and it also comes from the little texts section of the Sutra basket. Even though the Pali canon—remember those are the scriptures of the Theravada Buddhists—tends to be focused on monks, the Dhammapada has ethical advice and inspiration for all Buddhists. It consists of 423 verses divided into 26 sections, and it's relatively short; you can read the whole thing fairly carefully in just a couple of hours. There are no extended arguments, complicated doctrinal formulations, or lists of various principles or aspects of the dharma or such, so it's quite understandable; and because it was originally composed in Pali verse, with vivid images and repetitions, it was easy to memorize as well. It's been loved and memorized by Buddhists for over 2,000 years; and not just by Theravadans, but by Mahayana Buddhists as well. The prominence of the Dhammapada in Asia made it one of the first Buddhist texts to be translated into English. A partial translation appeared in 1840, but the first full translation into a Western language came in 1855; though in this case the Western language was Latin, and it was done by a Danish scholar, in fact. The first full translation into English was published in 1870, and the translation was done by Max Müller, the editor of the Sacred Books of the East. Since then, there have been more than 80 more English versions.

You can get a sense of the Dhammapada's contents by simply looking over the 26 section headings, which include titles like "Thought," "The Fool," "The Wise Man," "Old Age," "Self," "The World," "Happiness," "Pleasure," and "The Way." In general, the themes of the Dhammapada are moral action, observations about the fleeting nature of life, self-mastery, and warnings about desire. Some of its teachings refer to specifically Buddhist doctrines, such as the Four Noble Truths and the three refuges; but much of it might be applicable to almost anyone's life.

The Dhammapada tends to sound like a book of proverbs. Sometimes verses are paired, but usually they stand on their own. Buddhists have long considered each one a saying of the Buddha himself; and then later commentaries provided collections of anecdotes that they gave the story behind each of the sayings. For example, the tale of Kisa Gotami, which you just heard, was thought to have been the basis for verse number 287. After Kisa Gotami had come back to her right mind, buried her son, and returned to the Buddha, he told her, and this is the verse from the Dhammapada, "As a great flood carries off a sleeping village, death carries off the person whose mind is distracted, intoxicated by possessions and by children."

But the aphorisms work well on their own, even without the stories; and the stories may or may not be accurate as to their origins. Because the Dhammapada is so accessible and so quotable, I thought I'd give you a representative verse for seven major topics taken in the order in which they appear in the text; and just for fun, I'll use a different English translation for each quote. First, on the dangers of giving in to desire, this saying: "He who lives looking for pleasures only, his senses uncontrolled, immoderate in his food, idle, and weak, Mara (the tempter) will certainly overthrow him, as the wind throws down a weak tree." You can see an image there, an image that might stay in one's mind. The second theme is about disciplining one's mind: "The wise man guards his mind which is unruly and ever in search of pleasure. The mind well guarded brings great happiness." A third theme is about the impermanence; that everything's changing all the time. The quote is:

> A fool is troubled thinking,
> "I have sons, I have wealth"
> but even himself doesn't belong to himself—
> let alone sons, let alone wealth.

Can you see what's happening there? If your mind is caught up in possessions and in family, you're troubled by those, you're worried about those, but those aren't going to last forever; it's a mistake to dwell on those and worry about them.

A fourth theme from the Dhammapada is karma; so this quote: "Whoever offends a harmless, pure and innocent person, the evil falls back on that fool, like the light dust thrown up against the wind." Fifth theme, about how we should treat others: "Conquer anger through gentleness, unkindness through kindness, greed through generosity, and falsehood by truth." You can see how these are sort of general principles that might be applicable to anyone, not just to Buddhists. A sixth theme is the superiority of Buddhism; this is going to be a little more specific to the religious tradition: "The best of paths is the path of eight. The best of truths, the four sayings. The best of states, freedom from passions [basically nirvana]. The best of men, the one who sees." You can hear those references to the Four Noble Truths and the Eightfold Path.

> The seventh theme is individual effort; so the quote says:
> It is you who must make the effort.
> The masters [that is, the Buddhas] only point the way.
> But if you meditate
> And follow the law
> You will free yourself from desire.

I want to follow up on this last point. One of the things that's most striking about Theravada Buddhism is that it's not a savior religion. The Buddha can't rescue anyone from the consequences of karma. He can't give someone else enlightenment; it's something that each person has to do for him or herself. The Buddha can only show the way. There's a tough-minded realism here that I think might be attractive to some people in our own scientific, skeptical age. Don't misunderstand me: Buddhism is an ancient religion, and in the very earliest texts there's plenty of talk of miracles, gods, demons, and superhuman powers; but there's also a streak of practical empiricism that's worth considering, and it's perhaps most evident in our last Theravada sutra, the Discourse to the Kalamas, in which the Buddha argues against blind faith and dogmatism.

This sutra begins with Ananda reciting, "Thus have I heard," and then he tells the story of a time when the Buddha, traveling on foot with a large number of monks, arrived at the town of Kesaputta. The inhabitants there of the Kalama clan came out to greet him, for they'd heard reports of the Buddha's wisdom and of his spiritual attainment. But they had a question: There had been many holy men—so ascetics and sages—who'd come through their town, and each of those guys had praised his own doctrines while disparaging and condemning the teachers of others. "So," they asked, "how can we tell the difference between who's right and who's wrong? How can we tell the difference between truth and falsehood?" The first thing that the Buddha says is that it's appropriate to have doubts or be perplexed; and that in itself is probably worth noting, since some religions put such a premium on knowledge and faith that questioning itself is sometimes discouraged. Not so with Buddhism; the Buddha says "Question away, it's the right thing to do." Then he continued with these famous words; the Buddha said:

> Do not accept a thing by recollection [that's by repeated hearing], by tradition, by mere report, because it is based on the authority of scriptures, by mere logic or inference, by reflection on conditions, because of reflection on or a fondness for a certain theory, because it merely seems suitable, nor thinking "The religious wanderer is respected by us."

I know that was sort of a long quote with lots of reasons why you shouldn't believe something that someone says; but doesn't that cover most of the sources for religious belief? What's left outside of that? It's one of those Buddhist lists that seem to be comprehensive; to get all of the main options.

Then the Buddha switches things up a bit by telling them how they can know not what to accept, but what to reject. He says: "But when you know for yourselves: 'These things are unwholesome, blameworthy, reproached by the wise, when undertaken and performed lead to harm and suffering—these you should reject.'" In other words, he tells them that they should base their beliefs on personal experience and direct observation; if something isn't working, then don't do it.

He follows up by introducing them to the Buddhist doctrine of the Three Poisons; that suffering and sorrow in this world have three basic roots: greed, hatred, and ignorance. That's a very smart list. Think of all of the problems that result from those three things: greed, hatred, and ignorance. Even if you're not a Buddhist, he's got a point. The Buddha then gives several examples of these negative kinds of things; and then he asks, "Don't you know from your own experience that these three states of mind are trouble?" The Kalama clan agrees with that. Then the Buddha doubles back and suggests that they can know what to accept by looking for the opposites: "Look for things that are wholesome, unblameworthy, commended by the wise, that when put into practice lead to benefit and happiness. These are the sorts of things that will lead to an untroubled mind, pure and free from hatred." To paraphrase what's going on here, the Buddha says that you don't have to believe his teachings because they're traditional or because they're scriptural, or because they're popular or they're reasonable, or because the Buddha himself is a great guy. Instead, you should try out the practices that he recommends; try out the five precepts (remember, no killing, no stealing, no sexual immorality, no lying and no intoxicants); try out kindness, and meditation (there's lots of instruction about how to meditate); try out self-mastery and detachment and see if they bring good results. In fact, the Buddha goes on to say that whether there's an afterlife or not, this is still a good way to live; you can know that by your own experience.

Similarly, as we saw in the last lecture, the rules for monks and nuns aren't presented as revelation coming from on high; rather, the Buddha was making them up as he went along. It wasn't arbitrary; he had good reasons for it. He's an intelligent, insightful sort of fellow; but he was making them up in response to particular situations that came up. The Buddha was very wise, of course; but they're not to be seen as absolute commandments. They're training rules; they're sort of like the rules that athletes might voluntarily undertake while they're getting ready for a season. If you follow these precepts, you can make spiritual progress; and if not, you'll be entangled into suffering and samsara for a while longer.

It seems like Buddhism is a religion that would be well suited for our modern Western ideas of individual autonomy; for the freedom to choose or to act, to decide for ourselves. But then the Buddha undercuts it all with a paradox when he suggests that in the end, there's actually no self that chooses or acts; and later Buddhists in the Mahayana tradition will heighten the contradictions by arguing that actually there's no nirvana, no samsara, no salvation, and even no Buddha. But that's for the next lecture.

Mahayana Sutras
Lecture 16

The Mahayana division of Buddhism, predominant in East Asia, is the largest today. Mahayana Buddhists worship the Buddha as a god, look to bodhisattvas for assistance, and think that enlightenment can be attained by ordinary believers—not just monks and nuns—in this lifetime. This form of Buddhism had its origins between 100 B.C.E. and 100 C.E., when new sacred texts began to appear anonymously, texts that offered a slightly different take on the teachings of the Buddha. The origins of Mahayana Buddhism may have had something to do with the decision to commit the Theravada scriptures to writing in the 1st century B.C.E., giving the texts more of an independent life and making them more accessible to laypersons.

Perfection of Wisdom Sutras
- The earliest Mahayana sutras were concerned with the perfection of wisdom. These claimed to offer deeper insights into the meaning of the Buddha's teachings, or dharma. The first of these texts seems to have been the Sutra of Perfect Wisdom in 8,000 Lines. There were later versions in 18,000 lines, 25,000 lines, and even 100,000 lines.

- These sutras all purport to convey the words of the Buddha, and they explain the ways in which being a bodhisattva is superior to being a disciple. Ordinary disciples are assumed to simply want to gain enlightenment and escape the cycle of suffering for themselves, while bodhisattvas become enlightened and then renounce nirvana until they have assisted every other sentient being in attaining the same liberation. They undertake this great act of self-sacrifice for the good of others, exhibiting "perfect compassion."

- Six perfections characterize bodhisattvas: perfect generosity, perfect morality, perfect patience, perfect exertion, perfect meditation, and perfect wisdom. Taking a vow to become a bodhisattva is enough to get one started on the bodhisattva path and to begin working on the perfections. The idea is to aim for enlightenment but not for selfish reasons; instead, bodhisattvas seek to end the suffering of all beings throughout the universe.

- Perfect wisdom, which is attained by meditation rather than by logical analysis, means seeing thing as they actually are. In Mahayana Buddhism, this means recognizing that reality is beyond language and beyond such human concepts as being and nonbeing.
    o Indeed, nothing has a "self-existence," or a permanent identity or form. Instead, meditation leads one to an intuitive understanding that all things are intrinsically empty—empty of a permanent essence or self-existence. There's nothing really there, which means that there is nothing to hold on to or desire.

    o Taken to its logical limit, perfect wisdom means that there is ultimately no such thing as the Buddha, the Eightfold Path, bodhisattvas, or even enlightenment. All such phenomena are empty.

- Sometimes, the wisdom sutras can be rather obtuse, and they're often quite long. It seems paradoxical to use ever more words to try to explain something that is ultimately beyond words, but some interesting insights emerge from the sutras. If, in the end, everything is emptiness, then there is really no difference between things for which we make human distinctions. This is the doctrine of nonduality, which is illustrated in a story from the famous Vimalakirti Sutra (c. 100 C.E.).
    o Vimalakirti was a layperson who taught the dharma so authoritatively that the Buddha sent some of his disciples to talk with him. Through a series of dialogues, we see that Vimalakirti's understanding surpasses theirs and, indeed, is equaled only by that of the Buddha himself. These debates were witnessed by disciples, bodhisattvas, gods, and goddesses.

- At one point, a goddess showers heavenly flowers on all the spectators. Those that hit the bodhisattvas bounce off and fall to the floor, but they stick to the bodies of the Theravada monks. The goddess explains that the disciples still make distinctions between worldly and unworldly things, but because the bodhisattvas have gone beyond those conceptual categories, they are indifferent to the flowers and, thus, nothing sticks to them. Similarly, there is ultimately no difference between life and death, enlightened and unenlightened beings, even samsara (reincarnation) and nirvana (extinction).

- Later on in the sutra, Vimalakirti challenges 32 bodhisattvas to explain nonduality, and they all take a turn, each trying to best the one before. Finally, Vimalakirti offers his contribution, which is to say nothing, and Manjusri, a bodhisattva famous for his transcendent wisdom, says, "Excellent! This is indeed the entrance into the nonduality of the bodhisattvas. Here there is no use for syllables, sounds, and ideas" (Thurman, 77).

Reactions: Lotus Sutra

- There were several reactions to the new Mahayana Buddhist texts. The first was puzzlement: Where did these new scriptures come from? And how can they possibly be the words of the Buddha, given that they have appeared 500 years after his death?
  - Mahayana monks offered various explanations. These were the higher teachings of the Buddha, they said, which he entrusted only to his most advanced disciples, and they had been hidden away until the present age.

  - Another explanation was that the new scriptures had been heard and preserved by celestial bodhisattvas (rather than Ananda), who were now revealing them.

- Not everyone found these explanations convincing, but over time, the Mahayana sutras became more accepted, along with the distinctive doctrines of infinite compassion, bodhisattvas, multiple buddhas in multiple worlds, the buddha nature that is within each of us, the emptiness of all phenomena, and the three bodies of the Buddha: a transformation body (physical, historical Siddhartha Gautama), an enjoyment body (the heavenly buddha that oversees pure lands and whom believers see in visions), and a dharma body (the ultimate nature of reality, omnipresent truth body, with no limits or boundaries).

- Some sutras, such as the Lotus Sutra, asserted that Siddhartha Gautama had become a buddha eons ago, but he came to earth and pretended to be disillusioned with his princely life, gave it up, pretended to gain enlightenment, and then only seemed to die and enter nirvana—all for the benefits of others. This sort of theologizing answers some questions, but it created other problems.

- As the Mahayana sutras multiplied, so did the contradictions in their teachings. How could a Buddhist make sense of it all? The

The Lotus Sutra asserts Siddhartha Gautama was already a buddha when he came to earth and only pretended to gain enlightenment and reach nirvana for the benefit of others.

Lotus Sutra provided an answer in the famous parable of the burning house.

- Once there was a wealthy man who had many young sons, and they all lived in a large house with only one exit. One day, the house caught fire. The man managed to get his sons out by promising that he had presents for them outside the gate.

- A disciple of the Buddha explained that the man had not exactly lied to his sons because he gave each of them something much better than they could have imagined. This was not a case of telling falsehoods as much as using "expedient devices." Out of compassion, the man tailored his message to each son so that he could save them all.

- The Buddha himself goes on to explain that this life is like a burning house, and he came into the world to save people from "the fires of birth, old age, sickness and death, care, suffering, stupidity, misunderstanding, and the three poisons." But most people are so caught up in their day-to-day concerns and activities that they have no idea what danger they're in.

- Thus, he offers them three vehicles: that of the *arhat*, or disciple (basically, Theravada Buddhism); that of the solitary Buddha; and that of the bodhisattva (Mahayana). Each message appeals to different types of people, but in the end, they all receive the same wondrous gift of enlightenment.

- The moral of the tale is that the Buddha may have told some disciples one thing and other disciples another—his words may seem contradictory—but his teachings are all nevertheless part of one great truth, the truth of Mahayana Buddhism, the One Vehicle.

More Reactions: Diamond and Heart Sutras

- Even if the theological contradictions could be resolved, there remained the practical problem of a canon that includes hundreds of books, some of them quite long. Even monks and nuns couldn't master them all, and for Mahayana Buddhism, with its new emphasis on the spiritual progress of laypersons, the problem was even more acute.

- One response was to pick out a few sutras that were considered particularly insightful or advanced and focus on them as a sort of canon within the canon. Different schools of Buddhism championed different texts, but in East Asia, the Lotus Sutra became the most popular and widely read of the sacred texts of Buddhism.
    o The Lotus Sutra was originally compiled in the 1st century C.E. It was first translated from Sanskrit into Chinese in the 3rd century, then again much more accurately in the early 5th century, after which it became very popular, especially in Japan.

    o In China, it was adopted as the key scripture of the Tiantai school of Buddhism, which then spread to Japan as the Tendai school. In Japan, it was adopted by the imperial family and cultural elites, and its message was spread though art, music, sermons, ritual performances, protective charms, and Noh drama.

    o Eventually a 13th-century Japanese monk named Nichiren made the Lotus Sutra the center of his new form of Buddhism and taught his followers to look to it for salvation. The practices of Nichiren are still followed today in a Japanese lay Buddhist movement called Soka-gakkai.

- Another tactic, rather than focusing on a single text, was to try to distill the expanding versions of the perfection of wisdom sutras into something much shorter and more portable. Thus, for example, rather than the Perfection of Wisdom in 18,000 Lines, we find the Diamond Sutra, which is about the size of a pamphlet.
    o This sutra consists of a dialogue between the Buddha and a disciple, in which the Buddha explains repeatedly that the ordinary ways of thinking about Buddhism are undercut by the realization that all things are emptiness.

- o The Heart Sutra goes even further, reducing the Buddha's esoteric wisdom to a single page, which is recited daily by monks and lay Buddhists throughout East Asia.

- Mahayana sutras are often associated with what scholars term "the cult of the book." These texts were regarded as sacred objects, almost apart from their actual contents. They were seen as physical manifestations of the Buddha, and copying, reciting, reading, hearing, explaining, or even holding them were regarded as actions that brought great merit. The paradox here is worth noting: Mahayana scriptures are objects of veneration and care, but they have no ultimate value—the goal is to move beyond them.

Suggested Reading

Conze, trans., *The Large Sutra of the Perfect Wisdom*.

Lopez, *The Story of Buddhism*.

Strong, ed. and trans., *The Experience of Buddhism*.

Teiser and Stone, eds., *Readings of the Lotus Sutra*.

Thurman, *The Holy Teaching of Vimalakirti*.

Tsai, trans., *Lives of the Nuns*.

Watson, trans., *The Lotus Sutra*.

Williams, *Mahayana Buddhism*.

Questions to Consider

1. Why did the Buddhist canon of scripture expand dramatically some 400 years after the death of the Buddha?

2. How did Buddhists deal with a collection of sacred texts so large that it was difficult to read, let alone master, in a single lifetime?

Mahayana Sutras
Lecture 16—Transcript

The largest number of Buddhists today belong to the Mahayana division, which is predominant in East Asia. In contrast to Theravada Buddhism, which was the subject of the previous lecture, Mahayana Buddhists worship the Buddha as a god, they look to bodhisattvas for assistance, and they consider enlightenment something that can be attained by ordinary believers in this lifetime, not just monks and nuns.

This form of Buddhism had its origins sometime between 100 B.C.E. and 100 C.E., but there's no founder of Mahayana Buddhism. Instead, there are new sacred texts that begin to appear anonymously in India during those centuries. These texts offered a slightly different take on the teachings of the Buddha. Some monks accepted these new writings as authoritative and scriptural and others didn't, though they recited the same Vinaya, like the Pratimoksha that we talked about before; they recited that same Pratimoksha together and then often lived side by side in the same monasteries. For a long time, Mahayana Buddhism was a minority movement.

It may be that the origins of Mahayana Buddhism had something to do with the decision to commit the Theravada scriptures to writing in the 1st century B.C.E. Remember that written sacred texts were something of an innovation in India at the time. Hindus and early Buddhists had long held to the superiority of scriptures that were memorized and handed down from teacher to disciple, or from monk to monk, and then recited aloud. Transmitting oral texts through the centuries was definitely a collective project, with monks constantly teaching each other; they were memorizing and chanting, and then they were correcting the recitations as they were being made. A scripture needed to achieve widespread acceptance and consensus in order to survive. It has to be memorized and that takes time, and monks do that together.

But writing gave texts more of an independent life. A single monk working alone could create and refine a lengthy sutra, and then it could be spread far and wide without having to be memorized; that is, without having to be transmitted slowly, laboriously, and personally from a teacher to a student. A text that doesn't have to be memorized may lose something in immediacy, but it gains a great deal in portability, and it becomes much more accessible to laypersons who don't have the luxury of being able to study scripture and meditate fulltime. Altogether, there are about a hundred major Mahayana Sutras.

The earliest Mahayana Sutras were concerned with the "perfection of wisdom." These writings claimed to offer deeper insights into the meaning of the Buddha's teachings or dharma. The first of the texts seems to have been the Sutra of Perfect Wisdom in 8,000 Lines; so that's a pretty good-sized book. But there were later versions of the Sutra of Perfect Wisdom in 18,000 Lines, and then one in 25,000 lines, and there was even a version in 100,000 lines, which was actually a very repetitive version of this text. These sutras all purport to convey the words of the Buddha; they all start out "Thus I have heard. When the Buddha was staying at such and such a place," and then they go on. But then they explain how being a bodhisattva is superior to being a disciple. Ordinary disciples were assumed to simply want to gain enlightenment and escape from this cycle of suffering, death, birth, and death again—they wanted to escape from this cycle for themselves—while bodhisattvas become enlightened, and rather than moving on into nirvana they renounce that stage until they have assisted every other sentient being in attaining the same liberation. They undertake this great act of self-sacrifice, this staying in this world order, for the good of others, and hence they exhibit "perfect compassion."

There are actually six perfections that characterize bodhisattvas: The first is perfect giving; and then perfect morality; perfect patience; perfect exertion; perfect meditation; and then, finally, perfect wisdom. If these qualities seem utterly beyond you right now, then the sutras suggest that you can make a vow along the lines of something like "I vow that if I ever attain enlightenment, I won't immediately pass into nirvana but instead I promise that I will become a bodhisattva for the sake of others." Just that intention is enough to get a person started on the bodhisattva path, and then you can begin working on those perfections at whatever pace you can muster. Those are really lovely virtues. These are the kinds of lists that we encounter constantly in Buddhist texts, and they're worth thinking hard about: Is there anything missing from those six perfections? Is there any overlap? Do we need all six of them; are there any surprises there? Once again, the perfections that you'd be looking for as a future bodhisattva are giving, morality, patience, exertion, meditation, and wisdom. The point is that you'd, by making that vow, be aiming for enlightenment not for selfish reasons, not to free yourself from hardships and from sorrow, but rather in order to end the suffering of all beings throughout the universe.

"Perfect wisdom," and I'm talking now about something that's attained by meditation rather than by logical analysis, means seeing thing as they actually are. In Mahayana Buddhism, this means recognizing that reality is beyond language and beyond human concepts such as "being" and "non-being." Indeed, nothing has a self-existence or a permanent identity or form. Instead, by meditating, one can come to an intuitive understanding that all things are intrinsically empty; that is to say, they're empty of a permanent essence or self-existence. There's really nothing there, which means that there's nothing to hold onto and there's nothing to desire. You can see how this would tie into the Third Noble Truth. Remember that suffering comes from desire, and the Third Noble Truth is that if you stop desire you can stop suffering; and if you realize that there's really nothing to desire and no being that actually has desires, then it would be easier to bring those desires to a cessation. Indeed, taken to its logical limit, perfect wisdom says that there's ultimately no such thing as the Buddha, the eight-fold path, bodhisattvas, or even enlightenment. All such phenomena are empty. They're all caused by other things, and they only have temporary existence.

Sometimes these perfection of wisdom texts can be rather obtuse, and they often go on and on. For example, here's an excerpt that relies on a pun. In Sanskrit, the word *perfection* is *paramita*, and it means "to have gone to the other side, or beyond." Now the quotation:

> What then is the perfection of wisdom? With regard to the perfection of wisdom there is nothing on this or on yonder shore. If one could, with regard to the perfection of wisdom, apprehend this or yonder shore, the Tathagata [meaning the Buddha] would explain this or yonder shore of the perfection of wisdom; since, however, this shore of the perfection of wisdom cannot be apprehended, one cannot explain its beyond either.

It's a paradox, to use more and more words to try to explain something that's ultimately beyond words; but there are some interesting insights that come from this type of analysis. If everything in the end is emptiness, then they're all, from an ultimate perspective, equivalent. There's really no difference between the things that we make human distinctions about, that we get so wrapped up about. This is the doctrine of non-duality, which is illustrated in a story from a famous Mahayana sutra called the Vimalakirti Sutra (it was written about 100 C.E.). The Vimalakirti was a layperson (not a monk, but a lay Buddhist) who taught the dharma so authoritatively that the Buddha sent some of his disciples to go talk with him. Through a series of dialogues, we see that Vimalakirti's understanding surpasses theirs, and indeed is only equaled by that of the Buddha himself. These debates are witnessed by disciples, by bodhisattvas, by gods, and by goddesses.

At one point, a goddess showers heavenly flowers upon all the spectators. Those that hit the bodhisattvas simply bounce off and they fall to the floor, but they stick to the bodies of the Theravada monks. One of the most advanced of these monks, named Sariputra, tries to pull off these blossoms—since monks aren't allowed to wear decorative items, remember that from the Vinaya—but he can't pull them off; and when he asks the goddess why this is, she explains that the disciples still make distinctions between worldly and unworldly things, but because the bodhisattvas have gone beyond these conceptual categories, because they realize that all things are empty, they're completely indifferent to the flowers and thus none of this sticks to them. Similarly, there's ultimately no difference, no real difference, between life and death, between enlightened and unenlightened beings, or even between samsara (reincarnation) and nirvana (extinction).

Shortly thereafter (we're still in this Vimalakirti Sutra), when Sariputra asks her (the goddess) why she doesn't give up her female form—he assumes that women would want to be men if they had the power to choose, so he says "Why are you still in female form if you can do anything?"—and she responds not with words but by switching bodies with Sariputra who, as a monk who's been restraining his desires for many years, finds it very disconcerting to suddenly be within a female body. The goddess explains that gender is emptiness as well, and quotes the Buddha as saying, "In all things, there is neither male nor female." Later on in the sutra, Vimalakirti challenges 32 bodhisattvas to explain non-duality (that sort of difficult concept); and they all take a turn, each trying to best the last one. Finally, Vimalakirti himself offers his contribution, which is to say nothing; and Manjusri, a bodhisattva famous for his transcendent wisdom, says, "Excellent! This is indeed the entrance into the non-duality of the bodhisattvas. Here there is no use for syllables, sounds, and ideas."

There were several reactions to these sorts of Mahayana Buddhist texts. The first was simply puzzlement: Where do these new scriptures come from, and how can they possibly be the words of the Buddha, seeing as how they've only just now appeared, 500 years after his death? Mahayana monks offered various explanations. They said these were the higher teachings of the Buddha that he entrusted only to his most advanced disciples, and they'd been hidden away safely in heaven, or in earthly caves, or even in the underwater palaces of dragon spirits until the present age and now, at last, they've come forth. Or, they might say while the Theravada sutras were heard and remembered by Ananda, these new scriptures were heard and preserved by celestial bodhisattvas, who are now revealing them again. For instance, the second chapter of the Lotus Sutra recounts how just as the Buddha was about to teach the full dharma, 5,000 monks, nuns, laymen, and laywomen got up and just left because they were unable to comprehend his words. He kept speaking, and they weren't around to hear it, but there were still numberless heavenly beings, bodhisattvas and buddhas in multiple worlds, who heard the Buddha at that time, and they preserved his words in a line of supernatural transmission quite different from the memorizing monks behind the Theravada scriptures. Thus, monks in deep meditation might hear these teachings directly from celestial beings, from bodhisattvas, which they beheld in visions.

Not everybody found these explanations convincing. An early Mahayana sutra reports the reactions of its critics—so it's going to talk about people who are complaining about this sutra—and it says, "These [monks] are arrogant. ... It is a great wonder indeed that they should give the name of 'sutra' to that which was not spoken by the Buddha, that which they made themselves and is a poetic invention, that which is a motley of words and syllables." Of course, that sutra will go on to talk about how those criticisms aren't correct; but they're acknowledging the fact that not everybody was on board with these new Mahayana sutras when they first appeared.

Nevertheless, over time, the Mahayana sutras became more accepted, along with their distinctive doctrines of infinite compassion, of bodhisattvas, of multiple buddhas in multiple worlds, of the buddha-nature that is within each of us, the emptiness of all phenomena, and the three bodies of the Buddha. This is a theological innovation by which the Buddha can be thought to have gone into nirvana and thus be inaccessible to anyone in this world, but still the Buddha can be somebody that you pray to. The idea here is that the Buddha has three bodies: The first is a transformation body, this is the physical, historical Siddhartha Gautama; the second is an enjoyment body, which is a heavenly Buddha who oversees pure lands and that believers can see in vision; and then the dharma body is the third body of the Buddha, and this is the ultimate nature of reality, it's omnipresent, it's everywhere, it's the Buddha's truth body with no limits or boundaries. Indeed, some sutras, such as the Lotus Sutra, asserted that Siddhartha Gautama had become a Buddha eons ago, but he came to earth and then pretended to be disillusioned with his princely life; he gave that up and then pretended to gain enlightenment, and then only then seemed to die and enter nirvana, all for the benefit of others. As the scholar Donald Lopez puts it, "this was all a performance designed to inspire the world." It's an example of a concept we'll come to a little later in the lecture called "skillful means."

This sort of theology answers some questions—how can one expect help from the Buddha if he's already passed into Nirvana, for example—but it created some other problems. As the Mahayana sutras multiplied, so did the contradictions in their teachings. How could a Buddhist make sense of it all? The Lotus Sutra provided an answer in the famous parable of the burning house. I'll just note for a moment: The Lotus Sutra is probably the most significant sutra in East Asian Buddhism; it's a primary scripture in several types of Buddhism that we'll hear about in just a little bit with distinctive teachings about salvation, Buddhahood, proper worship, and there are lots of parables, and this parable of the burning house is probably the most famous of those.

The story is that there was once a wealthy man who had many young sons, and they all lived in a large house that had only one exit. One day the house caught fire. The father saw the danger, but his sons were happily playing games and entertaining themselves, and the father realized that they wouldn't understand his warnings and that he couldn't physically go and grab them all and get them out of the house in time. So he told them that he had presents for them outside the gate; and knowing their childish desires, some of them he promised a cart that was pulled by a goat, and others he promised carts pulled by deer, and still others an ox-cart (if we were going to update this for the modern world he might promise some of these kids tricycles, and some bicycles, and some pickup trucks depending how old they were). This promise of some carts, some vehicles, outside the gate got their attention, and all the boys rushed out of the burning house. When they saw their father, he gave them all ox carts; in our modern translation, that would be like he gave them all sports cars, Maseratis or something. Then the Buddha, after telling this story, asked his disciple, Sariputra, "Did this man lie to his sons?" Sariputra answers, "Not exactly; he got them all out of the burning house and he gave each of them something much better than what they could've imagined." It's not telling falsehoods so much as it's a case of what Buddhists call "expedient devices" or "skilful means." In other words, the Buddha took whatever action was necessary to get the job done. Out of compassion, he tailored his message to each son so that he could save them all.

Perhaps you can see where this is going, especially if you remember that the term *Mahayana* means "great vehicle." The Buddha goes on to explain that this life is like a burning house, and he came into the world to save people from, as the sutra says, "the fires of birth, old age, sickness and death, care, suffering, stupidity, misunderstanding, and the three poisons [desire, anger, and delusion or ignorance]." But most people are so caught up in their day-to-day concerns and activities that they have no idea what danger they're in; they don't understand the urgency and the need for them to be rescued and saved. So the Buddha offers people three vehicles: that of the *arhat* or disciple, and that's basically Theravada Buddhism where you hear the teachings of the Buddha and then individually try to put it into practice by becoming a monk or a nun and then hopefully gaining nirvana; the second vehicle is that of the solitary Buddhas (these are pretty rare), these are people who kind of figure out the Four Noble Truths on their own and then go into nirvana; and then that of the bodhisattva, this is the Mahayana vehicle, which will allow great numbers of people to gain salvation. Each message applies to different types of people, but in the end they all receive the same wondrous gift of enlightenment, of liberation from suffering. The moral of the tale is that the Buddha may have told some disciples one thing and other disciples another thing—so his words may seem contradictory—but his teachings are all nevertheless part of one great truth: the truth of Mahayana Buddhism, the one vehicle. So the Theravada scriptures aren't wrong; it's just that the truths they contain are only partial.

But even if the theological contradictions could be resolved, at least to some degree, there remains the practical problem of a canon that includes hundreds of books, some of them quite long. Even monks and nuns who spent a lifetime in study couldn't master them all; and for Mahayana Buddhism, with its new emphasis of the spiritual progress of laypersons with families and jobs, the problem was even more acute. One response was to pick out a few sutras that were considered particularly insightful or advanced and then focus on them as a sort of canon within the canon. Different schools of Buddhism championed different texts, but in East Asia the Lotus Sutra became the most popular and most widely read of the sacred texts of the Buddhism.

The Lotus Sutra was originally compiled in the 1st century C.E. It was first translated from Sanskrit into Chinese in the 3rd century, and then again much more accurately in the early 5th century, after which it became very popular, especially in Japan. In China, the Lotus Sutra was adopted as the key scripture of the Tiantai School of Buddhism, which then spread to Japan as the Tendai School. In Japan, it was adopted by the imperial family and cultural elites, and its message was spread though art, music, sermons, ritual performances, protective charms, and Noh drama, a very distinctive form of theater in Japan. Eventually, a Japanese monk named Nichiren—and he lived from 1222–1282; that makes him a contemporary of the Christian theologian Thomas Aquinas—made it the center of his new form of Buddhism; so much so that rather than reciting that traditional chant "Hail to the Lord Buddha" or "Homage to the Lord Buddha," Nichiren taught his followers to look to the Lotus Sutra for salvation and chant "Hail to the Lotus Sutra of the True

Dharma." Today, Soka-gakkai, a Japanese lay Buddhist movement that has some 12 million members around the world, continues this practice of giving homage to the Lotus Sutra. As a side note, the Lotus Sutra was the first Mahayana text translated in its entirety into a Western language; there was a French translation that was done in 1852.

Another tactic for dealing with this massive amount of sacred text in Mahayana Buddhism was rather than focusing on a single text, one could take the expanding versions of the Perfection of Wisdom sutras and try to distill the essence of them into something much shorter and more portable. These shorter Perfection of Wisdom texts started to appear between 300 and 500 C.E.; so rather than the Perfection of Wisdom in 18,000 or 25,000 lines, you get the Diamond Sutra, which is about the size of a pamphlet. You may remember a few lectures ago when I talked about a 9th-century copy of the Diamond Sutra that was found on the Silk Road at Dunhuang that was the world's oldest dated, printed book. This was also the text that the Chinese father burned as an offering to his small daughter who had died from smallpox.

The Diamond Sutra consists of a dialogue between the Buddha and his disciple Subhuti in which the Buddha explains again and again how the ordinary ways of thinking about Buddhism are undercut by the realization that all things are emptiness. The Buddha describes how a bodhisattva vows that he or she will lead all beings to final nirvana, but at the same time understands this; it says: "And yet, after I have thus delivered immeasurable beings, not one single being has been delivered." The Buddha continues, "And why? If, O Subhuti, a Bodhisattva had any idea of belief in a being, he could not be called a Bodhisattva. And why? He is not to be called a Bodhisattva, for whom there should exist the idea of a being, the idea of a living being, or the idea of a person." That is to say, someone with an enlightened mind knows that there are no selves to be liberated, no path to liberation, and no Buddha to show the way. There's nothing but emptiness.

The Heart Sutra goes even further, reducing this esoteric wisdom beyond ordinary comprehension to a single page, which is recited daily by monks and lay Buddhists throughout East Asia. It says, according to the Heart Sutra: "Form is emptiness and emptiness is form." Then checking off the five aggregates, the Four Noble Truths, and so forth, it pulls the rug out from under all of them. The Buddha tells Sariputra in the Heart Sutra:

> Where there is emptiness there is neither form, nor feeling, nor perception, nor impulse, nor consciousness; no eye, or ear, or nose, or tongue, or body, or mind; no form, nor sound, nor smell, nor taste, nor touchable, nor object of mind ... until we come to, there is no decay and death, no extinction of decay and death; there is no suffering, nor origination, nor stopping, nor path; there is no cognition, no attainment and no non-attainment.

It's hard to imagine what texts like these might've meant to the spirit of a recently deceased little daughter, but Mahayana sutras are often associated with what scholars term "the cult of the book." These texts were regarded as sacred objects, almost apart from their actual contents. They were seen as a physical manifestation of the Buddha; and copying them, reciting them, reading, hearing, explaining, or even holding them were regarded as actions that brought great merit. The Lotus Sutra promises that anyone who copies the text, or pays to have someone else copy it, will live a trouble-free life and after death will be reborn into a Buddhist paradise. The merit acquired from venerating these books could be transferred to others, and we saw an example of that in that oldest printed text where Hung Jen transferred the merit that he'd get for paying for the copy to be done to his deceased parents.

The Diamond Sutra makes it even easier. There are immeasurable benefits for anyone who receives, recites, and explains to others just these four lines of the text. The four lines say:

> All conditioned dharmas
> Are like dreams, illusions, bubbles, or shadows;
> Like drops of dew, or flashes of lightning;
> Thus should they be contemplated.

Just those four lines will get you a long way in your spiritual progress according to the Diamond Sutra.

You might be able to see a paradox here. Mahayana scriptures are objects of veneration and care—so there was incredible scholarly effort that went into studying, copying, translating, and printing such works—but ultimately they don't have value; the goal is to move beyond these texts. We'll see more of this in the next lecture when we take up Zen and Tibetan texts, but we can end with an example of what Mahayana sutras meant in the life of one particular Buddhist. This is a Chinese nun named Dào Yí, who lived in the 4th century. Her story is recorded in the Lives of the Nuns, a text that was compiled around 516 C.E., and that itself became part of the Chinese Buddhist Canon.

Dao Yi was married and then widowed at a young age; she was only 22. At that time, she decided that she'd become a nun; and because she was bright and gifted with an excellent memory, she was able to recite by heart the Lotus Sutra, the Vimalakirti Sutra, and the Smaller Perfection of Wisdom Sutra (all three of which I've mentioned in this lecture). She understood the doctrines behind them and was able to explain their nuances and their subtle meanings. Think of how unusual this level of learning and scholarship would've been for a woman in Ancient China, or anywhere in the ancient world for that matter.) When Dào Yí heard about a large project in the capital to collect, translate, and write commentaries on the Buddhist scriptures, she moved there and became an expert in the Vinaya (remember, those are the texts about regulations for monks and nuns). She gained esteem not only for her learning, but also her simple lifestyle and her humble demeanor.

Then the biography says this:

> When Dao-Yi was seventy-eight years old, she fell seriously ill. She even more fervently concentrated her mind and chanted the scriptures without becoming exhausted, but her disciples requested of her, "We wish that you would try to find a treatment for this disease so that you might overcome your debility." Dao Yi replied, "That is not a proper thing [for a Buddhist disciple] to say." As soon as she had spoken, she died.

To recover from personal tragedy (being in this case widowed at a young age), and then to live life fully and have the peace of mind to let go when the time comes, perhaps that indeed is the perfection of wisdom.

Pure Land Buddhism and Zen
Lecture 17

In 11th-century Japan, Buddhist monks had calculated that the year 1052 marked the beginning of a period when Buddhism would gradually decline. In response, people buried copies of sutras to preserve them for future generations. Among these sutras were the Lotus Sutra and the three Pure Land Sutras: the Larger Pure Land Sutra (or Sutra of Immeasurable Life), the Smaller Pure Land Sutra (or Amida Sutra), and the Sutra of Meditation on Amida Buddha. The message of these texts is that in a degenerate age, it's impossible to gain enlightenment through one's own efforts; thus, our only recourse is to rely on the grace of Amida Buddha (known as Amitabha in China), which means "infinite light."

Pure Land Sutras
- Mahayana Buddhism introduced the idea of multiple buddhas and bodhisattvas in other parts of the universe.
    - Some of these beings had created buddha-fields, or Pure Lands, and people of ordinary moral capacities or even grievous sinners could ask to be reborn in one of these celestial realms. The most famous of these was the Western Paradise of Amida, or the Land of Bliss.

    - This paradise is like heaven but not in the Christian sense because it doesn't last forever. Rather, it's a place where individuals can enjoy a pleasant environment in which to learn the dharma and gain enlightenment at their own pace; eventually, they will go directly from the Pure Land into nirvana.

- The Pure Land Sutras offer detailed accounts of the wonders of this region: filled with streams, flowers, fruits, bejeweled trees, parks, pools, and palaces. The air is filled with music and delightful fragrances, and everywhere, one hears the truths about

the six perfections, nonexistence, no-self, friendliness, compassion, sympathetic joy, and so forth.
- o The Pure Land Sutras are not particularly long texts, but there's enough detail that one can almost see the Pure Land—which is partly the point: These texts can be used as aids to meditation and visualization.

- o But the most prominent practice associated with Pure Land Buddhism is the *nembutsu*, that is, the invocation of Amida's name 10 times to achieve salvation.

- The Larger and Smaller Pure Land Sutras originated in India around 200 C.E., while the Meditation Sutra seems to have been written in Central Asia or China, but all these sutras gained their greatest popularity in medieval Japan during an era of political and spiritual crisis.
  - o A 12th-century Buddhist monk named Honen founded the Pure Land School when he encouraged his followers to disregard such traditional Buddhist practices as meditating, performing good works, and chanting scriptures and simply to focus on reciting the *nembutsu*.

  - o A generation later, Honen's disciple Shinran argued that true faith wouldn't feel the need for ceaseless repetitions; calling on Amida even once, in full sincerity, would be enough. Shinran gave up monasticism, married, and founded the True Pure Land school, perhaps the most widely practiced form of Buddhism in Japan today.

Zen Origins and Scriptures
- With so many scriptures in the Mahayana tradition advocating so many seemingly contradictory positions, some Buddhists looked for a more direct path to enlightenment. Zen focused on meditation under the personal guidance of someone who was already enlightened.

- The word *Zen* is a Japanese form of the Chinese *chan*, which in turn is derived from the Sanskrit *dhyana*, referring to a mind absorbed in meditation. The school had its origins in China, where Mahayana Buddhism was influenced by Daoism, especially its idea of wordless teaching. Legends trace its beginning to the Indian monk Bodhidharma, who came from the west to China in the early 5th century. He became known as the first patriarch.

- A famous definition of Zen is sometimes attributed to Bodhidharma, though it actually dates from several centuries later: "A special transmission outside the scriptures; / Without depending on words and letters; / Pointing directly to the human mind; / Seeing the innate nature, one becomes a Buddha."

- It is somewhat ironic that a religious tradition that is primarily inward looking and generally disregards scripture developed a body of authoritative sacred texts—scriptures—that eventually became part of the Chinese Buddhist canon.
    o The most famous of these texts is the Platform Sutra of the sixth patriarch, written about 780. This text is quite unusual because, unlike most sutras, it is not presented as the words of the historical Buddha or a bodhisattva. The Platform Sutra is a sermon given by the 7th-century Zen patriarch Huìnéng.

    o In this sermon, Huìnéng recounts that he was once an illiterate gatherer of firewood who happened to hear the Diamond Sutra being recited, and his mind was awakened. He traveled to a monastery, where he worked for eight months as help in the kitchen. When the fifth patriarch was about to die, he asked his disciples to write poems that would indicate the level of their spiritual progress. Everyone hesitated until finally, the head monk, Shenxiu, wrote a poem anonymously on a wall in the middle of the night.

    o Huìnéng realized that Shenxiu's poem, which offers a purification model of enlightenment, was insightful but didn't completely capture the whole truth. Huìnéng composed his own poem, suggesting that enlightenment comes from recognizing reality by seeing beyond the ordinary distinctions we make in life.

    o When the fifth patriarch saw Huinéng's poem, he recognized its profound understanding, and summoning Huinéng secretly, he explained the Diamond Sutra to him, gave him the robe of transmission and appointed him as his successor (the sixth patriarch), and then sent him away so as not to upset the monks.

- The Platform Sutra was written by later followers of Huinéng to defend his claims to leadership over those of Shenxiu. It is often regarded as promoting the idea of sudden enlightenment over gradual enlightenment, though some scholars have suggested that the Platform Sutra actually appears to transcend those theological distinctions and find room for both constant practice and liberating insight.

Zen Buddhism in Japan

- Zen became the dominant form of Buddhism in China in the 12th century, a time when Buddhist monks were traveling from Japan to China seeking the full dharma. Eventually, Zen declined in China with the rise of Neo-Confucianism, but it came into its own in Japan. Not only was its meditational and ethical discipline attractive to samurai, but its aesthetic sense became fundamental in Japanese art, music, drama, tea drinking, and even archery and swordsmanship.

- Two monks were chiefly responsible for bringing Zen to Japan: Eisai (late 12th century), who advocated the Rinzai school of sudden enlightenment, and Dogen (13th century), founder of the Soto school of gradual enlightenment. Both Zen traditions emphasized experiential understanding through meditation and downplayed scripture study, discursive thought, and philosophical analysis. Both schools also stressed the importance of the master-disciple relationship.

- o Monks would practice daily meditation and then have private interviews with their Zen teachers, who would evaluate and guide their practice.

- o These interviews often included rather cryptic exchanges, and Rinzai masters in particular were known for teaching through silence, shouting, or unexpected, even bizarre actions.

The aesthetic sense of Zen Buddhism has influenced many aspects of life in Japan, including gardening, art, and even swordsmanship.

- o Unlike the Soto school of gradual enlightenment, where students were encouraged to sit with an empty, calm mind, Rinzai teachers encouraged their disciples to meditate on koans—paradoxical sayings or narratives that could jolt one from ordinary modes of thinking.

- o Inevitably, stories of how famous Zen masters became enlightened and taught others were collected and canonized, along with classic examples of koans. Two of the most famous compilations are the *Blue Cliff Record* (12th century) and the *Gateless Barrier* (13th century).

- Despite its prominence in Japanese culture, Zen Buddhism is not uniquely Japanese; it's not the only type of Buddhism in Japan; it's not a major division of Buddhism; and it doesn't entirely reject doctrine or scriptures. Zen Buddhists believe that sacred texts are inadequate rather than worthless; a direct mind-to-mind transmission is needed for enlightenment.

Făxiăn's Pilgrimage

- Whether or not you believe that enlightenment or nirvana is accessible through meditation, calling upon Amida, or reciting the Diamond Sutra, clearly, the vast Buddhist canon asks and answers some of life's most profound questions: Is there a reality beyond ordinary existence? How does the mind shape and, perhaps, limit our perceptions of reality? What is the right balance between study and experience in learning something new? And, for our purposes, how important are sacred texts for gaining insight or wisdom?

- On the one hand, we have the Sutra of Perfect Enlightenment, much beloved by Zen Buddhists, which suggests that the scriptures can be a distraction. On the other hand, we have the example of such figures as Făxiăn, a Chinese monk who set out on a pilgrimage to India in 399 in search of authoritative Vinaya texts.
    o For at least two centuries, trade goods, along with the new religion of Buddhism, had been coming to China from unknown lands in the west. But the transmission of the religion was somewhat fragmentary. Although the Chinese had a number of Buddhist scriptures, the translations weren't good and the doctrines seemed contradictory.

    o In response to this situation, Făxiăn set off on foot, following the Silk Road through deserts and over mountains, crossing rivers, and at one point climbing down 700 ladders attached to cliffs. Făxiăn traveled through 30 different kingdoms in present-day China, Afghanistan, Pakistan, and India, visiting holy sites and studying with various teachers. Then he sailed home on ships that stopped at Sri Lanka and Indonesia, with his precious cargo of Buddhist relics, images, and scriptures.

    o At one point, a fierce storm arose, and Făxiăn's ship sprang a leak. The terrified merchants on the ship threw their goods and merchandise overboard to lighten the load. Făxiăn tossed his cup and wash basin into the sea, but he refused to part with anything else, praying fervently to the bodhisattva Guanyin to save the ship.

- o After 13 days, the voyagers finally reached a small island, and everyone survived. Eventually, Făxiăn made it back to China. Altogether, his journey took him 14 years and covered more than 8,000 miles. He spent the rest of his life translating into Chinese the Sanskrit texts he had so laboriously acquired, and he wrote an account of his travels, which itself became part of the Chinese Buddhist canon.

- Făxiăn's account of his visit to Vulture Peak, where the Buddha was thought to have taught the Lotus Sutra, is incredibly moving. Făxiăn realizes that all that remains in his era are "traces of the Buddha's presence," including the scriptures that preserve his words. But to Făxiăn, those sacred texts were worth a decade and a half of untold hardships and dangers, followed by a lifetime of meticulous study.

Suggested Reading

Chang, Chung-Yuan, trans., *Original Teachings of Ch'an Buddhism*.

Conze, et al., trans., *Buddhist Texts through the Ages*.

Gethin, *The Foundations of Buddhism*.

Inagaki and Steward, trans., *The Three Pure Land Sutras*.

Moerman, "The Death of the Dharma."

Olson, ed., *Original Buddhist Sources*.

Sekida, trans. and commentator, and Grimstone, ed., *Two Zen Classics*.

Questions to Consider

1. In what ways was Buddhism transformed when it became popular in Japan?

2. Why might a religion that explicitly rejects reliance on sacred texts, such as Zen Buddhism, eventually produce texts that are themselves revered?

Pure Land Buddhism and Zen
Lecture 17—Transcript

Hello, thanks for joining me again. In our last two lectures on Buddhism, we're going to focus on two regions where distinctive forms of the religion took root—in Japan and in Tibet—and along the way I'll try to dispel a few popular misconceptions. We can start with a little-known phenomenon.

In the 11th and 12th centuries, many people in Japan thought the world was coming to an end. This was a time of transition from imperial rule during the Heian Period to rule by the Shogun and warlords in the Kamakura Period, with their capital up near Tokyo. This was an age characterized by political upheaval, violence, destruction, and famine. Buddhist monks had calculated that the year 1052 marked the beginning of the last of the three long time periods predicted by the Buddha; this last one in which Buddhism itself would gradually decline and disappear.

During this third age, called Mappo, or "The Latter Day of the Law," people simply wouldn't be able to understand the dharma—that is, Buddhist teachings—and they certainly wouldn't be able to put them into practice. One response to these worries in medieval Japan was to bury copies of Buddhist sutras in mounds that looked like stupas—stupas are those traditional solid burial mounds that housed the relics of the Buddha—and indeed, these sacred texts were thought to be embodiments of the Buddha, just as much as a relic like a tooth or a finger bone might be that are inside these stupas; remember, stupas are solid, you don't go in them, there's just something buried inside. The sutras that were put inside were sometimes carved in stone, clay, bronze, and copper, but most often they were written on costly silks or indigo-dyed paper with inks of black, gold, or vermillion, sometimes mixed with blood. The paper and silk copies were placed inside ceramic, stone, or bronze containers; and all the sutras were then buried in underground chambers lined with rocks and then covered over with that earthen mound like a stupa. The idea was to preserve these sacred texts through the era of religious confusion until the time when a future Buddha would be able to use them to teach the Dharma once again to a receptive audience. In any case, it was thought that copying and preserving sutras were meritorious acts that would bring good karma; remember the cult of the book, from the last lecture. Over 200 of these sutra burial sites have been discovered all over Japan.

Then the question is: Which sutras were they transcribing and then hiding away for future generations? The most popular, of course, was the Lotus Sutra, which we talked about in a previous lecture; but also commonly buried were the three Pure Land Sutras. These are the Larger Pure Land Sutra that's sometimes called the Sutra of Immeasurable Life; then the Smaller Pure Land Sutra or the Amida Sutra; and finally, the Sutra of Meditation on Amida Buddha. These three texts constitute an alternative reaction to social breakdown and religious controversy. Their message is that the world is so corrupt and the scriptures are so hard to understand, and Buddhist principles are so difficult to put into practice, why even bother? Since in a degenerate age, it's impossible to gain enlightenment through one's own efforts, our only recourse is to rely on the grace of Amida Buddha—who's known in China as Amitabha—and that name means "infinite light."

Mahayana Buddhism had introduced the idea of multiple buddhas and bodhisattvas in other parts of the universe. Some of those beings had created buddha-fields or pure lands, and people of ordinary moral capacities, or even grievous sinners, could ask to be reborn not in this world of pain and sorrow—not to come back to this same world—but instead to be reborn in one of those celestial realms; and the most famous of those was the Western Paradise of Amida, or the Land of Bliss. It's like heaven, but not in the Christian sense, because it doesn't last forever. Rather, this Land of Bliss is a place where individuals can go—so you'll be reborn into this Buddhist paradise—and there you'll enjoy a pleasant environment in which to learn the dharma and to gain enlightenment at your own pace; and eventually beings reborn in the Pure Land will go directly from that paradise into nirvana, they won't pass go, they won't come back into this world.

The Pure Land Sutras offer detailed accounts of how wonderful this region is: It's lovely; it's fertile; it's filled with streams, flowers, fruits, and colorful bejeweled trees. There are beautiful parks, pools, and palaces. The air is filled with music and delightful fragrances. Everywhere one hears the truths about the six perfections: about non-existence and no-self; about friendliness, compassion, sympathetic joy, and so forth. Even the birds chirp the dharma it said, though these birds were magically conjured by Amida, they're not real birds. There are no animals in the Land of Bliss because those would be beings who'd been reborn in a lower karmic existence; only humans and gods exist in the Pure Land, and then maybe these illusions of birds. These Pure Land scriptures aren't terribly long texts; but there's enough detail that one can almost see the Pure Land in one's mind's eye, which is part of the point, these texts can be used as aids to meditation and visualization.

But the most prominent practice associated with Pure Land Buddhism is the *nembutsu*. Let me explain that term. The Larger Pure Land Sutra enumerates the 48 vows that Amida took in a previous lifetime before he became a bodhisattva; and the 18th of those vows states, "If, when I attain Buddhahood, sentient beings in the lands of the ten directions who sincerely and joyfully entrust themselves to me, desire to be born in my land, and call my Name even ten times, should not be born there, may I not attain perfect enlightenment." Whoever you are, whatever you've done, if you call on Amida 10 times in sincerity, then you're in; and the customary prayer to say is "Namu Amida Butsu," which is translated as "Hail to the Amida Buddha."

The Larger and Smaller Pure Land Sutras originated in India around 200 C.E., while the Meditation Sutra seems to have been written in Central Asia or in China; but it's in medieval Japan, in that era of political and spiritual crisis, it's there that they gained their greatest popularity. A 12th-century Buddhist monk named Honen founded the Pure Land School in Japan when he encouraged his followers to disregard traditional practices such as mediation, good works, and chanting scriptures and simply focus on reciting the *nembutsu*. If 10 times was the minimum—if someone calls on me 10 times in faith then Amida promises he'll save them—wouldn't 1,000 times be better just to hedge your bets? Or what about 1,000 times a day, or 10,000 times a day? Isn't rebirth in that Pure Land worth any effort? A generation later, Honen's disciple Shinran argued that true faith wouldn't feel the need for ceaseless repetitions—people started saying "Namu Amida Butsu" tens of thousands times a day—and he said calling on Amida even once in full sincerity would be enough. Shinran gave up monasticism, he married, and he founded the True Pure Land school; and this is perhaps the most widely practiced form of Buddhism in Japan today.

But the most famous type of Japanese Buddhism is probably Zen. Once again, it had its origins in China, and it also was a response to theological and scriptural perplexity. With so many scriptures in the Mahayana tradition advocating so many seemingly contradictory positions, some Buddhists looked for a more direct path to enlightenment. Zen Buddhism focused on meditation under the personal guidance of someone who himself or herself was already enlightened. The word *Zen* is a Japanese form of the Chinese *chan*, which in turn is derived from the Sanskrit *dhyana*; and that refers to a mind that's absorbed in meditation. The school had its origins in China, where Mahayana Buddhism was influenced by Daoism, especially in its idea of wordless teaching; and we'll hear more about Daoism in a future lecture. There were also legends that trace the beginning of this school to when the Indian monk Bodhidharma came from the West to China in the early 5th century. Bodhidharma became known as the first patriarch; and then this is important in Zen Buddhism: that there's a transmission lineage whereby the true teachings you can trace back to a teacher, who gets it from a teacher, from a teacher, all the way back to Bodhidharma.

A famous definition of Zen is sometimes attributed to Bodhidharma, though it actually dates from several centuries later. It says:

> A special transmission outside the scriptures;
> Without depending on words and letters;
> Pointing directly to the human mind;
> Seeing the innate nature, one becomes a Buddha.

It's a nice little description, and it talks about being beyond words and such, but it's ironic that a religious tradition that's primarily inward-looking, that generally disregards scripture itself developed a body of authoritative sacred texts; that is, there are Zen scriptures that eventually became part of the Chinese Buddhist canon.

The most famous of these scriptures is the Platform Sutra of the Sixth Patriarch, written about 780. This text is quite unusual because most sutras are presented as the words of the historical Buddha as heard and then recounted by Ananda or perhaps by a bodhisattva, a celestial being. This is true even of the Pure Land Sutras; they start out "Thus have I heard the Buddha is at a certain place and this is what he taught." The Platform Sutra, by contrast, is a sermon given by the 7th century by the Zen Patriarch Huineng. It doesn't even pretend to go back to Siddhartha Gautama. In this sermon, Huineng recounts how he was once an illiterate gatherer of firewood who happened to hear the Diamond Sutra being recited, and as he overheard this his mind was awakened. He travelled to a monastery, where he worked for eight months as help in the kitchen. When the Fifth Patriarch, who was in charge of the monastery, was about to die, he asked his disciples to write poems that would indicate the level of their spiritual progress. Everyone hesitated—they didn't really want to put themselves out there—and the finally the head monk, Shenxiu, eventually wrote a poem anonymously on a wall in the middle of the night (so he's going to try to sneak in something here), and his poem said this:

> The body is the tree of perfect wisdom,
> The mind is the stand of a bright mirror.
> At all times diligently wipe it.
> Do not allow it to become dusty.

The next morning, back in the kitchen, Huineng heard a boy recite this poem that had been found on this wall and that people had memorized; and Huineng realized that the verse was insightful, but it didn't seem to completely catch the whole truth. So Huineng composed his own poem and had somebody write it on the wall for him—remember that Huineng himself is illiterate—and Huineng's poem went this way:

> Fundamentally perfect wisdom has no tree.
> Nor has the bright mirror any stand.
> Buddha-nature is forever clear and pure.
> Where is there any dust?

So where the first poem offers a purification model of enlightenment through diligent practice—remember that it's wiping that mirror and keeping it clean—Huineng's poem suggests that enlightenment comes from recognizing reality, by seeing beyond the ordinary distinctions that we make in life; and that realization can come quickly, in a manner reminiscent of the perfection of wisdom sutras.

When the Fifth Patriarch saw Huineng's poem written there on the wall, he recognized its profound understanding, and then he summoned Huineng secretly. The Patriarch then explained the Diamond Sutra to Huineng, and he gave him the robe of transmission to show that he's his legitimate successor, and he appointed him as the next one in line (as the Sixth Patriarch), and then he sent him away. I think the idea was that he didn't want to upset the regular monks by promoting the kitchen help over them or by acknowledging the superiority of the understanding of the spiritual enlightenment of this illiterate young man. As you might imagine, this whole scripture, the Platform Sutra, was written by later followers of Huineng to defend his claims to leadership over those of Shenxiu, the monk who wrote the first poem. It's often regarded as promoting the idea of sudden enlightenment over gradual enlightenment, though some scholars have suggested that the Platform Sutra actually appears to transcend those theological distinctions and find room for both constant practice and for liberating insight.

The Platform Sutra continues for a couple dozen more pages explaining how meditation and wisdom can work together, how steady alertness should be matched by non-attachment, and how Zen understands Mahayana doctrines such as the three bodies of the Buddha, the bodhisattva vows, and perfect wisdom.

Zen became the dominant form of Buddhism in China in the 12th century at a time when Buddhist monks were traveling from Japan to China seeking the full dharma. Eventually, Zen declined in China with the rise of Neo-Confucianism (and we'll hear more about that philosophy in Lecture 21), but Zen really came into its own once it got to Japan. Not only was its meditational and ethical discipline attractive to samurai—samurai are that warrior class, and meditation is tough; it takes a lot of discipline, and the samurai respond to that—but also the aesthetic sense of Zen Buddhism became fundamental in Japanese art, music, and drama; in tea drinking; and even in archery and swordsmanship. In all of those art forms or activities, there's an emphasis on what's deliberate, spare, calm, and focused, and that's what's responded to in its connections with Zen Buddhism.

There were two monks who were chiefly responsible for bringing Zen to Japan: The first was Eisai, and he lived in the late 12th century, and he advocated the Rinzai school of sudden enlightenment; and the second monk was Dogen. He lived in the 13th century, and he's the founder of the Soto school of gradual enlightenment. Both Zen traditions emphasized experiential understanding through meditation and they downplayed scripture study, discursive thought, and philosophical analysis. Both schools also stressed the importance of the master-disciple relationship; so monks would practice daily meditation and then have regular private interviews with their Zen teacher, who could evaluate and guide their practice. These interviews often included rather cryptic exchanges, since enlightenment isn't something that can be attained through rational argument; and Rinzai masters—that's the sudden enlightenment school—in particular were known for teaching through silence, or shouting, or unexpected, even bizarre actions. Unlike the Soto school of gradual enlightenment where students were encouraged just to sit in the lotus position with an empty, calm mind, Rinzai teachers encouraged their disciples to meditate on koan. These are paradoxical sayings or narratives that could jolt one from ordinary modes of thinking.

Inevitably, stories of how famous Zen masters became enlightened and taught others were collected and then canonized. An example of this is the 30 volumes of something called the Transmission of the Lamp that was put together about 1004. Two of the most famous compilations are the 100 koan in the *Blue Cliff Record* from the 12th century, and the 48 koan of the *Gateless Barrier* in the 13th century. The *Gateless Barrier* is often known by its Japanese name, the *Mumonkan*. I'll give just one example from the *Mumonkan*, Koan Number Seven. It says this:

> A monk said to Joshu, "I have just entered this monastery. Please teach me." "Have you eaten your rice porridge?" asked Joshu. "Yes, I have," replied the monk. "Then you had better wash your bowl," said Joshu. With this the monk gained insight.

Clearly, this is more than just small talk about breakfast; something else much more profound is going on here. It's tempting to analyze this logically as a metaphor; to say, "Oh, that bowl must've represented his mind or his body, and the rice porridge maybe enlightenment or teachings," but I'm not sure that's quite the right way to go about all of this. This story somehow offers insight into ultimate reality. Somehow, the monk already has what he was looking for. The monk Mumon added this verse as a commentary to that particular story:

> It is too clear and so it is hard to see.
> A dunce once searched for a fire with a lighted lantern.
> Had he known what fire was,
> He could have cooked his rice much sooner.

It's kind of a striking image of somebody wandering around looking for fire when he has a flame within his lamp already; and the idea is that somehow this young monk who came to the monastery already had the enlightenment that he was looking for, he just didn't realize it yet. But perhaps even with that I'm trying to be too logical in my analysis.

Are you ready to dispel some misconceptions? Despite its prominence in Japanese culture, Zen Buddhism isn't uniquely Japanese; remember, it originally came from China. Zen isn't the only type of Buddhism in Japan; there's still Pure Land Buddhism and Nichiren Buddhism. It's not a major division of Buddhism; Zen is just one of many schools within the Mahayana tradition; and Zen doesn't entirely reject doctrine or scriptures. There's a famous story of the Zen master Takusan burning his commentaries on the Diamond Sutra, but the idea isn't that sacred texts are worthless, but rather inadequate. What's really needed is a direct mind-to-mind transmission; that's the only way that enlightenment can come about. Yet we've seen how Huineng, the Sixth Zen Patriarch, was first awakened when he heard the Diamond Sutra; and then he quoted regularly from the Vimalakirti Sutra in the sermon recorded in the Platform Sutra. You may remember that Vimalakirti was the enlightened layperson who exhibited his superior understanding of the principle of non-duality by saying nothing; and Huineng himself had been a layperson when he first heard the Diamond Sutra and his mind was first awakened. Huineng and other Zen masters such as Dogen assumed that their students would start their spiritual quest with the scriptures; and then Zen itself developed a large body of sacred texts to study and to meditate upon.

We've gone into a lot of details here, so it might be good to step back for a moment for a broader perspective. Whether or not you believe that enlightenment or nirvana is accessible through meditation, calling upon Amida, reciting the Diamond Sutra, or copying the Lotus Sutra, whether you hold to any of those, it's still clear that the Buddhist canon asks and then answers some of life's most profound questions; questions like: Is there a reality beyond the ordinary existence that we see day to day? How does the mind shape and perhaps limit our perceptions of reality? What's the right balance between study and experience in learning something new? That's a question that I often ask when I'm trying to arrange classes or activities for my students: How much are study and experience related? Another question: Can salvation, however one defines it, be gained through a one's own efforts, or is it necessary to rely on a higher power or a teacher? Are some of the most important truths in life unseen because they're right in front of us, if only we could recognize them, like looking for the fire with a lantern? For this course, how important really are sacred texts in gaining insight or wisdom? Are they ultimately dispensable, like a raft you can leave behind after you've reached the other shore of a river? (That's an image from the Diamond Sutra and it appears in earlier Theravada sutras.) Or are scriptures so crucial that they deserve elaborate ritual burials to preserve them for future generations, as we saw at the beginning of this lecture?

On the one hand, you get the Sutra of Perfect Enlightenment, much beloved by Zen Buddhists, which suggests that the scriptures can themselves be a distraction. That sutra says: "The teaching in the sutras is like a moon-pointing finger; on seeing the moon, one knows that what is marked as such (by the finger) is after all not the moon. The various speeches by all the Tathagatas for instructing the bodhisattvas are to be taken likewise." The idea of that quote is it's like a child seeing a parent point and saying, "Look at the moon"; that child might mistake the finger for the moon. Forget about the finger; don't focus on the scriptures, look at what they're pointing towards.

On the other side are people like the Chinese monk Făxiăn in 399. This side is people who take the scriptures very, very seriously. When Făxiăn was over 60 years old, he left the capital of China at Changan and headed west, out of China. For a couple of centuries, trade goods such as glass, coral, amber, perfumes, and precious metals had been coming in from unknown lands in the west along with this new religion of Buddhism. But the transmission was somewhat fragmentary. Although the Chinese had a number of Buddhist scriptures, the translations weren't very good and the doctrines in those books seemed to contradict each other. Fǎxiǎn, as an experienced monk, was particularly concerned that the Chinese were lacking authoritative Vinaya texts. He knew that he needed to get to India, so he set off on foot, following the Silk Road through deserts and over mountains covered in snow all year. He crossed rivers, and at one point he climbed down 700 ladders that were attached to cliffs, which must've been terrifying. Fǎxiǎn travelled through 30 different kingdoms in present day China, Afghanistan, Pakistan, and India. He visited holy sites and studied with various teachers, and then he sailed home on ships that stopped at Sri Lanka and Indonesia with his precious cargo of Buddhist relics, images, and scriptures that he'd collected over the years.

At one point on his return journey, a fierce storm arose and the ship sprang a leak. The merchants, terrified, threw their goods and their merchandise overboard to lighten the ship. Fǎxiǎn tossed his cup and his washbasin into the sea, but he refused to part with anything else, praying fervently to the bodhisattva Guanyin, saying "I have wandered far and wide in search of the Law. Oh! Would that by your spiritual power you would turn back the flowing of the water [I guess that's stop the leak], and cause us to reach some resting place." After 13 more days of being blown this way and that, they finally reached a small island and everyone survived. Eventually Fǎxiǎn made it back to China at the age of 77. Altogether, his journey had taken him 14 years, and he'd covered more than 8,000 miles. Fǎxiǎn spent the rest of his life translating into Chinese the Sanskrit texts that he'd so laboriously acquired; and he wrote an account of his travels, which itself became part of the Buddhist canon.

It's a great travel story. One of my favorite quotes from Fǎxiǎn's travel memoir is:

> In the desert were numerous evil spirits and scorching winds, causing death to anyone who would meet them. Above there were no birds, while on the ground there were no animals. One looked

as far as one could in all directions for a path to cross, but there was none to choose. Only the dried bones of the dead served as indications.

Kind of a harrowing journey, at least at some point.

I find myself incredibly moved by Făxiăn's account of his visit to Vulture Peak, where the Buddha was thought to have taught the Lotus Sutra originally. Speaking of himself in the third person, Făxiăn says:

> Făxiăn, having bought flowers, incense, oil, and lamps in New Town, procured the assistance of two aged monks to accompany him to the top of the peak. Having arrived there, he offered his flowers and incense, and lit his lamps, so that their combined luster illuminated the gloom of the cave.
>
> Faxian was deeply moved, even till the tears coursed down his cheeks, and he said, "Here it was in bygone days Buddha dwelt and delivered the Surangama Sutra. Faxian, not privileged to be born at a time when Buddha lived, can but gaze on the traces of his presence, and the place which he occupied." And taking his position in front of the cave, he recited the Surangama Sutra, and remained there the entire night.

But that's always the pilgrim's lament, isn't it? A pilgrim is somebody who says, "Here I am, finally, in the right place, but at the wrong time. If only I had been standing at this exact spot when (whatever happened that was important in that particular tradition)." Actually, I myself a few years ago was able to travel to Vulture Peak, and I stood there and realized that I'd missed not only the Buddha, but I'd missed Făxiăn as well. In Făxiăn's day, the time he was there, all that remained were, as he says, "traces of the Buddha's presence." But those traces included the scriptures that preserved his words, the scriptures that Făxiăn had decided while he was there; and those sacred texts, to Faxian, were worth a decade and a half of untold hardships and dangers as he made his way across Asia and back, followed by more years of meticulous study and translation.

So my last questions for you are: How far would you be willing to go for knowledge and wisdom? What risks would you take? If you thought there were books that were essential to that quest, how would you treat them?

Tibetan Vajrayana
Lecture 18

Tibetan Buddhism, or Vajrayana, is an esoteric tradition that includes practices that may at first seem strange, but to focus on those elements ignores the remarkable philosophical and scholarly accomplishments that are also part of this branch of the religion. Although Tibetan Buddhism receives a great deal of attention in the West, especially since the annexation of Tibet by China and the flight of the Dalai Lama and many of his followers to India in 1959, adherents of Vajrayana number only about 20 million out of 400 million Buddhists around the world. Numerically, Tibetan Buddhism is not terribly significant, but in terms of scholarship, it's enormously important.

Tibetan Vajrayana and Its Canon

- Vajrayana, which means the "Thunderbolt" or "Diamond Vehicle," is the third major Buddhist tradition, after Theravada and Mahayana. The term *Vajra* refers to the legendary thunderbolt weapon of the Hindu god Indra, which was thought to be indestructible, and to a small scepter-like object used in rituals.

- Vajrayana began in India in the 6th or 7th centuries, when Tantric techniques were added to Mahayana philosophy. Tantrism refers to physical or mental actions that can facilitate or accelerate the journey to enlightenment. Vajrayana, or Tantric Buddhism, is today mostly found in Tibet, but there is also an important offshoot in Japan known as Shingon ("True Word").

- As you may recall, the Tibetan canon is one of the three major collections of Buddhist sacred texts, the others being the Pali canon of Theravada in 48 volumes and the Chinese canon of 100 volumes, which is also used in Japan and Korea. The Tibetan canon, however, weighs in at 322 volumes and includes many translations of Sanskrit texts that have otherwise been lost.

- Buddhism first came to Tibet at the time of Songtsen Gampo, an early-7th-century king who had married two Buddhist princesses, one from Nepal and the other from China. Under his direction, a Tibetan script was developed, based on Sanskrit, so that translations could begin. Buddhism wasn't particularly influential, however, until the late 8th century, when another king invited an Indian monk to establish a monastery.
    - Buddhists soon faced intense hostility from the native Tibetan religion of Bon. The king invited the Indian Tantric master Padmasambhava to duel with demons and Bon priests through spectacular feats of magic.

    - This was the legendary "first dissemination" of Buddhism into Tibet, which is associated with the Nyingma sect, the oldest school of Tibetan Buddhism.

    - Tradition reports that about this time (c. 792), the king ordered a public debate between Chinese and Indian Buddhists. The Indians won, but another period of persecution followed not long after.

- In the 10th century, more monks came from India, bringing a "second dissemination" of Buddhism into Tibet, which picked up momentum with the arrival of Atisha in 1042. Atisha, an accomplished scholar, valued the discipline and insights of early forms of Buddhism, such as Theravada, along with Mahayana philosophy and its emphasis on the bodhisattva path and the latest Tantric techniques. He founded the Kadam school of Tibetan Buddhism, which was later followed by the Kagyu school and the Sakya school.

- Buddhist monks fleeing the Muslim conquest of India carried new scriptures to Tibet, where they were translated and eventually canonized. The Tibetan canon consists of two parts. The first is the Kangyur—the translation of the word of the Buddha—consisting of more than 600 texts in 98 volumes. The second, much longer part is the Tengyur—translations of treatises—which consists of

The great 14th-century Tibetan scholar and reformer Tsong Khapa wrote a multivolume elaboration of Atisha's "Lamp for the Path to Enlightenment."

more than 3,600 texts in 224 volumes. There is also a large body of commentaries written by Tibetans that are not included in the canon.

Atisha's "Lamp for the Path to Enlightenment"

- One influential, relatively accessible example of a Buddhist text written for Tibetans is Atisha's "Lamp for the Path to Enlightenment," a masterpiece of synthesis that combines the ethics of the Theravada Vinaya, the philosophy of Mahayana perfections of wisdom, and the Tantric ritual of Vajrayana. This scripture, with a commentary written by Atisha himself, was included in the Tengyur section of the Tibetan canon.

- Atisha addresses his words to those who seek enlightenment to benefit all beings, not just to end their personal suffering (the bodhisattva path). Ideally, one should take the vow to become a bodhisattva from a teacher, and Atisha stresses that the best path forward is that of a monk who purifies body, speech, and mind through strict morality and discipline (Vinaya). By practicing meditation, calm abiding and higher perceptions will arise.

- Atisha further explains the necessary combination of skillful means and wisdom (perfection of wisdom) and ends by acknowledging the efficacy of mantras, actions, and performances under the direction of a teacher or guru (Tantrism).

- But Atisha warns that even though monks can study the antras and make offerings, they are not allowed to receive secret or wisdom initiations. To do so would result in breaking their vows, defeat, and bad rebirths.

Tantrism

- Tantrism is a type of Buddhism that arose in India in the 6th or 7th centuries and combined Mahayana doctrines with secret rituals or practices that offered shortcuts to enlightenment. The bodhisattva path, with its six perfections, could take many lifetimes to complete. One of the six perfections was perfect meditation, which was generally understood to mean stilling the mind and body. Tantric teachers, by contrast, urged students to put the body and mind to work through mudras (ritual postures or gestures), mantras (sacred sounds or phrases), mandalas (sacred symbolic diagrams), and visualizations of multiple gods and goddesses.

- Tantrism is active rather than quiescent or passive. It uses physical and mental functions to transcend body and mind, like using fire to fight fire or desire to overcome desire.
  o Mahayana perfection of wisdom texts teach that in the end, there is no difference between samsara and nirvana, that attachment and aversion are both traps, that anything and everything can be a manifestation of the Buddha's dharma-body (ultimate reality).

  o Tantrism adds actions to those insights. Thus, we can see how using a bowl fashioned from a human skull or blowing a horn made from a human bone might demonstrate that one has stepped beyond ordinary conceptions.

- Tantrism is also known for rituals that involve drinking wine or eating meat in a cemetery at night or even engaging in sexual behavior without desire, while visualizing one's partner as a deity. It's easy to imagine how such practices might be abused, which is why it is crucial that they are undertaken under the direction of a qualified guru (Tibetan: *lama*).
    - Another reason that expert guidance is needed is that Tantric texts are often written in cryptic language that is unintelligible to outsiders; further, it's often unclear whether the rituals described are meant to be visualized in meditation or physically performed.

    - Many Tantric practices require a *yi-dam*, that is, a holy being chosen for a particular worshipper, appropriate to his or her nature. These deities may be male or female, wrathful or peaceful.

- It is common to categorize tantras into four stages: (1) action tantras, where adherents visualize themselves as servants of meditational deities and offer their devotions; (2) performance tantras, in which adherents see themselves as equal to a deity and perceive their own potential as enlightened bodhisattvas; (3) yoga tantras, or the gradual identification with deities to gain their perfections and wisdom; and (4) supreme yoga, that is, the transformation into a bodhisattva by learning to control energy channels, centers, winds, and drops within one's subtle body.
    - In supreme yoga, one experiences the bliss of the union of self and other, of wisdom and compassion (skillful means), which may be visualized as the sexual union of male and female.

    - Some forms of supreme yoga might involve ritualized sexual intercourse, with spouses in the case of lay Buddhists or Nyingmapa *lamas*, who are permitted to marry. Monks in other sects of Tibetan Buddhism, who have taken vows of celibacy, are allowed only to visualize such actions.

The Hevajra Tantra and Tibetan Book of the Dead

- About one-fifth of the Kangyur—the first part of the Tibetan canon—consists of Tantric texts, including a profusion of mantras, mudras, and mandalas that can put one in tune with a *yi-dam* and provide a focus for meditation and visualization.
  - The Hevajra Tantra, influential in the Sakya school, is one example of these texts. Hevajra is a popular chosen deity (*yi-dam*) of the wrathful variety and is often depicted with multiple arms holding weapons and skull bowls, embracing a female consort, and standing on a lotus and a corpse.

  - The tantra offers detailed instructions for multiple rituals and visualizations, but it's not really meant to be understood by outsiders; understanding requires a qualified guru. For us, it raises an interesting question that applies to many religions: Is the body a hindrance or a help to spiritual progress and salvation—however one might define it?

- The most famous text of Vajrayana Buddhism is the Tibetan Book of the Dead, although it is much better known in the West than in Tibet. The story of this text starts with theosophy, a sort of 19th-century New Age religion that taught the oneness of all beings, reincarnation, and karma, combined with an interest in mystical insight, esoteric teachings, and occult experiences.
  - In 1919, Walter Evans-Wentz, a theosophist, traveled to north India and bought an old Tibetan manuscript from a monk. Not knowing Tibetan himself, he found a translator and together, they produced what we know today as the Tibetan Book of the Dead, first published in 1927. It's important to note, however, than Evans-Wentz's volume was more a product of American spiritualism than Tibetan culture.

  - The manuscript Evans-Wentz came across was part of a larger cycle of texts known as Bardo Thodol ("Liberation in the

Intermediate State through Hearing"). The work belongs to a rather unique genre called *terma*, or "treasure texts." These are documents that were thought to have been written by Padmasambhava in the 8th century and then hidden so that they could survive centuries of persecution and be rediscovered in later generations.

o The text, which was read in the presence of someone who was dying, is more about rebirth than death. It gives a detailed description of what the dying person is about to experience and how he or she should respond. It speaks of three intermediate stages in the 49 days between death and rebirth, leading to either liberation from future rebirths or rebirth as a god, a demigod, a human, an animal, a hungry ghost, or a hell-being.

Suggested Reading

Davidson, "Atisa's *A Lamp for the Path to Awakening*."

Gyatso (Dalai Lama XIV, author) and Jinpa (trans.), *Essence of the Heart Sutra*.

———, *The World of Tibetan Buddhism*.

Harvey, *An Introduction to Buddhism*.

Lopcz, *The Tibetan Book of the Dead*.

Mitchell, *Buddhism: Introducing the Buddhist Experience*.

Power, *Introduction to Tibetan Buddhism*.

Rinchen (author) and Sonam (trans.), *Atisha's Lamp for the Path to Enlightenment*.

Snellgrove, *The Hevajra Tantra*.

Questions to Consider

1. What makes Tibetan Buddhism distinctive, and what is Tantrism?

2. Why is the Tibetan Book of the Dead better known in America than in Tibet?

Tibetan Vajrayana
Lecture 18—Transcript

Hello. It's always a pleasure to spend some time with you. I remember the first time I ever heard of Tibet. I was in the sixth or the seventh grade, and I came across a Ripley's *Believe It or Not!* comic book at a friend's house. This may seem to date me; Ripley's comics were most famous in the 1930s and 40s. The one I saw would've been a reprint in the 70s. Among those comic book panels of natural and human wonders was a description of Tibetan monks who used the tops of human skulls as cups and human thigh bones as flutes. It seemed very strange and more than a little eerie. That may well have been the first time I'd ever heard of Buddhism, which probably wasn't the best introduction to the religion.

First of all, I didn't know about the Buddha or his enlightenment, and the Four Noble Truths; that's the place to start. Second, I had no way of making sense of such a bizarre practice as drinking out of a bowl made out of a skull, for example. By the end of this lecture, you'll at least understand the thinking behind it. Third, I didn't realize that I had tapped into a rich vein of Western romanticism and sensationalism about Tibet that went back to the 19th century and then forward into 1930s when the novelist James Hilton coined the phrase "Shangri-la." For example, Sherlock Holmes was supposed to have spent two of his lost years in Tibet.) Tibetan Buddhism, or Vajrayana, is an esoteric tradition that does include things that may at first seem strange; but to focus on those elements ignores the remarkable philosophical and scholarly accomplishments that are also part of that branch of the religion. Finally, although Tibetan Buddhism gets a lot of attention in the West, especially since the annexation of Tibet by China and the flight of the Dalai Lama and many of his followers to India in 1959, adherents of Vajrayana only number about 20 million out of perhaps 400 million Buddhists around the world, so maybe five percent. Numerically, Tibetan Buddhism isn't terribly significant, though in terms of scholarship it's enormously important.

The term *Vajrayana* means the "Thunderbolt" or the "Diamond Vehicle," and this is the third major Buddhist tradition, after Theravada (The Way of the Elders) and Mahayana (the Great Vehicle). The term *Vajra* refers to the legendary thunderbolt weapon of the Hindu god Indra, which was thought to be indestructible like a diamond. It also refers to a small scepter-like object with five curved prongs at each end, and it's used in rituals. Vajrayana began in India in the 6th or the 7th centuries, when Tantric techniques were added to Mahayana philosophy. Tantrism refers to physical or mental actions that can facilitate or accelerate the journey to enlightenment. Vajrayana, or Tantric Buddhism, is today mostly found in Tibet, but there's also an important offshoot in Japan known as Shingon, translated it's the "True Word" school.

One of the things that makes Tibetan Buddhism distinct is that it has its own canon. As you may remember from an earlier lecture, the Tibetan canon is one of the three major collections of Buddhist sacred texts, the others being the Pali canon of Theravada Buddhism in 48 volumes and the Chinese canon of 100 volumes, which is also used in Japan and in Korea. The Tibetan canon, however, weighs in at 322 volumes and it includes many translations of Sanskrit texts that otherwise have been lost. We'll come back to this in a few moments.

Buddhism first came to Tibet at time of Songtsen Gampo, an early 7th-century king who'd married two Buddhist princesses, one from Nepal and the other from China. Under his direction, a Tibetan script was developed, based on Sanskrit, so that translations could begin. Buddhism wasn't particularly influential, however, until the late 8th century, when another king invited an Indian monk to establish a monastery. Buddhists soon faced intense hostility from the native Tibetan religion of Bon, and this religion has lots of gods, demons, magical spells, and shamanism. The Tibetan king invited an Indian Tantric master named Padmasambhava to duel with demons and Bon priests through spectacular feats of magic. This was the legendary "first dissemination" of Buddhism into Tibet, and it's associated with the Nyingma sect, the oldest school of Tibetan Buddhism. Tradition reports that about this time—so about 792 C.E.—the king ordered a public debate between Chinese Buddhists, who were proponents of sudden enlightenment and paying less attention to scriptures (basically like Zen Buddhism), and on the other side were Indian Buddhists, and they were arguing for the bodhisattva path of gradually refined wisdom and compassion. The Indians Buddhists won the debate, but then another period of persecution followed not long after.

Finally, in the 10th century, more monks were coming from India bringing a "second dissemination" of Buddhism into Tibet; and then that picked up momentum with the arrival of Atisha, the great monk, in 1042. Atisha, who was an accomplished scholar, had been the dean of Nalanda University in India, and he valued the discipline and insights of early forms of Buddhism such as Theravada, along with Mahayana philosophy and its emphasis on the bodhisattva path, and he also had an appreciation for the latest Tantric techniques. He founded the Kadam school of Tibetan Buddhism, which was later followed by the Kagyu school and the Sakya school (you can tell that this is kind of a complicated story).

Buddhist monks fleeing the Muslim conquest of India carried new scriptures when they came to Tibet, and eventually those new scriptures were translated and then canonized. Indeed, one of the great achievements of this second dissemination was the compilation of one of the world's largest collections of scripture. The Tibetan canon consists of two parts: The first is the Kangyur—and this is the translation of the word of the Buddha—and it consists of over 600 texts in 98 volumes, including 13 volumes of Vinaya and 13 volumes of sutras (about three-quarters of those sutras are Mahayana sutras), then 21 of Perfection of Wisdom texts, and finally 22 volumes of Tantra, and there are a dozen more volumes of odds and ends thrown in. The second, much longer part of the canon is the Tengyur, and these are translations of treatises. These consist of works by individual Indian masters, and they're divided into commentaries on the sutras and commentaries on the tantras; more than 3,600 texts in 224 volumes. Then there's a large body of commentaries written by Tibetans themselves, which aren't included in the canon. Tibetan Buddhism has a rich tradition of scholarship in Buddhist philosophy and logic.

You may have noticed two of the three Theravada baskets in the Kangyur: the Vinaya and the sutras. The third basket, the Abhidharma—and remember that's philosophical analysis of the constituent elements of phenomena and the mind—is absent from the Kangyur, but it's approached in Tibetan Buddhism through texts in the Tengyur, which include Abhidharma commentaries as well as many of the classics of Indian Buddhist philosophy translated into Tibetan. These would be works by Asanga, the founder of the

Yogacara or the Mind Only School; or works by Nagarjuna, the founder of the Madhyamaka or Middle Way School.

One influential, relatively accessible example of a Buddhist text written for Tibetans is Atisha's *Lamp for the Path to Enlightenment*, which is a masterpiece of synthesis at only 68 verses, and it combines the ethics of the Theravada Vinaya, the philosophy of Mahayana perfections of wisdom, and the Tantric rituals of Vajrayana. This scripture, with a commentary written by Atisha himself, was included in the Tengyur section of the Tibetan canon. Atisha addresses his words to those who seek enlightenment not just to end to their personal suffering, but to benefit all beings; so this is the bodhisattva path. Atisha says:

> Since you want to free these beings
> From the suffering of pain,
> From suffering and the cause of suffering,
> Arouse immutably the resolve to attain enlightenment.

Ideally, one should take this vow to become a bodhisattva from a teacher; and Atisha stresses that the best path forward is that of a monk who purifies body, speech, and mind through strict morality and discipline; this is the Vinaya part of this text. By practicing meditation, calm abiding and higher perceptions will arise. Atisha further explains the necessary combination of skilful means and wisdom, noting that, as he says:

> Wisdom is fully explained as knowing the emptiness of own-being in the non-arising of the Five Aggregates, the sense fields and elements of existence ... Samsara arises from conceptual thought ... The complete removal of that conceptual thought is the highest Nirvana.

Atisha ends by acknowledging the efficacy of mantras, actions, and performances under the direction of a teacher or a guru; so this is the Tantric part of that. But Atisha warns even though monks can study the tantras and make offerings, they're not allowed to receive secret or wisdom initiations. To do so would result in breaking their vows, in defeat (remember that's the worst category of offenses in the Vinayas), and it would result in bad rebirths for the monks. What's going on here, and why would aiming at enlightenment be bad for a monk? What does Atisha have in mind when he's warning against certain types of Tantric practices?

With this, we get to some of the stranger elements of Tibetan Buddhism. The key term here is *Tantrism*, which refers to a type of Buddhism that arose in India in the sixth or the 7th centuries and combined Mahayana doctrines with secret rituals or practices that offered shortcuts to enlightenment. The bodhisattva path could take many lifetimes to complete with its six perfections: You remember those are generosity, morality, patience, exertion, meditation, and wisdom. One of those six perfections is perfect meditation, which was generally understood to mean stilling the mind and the body. Tantric teachers, by contrast, urged students to put the body and the mind to work through *mudras*, those are ritual postures or gestures; mantras, sacred sounds or phrases; mandalas, and those are sacred symbolic diagrams; and visualizations of multiple gods and goddesses. If you think this sounds like things we've already encountered in Hindu texts, you're right; there are also Tantric forms of Hinduism.

Tantrism is active rather than quiescent or passive. It uses physical and mental functions to transcend the body and the mind, sort of like using fire to fight fire, or desire to overcome desire. It may remind us of the Lotus Sutra, where the father of that burning house appealed to his sons' desire for carts in order to rescue them from the danger that they were in; so you can use desire in order to help people escape from desire. Mahayana perfection of wisdom texts teach that in the end, there's no difference between samsara and nirvana; that attachment and aversion are both traps; that anything and everything can be a manifestation of the Buddha's dharma-body. Remember the doctrine of the three bodies of the Buddha, and the dharma-body is ultimate reality that encompasses everything. Tantrism takes those insights and then puts them into action. So you can see how using a bowl that was fashioned from a human skull without it bothering you in the least, or blowing a horn made from a human bone with perfect calmness might demonstrate that one has stepped beyond ordinary conceptions; one has moved into that realm of non-duality where one realizes the kinds of distinctions we normally make are artificial and that everything ultimately is emptiness.

Tantrism is also known for rituals that involve drinking wine or eating meat in a cemetery at night; so this is going to go against ordinary taboos. Many forms of Buddhism encourage vegetarianism—not all of them, but some of them—though all Buddhists should prescribe to the five precepts, and remember the fifth one is no intoxicants. In this case, there are some practices that seem to go against ordinary Buddhist morality. There are some Tantric practices that even encourage engaging in sexual behavior without desire while visualizing one's partner as a deity. It's easy to see how such practices might be abused as well, which is why it's crucial that they're undertaken under the direction of a qualified guru; and the word *guru* is translated as *lama*, in Tibetan. You may recall the classic Ogden Nash poem about "one-L" and "two-L" lamas. Here we're taking about the "one-L" lama; the priest, not the beast. Another reason why expert guidance is needed is that Tantric texts are often written in cryptic language that's unintelligible to outsiders. It's an esoteric tradition, a secret transmission; and it is often unclear whether the rituals that are described in these texts are only meant to be visualized in meditation or physically performed. Many Tantric practices require a *yi-dam*; that is, a holy being chosen for a particular worshipper, appropriate to his or her nature. These deities may be male or female; they may be wrathful or peaceful.

It's common to categorize tantras into four stages: The first are "action tantras," where adherents visualize themselves as servants of meditational deities and offer their devotions. The second type are "performance tantras," in which one sees oneself as equal to a deity, like a friend, and where one perceives his or her own potential as enlightened bodhisattvas. The third type is "yoga tantras," or the gradual identification with deities to gain their perfections and wisdom; so we're going from equality to identification. The fourth kind of tantra is "supreme yoga"; that is, being transformed into a bodhisattva by learning to control energy channels, centers, winds, and drops within one's subtle body, and there are lots of instructions about how to do this.

One experiences the bliss of the union of self and other, of wisdom and compassion, which may be visualized as the sexual union of male and female. Some forms of supreme yoga might involve ritualized sexual intercourse, with spouses, in the case of lay Buddhists or Nyingmapa lamas, who are permitted to marry. Monks in the other sects of Tibetan Buddhism, who have undertaken vows of celibacy, are only allowed to visualize such actions. This seems to be what Atisha was worried about in his *Lamp for the Path to Enlightenment*; that some monks would move beyond visualizations to actually enact these practices.

I mentioned earlier that about a fifth of the Kangyur—the first part of the Tibetan canon—consists of Tantric texts, some 22 volumes worth. They feature a profusion of mantras, so those are incantations and magical spells; they also have *mudras*, ritualized hand gestures; and mandalas, those mystical diagrams; all of which can put one in tune with a *yi-dam*, one's chosen deity, and provide a focus for meditation and visualization.

For just one example, we could turn to the Hevajra Tantra, which is very influential in the Sakya school, and which was the first major tantra to be published in English in 1959. Hevajra, a popular chosen deity of the wrathful variety, is often depicted with multiple arms holding weapons and skull bowls, and he's embracing a female consort and standing on a lotus and a corpse.

The Tantra offers detailed instructions for multiple rituals and visualizations, explaining that:

> From self-experiencing comes this knowledge, which is free from ideas of self and other; like the sky it is pure and void, the essence supreme of non-existence and existence, a mingling of Wisdom and [Skillful] Means, a mingling of passion and absence of passion.

The Hevajra Sutra continues:

> Then the master should enter the mandala as a two-armed Hevajra, and assuming the majestic bearing of Vajrasattva, he should adopt the alidha posture. He is washed and purified and perfumed, and adorned with the various adornments. HUM HUM he cries majestically, HI HI he cries to terrify. Then the essence is declared, pure and consisting in knowledge, where there is not the slightest difference between samsara and nirvana.

Some of the imagery from that text seems to break taboos. It goes on to say:

> Into the mandala one should cause to enter the eight blissful Spells, twelve or sixteen years of age, and adorned with necklaces and bangles. They are called wife, sister, daughter, niece, [mother-in-law, aunt, etc.]. ... He should cause them to drink [camphor] and he should quickly gain siddhi [magical powers]. Wine is drunk and meat and herbs are eaten. Next he removes their garments and kisses them again and again. They honour him in return and sing and dance to their best, and they play there together in the union of vajra and lotus.

I don't really understand what's going on there; but then again, I'm not supposed to. This is written for insiders, and you need a qualified guru or a lama to take you through it.

One more quote from the Hevajra Tantra: "Those things that bind people of evil conduct, others use as a skillful means to gain freedom from the bonds of samsara. The world is bound by passion, but by passion too it can be freed." Once again, "The world is bound by passion, but by passion too it can be freed." This raises an interesting question that applies to many religions, and not just Buddhism: Is the body a hindrance or a help to spiritual progress and salvation, however one might define salvation? Is the body something that needs to be overcome in asceticism, or is it something that can be used; is it necessary for spiritual progress? Indeed, that's one of the questions that first started the Buddha on his spiritual path: where he was an ascetic for a while, giving up eating and living a very restrictive life; and then he decided that that wasn't working out so well; of course his earlier life of being a prince in a palace and enjoying everything in life hadn't worked out; and Buddhism was the middle way. He found the right balance between asceticism and ordinary life; between not having passions and having passions.

Thus far, I haven't talked about the most famous text of Vajrayana Buddhism, the Tibetan Book of the Dead. That's probably because most Tibetans have probably never heard of it; it's much better known in the West than in Tibet. How can that be? The story starts with theosophy, a sort of 19th-century New Age religion that taught the oneness of all beings as well as reincarnation and karma—it was very much influenced by Hinduism—and then theosophy took those ideas and combined those with an interest in mystical insight, in esoteric teachings, and occult experiences. In 1919, Walter Evans-Wentz, a theosophist, traveled to North India and bought an old Tibetan manuscript from a monk. Not knowing Tibetan himself, he found a translator and together they produced what we know today as the Tibetan Book of the Dead, which was first published in 1927. Although the text that he'd found wasn't particularly significant in Tibet—it wasn't even part of the Tibetan Canon—it did speak to Evans-Wentz's theosophical sensibilities, and to many other in the West as well. The psychiatrist Carl Jung wrote a brief commentary, and Timothy Leary used it as the basis for a guidebook of LSD tripping, which in turn inspired the Beatle's song "Tomorrow Never Knows." In various translations, the Tibetan Book of the Dead has sold more than a million copies.

Yet the scholar Donald Lopez has noted that "the work by Walter Evans-Wentz entitled the Tibetan Book of the Dead is not really Tibetan, it is not really a book, and it is not really about death." That cryptic statement probably needs a little more explanation. Evans-Wentz's volume was more a product of American Spiritualism than Tibetan culture. He'd added a long theosophical introduction to the translation, and the Tibetan text itself would've been used by only one of the four major schools, the Nyingma school, founded by Padmasambhava, as a supplement to more authoritative, canonical texts. The manuscript that Evans-Wentz had come across was part of a larger cycle of texts known as parto thotrol, literally, "Liberation in the Intermediate State Through Hearing." It's not really a distinct book, and the text has never been fixed; there are many versions of varying lengths.

The work belongs to a rather unique genre called *terma*, or "treasure texts." These are documents that were thought to have been written by Padmasambhava back in the 8th century and then hidden by him in caves, lakes, pillars, or even in the minds of his future disciples so that they could survive centuries of persecution and be rediscovered in later generations. Thousands of such texts have come to light since the 11th century, with the majority appearing in the 14th century. That was the time when an obscure mystic named Karma Lingpa claimed to have found a number of funereal texts, some of which would become known in the West as the Tibetan Book of the Dead.

But it's not really about death either; it's about rebirth. The text, which was read in the presence of someone on the verge of death, gave a detailed description of what they were about to experience and how they should respond. It speaks of three intermediate stages in the 49 days between death and rebirth. The first, at the moment of death, will be seen as clear light. If a person is able to recognize that as reality, he or she can be liberated from all future rebirths. But the temptation will be to flee in terror; and if that happens, over the next few weeks the deceased will see a succession of 42 peaceful deities and 58 wrathful deities. Again, it's natural to feel confusion and fear; and if a person doesn't grasp the chance to join those deities in their buddha-worlds, then karma will take over and he or she will be attracted by lights that lead back to the six realms of this world-system, to be reborn as a god, a demi-god, a human, an animal, a hungry ghost, or a hell-being. As someone is dying, you read them this text and then they can understand what to expect and they can plan out how they're going to respond to what's going to happen to them.

I hope at this point that you have a sense of the tremendous variety of sacred texts within the three Buddhist canons, but I want conclude with a quotation that conveys one Buddhist's heartfelt response to the scriptures in his tradition. He's not any random Buddhist; I'm going to talk about Tsong Khapa, the great 14th-century Tibetan scholar and reformer who wrote massive commentaries on classic works of Buddhist philosophy, as well as a multivolume elaboration of Atisha's *Lamp for the Path to Enlightenment*. At a time when there were all sorts of problems within the monastic orders, Tsong Khapa put equal emphasis on mainstream Buddhist teachings and on Tantra, and he required strict discipline of the monks; so no alcohol, no sex, no evening meals, no long naps, no magic. Eventually, Tsong Khapa founded the Geluk school, probably the dominant sect of Tibetan Buddhism in the modern era. The Dalai Lama, for instance, is a prominent line of incarnation within the Geluk school; though he's hardly the leader of all Buddhists all over the whole, despite the well-deserved prominence of the current, 14th Dalai Lama.

A few years ago, the Dalai Lama wrote a commentary on the Heart Sutra; and you may remember that's the short one-page summary of perfection of wisdom teachings that's recited daily throughout China, Korea, Japan, and Tibet. The Dalai Lama tried to express the depths of his own feelings by citing these lines from Tsong Khapa, his spiritual mentor, addressing the Buddha and thinking of his teachings preserved in the Sutras and the Vinaya:

> And yet, as I contemplate your words,
> the thought arises in me:
> "Ah, this teacher, enveloped in a halo of light
> and brilliant with the glorious major and minor marks,
> has taught thus in his perfect brahma melody."
> O Buddha, as your image reflects in my mind,
> it brings solace to my weary heart,
> like the cool moon rays to one tormented by heat.

That's the sort of devotion, that's the sort of gratitude that comes when he thinks of the Buddha and the traces that he's left in the present world in the scriptures.

Recommended Texts and Translations

Hinduism
Flood, Gavin, and Charles Martin, trans. *The Bhagavad Gita: A New Translation*. New York: W.W. Norton, 2012.

Miller, Barbara Stoler, trans. *The Bhagavad-Gita: Krishna's Counsel in Time of War*. New York: Bantam, 1986.

Olivelle, Patrick, trans. *Upanisads*. Oxford World's Classics. Oxford: Oxford University Press, 1996.

Patton, Laurie L., trans. *The Bhagavad Gita*. London: Penguin, 2008.

Roebuck, Valerie J., trans. *The Upanishads*. London: Penguin, 2003.

Judaism
Danby, Herbert, trans. *The Mishnah*. London: Oxford University Press, 1933.

Neusner, Jacob, trans. *The Mishnah: A New Translation*. New Haven: Yale University Press, 1988.

Note on the Bible: The New American Bible (Catholic), the New International Version (evangelical), the New Jerusalem Bible (Catholic), and the Revised English Bible (ecumenical) are all good translations, though the New Revised Standard Version (NRSV) is the most ecumenical and also the widely used version in academia. If you're new to the Bible, the NRSV is recommended. For the Hebrew Bible, be sure to take a look at the Jewish Publication Society Tanakh.

Buddhism
Carter, John Ross, and Mahinda Palihawadana, trans. *The Dhammapada: The Sayings of the Buddha*. Oxford World's Classics. Oxford: Oxford University Press, 2008.

Hurvitz, Leon, trans. *Scripture of the Lotus Blossom of the Fine Dharma (The Lotus Sutra)*. Rev. ed. New York: Columbia University Press, 2009.

Roebuck, Valerie J., trans. *The Dhammapada*. London: Penguin, 2010.

Sekida, Katsuki, trans. and commentator, and A. V. Grimstone, ed. *Two Zen Classics: Mumonkan and Hekiganroku*. New York and Tokyo: Weatherhill, 1977.

Shibayama, Zenkei. *Zen Comments on the Mumonkan*. Translated by Sumiko Kudo. New York: Harper & Row, 1974.

Watson, Burton, trans. *The Lotus Sutra*. New York: Columbia University Press, 1993.

East Asian Religions

Dawson, Raymond. *Confucius: The Analects*. Oxford World's Classics. Oxford: Oxford University Press, 2008.

Ivanhoe, Philip J., trans. *The Daodejing of Laozi*. Indianapolis, IN: Hackett, 2002.

Lau, D. C., trans. *Confucius: The Analects*. London: Penguin, 1979.

———, trans. *Lao Tzu: Tao Te Ching*. London: Penguin, 1963.

Leys, Simon, trans. *The Analects of Confucius*. New York: Norton, 1997.

Mair, Victor H., trans. *Tao Te Ching: The Classic Book of Integrity and the Way*. New York: Bantam, 1990.

Christianity

"The Gospel of Thomas." In *Lost Scriptures: Books That Did Not Make It into the New Testament*, edited by Bart D. Ehrman, pp. 19–28. New York: Oxford University Press, 2003.

Note on the Bible: The New American Bible (Catholic), the New International Version (evangelical), the New Jerusalem Bible (Catholic), and the Revised English Bible (ecumenical) are all good translations, though the New Revised Standard Version (NRSV) is the most ecumenical and also the widely used version in academia. If you're new to the Bible, the NRSV is recommended.

Islam

Abdel Haleem, M. A. S., trans. *The Qur'an: A New Translation*. Oxford: Oxford University Press, 2004.

Ali, Maulana Muhammad, trans. *The Holy Qur'an with English Translation and Commentary*. 7th rev. ed. Lahore: Ahamadiyya Anjuman Ishaat Islam, 2002.

———, trans. *A Manual of Hadith*. 2nd ed. Lahore: Ahamadiyya Anjuman Ishaat Islam, 1990.

Ibrahim, Ezzeddin, and Denys Johnson-Davies, trans. *An-Nawawi's Forty Hadith*. Cambridge: Islamic Texts Society, 1997.

Khalidi, Tarif, trans. *The Qur'an*. New York: Penguin, 2008.

Newer Religions

Abdu'l-Baha. *Some Answered Questions*. Translated by Laura Clifford Barney. Wilmette, IL: Baha'i Publishing Trust, 1990.

Baha'u'llah. *The Hidden Words of Baha'u'llah*. Translated by Shoghi Effendi. Wilmette, IL: Baha'i Publishing Trust, 2003

Dass, Nirmal, trans. *Songs of the Saints from the Adi Granth*. Albany: State University of New York Press, 2000.

Hardy, Grant, ed. *The Book of Mormon: A Reader's Edition*. Urbana, IL: University of Illinois Press, 2003.

Singh, Nikky-Guninder Kaur, trans. *The Name of My Beloved: Verses of the Sikh Gurus*. San Francisco: Harper San Francisco, 1995.

Bibliography

Abdel Haleem, M. A. S., trans. *The Qur'an: A New Translation*. Oxford: Oxford University Press, 2004.

Abdu'l-Baha. *Some Answered Questions*. Translated by Laura Clifford Barney. Wilmette, IL: Baha'i Publishing Trust, 1990 (1908).

Alexander, Philip S., ed. and trans. *Textual Sources for the Study of Judaism*. Chicago: University of Chicago Press, 1990.

Ali, Maulana Muhammad, trans. *The Holy Qur'an with English Translation and Commentary*. 7th rev. ed. Lahore: Ahamadiyya Anjuman Ishaat Islam, 2002.

Alter, Robert, trans. *The Five Books of Moses*. New York: Norton, 2004.

Alter, Robert, and Frank Kermode, eds. *The Literary Guide to the Bible*. Cambridge, MA: Harvard University Press, 1987.

American Bible Society, "The State of the Bible, 2013." http://www.americanbible.org/state-bible.

———. *Synopsis of the Four Gospels, Revised Standard Version*. Rev. ed. New York: American Bible Society, 2010.

Armstrong, Karen. *The Bible: A Biography*. New York: Grove Press, 2007.

Aston, William George, trans. *Nihongi: Chronicles of Japan from the Earliest Times to A.D. 697.* 2 vols. London: Kegan Paul and Japan Society of London, 1896.

Attar, Farid Ud-Din. *Conference of the Birds*. Translated by Afkham Darbandi and Dick Davis. London: Penguin, 1984.

———. *Farid ad-Din 'Atar's Memorial of God's Friends: Lives and Sayings of Sufis*. Translated by Paul Losensky. New York: Paulist Press, 2009.

Attridge, Harold W. ed. *Harper Collins Study Bible*. Rev. ed. New York: HarperCollins, 2006. (Includes the New Revised Standard Version, with the Apocrypha.)

Baha'i Prayers: A Selection of Prayers Revealed by Baha'u'llah, the Bab, and Abdu'l-Baha. Wilmette, IL: Baha'i Publishing Trust, 1991.

Baha'u'llah. *Gleanings from the Writings of Baha'u'llah*. Wilmette, IL: Baha'i Publishing Trust, 1976.

———. *The Kitab-i-Aqdas: The Most Holy Book*. Wilmette, IL: Baha'i Publishing Trust, 1992.

———. *Writings of Baha'u'llah: A Compilation*. Rev. ed. New Delhi: Baha'i Publishing Trust, 1994.

Barlow, Philip. *Mormons and the Bible: The Place of the Latter-day Saints in American Religion*. New York: Oxford University Press, 1991.

Barton, Stephen C., ed. *Cambridge Companion to the Gospels*. Cambridge: Cambridge University Press, 2006.

Berlin, Adele, and Marc Zvi Brettler, eds. *The Jewish Study Bible*. Oxford: Oxford University Press, 2004. (Includes the JPS Tanakh translation.)

Blenkinsopp, Joseph. *The Pentateuch: An Introduction to the First Five Books of the Bible*. New York: Doubleday, 1992.

Bock, Felicia Gressitt, trans. *Engi-Shiki: Procedures of the Engi Era*. Books I–X. 2 vols. Tokyo: Sophia University, 1970–1972.

Bokenkamp, Stephen R. *Early Daoist Scriptures*. Berkeley: University of California Press, 1997.

Bokser, Ben Zion, ed. and trans. *The Talmud: Selected Writings*. New York: Paulist Press, 1989.

Bowman, Matthew. *The Mormon People: The Making of an American Faith*. New York: Random House, 2012.

Boyce, Mary, ed. and trans. *Textual Sources for the Study of Zoroastrianism*. Chicago: University of Chicago Press, 1990.

———. *Zoroastrians: Their Religious Beliefs and Practices*. London: Routledge, 2001.

Breen, John, and Mark Teeuwen. *A New History of Shinto*. Malden, MA: Wiley-Blackwell, 2010.

Brettler, Marc Zvi. *How to Read the Bible*. Philadelphia: Jewish Publication Society, 2005.

Brettler, Marc Zvi, Peter Enns, and Daniel J. Harrington. *The Bible and the Believer: How to Read the Bible Critically and Religiously*. New York: Oxford University Press, 2012.

Brockington, John, and Mary Brockington, trans. *Rama the Steadfast: An Early Form of the Ramayana*. London: Penguin, 2007.

Brown, Jonathan A. C. *Hadith: Muhammad's Legacy in the Medieval and Modern World*. Oxford: Oneworld, 2009.

Burton, John. *An Introduction to the Hadith*. Edinburgh: Edinburgh University Press, 1994.

Burtt, E. A., ed. *The Teachings of the Compassionate Buddha: Early Discourses, the Dhammapada, and Later Basic Writings*. New York: Penguin, 1982.

Bushman, Richard L. *Joseph Smith: Rough Stone Rolling*. New York: Knopf, 2005.

———. *Mormonism: A Very Short Introduction*. New York: Oxford University Press, 2008.

Calder, Norman, Jawid Mohaddedi, and Andrew Rippin, eds. and trans. *Classical Islam: A Sourcebook of Religious Literature*. London: Routledge, 2003.

Chan, Wing-tsit, trans. *A Source Book in Chinese Philosophy*. Princeton: Princeton University Press, 1963.

Chang, Chung-Yuan, trans. *Original Teachings of Ch'an Buddhism, Selected from the Transmission of the Lamp*. New York: Pantheon, 1969.

Charlesworth, James H., ed. *The Old Testament Pseudepigrapha*. 2 vols. Garden City, NY: Doubleday, 1983.

Chien-hsing Ho. "The Finger Pointing toward the Moon: A Philosophical Analysis of the Chinese Buddhist Thought of Reference." *Journal of Chinese Philosophy* 35(1): 159–177.

Christenson, Allen J., trans. *Popol Vu: Literal Poetic Version: Translation and Transcription*. Norman, OK: University of Oklahoma Press, 2004.

Church of Jesus Christ of Latter-day Saints, *Book of Mormon, Doctrine and Covenants, Pearl of Great Price*. Rev. ed. Salt Lake City, UT: Church of Jesus Christ of Latter-day Saints, 2013.

Cohen, Abraham. *Everyman's Talmud*. New York: Schocken, 1995.

Collins, John J. *The Dead Sea Scrolls: A Biography*. Princeton: Princeton University Press, 2013.

Collins, Raymond F. *Introduction to the New Testament*. Garden City, NY: Doubleday, 1983.

Conze, Edward, trans. *The Large Sutra of the Perfect Wisdom*. Berkeley, CA: University of California Press, 1975.

Conze, Edward, I. B. Horner, D. Snellgrove, and A. Waley, eds. *Buddhist Texts through the Ages*. Boston: Shambala, 1990.

Coogan, Michael D. *The Old Testament: A Historical and Literary Introduction to the Hebrew Scriptures*. Oxford: Oxford University Press, 2006.

———, ed. *The New Oxford Annotated Bible*. 4th ed. Oxford: Oxford University Press, 2010. (Includes the New Revised Standard Edition, with the Apocrypha.)

———. *The Old Testament: A Very Short Introduction*. Oxford: Oxford University Press, 2008.

Cook, Michael. *The Koran: A Very Short Introduction*. Oxford: Oxford University Press, 2000.

Cowell, E. B., ed. *The Jataka*, 6 vols. Cambridge: Cambridge University Press, 1895–1907.

Darmsteter, James, trans. *The Zend-Avesta*. 3 vols. Oxford: Oxford University Press, 1880–1887.

Dass, Gucharan. *The Difficulty of Being Good: On the Subtle Art of Dharma*. Oxford: Oxford University Press, 2009.

Dass, Nirmal, trans. *Songs of Kabir from the Adi Granth*. Albany: State University of New York Press, 1991.

———, trans. *Songs of the Saints from the Adi Granth*. Albany: State University of New York Press, 2000.

Davidson, Ronald, M. "Atisa's *A Lamp for the Path to Awakening*." In *Buddhism in Practice*, edited by Donald S. Lopez, Jr., pp. 290–301. Princeton: Princeton University Press, 1995.

Davies, Douglas J. *An Introduction to Mormonism*. Cambridge: Cambridge University Press, 2003.

Denny, Frederick M., and Rodney L. Taylor, eds. *The Holy Book in Comparative Perspective*. Columbia, SC: South Carolina University Press, 1985.

Despeux, Catherine, and Livia Kohn. *Women in Daoism*. Cambridge, MA: Three Pines, 2003.

Dimmitt, Cornelia, and J. A. B. van Buitenen, eds. and trans. *Classical Hindu Mythology: A Reader in the Sanskrit Puranas*. Philadelphia: Temple University Press, 1978.

Doniger, Wendy, trans. *The Rig Veda*. London: Penguin, 1981.

———. *The Hindus: An Alternative History*. New York: Penguin, 2009.

Dreazen, Yochi. "The Brazen Bibliophiles of Timbuktu: How a Team of Sneaky Librarians Duped Al Qaeda." *New Republic*. April 29, 2013, 34–37.

Duchesne-Guillemin, Jacques, trans. *The Hymns of Zarathustra*. Translated by M. Henning, Boston: Beacon Hill, 1952.

Dundas, Paul. *The Jains*. 2nd ed. London: Routledge, 2002.

Dunn, James D. G. *Cambridge Companion to St. Paul*. Cambridge: Cambridge University Press, 2003.

Earhart, H. Byron. *Japanese Religion: Unity and Diversity*. 5th ed. Boston: Wadsworth, 2013.

Edgerton, Franklin, trans. *The Beginnings of Indian Philosophy: Selections from the Rig Veda, Atharva Veda, Upanisads, and Mahabharata*. Cambridge, MA: Harvard University Press, 1865.

Ehrman, Bart D. *Lost Christianities: The Battles for Scripture and the Faiths We Never Knew*. New York: Oxford University Press, 2003.

———. *The New Testament: A Historical Introduction to the Early Christian Writings*. 5th ed. New York: Oxford University Press, 2011.

———, ed. *Lost Scriptures: Books That Did Not Make It into the New Testament*. New York: Oxford University Press, 2003.

Ehrman, Bart D., and Zlatko Pleše, trans. *The Apocryphal Gospels: Texts and Translations*. New York: Oxford University Press, 2011.

Esack, Farid. *The Qur'an: A User's Guide*. Oxford: Oneworld, 2005.

Faulkner, Raymond O., trans. *The Ancient Egyptian Book of the Dead*. Rev. ed. Edited by Carol Andrews. New York: Macmillan, 1985.

Feiser, James, and John Powers, eds. *Scriptures of the World's Religions*. 4th ed. New York: McGraw-Hill, 2012.

Flood, Gavin, ed. *The Blackwell Companion to Hinduism*. Oxford: Blackwell, 2003.

———. *An Introduction to Hinduism*. Cambridge: Cambridge University Press, 1997.

Flood, Gavin, and Charles Martin, trans. *The Bhagavad Gita: A New Translation*. New York: W.W. Norton, 2012.

Ford, David F. "An Interfaith Wisdom: Scriptural Reasoning between Jews, Christians and Muslims." In *The Promise of Scriptural Reasoning*, edited by David F. Ford and C. C. Pecknold, pp. 1–22. Malden, MA: Blackwell, 2006.

Foster, Paul. *The Apocryphal Gospels: A Very Short Introduction*. Oxford: Oxford University Press, 2009.

Friedman, Matti. *The Aleppo Codex: A True Story of Obsession, Faith, and the Pursuit of an Ancient Bible*. Chapel Hill, NC: Algonquin Books of Chapel Hill, 2012.

Friedman, Richard Elliot. *Who Wrote the Bible?* New York: Summit Books, 1987.

Gager, John G. *Reinventing Paul*. New York: Oxford University Press, 2000.

Gardner, Daniel K., trans. *The Four Books: The Basic Teachings of the Later Confucian Tradition*. Indianapolis, IN: Hackett, 2007.

Gernet, Jacques. "Christian and Chinese Visions of the World in the Seventeenth Century." *Chinese Science* 4 (1980): 17.

Gethin, Rupert. *Sayings of the Buddha: A Selection of Suttas from the Pali Nikayas*. Oxford: Oxford University Press, 2008.

———. *The Foundations of Buddhism*. Oxford: Oxford University Press, 1998.

Giller, Pinchas. *Reading the Zohar: The Sacred Text of the Kabbalah*. Oxford: Oxford University Press, 2001.

Givens, Terryl L. *By the Hand of Mormon: The American Scripture That Launched a New World Religion*. New York: Oxford University Press, 2002.

Goldman, Robert P., Sally Goldman, and Barend A. van Nooten, trans. *The Ramayana of Valmiki: An Epic of Ancient India*. Princeton: Princeton University Press, 1984.

Goodall, Dominic, ed. and trans. *Hindu Scriptures*. Berkeley: University of California Press, 1996.

Graham, William A. "Scripture." In *The Encyclopedia of Religion*, 2nd ed., edited by Lindsay Jones, pp. 8194–8205. Detroit: Thompson Gale, 2005.

Griffith, Ralph T. H., trans. *The Hymns of the Rig Veda*. London: 1889.

Guru Granth Sahib, Khalsa Consensus Translation, http://www.sikhs.org/english/eg_index.htm.

Gutjahr, Paul. *The Book of Mormon: A Biography*. Princeton: Princeton University Press, 2012.

Gyatso, Tenzin (Dalai Lama XIV). *Essence of the Heart Sutra: The Dalai Lama's Heart of Wisdom Teachings*. Translated by Geshe Thupten Jinpa. Boston: Wisdom Publications, 2002.

———. *Toward a True Kinship of Faiths: How the World's Religions Can Come Together*. New York: Doubleday Religion, 2010.

———. *The World of Tibetan Buddhism: An Overview of Its Philosophy and Practice*. Boston: Wisdom Publications, 1995.

Halbertal, Moshe. *People of the Book: Canon, Meaning and Authority*. Cambridge, MA: Harvard University Press, 1997.

Hardy, Grant, ed. *The Book of Mormon: A Reader's Edition*. Urbana, IL: University of Illinois Press, 2003.

———. *Understanding the Book of Mormon*. New York: Oxford University Press, 2010.

Harris, Stephen L. *The New Testament: A Student's Introduction*. 7th ed. New York: McGraw-Hill, 2012.

Harris, Stephen L., and Robert L. Platzner. *The Old Testament: An Introduction to the Hebrew Bible*. 2nd ed. Boston: McGraw-Hill, 2008.

Harvey, Peter. *An Introduction to Buddhism: Teachings, History and Practices*. Cambridge: Cambridge University Press, 1990.

Hatcher, William S., and J. Douglas Martin. *The Baha'i Faith: The Emerging Global Religion*. San Francisco: Harper & Row, 1984.

Hendricks, Robert G., trans. *Lao-Tzu: Te-Tao Ching*. New York: Ballantine, 1989.

Hendrischke, Barbara. *The Scripture on Great Peace: The Taiping jing and the Beginnings of Daoism*. Berkeley: University of California Press, 2006.

Hoffman, Adina, and Peter Cole. *Sacred Trash: The Lost and Found World of the Cairo Geniza*. New York: Schocken, 2011.

Holder, John J., trans. *Early Buddhist Discourses*. Indianapolis, IN: Hackett, 2006.

Holm, Jean, ed. *Sacred Writings*. London: Pinter, 1994.

Holtz, Barry W. *Back to the Sources: Reading the Classic Jewish Texts*. New York: Summit Books, 1984.

Inagaki, Hisao, and Harold Steward, trans. *The Three Pure Land Sutras: A Study and Translation from Chinese*. 3rd ed. Kyoto: Nagata Bunshodo, 2000.

The Israel Museum, *The Digital Dead Sea Scrolls*. http://dss.collections/imj.org.il/.

Ivanhoe, Philip J., trans. *The Daodejing of Laozi*. Indianapolis, IN: Hackett, 2002.

Jacob, Louis. *The Talmudic Argument: A Study in Talmudic Reasoning and Methodology*. Cambridge: Cambridge University Press, 1984.

Jacobi, Hermann, trans. *Jaina Sutras*. 2 vols. Oxford: Oxford University Press, 1884, 1895.

Jaini, Padmanabh S. *The Jaina Path of Purification*. Berkeley: University of California Press, 1979.

Jamal, Mahmood, ed. and trans. *Islamic Mystical Poetry: Sufi Verse from the Early Mystics to Rumi*. London: Penguin, 2009.

Jewish Publication Society. *JPS Torah Commentary*. 5 vols. New York: Jewish Publication Society, 1989–1996.

Johnson, Luke Timothy. *The New Testament: A Very Short Introduction*. Oxford: Oxford University Press, 2010.

Johnston, Sarah Iles, ed. *Religions of the Ancient World: A Guide*. s.v. "Sacred Texts and Canonicity." Cambridge, MA: Harvard University Press, 2004.

Kammen, Michael, ed. *The Origins of the American Constitution: A Documentary History*. New York: Penguin, 1986.

Kemp, Barry. *How to Read the Egyptian Book of the Dead*. New York: Norton, 2007.

Khalidi, Tarif, trans. *The Qur'an*. New York: Penguin, 2008.

Khoroche, Peter, trans. *Once the Buddha Was a Monkey: Arya Sura's Jatakamala*. Chicago: University of Chicago Press, 1989.

Kirkland, Russell. *Taoism: The Enduring Tradition*. New York: Routledge, 2004.

Klein, William W., Craig L. Blomberg, and Robert I. Hubbard, Jr. *Introduction to Biblical Interpretation*. Rev. ed. Nashville, TN: Thomas Nelson, 2004.

Kohn, Livia, ed. *The Taoist Experience: An Anthology*. Albany: State University of New York Press, 1993.

———. *Daoism and Chinese Culture*. Cambridge, MA: Three Pines Press, 2001.

———. *Introducing Daoism*. London: Routledge, 2009.

Kohn, Livia, and Michael LaFargue, eds. *Lao-tzu and the Tao-te-ching*. Albany, NY: State University of New York Press, 1998.

Kugel, James. L. *How to Read the Bible: A Guide to Scripture, Then and Now*. New York: Free Press, 2007.

Lao, D. C., trans. *Lao Tzu: Tao Te Ching*. London: Penguin, 1963.

Lau, D. C., trans. *Confucius: The Analects*. London: Penguin, 1979.

———, trans. *Mencius*. Rev. ed. London: Penguin, 2003.

Lawrence, Bruce. *The Qur'an: A Biography*. New York: Atlantic Monthly Press, 2006.

Layton, Bentley, trans. *The Gnostic Scriptures*. Garden City, NY: Doubleday, 1987.

Legge, James, trans. *The Chinese Classics*. 5 vols., 2nd rev. ed. (Four Books, *Documents*, *Odes*, *Spring and Autumn Annals*, with *Zuo Commentary*.) Oxford and London: Clarendon Press and Oxford University Press, 1893–1895.

———, trans. *The Chinese Classics*. 2 vols., 2nd rev. ed. (Four Books.) Oxford: Clarendon Press, 1893–1895.

———, trans. *The Li Ki* (*Records of Rites*). 2 vols. Oxford: Oxford University Press, 1885.

Levering, Miriam, ed. *Rethinking Scripture: Essays from a Comparative Perspective*. Albany, NY: State University of New York Press, 1989.

———. "Scripture and Its Reception: A Buddhist Case." In *Rethinking Scripture: Essays from a Comparative Perspective*, edited by Miriam Levering. Albany, NY: State University of New York Press, 1989.

Levinson, Sanford. *Constitutional Faith*. Princeton: Princeton University Press, 1988.

Leys, Simon, trans. *The Analects of Confucius*. New York: Norton, 1997.

Littlejohn, Ronnie L. *Confucianism: An Introduction*. London: I. B. Tauris, 2011.

Lopez, Donald S., Jr. *The Story of Buddhism: A Concise Guide to Its History and Teachings*. New York: HarperCollins, 2001.

———. *The Tibetan Book of the Dead: A Biography*. Princeton: Princeton University Press, 2011.

Mair, Victor H., trans. *Tao Te Ching: The Classic Book of Integrity and the Way*. New York: Bantam, 1990.

Major, John S., Sarah Queen, Andrew Meyer, and Harold Roth, trans. *The Huainanzi: A Guide to the Theory and Practice of Government in Early Han China, by Liu An, King of Huainan*. New York: Columbia University Press, 2010.

Mann, Gurinder Singh. *The Making of Sikh Scripture*. Oxford: Oxford University Press, 2001.

Matt, Daniel Chanan, trans. *Zohar: The Book of Enlightenment*. New York: Paulist Press, 1983.

Mattson, Ingrid. *The Story of the Qur'an: Its History and Place in Muslim Life*. 2nd ed. Malden, MA: Blackwell, 2008.

McLeod, W. H., trans. *Textual Sources for the Study of Sikhism*. Chicago: University of Chicago Press, 1990.

Meier, Pauline. *American Scripture: Making the Declaration of Independence*. New York: Knopf, 1997.

Miller, Barbara Stoler, trans. *The Bhagavad-Gita: Krishna's Counsel in Time of War*. New York: Bantam, 1986.

Mitchell, Donald W. *Buddhism: Introducing the Buddhist Experience*. New York: Oxford University Press, 2002.

Mittal, Sushil and Gene Thursby, eds. *The Hindu World*. New York and London: Routledge, 2007.

Moerman, D. Max. "The Death of the Dharma: Buddhist Sutra Burials in Early Medieval Japan." In *The Death of Sacred Texts*, edited by Kristina Myrvold. Burlington, VT: Ashgate, 2010.

Momen, Moojan. *The Baha'i Faith: A Beginner's Guide*. London: Oneworld, 2007.

Murcott, Susan, trans. *The First Buddhist Women: Translations and Commentaries on the Therigatha*. Berkeley: Parallax Press, 1991.

Nakayama, Miki. *Ofudesaki: The Tip of the Writing Brush*. 6th ed. Tenri, Japan: Tenrikyo Church Headquarters, 1993.

Narasimhan, Chakravarthi V., trans. *The Mahabharata*. Rev. ed. New York: Columbia University Press, 1998.

Nesbitt, Eleanor. *Sikhism: A Very Short Introduction*. New York: Oxford University Press, 2005.

Neuser, Jacob, trans. *The Mishnah: A New Translation*. New Haven: Yale University Press, 1988.

———. *Making God's Word Work: A Guide to the Mishnah*. New York: Continuum, 2004.

Nickelsburg, George W. E. *Jewish Literature between the Bible and the Mishnah: A Historical and Literary Introduction*. Philadelphia: Fortress Press, 1981.

Nigosian, S. A. *Islam: Its History, Teaching, and Practices*. Bloomington, IN: Indiana University Press, 2004.

Novak, Philip, ed. *The World's Wisdom: Sacred Texts of the World's Religions*. New York: HarperCollins, 1994.

Nylan, Michael. *The Five "Confucian" Classics*. New Haven: Yale University Press, 2001.

Nylan, Michael, and Thomas Wilson. *Lives of Confucius*. New York: Doubleday, 2010.

O'Flaherty, Wendy Doniger, ed. and trans. *Textual Sources for the Study of Hinduism*. Chicago: University of Chicago Press, 1990.

Olivelle, Patrick, trans. *The Law Code of Manu*. Oxford: Oxford University Press, 2004.

———, trans. *Upanisads*. Oxford World Classics. Oxford: Oxford University Press, 1996.

Olson, Carl, ed. *Original Buddhist Sources: A Reader*. New Brunswick, NJ: Rutgers University Press, 2005.

Pagels, Elaine. *Revelations: Visions, Prophecy, and Politics in the Book of Revelation*. New York: Viking, 2012.

———. *Beyond Belief: The Secret Gospel of Thomas*. New York: Random House, 2003.

———. *The Gnostic Gospels*. New York: Random House, 1979.

Palmer, Martin, trans. *The Book of Chuang Tzu*. London: Penguin, 1996.

Patton, Laurie L., trans. *The Bhagavad Gita*. London: Penguin, 2008.

Peters, F. E. *The Voice, the Word, the Books: The Sacred Scripture of the Jews, Christians, and Muslims*. Princeton: Princeton University Press, 2007.

Philippi, Donald L., trans. *Kojiki*. Tokyo and Princeton: Tokyo University Press and Princeton University Press, 1969.

———, trans. *Norito: A Translation of the Ancient Japanese Ritual Prayers*. Princeton: Princeton University Press, 1990.

Power, John. *Introduction to Tibetan Buddhism*. Ithaca, NY: Snow Lion, 1995.

Pregadio, Fabrizio, ed. *The Encyclopedia of Taoism*. 2 vols. London: Routledge, 2008.

Puskas, Charles B., and David Crump. *An Introduction to the Gospels and Acts*. Grand Rapids, MI: Eerdmans, 2008.

Radhakrishnan, S., trans. *The Principal Upanishads*. London: Allen & Unwin, 1953.

Rakov, Jack N., ed. *The Annotated U.S. Constitution and Declaration of Independence*. Cambridge, MA: Harvard University Press, 2009.

Ravitch, Diane, and Abigail Thernstrom, eds. *The Democracy Reader: Classic and Modern Speeches, Essays, Poems, Declarations, and Documents on Freedom and Human Rights Worldwide*. New York: HarperCollins, 1992.

Rhys Davids, Caroline, trans. *Psalms of the Sisters*. London: Oxford University Press, 1909.

Rhys Davids, T. W., and Hermann Oldenberg, trans., *Vinaya Texts*. 3 vols. Oxford: Oxford University Press, 1881–1885.

Rinchen, Geshe Sonam, and Ruth Sonam, author and trans. *Atisha's Lamp for the Path to Enlightenment*. Ithaca, NY: Snow Lion, 1997.

Rippin, Andrew, ed. *The Blackwell Companion to the Qur'an*. Malden, MA: Blackwell, 2006.

Robinet, Isabelle. *Taoism: Growth of a Religion*. Translated by Phyllis Brooks. Stanford, CA: Stanford University Press, 1997.

Robinson, George. *Essential Judaism: A Complete Guide to Beliefs, Customs, and Rituals*. New York: Pocket Books, 2000.

Roebuck, Valerie J., trans. *The Dhammapada*. London: Penguin, 2010.

———, trans. *The Upanishads*. London: Penguin, 2003.

Rogerson, John, ed. *The Oxford Illustrated History of the Bible*. Oxford: Oxford University Press, 2001.

Rogerson, J. W., and Judith M. Lieu, eds. *The Oxford Handbook of Biblical Studies*. Oxford: Oxford University Press, 2006.

Rose, Jenny. *Zoroastrianism: An Introduction*. London: I. B. Tauris, 2011.

Rosenberg, David, ed. *Congregation: Contemporary Writers Read the Jewish Bible*. San Diego: Harcourt Brace Jovanovich, 1987.

Roth, Harold D. *Original Tao and the Foundations of Taoist Mysticism*. New York: Columbia University Press, 1999.

Rumi, Jalal al-Din. *The Masnavi, Book 1*. Translated by Jawid Mojaddedi. New York: Oxford University Press, 2008.

Ruthven, Malise. *Islam in the World*. 3rd ed. Oxford: Oxford University Press, 2006.

Saeed, Abdullah. *The Qur'an*. London: Routledge, 2008.

Sailey, Jay. *The Master Who Embraces Simplicity: A Study of the Philosopher Ko Hung, A.D. 283–343.* San Francisco: Chinese Materials Center, 1978. (Includes 21 of the 50 Outer Chapters.)

Sardar, Ziauddin. *Reading the Qur'an.* Oxford: Oxford University Press, 2012.

Schipper, Kristofer, and Franciscus Verellen, eds., *The Taoist Canon: A Historical Companion to the Daozang.* 3 vols. Chicago: University of Chicago Press, 2004.

Scholem, Gershom, ed. *Zohar: The Book of Splendor.* New York: Schocken Books, 1963.

Schweig, Graham M. *Dance of Divine Love: The Rasa Lila of Krishna from the Bhagavata Purana, India's Classic Sacred Love Story.* Princeton: Princeton University Press, 2005.

Sekida, Katsuki, trans. and commentator, and A. V. Grimstone, ed. *Two Zen Classics: Mumonkan and Hekiganroku.* New York and Tokyo: Weatherhill, 1977.

Sells, Michael. *Approaching the Qur'an: The Early Revelations.* 2nd ed. Ashland, OR: White Cloud Press, 2007.

Shackle, Christopher, and Arvind-pal Singh Mandair, eds. and trans. *Teachings of the Sikh Gurus: Selections from the Sikh Scriptures.* New York: Routledge, 2005.

Shaughnessy, Edward L., trans. *I Ching: The Classics of Changes.* New York: Ballantine, 1996.

Siddiqui, Mona. *How to Read the Qur'an.* New York: Norton, 2007.

Silver, Daniel Jeremy. *The Story of Scripture: From Oral Tradition to the Written Word.* New York: Basic Books, 1990.

Singh, Nikky-Gurinder Kaur. *Sikhism: An Introduction*. London: I. B. Tauris, 2011.

Skjærvø, Prods Octor, trans. and ed. *The Spirit of Zoroastrianism*. New Haven: Yale University Press, 2011.

Skousen, Royal, ed. *The Book of Mormon: The Earliest Text*. New Haven: Yale University Press, 2009.

Smart, Ninian, and Richard D. Hecht, eds. *Sacred Texts of the World: A Universal Anthology*. Bristol: Macmillan, 1982.

Smith, John D., trans. *The Mahabharata*. London: Penguin, 2009.

Smith, Peter. *An Introduction to the Baha'i Faith*. Cambridge: Cambridge University Press, 2008.

Smith, Richard J. *The I Ching: A Biography*. Princeton: Princeton University Press, 2012.

Smith, Wilfred Cantwell. *What Is Scripture? A Comparative Approach*. Minneapolis: Fortress Press, 1993.

Snellgrove, D. L. *The Hevajra Tantra: A Critical Study*. London: Oxford University Press, 1959.

Solomon, Norman, ed. and trans. *The Talmud: A Selection*. London: Penguin, 2009.

Sprong, John Shelby. *Re-Claiming the Bible for a Non-Religious World*. New York: HarperCollins, 2011.

Stausberg, Michael. *Zarathustra and Zoroastrianism: A Short Introduction*. Translated by Margaret Preisler-Weller. London: Equinox, 2008.

Steinsaltz, Adin. *The Essential Talmud*. Rev. ed. New York: Basic Books, 2006.

Strong, John S., ed. and trans., *The Experience of Buddhism: Sources and Interpretations*. 2nd ed. Belmont, CA: Wadsworth, 2002.

Tatia, Nathmal, trans. *Tattvartha Sutra: That Which Is*. New York: HarperCollins, 1994.

Taylor, John. H., ed. *Journey through the Afterlife: Ancient Egyptian Book of the Dead*. Cambridge, MA: Harvard University Press, 2010.

Tedlock, Dennis, trans. *Popol Vuh: The Definitive Edition of the Mayan Book of the Dawn of Life and the Glories of Gods and Kings*. New York: Simon & Schuster, 1985.

Teiser, Stephen F., and Jacqueline I. Stone, eds. *Readings of the Lotus Sutra*. New York: Columbia University Press, 2009.

Thompson, Laurence G. "Taoism: Classic and Canon." In *The Holy Book in Comparative Perspective*, edited by Frederick M. Denny and Rodney F. Taylor, pp. 204–223. Columbia, SC: University of South Carolina Press, 1985.

Thomsen, Harry. *The New Religions of Japan*. Rutland, VT: Charles E. Tuttle, 1963.

Throckmorton, Burton H., Jr. *Gospel Parallels: A Comparison of the Synoptic Gospels*. Nashville, TN: Thomas Nelson, 1989.

Thurman, Robert A. F. *The Holy Teaching of Vimalakirti*. University Park, PA: Pennsylvania State University Press, 1976.

Tsai, Kathryn Ann, trans. *Lives of the Nuns: Biographies of Chinese Buddhist Nuns from the Fourth to Sixth Centuries*. Honolulu: University of Hawaii Press, 1994.

Van Voorst, Robert E., ed. *Anthology of World Scriptures*. 8th ed. Boston: Wadsworth, 2013.

VanderKam, James C. *The Dead Sea Scrolls Today*. 2nd ed. Grand Rapids, MI: Eerdmans, 2010.

Venkatesananda, Swami. *The Concise Ramayana of Valmiki*. Albany, NY: State University of New York Press, 1988.

Vermes, Geza, trans. *The Complete Dead Sea Scrolls in English*. Rev. ed. London: Penguin, 2004.

Waley, Arthur, trans. *The Book of Songs: The Ancient Chinese Classic of Poetry*. New York: Grove Press, 1987 (1st ed., 1937).

Ware, James R. *Alchemy, Medicine and Religion in the China of A.D. 320: The Nei Pien of Ko Hung*. Cambridge, MA: MIT Press, 1966.

Watson, Burton, trans. *The Complete Works of Chuang Tzu*. New York: Columbia University Press, 1968.

——, trans. *The Lotus Sutra*. New York: Columbia University Press, 1993.

——, trans. *The Tso Chuan: Selections from China's Oldest Narrative History*. (*Zuo Commentary*.) New York: Columbia University Press, 1989.

West, E. W., trans. *Pahlavi Texts*. 5 vols. Oxford: Oxford University Press, 1880–1897.

Wilhelm, Richard, and Cary Baynes, trans. *The I Ching or Book of Changes*. 3rd ed. Princeton: Princeton University Press, 1967.

Williams, Paul. *Mahayana Buddhism: The Doctrinal Foundations*. London: Routledge, 1989.

Wright, N. T. *Paul in Fresh Perspective*. Minneapolis: Fortress, 2005.

Yates, Robin D. S., trans. *Five Lost Classics: Tao, Huang-lao, and Yin-yang in Han China*. New York: Ballantine, 1997.

Notes

Notes